African Cities and the Development Conundrum

International Development Policy

Editor-in-Chief

Gilles Carbonnier /Ugo Panizza

Guest Editors

Carole Ammann
Till Förster

VOLUME 10

The titles published in this series are listed at *brill.com/idp*

Visit *International Development Policy* and associated documents online
http://devpol.org.

International Development Policy
Previous Titles
Africa: 50 Years of Independence, No. 1, Geneva: Graduate Institute Publications, 2010, ISSN print 1663–9383 | ISSN online 1663–9405 | EAN 9782940415274.
Energy and Development, No. 2, Basingstoke/Geneva: Palgrave Macmillan/Graduate Institute Publications, 2011, EAN 9780230282483.
Aid, Emerging Economies and Global Policies, No. 3, Basingstoke/Geneva: Palgrave Macmillan/Graduate Institute Publications, 2012, EAN 9781137003409.
Religion and Development, No. 4, Basingstoke/Geneva: Palgrave Macmillan/Graduate Institute Publications, 2013, EAN 9781137329370.
Education, Learning, Training: Critical Issues for Development, No. 5, Leiden|Boston/Geneva: Brill Nijhoff/Graduate Institute Publications, 2014, EAN 9789004281141.
Large-Scale Land Acquisitions, Focus on South-East Asia, No. 6, Leiden|Boston/Geneva: Brill Nijhoff/Graduate Institute Publications 2015, EAN 9789004304741.
Combining Economic and Political Development, The Experience of MENA, No. 7 Leiden|Boston/Geneva: Brill Nijhoff/Graduate Institute Publications 2017, EAN 9789004336452.
Development as a Battlefield, No. 8 Leiden|Boston/Geneva: Brill Nijhoff/Graduate Institute Publications 2017, EAN 9789004349520.
Alternative Pathways to Sustainable Development Lessons from Latin America, No. 9 Leiden|Boston/Geneva: Brill Nijhoff/Graduate Institute Publications 2017, EAN 9789004351660.

THE GRADUATE INSTITUTE | GENEVA
Graduate Institute of International and Development Studies
Institut de hautes études internationales et du développement
Research Office
P.O. Box 1672
CH–1211 Geneva 1
Switzerland
publications@graduateinstitute.ch
http://www.graduateinstitute.ch/home/research/publications.html

African Cities and the Development Conundrum

Edited by

Carole Ammann
Till Förster

BRILL
NIJHOFF

LEIDEN | BOSTON

Cover illustration: Street scene in Korhogo, Côte d'Ivoire, courtesy Till Förster (2015).

Library of Congress Cataloging-in-Publication Data

Names: Ammann, Carole, editor. | Förster, Till, editor.
Title: African cities and the development conundrum / edited by Carole Ammann, Till Forster.
Description: Leiden ; Boston : Brill, [2018] | Series: International development policy, ISSN 1663-9383 ; VOLUME 10 | Includes index.
Identifiers: LCCN 2018040919 (print) | LCCN 2018041920 (ebook) | ISBN 9789004387942 (E-book) | ISBN 9789004387928 (pbk. : alk. paper)
Subjects: LCSH: Urbanization--Africa. | Urban policy--Africa. | City planning--Africa.
Classification: LCC HT384.A35 (ebook) | LCC HT384.A35 A3195 2018 (print) | DDC 307.76096--dc23
LC record available at https://lccn.loc.gov/2018040919

Typeface for the Latin, Greek, and Cyrillic scripts: "Brill". See and download: brill.com/brill-typeface.

ISSN 1663-9383
ISBN 978-90-04-38792-8 (paperback)
ISBN 978-90-04-38794-2 (e-book)

This book is printed on acid-free paper and produced in a sustainable manner.

Contents

PART 3
Planning, Politics and the Urban Grey Zone

PART 4
The Rural-Urban Continuum

Foreword

We are pleased to introduce this new thematic issue of *International Development Policy*. This issue, number 10, explores some of the complex development challenges associated with Africa's relatively recent and rapidly-progressing urbanisation. Analysing urban settings through the diverse experiences and perspectives of inhabitants and stakeholders in cities from Addis Ababa and Johannesburg to mid-sized cities such as the mining boomtowns of Eastern Congo, this collection of articles invites readers to ponder the evolution of international development policy responses across the region.

The contributions are organised in four parts. Part one includes an introduction by the guest editors, Carole Amman and Till Förster, and a scene-setting chapter by Edgar Pieterse. Part two looks at urban governance and is followed by chapters addressing policy, planning and informality in part three. The rural-urban continuum is explored in the fourth and final part. Sixteen authors and co-authors have contributed, several of whom are based in the Africa region itself, and all offering a rich variety of expertise and viewpoints drawing on anthropology, economics, geography, political science and sociology.

Articles in this issue were the subject of lively exchanges during the 7th European Conference on African Studies (ECAS), held in Basel in late June and early July 2017. The editors are grateful for the substantive comments of the anonymous reviewers and others who commented on earlier drafts.

Taken together, the articles challenge readers to reconsider the relationship between urbanisation in Africa and conventional development narratives, and make an important contribution to the existing literature. We hope this collection will resonate especially with new readers across the Africa region as well as among our regular readership of scholars and practioners, thanks to its timely and relevant focus on a region whose population is set to shift from predominantly rural to urban in just over a decade.

The Editors,
Basel, Bern and Geneva, July 2018

Preface

International Development Policy is a critical source of analysis of development policy and international cooperation trends and is aimed at scholars, policy makers and development professionals. It offers a diverse range of academic views from both industrialised countries and emerging economies.

International Development Policy is edited by the Graduate Institute of International and Development Studies, an institution of research and higher education dedicated to advancing world affairs. Located in Geneva at the heart of an international centre of multilateral governance, the Graduate Institute benefits from a rich legacy linked to the founding of the international system and the League of Nations in the 1920s, and the emergence of the developing world in the 1960s.

http://devpol.org

http://graduateinstitute.ch/research

We extend our thanks to the Swiss Agency for Development and Cooperation (SDC) and Geneva Canton's Service de la Solidarité Internationale (SSI) for their financial support.

Schweizerische Eidgenossenschaft
Confédération suisse
Confederazione Svizzera
Confederaziun svizra

List of Illustrations

Figures

Tables

Acronyms and Abbreviations

AACRA	Addis Ababa City Roads Authority
AAPS	Association of African Planning Schools
AASHTO	American Association of State Highway and Transport Officials
ACC	African Centre for Cities
AFD	Agence Française de Développement
AfDB	African Development Bank
AFSUN	African Food Security Urban Network
AMA	Accra Metropolitan Assembly
AMS	Association des Maires du Sénégal
ANT	actor–network theory
APCLS	Alliance of Patriots for a Free and Sovereign Congo (DRC)
AR	Affirmative Repositioning movement (Namibia)
AU	African Union
AURI	African Urban Research Initiative
CBDS	central business districts
CID	City Improvement District
CLO	community liaison officers
CORD	Coalition for Reforms and Democracy (Kenya)
CNDP	National Congress for the Defence of the People (DRC)
CRBC	China Road and Bridge Corporation
CSOS	civil society organisations
DBSA	Development Bank of Southern Africa
DRC	Democratic Republic of the Congo
EABI	East African Bribery Index
EIU	Economist Intelligence Unit
EPWP	Expanded Public Works Programme (South Africa)
ERA	Ethiopian Roads Authority
FARDC	Armed Forces of the Democratic Republic of the Congo
FGDS	focus group discussions
FroK	Friends of Kloofendal
GAMA	Greater Accra Metropolitan Area
GaWC	Globalization and World Cities Research Network
IAGU	Institut Africain de Gestion Urbaine
ICLEI	International Council for Local Environmental Initiatives
ICT	Information and communications technology
IDPS	internally displaced persons
IDRC	International Development Research Centre

IMF	International Monetary Fund
IPCC	Intergovernmental Panel on Climate Change
ISUD-Plan	Integrated Strategic Urban Development Plan
JCPZ	Johannesburg City Parks and Zoo
KAT	Kisumu Action Team (Kenya)
KIWASCO	Kisumu Water and Sewerage Company (Kenya)
KLIP	Kisumu Local Interaction Platform
KPAS	Key Performance Areas
KPIS	Key Performance Indicators
MDGS	Millennium Development Goals
MoA	Memorandum of Agreement
MONUSCO	United Nations Organization Stabilization Mission in the Democratic Republic of the Congo
MoU	Memorandum of Understanding
NGOS	non-governmental organisations
NHP	National Housing Policy (Ghana)
NSDF	National Spatial Development Framework (Ghana)
NUs	neighbourhood units
NUPF	National Urban Policy Framework (Ghana)
ODM	Orange Democratic Movement (Kenya)
OECD	Organisation for Economic Cooperation and Development
ORNS	Overseas Road Notes
PARECO	Coalition of Congolese Patriotic Resistance
PRD	Pearl River Delta
RCD	Rassemblement Congolais pour la Democratie (DRC)
SACN	South African Cities Network
SDGS	Sustainable Development Goals
SDSN	Sustainable Development Solutions Network
SJC	Social Justice Coalition
SLAS	Service Level Agreements
SLOS	Stakeholder Liaison Officers
SMMES	Small Micro and Medium Enterprises
TRL	British Transport and Road Laboratory
UCLG	United Cities and Local Governments
UCT	University of Cape Town
UN	United Nations
UNDP	United Nations Development Programme
UNECA	United Nations Economic Commission for Africa
UNEP	United Nations Environment Programme
UNESCO	United Nations Educational, Scientific and Cultural Organization

Notes on Contributors

Carole Ammann

is a postdoctoral researcher at the Institute of Geography at the University of Bern and at the Institute of Sociology, University of Fribourg. She recently completed her dissertation—entitled 'Silent Politics. Gender, Imagination and the State in Kankan, Guinea'—at the University of Basel. Carole Ammann is interested in questions of urbanity, secondary cities, transformations of the state, political participation, everyday life, and gender in West Africa and France.

Claudia Baez Camargo

holds a PhD in Political Science from the University of Notre Dame, USA and a graduate degree in Economics from the University of Cambridge, England. She is Head of Governance Research at the Basel Institute on Governance/University of Basel, where she is responsible for the development, oversight and management of the Institute's research activities as well as delivering technical assistance projects aimed at preventing corruption in the public sector.

Claire Bénit-Gbaffou

is an Associate Professor in the School of Architecture and Planning at Wits University (South Africa) and a member of the Centre for Urbanism and Built Environment Studies (CUBES). Her research expertise lies in urban politics, community participation, local leadership and urban governance. She is currently coordinating a research programme focusing on 'Practices of the State in Urban Governance', based on South African city case studies.

Karen Büscher

is an Assistant Professor at the Conflict Research Group, Ghent University, Belgium. Her research focuses on different aspects of the relationship between violent conflict and urbanisation in the Democratic Republic of Congo.

Aba Obrumah Crentsil

is a research fellow at the Institute of Statistical, Social and Economic Research (ISSER) at the University of Ghana. A multidisciplinary researcher, her research interests include renewable energy, the energy–health nexus, climate change, urbanisation and sustainable development.

Sascha Delz

holds a Doctor of Sciences and a Master's degree in Architecture from ETH Zurich. After practicing as an architect in New York and Switzerland, he worked as design instructor and researcher at the Department of Architecture of ETH Zurich, and the Future Cities Laboratory in Singapore. While his dissertation investigated urban transformations under the premise of international development cooperation in Ethiopia, his current postdoctoral research explores models of cooperative housing for low-income contexts.

Ton Dietz
was Director of the African Studies Centre Leiden (ASCL) and a member of the Board of African Studies in Europe (AEGIS) until September 2017. He was one of the initiators of oursus.org, a website about sustainable city initiatives developed under the umbrella of the International Geographical Union. Currently, Ton Dietz is a senior researcher at the ASCL and Emeritus Professor of African Development at Leiden University.

Till Förster
is an anthropologist. He holds a PhD from the Freie Universität Berlin. Since 2001 he has been Chair of Social Anthropology at the University of Basel. Till Förster has specialised in art, visual culture and political transformations in West and Central Africa. Since 1979, he has conducted field research in Côte d'Ivoire and Cameroon. His recent publications focus on visual culture, social creativity and the postcolonial state, as well as on politics and governance in African cities.

Lucy Koechlin
is Senior Lecturer at the Institute of Social Anthropology, University of Basel. Her research and teaching focuses on political transformations in Africa, with a particular focus on urban politics, democratic spaces and governance. As a consultant, Dr Koechlin has been involved in a wide range of cross-sectoral mandates on anti-corruption, accountability and governance.

Lalli Metsola
received his Master's degree in Cultural Anthropology and his doctorate in Development Studies at the University of Helsinki, where he works as a postdoctoral researcher examining claim-making dynamics related to urban land, basic services and housing in Namibia and Botswana. His earlier studies focused on former exiles, ex-combatants and veterans in Namibia. He specialises in political anthropology, state formation, citizenship, post-conflict transformations and southern Africa.

Garth Myers
is the Paul E. Raether Distinguished Professor of Urban International Studies and Director of the Urban Studies Program at Trinity College in Hartford,

Connecticut, USA. He is the author of four books and co-editor of two other books on urban Africa, along with more than 65 articles and book chapters. His primary areas of expertise concern the historical and political geography of urban and environmental planning in cities in Africa.

George Owusu
is a Professor at the Institute of Statistical, Social and Economic Research (ISSER) and the Director of the Centre for Urban Management Studies (CUMS) at the University of Ghana. His main areas of research include urban and regional development, urban crime, urban land use and administration, local governance and decentralisation, and civil society and participatory approaches to development.

Edgar Pieterse
holds the South African Research Chair in Urban Policy and is founding director of the African Centre for Cities at the University of Cape Town, South Africa. His most recent co-authored book is: *New Urban Worlds. Inhabiting Dissonant Times* (Polity, 2017).

Sebastian Prothmann
studied geography, social anthropology and sociology at the Georg-August-Universität Göttingen and received a doctorate in 2015 at the Johann Wolfgang von Goethe-Universität Frankfurt with a thesis entitled 'Youth in "Kinpi Corner": Lifeworlds of Young Men beyond Migration and Immobility in Pikine, Senegal.' His main research interests centre around topics of Senegalese (im)mobilities and transnationalism, and African migration in general.

Warren Smit
is a senior researcher at the African Centre for Cities, an urban research institute based at the University of Cape Town in South Africa. Smit's background is in urban planning, and he has been a researcher on urban issues in Africa since 1993. His main research interests are urban governance, urban health, and housing policy.

Florian Stoll
has been working since May 2013 in the sociological wing (with Prof. Dieter Neubert) of the project 'Middle Classes on the Rise' at the Bayreuth Academy of Advanced African Studies, Germany. From October 2016 to October 2017 he was a visiting scholar at the Center for Cultural Sociology, Yale University. Stoll's main research areas are the sociology of the global South (Foci Kenya/Brazil), cultural sociology, social stratification/milieus, globalisation theories, and urban theory/the sociology of space.

PART 1

Introduction

CHAPTER 1

African Cities and the Development Conundrum: Actors and Agency in the Urban Grey Zone

Till Förster and Carole Ammann

Abstract

Africa is urbanising faster than any other continent. The stupendous pace of urbanisation challenges the usual image of Africa as a rural continent. The sheer complexity of African cities contests conventional understandings of the urban as well as standard development policies. Lingering between chaos and creativity, Western images of African cities seem unable to serve as a basis for development policies. The diversity of African cities is hard to conceptualise—but at the same time, unbiased views of the urban are the first step to addressing the urban development conundrum. International development cooperation should not only make African cities a focus of its engagement—it should also be cautious not to build its interventions on concepts inherited from Western history, such as the formal/informal dichotomy. We argue that African cities are more appropriately regarded as urban grey zones that only take shape and become colourful through the actors' agency and practice. The chapters of this special issue offer a fresh look at African cities, and the many opportunities as well as limitations that emerge for African urbanites—state officials, planners, entrepreneurs, development agencies and ordinary people—from their own point of view: they ask where, for whom and why such limitations and opportunities emerge, how they change over time and how African urban dwellers actively enliven and shape their cities.

1 The Urban Challenge in Africa

Cities produce difference—and they accommodate difference. African cities are no exception. They rather seem to accelerate processes of differentiation to a degree that makes it difficult to conceive them as an entity, to understand their social complexities and, not least, to govern them. The pace of urbanisation in Africa currently exceeds that of all other continents. Soon, more Africans will live in cities than in rural areas. As reliable statistics are hard to establish, estimations vary, but 2030 seems to be a safe bet for the turning point (UN DESA, 2014; UN-Habitat, 2008, 2016; ADB, 2016a; also Chapter 6, this issue).

Other estimates claim that the watershed could already be reached by 2022—a mere blink of an eye from a historical perspective.[1] To some extent, this incredible acceleration is due to the belated beginning of mass urbanisation in Africa (see below).[2] But besides its historical framework, urbanisation in Africa today presents multiple challenges, which—regardless of its inherent problems—also find expression in Sustainable Development Goal (SDG) number 11, from the UN (2015). African urbanism is a challenge for our scholarly understanding of social change, the status of such cities and what they are about to become, and of their role in national, regional and world development, and last but not least, contemporary African cities raise questions of how they can be governed and planned. As conventional forms of governance often fail, new, '…hybrid institutional forms have to be developed' (Smit and Pieterse, 2014, 160). African cities thus challenge conventional concepts of development and social theory. Mario Pezzini, director of the OECD development centre, says that 'it is not possible to separate these issues' (*The Guardian*, 2016; ADB, 2016b, 143–189). Social theory and development practice have to be thought of as one.

Cities and their relationship with their hinterland must be understood in their full complexity—else all attempts to govern them will fail. Hence the significance of the urban and urban studies for the national, regional and eventually global future (Pieterse, 2008; Parnell and Pieterse, 2014). Very much the same holds true for development agendas. Ignoring the urban dimension would mean conceiving the future without one of its most important, if not the most important of its dimensions. Cities can drive development by providing education, work and consumption opportunities. At the same time, they can also drain their hinterland by drawing resources into the exploding African megacities: rural areas lose their best minds as they move into cities—very much as the global North attracts the best brains.

For many, cities are at the centre of a new world geography (Robinson, 2005). They are also the sites where new social theories have to prove whether and how they can be translated into policies that advance the lives of ordinary people. Without thorough, empirically based and theoretically informed

1 Comparing estimations over the past two decades shows how volatile estimations are (e.g. Kessides, 2006; Potts, 2012; and Chénal, 2016; also Chapter 6, this issue).

2 It took Europe 110 years to move from 15 per cent urban dwellers in 1800 to 40 per cent in 1910. Well into the twentieth century, urbanisation was mainly a phenomenon of the industrialised global North. But in 2013, a little more than a hundred years later, six of the ten countries with the highest urbanisation rates in the world are in sub-Saharan Africa (World Bank, 2014). In Africa, 14 per cent of the population lived in cities in 1950, and in 2010, 60 years later, the percentage was estimated to be 48 per cent—roughly twice the nineteenth and early twentieth century growth rates of urbanisation in Europe (ADB, 2012).

knowledge, we might only address the symptoms and ignore the real problems. One of the targets of SDG 11 is to ensure access to basic services and housing for all urbanites by 2030 (UN, 2015). However, it is '...surprisingly difficult to secure accurate data of access to basic services in rural and urban areas in African countries' (Pieterse and Parnell, 2014, 11). Again, there is a need for much more empirical research and theoretical reflection on African cities. Admittedly, this collection cannot fill that gap—but it contributes to rethinking African cities by raising key questions that need answers. How the urban revolution in Africa is handled will depend on how well it is understood and how—besides the political participation of the populace (Smit and Pieterse, 2014; Oldfield, 2015)—the continent's intellectuals will be able to engage in this debate (Pieterse and Parnell, 2014; Watson, 2014; Oldfield, 2015). We would gamble with our shared future—not only with that of the estimated half a billion Africans who currently live in these cities—if we did not engage with these issues (UN DESA, 2014; Datta and Shaban, 2016).

Writings on urbanisation in Africa tend to be normative; many views are either overly optimistic or pessimistic while balanced perspectives seem to be the exception. One strand of literature over-romanticises the African city. This focus stresses the innovative potential, the creativity and the entrepreneurial attitudes of African urbanites. It considers the African city as a particularly vital space from where, for example, a huge variety of artistic expressions emerge (Pinther et al., 2012). The other strand, in contrast, focuses on what African cities lack compared to metropolitan areas in the global North and accordingly develops a crisis narrative by depicting African cities as not working—while claiming at the same time that urbanisation is a prerequisite for development. For authors like Mike Davis (2006), the bustling cities in the global South consist mainly of chaotic slums where poverty, frustration, corruption, crime and violence thrive due to a lack of housing and basic infrastructure and to the limited opportunities they offer their inhabitants. This Afro-pessimistic doomsday scenario depicts African cities primarily as violent and ungovernable and eventually as a mirror of the whole continent.

African cities and their inhabitants do face numerous challenges (see UN, 2015). However, to understand cities and urbanisation in Africa, normative approaches will neither work as heuristic instruments nor produce the insights needed to advance urban development. At best, they may highlight a particular perspective, but they will also restrict the spectators' view to that one aspect—namely, that cities in Africa fail to meet expectations based on the historical experience of Western urbanisation. In this issue, we thus look for the many opportunities as well as limitations that exist for African urban dwellers from their own point of view. We ask where, for whom and why such limitations and opportunities emerge and how they change over time (Pieterse, 2008; Chapter 2, this issue). By acknowledging the prevalent tension between invention and intervention (Obrist et al., 2013) and applying an actor-centred approach that analyses the wide range of urban practices, we aim at moving beyond a simplistic discourse of modernity and development. Therefore, we focus on how various actors bargain, manoeuvre, resist, mediate and flexibly adapt their everyday lives in an ever-changing African urban environment (Chapters 11 and 13, this issue).

African cities are 'works in progress' (Simone, 2004a, 1); they are fluid, complex, and marked by a huge breadth, diversity and heterogeneity—both across and within cities. What is more, cities in Africa are not exceptional and are as ordinary as any (Robinson, 2006). They are confronted with many problems such as vulnerability, poverty and inequality and are characterised by a constant competition over resources (Kennedy, 2015) and the making and control of urban spaces (Massey, 2005; Healey, 2007) just like many other urban areas all over the world (Myers, 2011). But they also produce that specific urban mixture: the connections and disconnections that breed new ideas and opportunities (Amin and Thrift, 2002, 3).

Edgar Pieterse and Susan Parnell (2014) point to some commonalities that might be typical features of African cities; namely, a) rapid urbanisation (Chapters 6 and 10, this issue); b) the strong link between the rural and the urban due to circular migration patterns (Chapter 13, this issue); c) large peri-urban areas that characterise the cities' outskirts (Chapters 10 and 11, this issue); d) the informality of urbanisation that affects the economic and the social sphere (Chapters 9 and 11, this issue); e) urban primacy, a particularity rooted in the colonial past due to which many countries have one large urban centre typically three to four times larger than the second largest city; f) rivalling and partly overlapping power poles (Chapter 13, this issue) that make it difficult for ordinary citizens to know whom they should address to achieve certain goals; g) land and housing as major issues due to unclear legal situations; h) huge inequality between cities' inhabitants, which results in almost no interactions between the urban elite (Chapter 12, this issue) and poor citizens; and finally j) urban youth constitutes a particularly vulnerable large cohort in many African cities (Pieterse and Parnell, 2014, 9–15; Chapter 11, this issue).

The current state of urbanisation in Africa has its roots in the history of the continent. It is no less related to the present economic, social and political settings that African cities have to cope with. A fundamental and still influential characteristic is the comparatively short history of urbanisation on the African continent. A handful of bigger towns had emerged in medieval West Africa, and smaller urban areas persisted there through the first part of the nineteenth century, while eastern and southern Africa stayed mostly rural, with the exception of a few scattered Swahili trading towns (Iliffe, 1995, 118). The situation did not change much when the continent came under colonial domination by the end of the century. Throughout the incipient phase of the colonial era, the African continent remained mostly rural, intermingled with some small but growing colonial trading towns along the coasts. At that time, only Cairo had more than 900,000 inhabitants. Ibadan, Tunis and Johannesburg, which followed next, counted between 100,000 and 210,000 residents each. This picture changed rapidly after World War II when urban areas began to expand at an unprecedented pace. Between 1940 and 1960, the population of many African cities more than doubled. Simultaneously, new cities emerged, for instance the mining towns of the Copperbelt (Chapter 13, this issue). However, other towns also shrank when the colonial powers withdrew or because caravan routes became less important (Freund, 2007, 65–67).

In the postcolonial era, the pace of urbanisation accelerated enormously because of the rural–urban migration that drew masses of peasants to cities that were increasingly unable to absorb them. By the end of the millennium, large African cities like Lagos, Cairo or Kinshasa had become endless urban agglomerations of over five million people (Freund, 2007, 143–145; Burdett and Sudjic, 2007). Nevertheless, Europeans perceived and often continue to perceive Africa as a rural continent; and so did development cooperation well into the twenty-first century, where the image of rural Africa remained the basis for development aid and later development cooperation. The reduction of poverty in Africa was thought of, conceived and planned as technical cooperation in rural areas, largely ignoring the urban realities of the continent.[3] For a long time, applied research and development policies focused on agrarian and pastoral issues. Thus, many programmes assisted and still support African farmers to increase their harvest, to promote sustainable land management and to develop strategies to deal with climate change. The aim of many governments—supported by international development agencies—was to reduce circular rural–urban migration patterns. We do not claim that such programmes are irrelevant.[4] However, we advocate readjusting the focus away from the rural to

3 Michael Lipton (1977) popularised the term 'urban bias' in development since the late 1970s. He claimed that development cooperation focused almost exclusively on cities and neglected rural areas—a misjudgement that has had an enormous and devastating influence (e.g. Riddell, 1985).

4 The interdependence of local subsistence and cash crop production with international value chains has been a central theme of economic anthropology since the 1960s (e.g. Meillassoux, 1981). International development agencies recently rediscovered this link but framed it—unlike the critical studies of the 1960s and 1970s—no longer in terms of rural dependency but

Africa's urban areas as sooner rather than later, this is where the majority of the continent's population will live.

As recently as 2007, political scientist Goran Hyden wrote: 'After 40 or more years of trying to assist sub-Saharan Africa to develop and modernize, the region remains an enigma to the international policy community. [...] The proverbial elephant has been examined from all possible angles with only a minimal discovery of what really works in Africa. The main reason is that the international development community has been reluctant to learn what the elephant is all about when up close' (Hyden, 2007, 16751). We share his view and believe that urban Africa is part of that elephant sitting squarely in the room. There is an urgent need to engage more in basic as well as applied research on African cities—and to look at them as ordinary cities facing ordinary problems. Thus, we need to thoroughly understand how local actors live and engage in African cities. Most of the contributions to this issue mirror this shift in development studies and put local actors and their agency first.

From a foreign, in particular Northerners' perspective, the ordinary, 'normal' African city is an informal city. While the former colonial centre often turned into a business district with metallised window panes, the areas where the local population lived soon transformed into mushrooming neighbourhoods that no planning could keep up with. Behind the restricted zones once meant to protect the white colonisers and later the privileged state bourgeoisie, shanty towns extended in all directions. As early as in the 1920s, the colonisers perceived these 'spontaneous settlements' as a challenge to their visions of an emerging urban Africa (Njoh, 2009). Well-organised towns were supposed to serve as showcases for the attempts of Western powers to order African societies. In new political contexts, such ambitions to some extent continued to inform development policies—including those of the UN, whose target is to upgrade slums and provide safe and affordable housing for all by 2030 (UN, 2015), the new donor countries as well as postcolonial administrations (Jones, 2012a). 'Slum upgrading' is only the most obvious intervention in areas that are usually considered 'informal' (Jones, 2012b; Chapters 6, 7 and 9, this issue).

Since late colonial times, these 'informal' settlements grew faster than any other part of the respective cities. These settlements' populace was difficult to control; and, probably more important, unlike the 'formal' centres, which often looked like cities in the motherland, these areas were hardly legible to planners and civil servants. The difference was often cast in the grand binary distinction of the time: the 'old, traditional, African' ways of living and housing

---

in a more euphemistic perspective as food security for the urban populace (ADB, 2016b, 2; African Center for Economic Transformation, 2017).

were represented by the unordered, spontaneous, poor and unstructured settlements while the well-built 'modern' centre stood for a promising African future (Drakakis-Smith, 2000).

The dichotomy transformed repeatedly and adopted more than once another shape after independence. The most prominent is certainly the opposition of 'formal' vs. 'informal' that, at first sight, still divides most African cities. In the 1970s, the economic anthropologist Keith Hart (1973, 1985) and others[5] had derived the term 'informal economy' from the enormous cleavage between those who paid taxes and profited from official, legal, waged, regulated employment and its many benefits and the masses who had no official employment and who had to make a living as 'autonomous'—that is, self-employed—workers in the unregulated, often illegal, small-scale spheres of the urban arena. Broadly defined, informality covers all unregistered or officially unobserved economic activities. This definition implies that there is an agency, usually the state, that registers and observes. In the end, the binary distinction juxtaposes state-regulated economic activities to all others that the state is unable or unwilling to control. Because of the—from a Western perspective—'weakness' of most African states, the 'informal sector' is sometimes identified as Africa's most prominent contribution to economic theory (Collier, 1993).[6]

This opposition made Africa's cityscapes legible to planners and development experts. Slums and the infamous *bidonvilles* in French-speaking Africa (Balandier, 1955, 1957) were redefined as 'informal' settlements that were not recognised or addressed by the administration '...as an integral part of the city' (UN-Habitat, 2008, 7). Hence the assumption that informality is directly related to poverty (e.g. Rauch, 1991). Of course, this definition comes with real disadvantages for the people living in these areas, who often account for three fourths of the urban populace. They frequently have no access to public services, no electricity or water supply and only insufficient living areas, and their houses are constructed of inadequate materials and thus easily affected by natural disasters (UN, 2015). No less important is that they often do not have a right to the places and houses where they live. They usually have no title deeds

5 More generally first outlined by W. Arthur Lewis (1955), who coined the term 'shadow economy'. As 'informal economy', the concept was popularised in the 1970s and 1980s (de Soto, 1989). Ilda Lindell (2010a, 2010b) and Rafael La Porta and Andrei Shleifer (2014) provide overviews.

6 Statistics and quantitative data on the informal sector are notoriously unreliable. Estimations for sub-Saharan Africa currently vary between 20–25 per cent for South Africa and Namibia and 50–65 per cent for Nigeria, Benin and Tanzania (Medina et al., 2017). The urban informal economy is usually larger than the national informal economy, in terms of how these relate, proportionally, to the urban and national economy at large.

and in many cities they are regularly expelled whenever the urban council sees a need to do so (Chapter 9, this issue).

From a critical perspective, the facts are obvious. The inhabitants of 'informal' settlements have no right to the city—their city is not theirs (Lefebvre, 1968; Purcell, 2014; on South Asia see Anjaria and McFarlane, 2011). The 'formal–informal' bifurcation thus has immediate relevance for urban governance and, by extension, for any development policy (Chapters 4 and 9, this issue). It creates an administrative reality that no actor, whatever their background and intentions, can ignore. Having no deed for the place where one lives makes one extremely vulnerable to expulsion, which not only implies the loss of one's home but more often than not the loss of all belongings. It is no surprise that most slum dwellers would do almost everything to get their shacks registered as private property—even if their home does not consist of much more than the two or three corrugated iron sheets of the roof and sun-dried mud bricks (Chapter 7, this issue).

If there is a chance to do so, people who construct 'illegally' at the margins of 'formally' recognised areas try to reproduce the patterns that they believe a 'formal' planning of the urban council would have produced. That will, they presume, ease their recognition as a 'formal' settlement at a later date: urban and development planners must learn to work with these areas—regardless of whether they emerged as unregistered or as registered settlements (Roy, 2005). Though entirely illegal from an official point of view, such neighbourhoods may look as if they were constructed by a construction company under government supervision. They often have the same street grid and reproduce housing patterns very similar to those of the officially recognised neighbourhoods next to them. In an act of 'inverse governmentality', they thus breed similar forms of urban housing and governance (Nielsen, 2011). The street vendor, the market, the tiny shops at the street corner, or illicit drinking spots—they all work in the grey zone that such apparently informal neighbourhoods provide and protect.

Unlike the formal–informal divide, which projects the normativity of Western tax- and state administration on African cities,[7] the grey zone is an open concept. It recognises that neither urban economies and practices nor the roles of the many different actors are fixed. Actors can adopt one or other role according to how they judge a particular situation and what suits them best. They may be tax collectors when meeting a stall owner on the market—and a friend or patron a minute later when they exchange a few words with the

7 To conceive the 'formality' and 'informality' dichotomy as two types of practice (McFarlane, 2012) is a step forward but does not solve the problem as practices may merge as much and as often as the actors change their position in an ongoing interaction.

trader. Living in a grey zone means that that one has to judge and to weigh repeatedly one's interactions with others as people are the institutional infrastructure that one must most often rely on (Simone, 2004b). Only when having engaged in an interaction does the grey give way to colours: the 'formal' and the 'informal' are at best extreme positions on a sliding scale.

Unsurprisingly, the dichotomy of 'formal' vs. 'informal' does not play a decisive role outside the narrower administrative context. Most urban actors do not care whether a particular practice is 'formally' recognised or not. However, that does not mean that there are no rules or that they are living in a chaotic setting. Although development experts perceive the 'informal' sector as 'chaotic' because it is unregulated, that is a big misunderstanding. Unregulated does not mean disordered nor does it necessarily mean confused. Indeed, most people living and working in settings that development experts qualify as 'informal' do have to follow strict rules and regulations. The difference is that these rules are neither written nor necessarily registered and enforced by the city and its administration. They emerge out of the myriad of interactions that ordinary urban dwellers engage in day in, day out. They grow out of the everyday politics of urban governance.

Notwithstanding its opaqueness, the urban grey zone can be a strictly regulated space. The grey zone thus sets itself apart from the usual understanding of the 'informal' sector as an unregulated market. The street vendors in front of a church, mosque or supermarket usually have to respect invisible limits. They must not sell things that other vendors offer next to them—or that the supermarket sells—and they must not intrude into the territory of neighbouring vendors who sell the same stuff. More often than not, they also pay 'taxes'—that is, a daily fee collected by the 'owner of the place'. Often, street vendors do not know why a particular person claims to be the 'owner' of the place—but they know that the man gets angry if he does not get the daily fee. It may be small and insignificant for a shop owner—but it may be very high for vendors with no capital and no other income than the little that they sell over the day. In addition, they sometimes have to pay twice: first to the 'informal' owner and second to the 'formal' tax collector of the urban council. Living in the grey zone is not easy. 'One has to struggle to survive', many of these people say. Rules in the 'informal' sector can be much stricter than the 'formal' rules of the urban council—and may extend right into the heart of global cities such as New York (Touré, 1985; Stoller, 1996; in general Brown, 2006; Bhowmik, 2010).

Does it really make sense to divide urban economies into 'formal' and 'informal' sectors? Or a city's neighbourhoods into 'formal' and 'informal' ones? To characterise African cities as 'informal' cities? In addition to what we have already outlined, other processes also put the 'formal–informal' divide into question. The grey zones may become dominant when an institution disintegrates or when it loses interest in a particular area. Such transformations were sometimes labelled as 're-informalisation' (Myers, 2010, 2011, 89–97). Very much as the processes of inverse governmentality, they may lead to partial formalisation—that is, to hybrid forms where 'formal' and 'informal' rules coexist or overlap (Oldfield, 2002). But that is not the main characteristic of the urban grey zone. 'Informal' as well as 'formal' practices are indistinguishable as long as the actors do not specify them as such—or, to use a metaphor, when they, through their practice, morph the grey into clearer, legible colours.

Using conventional development language thus leads to contradictory statements: 'formal' and 'informal' often merge in everyday life. Myriad forms of 'informal' practices exist within the 'formal' economy. At the same time, the activities in the 'formal' sector very much depend on those in the 'informal' one (Chapter 3, this issue). Not only the urban poor make a living from the 'informal' sector; better-off urbanites also profit from unregulated forms of production, distribution and service provision, especially since the structural adjustment reforms imposed by the International Monetary Fund and the World Bank (Murray and Myers, 2006, 13–15). The emerging urban middle class and its interaction with local state employees and politicians (for India see Fernandes and Heller, 2006; Baud, 2015) is of increasing importance to development cooperation—though the highly loaded term 'class' may not apply in Marxist terms. Again, empirical research is lacking, and much still needs to be clarified. The contribution of Chapter 3 of this issue is an important step towards such a clarification.

Obviously, it is impossible to draw a clear line between the 'informal' and the 'formal' in African cities (Pieterse and Simone, 2013). It depends on the actors and the situation whether a particular practice may fall under the Western rubric of 'formal' and state governed or 'informal' and regulated by others, but it is also possible—and often much more likely—that it merges the two. So, if we have to learn what the elephant is all about, we have to learn it from the actors.

If the distinction of 'formal' versus 'informal' is flawed, what does that mean for development cooperation? The many panels on 'informality' and urbanity in Africa at the European Conference on African Studies 2017 show that the large and ongoing scholarly debates about the meaning and the consequences of 'informality' and development cooperation have not ended. Our notion of the grey zone meets to some extent Oren Yiftachel's (2009b) concept of 'gray space' in the context of Bedouin Arabs' struggles in Israel and Palestine. According to Yiftachel, 'gray spacing' is 'the practice of indefinitely positioning populations between the "lightness" of legality, safety and full membership, and the "darkness" of eviction, destruction and death' (2009a, 247). His example shows that the actors not only have to deal with economic constraints and attempts to extract fees or taxes from them—they are deeply entangled in urban politics. Our concept of the urban grey zone takes this understanding a step further. We take the grey zone as an opaque space that the actors not only confront but through their daily social practice incrementally morph into a colourful cityscape. By positioning themselves in interactions with other urbanites, they create the colours that allow them to perceive the city as a life-world of their own agency.

Development agencies have to rethink conventional concepts that their interventions build on—and their own position in the social and political urban space. Any intervention in such a context is inevitably a political statement. There is no purely 'technical assistance' or 'technical cooperation', as the name of some big development agencies suggests. The materiality of the infrastructure is not a technical instrument only. The segregated colonial city with its *cordons sanitaires* that separated the white urban centre from the periphery and the 'indigenous' population is only the most obvious case in point (Eckert, 2002, 2011). The congestion between the city centre and a suburban neighbourhood today may have a similar effect. On the one hand, not to construct a street means to seal the neighbourhood off from the city as a political space, but it also fosters the emergence of an autonomous suburban social and political space where new actors may emerge (Chapter 11, this issue). On the other hand, constructing a four-lane expressway that cuts the neighbourhood into two also has a double-sided effect. Besides inhibiting the formation of a cohesive community, it may easily bring local actors into the city centre, where they may articulate their political claims in unexpected ways, often to the dislike of those in power (Merrifield, 2013; Diouf and Fredericks, 2014; Chapter 8, this issue).

Cityscapes mirror urban politics (e.g. Habitat International 2015 on urban megaprojects). African cities as 'sites of assemblages and centrality, territorialisation and connectedness' (Robinson, 2013, 1) are characterised by stark contrasts. Today, many African cityscapes display an 'additive' and 'poly-nucleated' urbanism (Brenner and Schmid, 2011, 2015): one neighbourhood after the other is added—but they often remain disconnected, rather focused on themselves. Only a few major axes run through the endlessly urbanised landscape, congested throughout the entire day and much of the night. Moving from one neighbourhood to the other is often extremely time consuming and especially challenging for vulnerable people such as disabled or old persons (UN, 2015). There is no public transport system except tardy minibuses that cannot advance because of traffic and because people enter and exit the buses every few hundred metres—eventually congesting the street as much as private cars do.

Hence, many tiny shops and street vendors persist for all those who cannot afford a car to drive to the main market or the next mall. Africa's urbanites are actors and subjects of continuous social, political and economic transformations and actively situate themselves in their cities as economic, social and political spaces. To move or not to move, to walk or to take a minibus ride is not only a pragmatic judgment of the current situation, it is also an act of articulating one's claims to the city as a social and political space.

Development policies are neither neutral tools nor instruments of social engineering—and neither are remittances, which have become the largest flow of foreign investment in many African countries (Gupta et al., 2009; Nyamongo et al., 2012).[8] They are an important part of and play a multifaceted role in urban politics. Therefore, they require a thorough knowledge of the inhabitants and how they act and articulate their claims to the city. That makes urban development a highly intricate venture that goes far beyond planning exercises. Continuous and critical reflection on the all too often mixed impacts of development policies is an imperative to bring urban change in a good way. The contributions to this issue address this conundrum—they aim to provide insights into the urban life-worlds that African urbanites create, and ask how that local, urban knowledge relates to three themes in African urbanism; urban governance; planning, politics and the urban grey zone; and the urban-rural continuum.

2 The Contributions to This Thematic Issue

The contributions to this issue approach African cities from cross-cutting and interdisciplinary perspectives. They avoid normative, preconceived categories and look at African cities as they are experienced and lived by actors on the continent. We understand urbanity as a social practice of urban dwellers who, through their interactions, create encounters and distanciation in urban social spaces (Förster, 2013). They thus set the frame for urban governance, politics, planning, economics and not least how African cities relate to their outer, rural conurbation area. We structure the chapters around the themes mentioned above.

2.1 *Urban Governance*

Among the many problems that cities are facing in Africa, governance is a key issue. 'Policies do not occur in a vacuum', as the World Development Report

8 Here, the flow of remittances within and between African countries should not be neglected (Sander and Maimbo, 2005).

aptly notes. They are the outcome of complex political and social settings within ever changing rules that are influenced by various actors (World Bank, 2017, 29). As municipalities are, with few exceptions, financially and institutionally weaker than their counterparts in the global North, they often cannot plan and order urban space as urban administrations would do elsewhere. They have to engage in novel forms of governance that are not based on Western models and their history. Research on urban governance in Africa thus has turned into a fascinating field that calls for new concepts and urban theories to analyse the entanglement of the many actors that engage in and deal with cities and the urban. The author of Chapter 2 looks at different levels and scales of urban governance in Africa. Having been part of international, regional and national bodies responsible for drafting new policies, he is intimately familiar with urban agendas in numerous African cities and analyses how they relate to global policy frameworks—namely, the New Urban Agenda adopted by the United Nations at Habitat III, 2016. The author's analyses also address the local level, including Khayelitsha, a suburb and former township of Cape Town, South Africa. As director of the African Centre for Cities, also domiciled in Cape Town, he has a deep insight into urban policies and the formation of urban governance in other parts of the continent. The author proposes a radical change in the future political and institutional landscape: territorial, macroeconomic and infrastructure investment regimes should be thought of as one. In his contribution, he outlines how this new landscape could—and should—look and what conditions need to be fulfilled to extend such multiscalar politics in Africa.

The author of Chapter 3 adopts another, complementary perspective on urban governance in Africa. He mainly looks at Kisumu in Kenya as an example of the urban middle ground—the many ordinary, medium-sized cities on the continent that are neither sprawling megacities nor country capitals with their extraordinary responsibilities and corresponding budgets. The author's analytical lens focuses on three basic fields of governance: land use management, the provision of basic services, and mobility. His basic findings are obvious: the World Bank's concept of good governance, largely based on normative Western understandings of the Westphalian state as an institution of superior legitimate power, does and will not work in Africa. One has to recognise, he argues, that neither the state as an institution nor state actors as individuals occupy the same dominant position in African cities as they do in the global North. Therefore, he uses governance mainly as a lens to analyse how decisions are made in African cities and how they are eventually implemented. By juxtaposing a general typology of actors to the three basic themes of governance, the author concludes that there is no alternative to collaborative forms of governance—as messy and conflictual as they often are, they take the deeply political character of governance into account while government-oriented models will fail to depoliticise governance.

In Chapter 4, the authors examine a practical case of urban governance: the effectiveness of conventional anti-corruption and good-governance policies in Rwanda, Uganda and Tanzania, East Africa. As many state actors and also development agencies still make use of the formal–informal dichotomy, the authors look at how such basic convictions shape the perception of corruption and how corruption is related to informal practices blurring its presence in the daily lives of the populace. They identify three such practices: a) co-optation as the recruitment into social networks where corruption is sustained, b) control as a practice of normalising and securing the persistence of corruption by disciplining those who might deviate from corrupt patterns of behaviour, and c) camouflage as a way of obscuring where corruption actually plays a role in the administration and its subordinate bodies. Corruption sustains, the authors conclude, a moral economy that, on its part, also legitimises these practices. As a normalised form of interaction, corruption depends on political regimes that build on clientelist networks. To claim that corruption is 'endemic'—as some politicians repeatedly do—is no more than a shortcut. Bypassing a thorough empirical analysis, it labels corruption as a disease for which no cure exists. The authors show that such analyses are possible and need to be done.

Chapter 5 addresses one of the SDG 11 targets, namely the provision of inclusive, green and public spaces (UN, 2015). The author zooms in on a failure of collaborative governance and thus counterbalances to some degree the more general statements of the preceding contributions. The author asks why the co-management of parks in Johannesburg, South Africa, does not work in the post-apartheid era. Since the budget allocated to such sites by the city council is limited, many neighbourhoods in middle-class areas engage in a sort of community management of already existing parks. Opposing agendas are fostered by the deep mistrust between certain actors, in particular the mainly white middle classes and the City Park authorities dominated by black South Africans. This opposition provokes the emergence of political articulations and creates a discursive space where the voices of other actors, in particular those of lower-income communities are often not heard. This deeply conflictual, political configuration makes the management of the parks extremely complex and eventually marginalises other, private actors and their initiatives.

2.2 *Planning, Urban Politics and the Urban Grey Zone*

The second section of this special issue looks at planning, urban politics and the urban grey zone, which all feed into what is usually known as the 'informality' of urbanisation in Africa. Rapid urbanisation processes are highly sensitive issues for the actors involved. Politicians, planners, local entrepreneurs, development experts as well as ordinary urbanites have different and often contesting visions for their city. The African city is characterised by stark contrasts within itself. Thus, the same city looks very different from one neighbourhood to the next. While glittering skyscrapers might dominate the central business districts where governmental buildings are located and where the country's financial centre lies, many areas of the city's grey zone are marked by modest houses and insufficient, decaying infrastructure. These are the areas where upgrading and transformation processes are frequent—and where development policies are most relevant, as the following chapters demonstrate.

Chapter 6 provides an overview of urbanisation in Africa and relates it to general demographic trends on the continent and elsewhere. The prospects of an extremely rapidly growing urban population point at future challenges of development cooperation and, indeed, at what these changes in Europe's global neighbourhood will mean for the aging population of the global North. The author does not come up with easy answers; he just points at the dimensions of the long-term tendencies. It is clear that, already today, the image of Africa as a rural continent no longer reflects realities on the continent. The author then analyses the wide variety of cities in Africa and introduces the Sustainable Cities Initiatives in Africa that aim at answering the challenges of urbanisation, focusing particularly on the environment, land use, public transport, water and sanitation as the most burning issues in Africa's exploding megacities. He shows that regional and international networks of cities may lead to a more sustainable development of African cities, but it is also clear that some cities and urban agglomerations on the continent are not visible in these networks—indicating the importance of expanding and strengthening these networks. The same holds true for thorough, empirically grounded research on urbanisation in Africa, which is done by only a few institutions on the continent.

Chapter 7 takes a close look at how inhabitants who live at the fringes of Namibia's capital Windhoek make claims in the context of upgrading policies that have been ongoing for over 15 years. The author demonstrates that while some campaigning and sporadic movements have received wider attention, most forms of claim-making over land, services and housing emerge from the residents' everyday experiences. The contribution nicely illustrates the diversity of the settlements and actors involved as well as the blurred boundaries between tolerated and non-tolerated practices, licit and illicit procedures, and between formality and informality more generally. The author concludes that contrary to all too many other, more autocratic settings, the relationship between state representatives and the poor inhabitants in Namibia is not marked by opposition but by mutual dependency, which leads to co-optation and collusion.

Addis Ababa, Ethiopia's capital, is an example of a rapidly growing city in an authoritarian development state. In Chapter 8, the author analyses the formation of physical and social spaces and how these processes relate to social and economic differentiation. The formation of such spaces is key to understanding the range of urbanisation in Africa. In practical terms, this may mean looking more attentively at the impact that, for instance, the construction of streets and other infrastructure has on how the urban populace can dwell, make a living and articulate their interests. In particular, large streets with separate lanes and heavy traffic may affect the ways urbanites as social actors can situate themselves in the city. They can prevent, as the author writes, 'spatial dialogics' and dialogic articulations that would sustain the city as a collective social space. An approach that looks more carefully at how common ground emerges in the formation of urban social spaces would no longer follow the usual, linear model of development to solve specific economic, environmental or social problems. It would rather foster a circular approach—a continuous engagement with different concepts and ideas as they are articulated by the people in different spaces in the city.

In Chapter 9, the authors are also interested in the impacts of major spatial transformations that significantly influence the everyday lives of ordinary urbanites. The authors analyse decongestion policies applied in Accra, Ghana, over the last decades to remove unwanted urban dwellers and activities within the city centre. The municipality argued that the policies were aimed at beautifying the city, easing traffic flows, reducing crime and preventing the regular flooding of large areas. In their contribution, the authors analyse the effects of these policies with regard to inclusiveness, sustainable development and the promotion of the right to the city more generally.

2.3 *The Urban-Rural Continuum*

The last section in this special issue focuses on the rural–urban continuum. In discursive formations of many African urbanites, a huge discrepancy between urban and rural modes of living and lifestyles is noticeable. While the city is related to 'modern' ways of life, the village is considered the representation of 'traditional' values. However, such a clear-cut binary distinction between the two is utterly impossible: the rural and the urban are interlinked in manifold ways. The footprints of the city are visible in rural areas—very much as rural ways of living shape urban areas. One such example is urban agriculture, which replenishes the food basket of many a household in urban Africa. As cities expand, they extend more and more into the surrounding rural area, adding to the expansion of what can be labelled the city's outskirts, the city's fringes, suburbs, peri-urban areas or peripheral neighbourhoods. Consequently, it is often not clear where a city begins and where it ends. Ash Amin and Nigel Thrift (2002, 1) go as far as to claim that '[w]e can no longer even agree on what counts as a city... The city is everywhere and in everything'.

In Chapter 10, the author foregrounds exactly such urbanisation processes, analysing former villages that have merged with the city. The author critically distances himself from research that analyses urban phenomena in the global South from a 'Western' perspective as done for example by the Globalization and World Cities (GAWC) research network or the work informed by Lefebvre's idea of planetary urbanisation. In contrast, he utilises urban theory from the global South for the global South, applying Chinese concepts to explain urban transformations in Senegal and Zanzibar. When analysing villages swallowed up by the cities in the Pearl River Delta, Chinese urbanists distinguish three forms: villages in the city, villages on the edge and villages in the suburbs. The author utilises these three concepts as lenses to explain what has recently been happening in the West District of Zanzibar and Dakar's satellite city of Pikine. The author's comparison is a convincing example of how African cities can be thought through the urban elsewhere (Robinson, 2016).

In Chapter 11, the author zooms in on this same city—Pikine. He examines the various ways through which young men live and shape their city and vice versa. Even though Pikine lacks basic infrastructure and is characterised by a high degree of urban poverty, its young urbanites take pride in being from this place. Through the explanation of specific expressions young men frequently use in the vernacular language, the author demonstrates how they situationally adapt to the daily challenges they face. Male youth does this by, among other practices, switching between different identities and appearances and by applying specific coping strategies. They typically characterise themselves as being smart, having stamina and making the best of every situation thanks to their improvisational capacities. Like this, young men are able to make a living and get by in the challenging everyday life-worlds of urban Africa.

The author of Chapter 12 is also interested in urban milieus, this time in East Africa. More specifically, he applies the *distinctiveness of cities*-concept developed by German sociologists to examine the particularities of a growing segment in almost all African cities, namely the middle-income strata. In his study, the author identifies six different, but partly overlapping milieus in Nairobi and explains their connections to rural areas: the Neo-Traditionals, the Social Climbers, the Cosmopolitan-Liberals, the Christian Religious and the Young Professionals. The last two are analysed in more detail. The Christian Religious are active church members and strictly follow religious rules. At the same time, they are highly ambitious and convinced that they will—thanks to spiritual support—socially advance. For Young Professionals, in contrast, conspicuous consumption and individual lifestyles are essential. These milieus, so the author argues, are bound to their city in particular ways just as, vice versa, the different cities shape the lifestyles of these milieus.

In Chapter 13, the author is also interested in rural–urban transformations but approaches them through mining 'boomtowns' in the conflict-ridden area of the Kivu provinces, Democratic Republic of Congo. In an ethnographically rich description, the author demonstrates how three emerging mining towns have become important political, economic and social resources for the actors involved. These 'boomtowns' offer fascinating lenses with which to explore how different political, economic, humanitarian, civil and military actors (violently) struggle for power, authority and control. The author argues that due to their urban character and the natural resources they contain, emerging 'boomtowns' have intensified the already existing conflict dynamics in the Kivu provinces.

References

ADB (African Development Bank) (2016) *Annual Report 2016*, https://www.afdb.org/fileadmin/uploads/afdb/Documents/Generic-Documents/AfDB_Annual_Report_2016_EN.pdf, (accessed on 16 January 2018).

ADB (2016) *Sustainable Cities and Structural Transformation* (African Economic Outlook 2016), DOI: http://dx.doi.org/10.1787/aeo-2016-en, (accessed on 16 January 2018).

ADB (2012) *Urbanisation in Africa*, https://www.afdb.org/en/blogs/afdb-championing-inclusive-growth-across-africa/post/urbanization-in-africa-10143/ (accessed on 16 January 2018).

African Center for Economic Transformation (2017) *African Transformation Report. Agriculture Powering Africa's Economic Transformation*, http://acetforafrica.org/acet/wp-content/uploads/publications/2017/10/ATR17-full-report.pdf, (accessed on 16 January 2018).

Amin, A. and N. Thrift (2002) *Cities: reimagining the urban* (Cambridge: Polity Press).

Anjaria, J.S. and C. McFarlane (eds.) (2011) *Urban Navigations* (London: Routledge).

Balandier, G. (1957) *Afrique ambiguë* (Paris: Plon).

Balandier, G. (1955) *Sociologie actuelle de l'Afrique noire* (Paris: Presses Universitaires de France).

Baud, I. (2015) 'The emerging middle classes in India: Mobilizing for inclusive development?' *The European Journal of Development* Research 27(2), pp. 230–237, DOI: 10.1057/ejdr.2015.1.

Bhowmik, S. (ed.) (2010) *Street Vendors in the Global Urban Economy* (New Delhi: Routledge).

Brenner, N. and C. Schmid (2015) 'Towards a New Epistemology of the Urban?' *City* 19(1–2), pp. 151–182.

Brenner, N. and C. Schmid (2011) 'Planetary Urbanisation', in Gandy M., (ed.) *Urban Constallations* (Berlin: Jovis), pp. 10–13.

Brown, A. (ed.) (2006) *Contested Space: Street Trading, Public Space, and Livelihoods in Developing Cities* (Rugby: ITDG Publishing).

Burdett, R. and D. Sudjic (eds.) (2007) *The Endless City: an authoritative and visually rich survey of the contemporary city* (London: Phaidon Press).

Chénal, J. (2016) 'Capitalizing on Urbanization'. In *Foresight Africa: top priorities for the continent in 2016,* edited by Brookings Institution (Washington DC: Brookings), pp. 59–72.

Kessides, C. (2006) *The Urban Transition in Sub-Saharan Africa* (Washington DC: Cities Alliances).

Collier, P. (1993) 'Africa and the Study of Economics', in R. Bates, V.Y. Mudimbe and J. O'Barr (eds.) *Africa and the Disciplines* (Chicago: University of Chicago Press), pp. 58–82.

Datta, A. and A. Shaban (2016) *Mega-Urbanisation in the Global South* (London: Routledge).

Davis, M. (2006) *Planet of Slums* (London: Verso).

De Soto, H. (1989) *The Other Path: The invisible revolution in the Third World* (New York: Harper and Row).

Diouf, M. and R. Fredericks (2014) 'Introduction: Decolonizing Urban Theory', in M. Diouf and R. Fredericks (eds.) *The Arts of Citizenship in African Cities* (New York: Palgrave Macmillan), pp. 1–23.

Drakakis-Smith, D. (2000) *Third World Cities* (New York: Routledge).

Eckert, A. (2011) '"Bright Lights—Big City": Zur Geschichte und Gegenwart der Städte in Afrika', *Globalisierung Süd.* Sondernummern Leviathan: Zeitschrift für Sozialwissenschaften (Wiesbaden: VS Verlag für Sozialwissenschaften), pp. 314–330.

Eckert, A. (2002) 'Städte und Urbanisierung in Afrika in historischer Perspektive', *Africa Spectrum* 37(1), pp. 81–97.

Fernandes, L. and P. Heller (2006) 'Hegemonic aspirations: New middle-class politics and India's democracy in comparative perspective' *Critical Asian Studies* 38(4), pp. 495–552, DOI: 10.1080/14672710601073028.

Förster, T. (2013) 'On Urbanity: Creativity and Emancipation in African Urban Life', in B. Obrist, V. Arlt and E. Macamo (eds.) *Living the City in Africa* (Zürich: Lit-Verlag), pp. 235–251.

Freund, B. (2007) *The African City: A History* (Cambridge: Cambridge University Press).

Gupta, S., C.A. Pattillo and S. Wagh (2009) 'Effect of Remittances on Poverty and Financial Development in Sub-Saharan Africa', *World Development* 37(1), pp. 103–115, DOI: 10.1016/j.worlddev.2008.05.007.

Hart, K. (1985) 'The informal economy', *Cambridge Anthropology* 10(2), pp. 54–58.

Hart, K. (1973) 'Informal income opportunities and urban employment in Ghana', *Journal of Modern African Studies* 11(1), pp. 61–89, http://www.jstor.org/stable/159873.

Healey, P. (2007) 'Urban complexity and spatial strategies: Towards a relational planning for our times' (New York: Routledge), https://trove.nla.gov.au/version/31316342.

Hyden, G. (2007) 'Governance and Poverty Reduction in Africa', *Proceedings of the National Academy of Sciences of the United States of America* 104(43): 16751–16756, DOI: 10.1073/pnas.0700696104.

Iliffe, J. (1995) *Africans: The History of a Continent* (Cambridge: Cambridge University Press).

Jones, B.G. (2012a) 'Civilising African Cities: International Housing and Urban Policy from Colonial to Neoliberal Times'. *Journal of Intervention and Statebuilding* 6(1), pp. 23–40, DOI: 10.1080/17502977.2012.655560.

Jones, B.G. (2012b) '"Bankable" Slums: The global politics of slum upgrading' *Third World Quarterly* 33(5), pp. 769–798.

Kennedy, L. (2015): 'The politics and changing paradigm of megaproject development in metropolitan cities', *Habitat International* 45, pp. 163–168, http://www.sciencedirect.com/science/journal/01973975/45/supp/P3.

La Porta, R. and A. Shleifer (2014) 'Informality and Development', *Journal of Economic Perspectives* 28(3), pp. 109–126.

Lefebvre, H. (1968) *Le droit à la ville* (Paris: Anthropos).

Lewis, W. (1955) *The Theory of Economic Growth* (London: Allen and Unwin).

Lindell, I. (ed.) (2010a) *Africa's Informal Workers* (London: Zed).

Lindell, I. (2010b) 'Between Exit and Voice: Informality and the Spaces of Popular Agency', *African Studies Quarterly* 11(2–3), pp. 1–11.

Lipton, M. (1977) *Why Poor People Stay Poor: A study of urban bias in world development* (London: Temple-Smith).

Massey, D. (2005) *For Space* (London: Thousand Oaks).

McFarlane, C. (2012) 'Rethinking Informality: Politics, Crisis, and the City', *Planning Theory and Practice* 13(1), pp. 89–108.

Medina, L., A. Jonelis, and M. Cangul (2017) *The Informal Economy in Sub-Saharan Africa.* (IMF Working Papers 17/156), https://www.imf.org/en/Publications/WP/Issues/2017/07/10/The-Informal-Economy-in-Sub-Saharan-Africa-Size-and-Determinants-45017, (accessed on 16 January 2018).

Meillassoux, C. (1981) *Maidens, Meal and Money: Capitalism and the Domestic Community* (Cambridge: Cambridge University Press).

Merrifield, A. (2013) *The Politics of the Encounter* (Athens, GA: University of Georgia Press).

Murray, M. and G. Myers (eds.) (2006) *Cities in Contemporary Africa* (New York: Palgrave Macmillan).

Myers, G. (2010) *Seven Themes in African Urban Dynamics* (Uppsala: Nordiska Afrikainstitutet).

Myers, G. (2011) *African Cities: Alternative Visions of Urban Theory and Practice* (London: Zed).

Nielsen, M. (2011) 'Inverse Governmentality: The paradoxical production of peri-urban planning in Maputo, Mozambique', *Critique of Anthropology* 31(4), pp. 329–358, DOI: 10.1177/0308275X11420118.

Njoh, A. (2009) 'Urban planning as a tool of power and social control in colonial Africa', *Planning Perspectives* 24(3), pp. 301–317, DOI: 10.1080/02665430902933960.

Nyamongo, E.M., R.N. Misati, L. Kipyegon and L. Ndirangu (2012) 'Remittances, Financial Development and Economic Growth in Africa', *Journal of Economics and Business* 64, pp. 240–226, DOI: 10.1016/j.jeconbus.2012.01.001.

Obrist, B., A. Veit and M. Elisio (eds.) (2013) *Living the City in Africa: Processes of Invention and Intervention* (Münster: lit Verlag).

Oldfield, S. (2015) 'Between Activism and the Academy: The Urban as Political Terrain', *Urban Studies* 52(11), pp. 2072–2086, DOI: 10.1177/0042098013515942.

Oldfield, S. (2002) 'Partial Formalization and Its Implications for Community Governance in an Informal Settlement', *Urban Forum* 13(2), pp. 102–115.

Parnell, S. and E. Pieterse (eds.) (2014) *Africa's Urban Revolution* (London: Zed).

Pieterse, E. (2008) *City Futures: confronting the crisis of urban development* (London: Zed).

Pieterse, E. and S. Parnell (2014) 'Africa's urban revolution in context', in S. Parnell and E. Pieterse, *Africa's Urban Revolution* (Zed Books: London), pp. 1–17.

Pieterse, E. and A. Simone (eds.) (2013) *Rogue Urbanism: Emergent African Cities* (Johannesburg: Jacana Media).

Pinther, K., L. Förster and C. Hanussek (eds.) (2012) *Afropolis: City, Media, Art* (Johannesburg: Jacana Media).

Potts, D. (2012) *Whatever Happened to Africa's Rapid Urbanisation?* (Africa Research Institute: London) http://africaresearchinstitute.org/newsite/wp-content/uploads/2013/03/Whatever-happened-to-Africas-rapid-urbanisation.pdf (accessed on 16 January 2018).

Purcell, M. (2014) 'Possible Worlds: Henri Lefebvre and the right to the city', *Journal of Urban Affairs* 36(1), pp. 141–154.

Rauch, J. (1991) 'Modelling the informal sector formally', *Journal of Development Economics* 35(1), pp. 33–47.

Riddell, R. (1985) *Regional Development Policy* (Gower: Aldershot).

Robinson, J. (2016). Thinking cities through elsewhere: Comparative tactics for a more global urban studies. *Progress in Human Geography* 40(1), 3-29.

Robinson, J. (2013) '"Arriving at" Urban Policies/the Urban: Traces of Elsewhere in Making City Futures', in O. Söderström, S. Randeria, D. Ruedin, G. d'Amato and F. Panese (eds.), *Critical Mobilities* (Oxford: Routledge), pp. 1–28.

Robinson, J. (2006) *Ordinary Cities: Between Modernity and Development* (New York: Routledge).

Robinson, J. (2005) 'Urban geography: world cities, or a world of cities', *Progress in Human Geography* 29(6), pp. 757–765.

Roy, A. (2005) 'Urban Informality: Toward an Epistemology of Planning', *Journal of the American Planning Association* 71(2), pp. 147–158, DOI: 10.1080/01944360508976689.

Sander, C. and S.M. Maimbo (2005) 'Migrant Remittances in Africa. A Regional Perspective' in S.M. Maimbo, and D. Ratha (eds.) *Remittances. Development Impact and Future Prospects* (Washington: The World Bank), pp. 53–79.

Simone, A. (2004a) *For the City Yet to Come: Changing African Life in Four Cities* (Durham: Duke University Press).

Simone, A. (2004b) 'People as Infrastructure: Intersecting fragments in Johannesburg', *Public Culture* 16(3), pp. 407–429, DOI: 10.1215/08992363-16-3-407.

Smit, W. and E. Pieterse (2014) 'Decentralisation and institutional reconfiguration in urban Africa' in S. Parnell and E. Pieterse (eds.) *Africa's Urban Revolution* (London: Zed), pp. 148–166.

Stoller, P. (1996) 'Spaces, Places, and Fields: the politics of West African trading in New York City's informal economy', *American Anthropologist* 98(4), pp. 776–788, DOI: 10.1525/aa.1996.98.4.02a00080.

The Guardian (2016) *'Africa's urbanisation 'megatrend' needs to deliver growth, says report',* https://www.theguardian.com/global-development/2016/jun/07/africa-urbanisation-megatrend-needs-to-deliver-growth-says-report, (accessed on 16 January 2018).

Touré, A. (1985) *Les petits métiers à Abidjan: l'imagination au secours de la conjuncture* (Paris: Karthala).

UN (United Nations) (2015) 'Sustainable Development Goals, Goal 11: Make cities inclusive, safe, resilient and sustainable', http://www.un.org/sustainabledevelopment/cities/ (accessed on 16 January 2018).

UN DESA (United Nations Department of Social and Economic Affairs) (2014) *World Urbanization Prospects: The 2014 Revision* (New York: United Nations).

UN-Habitat (2016) *Urbanization and Development: Emerging Futures. World Cities Report 2016* (New York: United Nations).

UN-Habitat (2008) *The State of African Cities 2008: A framework for addressing urban challenges in Africa* (New York: United Nations).

Watson, V. (2014) 'The Case of a Southern Perspective in Planning Theory', *International Journal of E-Planning Research* 3(1), pp. 23–37, DOI: 10.4018/ijepr.2014010103.

World Bank (2017) World Development Report 2017. Governance and the Law, http://www.worldbank.org/en/publication/wdr2017, (accessed on 16 January 2018).

World Bank (2014) *Africa's urban population growth: trends and projections*, https://blogs.worldbank.org/opendata/africa-s-urban-population-growth-trends-and-projections, (accessed on 16 January 2018).

Yiftachel, O. (2009a) 'Critical theory and "gray space": Mobilization of the colonized', *City* 13(2–3), pp. 246–263, DOI: 10.1080/13604810902982227.

Yiftachel, O. (2009b) 'Theoretical notes on "gray cities": the coming of urban apartheid?' *Planning Theory* 8(1), pp. 88–100, DOI: 10.1177/1473095208099300.

CHAPTER 2

The Politics of Governing African Urban Spaces

Edgar Pieterse

Abstract

Drawing on the author's direct experiences in urban policy formulation processes on various scales, this chapter makes a case for a more intimate reading and account of macro policy shifts that may hold the potential to advance transformative politics on the national and the urban scale. It argues that new policy concepts and frameworks can advance a more focused politics based on an analysis of the nature and terms of infrastructure investments and considers whether such investments are advancing a more inclusive, labour intensive and sustainable pattern of development in African cities and towns. The chapter asserts that urban governance policy discourses are now connecting urban investments and regulation with macroeconomic imperatives, which could lead to a greater awareness of urban governance within centres of state power. Structurally the chapter identifies examples of policy artefacts on the global, pan-African and national scales to demonstrate the shared potential for a new kind of transformative politics. Thereafter, the chapter sets out a potential methodological register to track, analyse and engage these processes on the urban scale in order to arrive at a propositional sensibility with regard to governing diverse spaces. It calls for a form of research and analysis that is not merely evaluative, after the fact, but rather positioned in the processes of unfolding. There are not enough of these kinds of scholarly accounts that can enrich and deepen debates about the politics and practice of multi-scalar urban governance reform in diverse African settings.

1 Introduction

My experiences in conducting urban policy advocacy and advisory work over the past three years are the entry point for this chapter, accumulated in the run-up to the bi-decennial convening of the United Nations Conferences on Housing—Habitat III. This chapter offers a reflection on why formal discursive shifts at both the global and the African level, about the territorial underpinnings of sustainable development, offer new opportunities to both imagine and instantiate a fresh politics on how urban areas are governed. It seeks to sidestep the typical approaches to the dynamics of multi-scalar urban

© EDGAR PIETERSE, 2018 | DOI:10.1163/9789004387942_003

governance in Africa, which either provide neo-Marxian accounts of macroeconomic processes of neo-liberalisation (Miraftab, 2004; Obeng-Odoom, 2015; Ferguson 2011) or constructivist perspectives on the significance of everyday urbanism in shaping forms of rule, government and counter-governmentality (Bayat, 2010). This chapter relates to both strands in the literature but seeks to offer a closer reading of formal policy shifts with an eye to the kinds of critical politics that might emerge, building on the conceptual framework proposed by Scoones et al. (2015) and Swilling (2016).

The chapter starts by briefly rehearsing the various policy formulation processes I have been active in since 2015 to provide a contextual reference point for what follows. The following section traces some of the emblematic milestones in this policy reorientation with an eye to what it might mean for the imperative to rethink and remake multilevel governance arrangements animated by new normative policy imperatives such as 'infrastructure-led growth', closely linked to the macroeconomic imperative to achieve 'structural transformation'. These policy imperatives matter because they are forging and foregrounding a more explicit spatial articulation of macroeconomic policy. This articulation in turn instigates significant institutional reforms that announce, I believe, novel political opportunities for deep democracy and cultural citizenship (Pieterse, 2008; Mbembe, 2016). The second half of the chapter sets out a potential methodological register—in the broadest sense—to track, analyse and engage these processes on the urban scale in order to arrive at a propositional sensibility with regard to governing diverse spaces. It therefore calls for a form of research and analysis that is not merely evaluative after the fact, but is applied in the processes of unfolding. There is a dearth of these kinds of scholarly accounts that can enrich and deepen debates about the politics and practice of multi-scalar urban governance reform in diverse African settings.

2 Policy Artefacts to Reshape Urban Governance

This section situates my positioning in relation to the production of a number of policy artefacts on the pan-African and national (South Africa) scales during the last few years. Specifically, at the global level, I contributed to the technical research processes of UN-Habitat to formulate an overarching narrative about the state of the world's cities, with an eye to proposing comprehensive reforms to effect structural change. More specifically, I worked on Chapter Six of the *World Cities Report 2016* (UN-Habitat, 2016), which deals with governance. Another global report that was published in 2016 was the GOLD IV report, by United Cities and Local Government (UCLG 2016). I collaborated with two colleagues to draft the synthesis and recommendations of this report, which explored the implications of the 2030 Agenda for Sustainable Development and its goals (SDGs) for different categories of territorial organisation: metropolitan areas, intermediary cities, regions, small towns and rural areas.

At the African level, I collaborated with colleagues at the African Centre for Cities (ACC)—an interdisciplinary research hub at the University of Cape Town—to craft a primer on what an African perspective might comprise regarding a new urban agenda for the world as governments were preparing for Habitat III, the United Nations convening on urbanisation that happens every twenty years. This work was published in early 2015. It was crafted to serve as a resource for governmental preparatory processes at national and sub-regional (e.g. West African, Southern African) levels to clarify the African perspective for Habitat III (UN Habitat and UNECA, 2015). Questions of governance, institutional design and politics were central to this paper, published under the auspices of UN-Habitat and the UN Economic Commission for Africa (UNECA). A second pan-African intervention took the form of a background research paper for the Organisation for Economic Cooperation and Development (OECD) and the African Development Bank (AfDB) as they were drafting the *Africa Economic Outlook 2016*, themed: Sustainable Cities and Structural Transformation (OECD, et al., 2016). The two Africa-focused policy papers had to confront the articulation of African specificities with emerging global discourses generated by the SDGs and the Paris Agreement, or Paris climate accord. This meant addressing systemic dysfunctionality as detailed by academic commentators, and the routine violation of rights and obligation (Davis, 2006; Myers, 2011; Swilling and Annecke, 2012).

Alongside this work on a global and African scale, I was deeply involved in national policy drafting processes in South Africa that sought to formulate the *Integrated Urban Development Framework* (RSA, 2016). This framework was a forerunner of National Urban Policies, or recognised tools toward global urban agendas as sanctified by the New Urban Agenda adopted at Habitat III. This experience gave me an opportunity to work through the discursive gymnastics required to articulate highly localised demands, histories and institutional imperatives with African and global discourses about urban governance, regulation and politics.

Lastly, and in anticipation of criticisms that I am simply the 'bagman' for what academics call free-floating or 'travelling' discourses (Harris and Moore, 2013), during this time I also worked closely with a social movement called the Social Justice Coalition (SJC). The SJC is operative around safety and sanitation issues in areas of Khayelitsha, one of the largest suburbs of Cape Town.[1] Strictly speaking, this was not conventional research but rather a process of mutual socialisation and exchange. I spent time with a cross-section of the leadership of the SJC, on a periodic basis, to creatively explore dilemmas of strategy and tactics, drawing on social history methods in a focus group setting. In return, I offered my experience and knowledge of comparable social movement practices in other urban settings of the world, as well as earlier periods of social struggle in Cape Town. These intimate conversations were profoundly important as an anchoring device while I was plying my policy craft on these other scales of policy politics.

One of the insights gained over the course of this work was into the ways in which the political/policy ground on questions of urbanisation in sub-Saharan Africa had shifted from only a few years before this engagement. In 2014, Sue Parnell and I published the edited volume *Africa's Urban Revolution*; many chapters in that volume confirm the long-standing lament about the anti-urban bias practised by most African governments, manifested in mired devolution efforts combined with futile anti-migration policies (UN-Habitat, 2014). However, over only a few years there has been a sea change at various levels of formal governance across the continent. Most significantly, at a pan-African level, the African Union, UNECA and the AfDB have all been driving a much more aggressive line around the imperative to rethink, remake and reinvest multilevel governance arrangements to improve the prospects of 'structural economic transformation' and inclusive growth. These gestures towards an African-centred perspective on inclusive modernisation rest on an acknowledgement of urbanisation as evident in *Agenda 2063*—the signature political programme and ideological frame of the African Union, initiated in 2013 in Addis Ababa on the occasion of the 50th anniversary of the establishment of the Organisation of African Unity (African Union, 2014). This 50th milestone informed the 50-year horizon of the revitalised pan-African vision as reflected in the designator: *Agenda 2063*.

Embedded in this new policy discourse is an unmistakable recognition that unless a stronger territorial or spatial understanding begins to drive routine processes of infrastructure investment and economic development, most African countries will remain low-income and marginal in global value chains (UNECA, 2015; 2017). Furthermore, it is recognised that the imperative to coordinate, sequence and calibrate disparate investments in highly

1 See the Social Justice Coalition website http://www.sjc.org.za (accessed on 18 April 2018).

complex and volatile systems requires a territorial proximity, for which the traditional model of national-centric planning and management is not well suited.

3 Major Discursive Shifts

The 2030 Agenda for Sustainable Development (United Nations 2015), as embodied in the 17 sustainable development goals (SDGs), is highly significant and reflects the culmination of at least two decades of sustained human rights struggles to push back on the narrow economistic precepts of neo-liberal managerialism.[2] For example, there is an explicit recognition that growing intra- and inter-country inequality is a major impediment to inclusivity. This is a profound break with the reformist 'poverty reduction' orientation of the Millennium Development Goals of 2000. The SDGs also acknowledge the environmental limits of the dominant growth model that remains the de facto reference point for governments and companies. Thus, there is a strong push to mainstream the work and perspective of the United Nations Environment Programme (UNEP) on sustainable production and consumption, linked to a separate set of goals on changing the carbon intensity and resource consumption patterns that underpin global value chains across all domains of economic activity. In other words, in the SDGs there is a mainstreaming of the long-established political claims and policy proposals to internalise negative environmental and social costs, opening up a line of politics to build a broad-based front against extractive and exploitative capitalist processes. It is precisely these ambitions that have reinforced a more popular discourse and imagination about post-capitalist futures and trajectories (Mason, 2015; Srnicek and Williams, 2015). Lastly, the SDGs also recognise the importance

2 It is important to keep in mind that since 1990, with the publication of the first Human Development Report by UNDP, there has been a fierce ideological contestation between the Bretton Woods institutions and the United Nations. Fundamentally it turned on Amartya Sen's human capabilities approach versus a narrow neoclassical perspective on market-led development. After Rio+20, the green economic perspective, riding on the momentum of the environmental limits work of the IPCC, was able to broaden the mainstream debates to incorporate various shades of green analysis (Swilling and Annecke, 2012). Throughout these processes, the human rights struggle of social movements and watchdog bodies have been instrumental in keeping up the political pressure necessary for mainstream arguments to shift away from crass neo-liberalism to a broader, more heterodox perspective as manifest in the SDGs and the Paris Climate Accord of 2015.

of sustainable urbanisation as a precondition for a more green and inclusive economic patterning of development. This is a major departure from the aspatial and implicitly anti-urban orientation of the MDGs (Parnell, 2016) and has created room for a pointed argument that the SDGs must be 'localised'—that is to say, driven from the grassroots by municipalities and citizens' movements—to find resonance and sustained traction in diverse contexts (Pieterse, et al. 2017).

A number of broader dynamics made it possible for the SDGs to break with the welfarist reformism of the MDGs. Firstly, the damaging environmental impacts of existing economic globalisation processes have been argued convincingly through climate change evidence and its calculation-driven discourse, creating an opening for the broader sustainable development perspective of yonder to stage a comeback after being unable to substantively shift the economist reference points of international and national developmentalism (Scoones et al., 2015). Secondly, the exclusionary and alienating aspects of neoliberal globalism were made evident through the lingering effects of youth unemployment and political volatility across many OECD countries, especially in southern Europe, linked to the decentralised impacts of terrorist violence related to so-called alienated youth. Populist ideologues on both the left and the right stepped into this disjuncture, unsettling traditional centrist parties (and coalitions) across the OECD world, but also deeply entrenched political parties that have been in power since independence in many African countries. The post-2008 era spelled political uncertainty, volatility and changing public attitudes towards incumbent political parties, undermining the hegemony of economic globalists and the political parties who grew fat off those ideological regimes (Castells and Himanen, 2014).

These broader trends played out in interesting ways in much of sub-Saharan Africa. The 'boosterism' narrative that Africa's economic time had come, which took hold and flourished post 2000, was starting to experience strain. GDP growth rates started to slow and stagnate, and substantial investment gaps remained. Two structural breaks on sustained and high economic growth were identified across development and private sector think tanks: limited and inefficient infrastructure and weak governance and regulatory practices that constituted systemic risk for large-scale investment (McKinsey Global Institute, 2016; PwC, 2015). Of course, these two dynamics are inextricably linked. It is against this background that my focus turns to the announcement and promotion of *Agenda 2063*. In keeping with the nature of these aspirational and norm-setting policy frameworks, *Agenda 2063* envisages a profoundly transformed Continent, people and economy: 'an integrated, prosperous and peaceful Africa, driven by its own citizens and representing a dynamic force in the international arena' (African Union, 2015, 1). This vision is meant to be realised through a highly focused, strongly normative and popular agenda that is cognisant of the importance of

> ... mobilization of the people and their ownership of continental programmes at the core; the principle of self-reliance and Africa financing its own development; the importance of capable, inclusive and accountable states and institutions at all levels and in all spheres; the critical role of Regional Economic Communities as building blocks for continental unity.
>
> African Union, 2015, 1

This assertion hints at the seductive yearning for a uniquely African social solidarity, rooted in long-standing (perhaps imagined?) cultural values and practices that have endured despite the horrors of colonialism, ready to be mobilised for a modernised version of what Africa was always meant to be: united 'to realize its Renaissance'. It would be the easiest thing in the world to poke holes in the kitsch fabric of this obvious fiction. But that would be to miss the point about the importance of *animating narratives* that create a semblance of a shared footing in order to have certain kinds of political conversations that may, or may not, lead to coordinated action across profound differences and disagreements. I will return to the notion of shared narratives and the work they do in the fabrication of political and public spaces.

Notably, *Agenda 2063* is certainly a product of its time. At least since the MDGs there has been an unmistakable adoption of performance management rhetoric and planning across most development frameworks and agreements. For example, the 2030 Agenda for Sustainable Development has 17 goals and 169 targets that all nation states will be measured against on an annual basis in anticipation of achievements by 2030. Similarly, *Agenda 2063* must be read alongside the 'First Ten Year Implementation Plan 2014–2023', published by the African Union. This 140-page compendium of goals, targets, indicators and so forth set out in meticulous detail—even if some are wildly optimistic—how the seven aspirations (see Box 1) of Agenda 2063 will be realised. This is not the occasion to delve into the function of these kinds of policy artefacts, but it is important to recognise their existence and how they might provide a staging ground for a nuanced politics of critique, collaboration, learning and experimentation and the forging of novel coalitions across sectors and scales. These artefacts are not meant to be taken literally. They are discursive mechanisms aimed at instilling confidence and purpose in a sea of uncertainty and uncontrollable factors that will scupper the most well-laid plans (Roe, 1993).

Box 1: Aspirations of Agenda 2063

1. A prosperous Africa based on inclusive growth and sustainable development
2. An integrated continent, politically united, based on the ideals of Pan-Africanism and the vision of Africa's renaissance
3. An Africa of good governance, democracy, respect for human rights, justice, and the rule of law
4. A peaceful and secure Africa
5. An Africa with strong cultural identity, common heritage, values, and ethics
6. An Africa whose development is people-driven, relying on the potential of African people, especially its women and youth, and caring for children
7. Africa as a strong, united, and influential global player and partner.

Source: African Union (2015)

One of the most important impacts of *Agenda 2063* is that it has made a clearing for a more grounded and politically astute macroeconomic policy discussion under the sign of the concept of structural transformation (UNECA, 2015). This concept represents an attempt by African economists to confront the deep-seated legacies of colonial exploitation and the ways in which these laid the tracks for the asymmetrical incorporation of African economies into globalisation. It then follows that extraordinary policy focus and discipline is required to deploy macroeconomic and fiscal levers of the state to escape historical traps of dependency in favour of a more dynamic and inclusive trajectory. However, this cannot be done without leveraging the collective power of supranational regions in Africa and, ultimately, the African continent as a single economic organism characterised by the 'Free movement of people, goods, capital and services to increase trade and investment among countries' (African Union, 2015). If *Agenda 2063* does nothing else but give genuine impetus to a single economic and labour market for Africa, it can be regarded a success. Furthermore, structural transformation is linked to a more explicit consideration of space and territoriality in meeting the lofty aspirations of the African Union and its member states. The rapidly expanding work from UNECA (2015, 2016, 2017) has been the most significant body of development thought to substantiate the political, policy and regulatory implications of the lofty ideals of *Agenda 2063*.

Box 2: Structural Transformation
Structural transformation is the defining characteristic of the development process. It entails the allocation of resources—especially new investments—from low- to high-productivity activities within and across sectors, especially the agriculture, industry and services sectors. [...] Four quite relentless and interrelated processes define the structural transformation process: (a) a declining share of agriculture in gross domestic product (GDP) and employment; (b) the rapid process of urbanization as people migrate from rural to urban areas; (c) the rise of a modern industrial and service economy; and (d) a demographic transition from high to low rates of births and deaths. The final outcome of structural transformation is an economy and society in which agriculture as an economic activity has no distinguishing characteristics from other sectors, at least in terms of the productivity of labour and capital or the location of poverty.

Source: UNECA (2015)

UNECA has produced a series of development reports on various dimensions of structural transformation. This output ranges from an analysis of trade policy (UNECA, 2015) to an exploration of why an explicit green economic approach is the most promising for realising the ideals of structural transformation (UNECA, 2016), and the most recent focus on the connections between urbanisation and structural transformation (UNECA, 2017). It is this last report that I draw upon to illustrate the policy narrative that UNECA is driving, which is achieving significant traction with key infrastructure financing institutions such as the AfDB, the World Bank, various Chinese banks and the Development Bank of Southern Africa (DBSA).

But first, a few words on the policy meaning of structural transformation. At its core, structural transformation denotes processes to 'shift labour out of low-productivity agriculture into higher-productivity manufacturing and modern services' (UNECA, 2017, 20). Across most of sub-Saharan Africa, this shift is not occurring fast enough and many countries display an economic structure almost unchanged since the postcolonial era (see Figure 2.1). Thus, the relative shares of agriculture, industry and services have remained more or less the same—with the exception of manufacturing as a component of industry, which has actually declined since 1960 in relative terms. These patterns persist despite a dramatic expansion of the labour force and educational improvements, particularly over the past two decades. Large-scale, labour intensive and productive industrialisation is not on the cards for most African economies, a situation that leaves them marginal and vulnerable in an increasingly

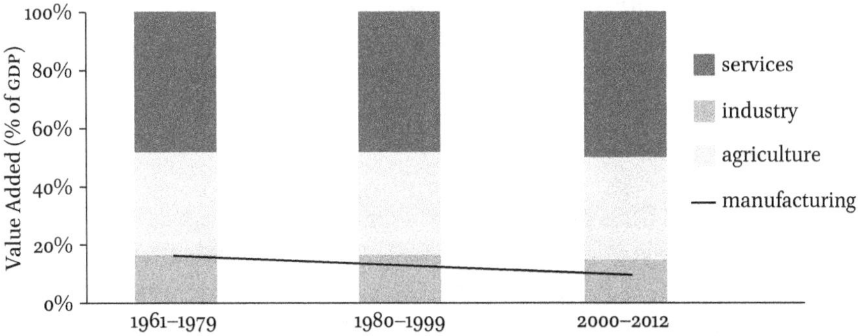

FIGURE 2.1 GDP composition by sector, Africa, 1961–2012.
SOURCE: UNECA (2015, 47)

integrated global economy and, most importantly, unable to absorb new entrants into the formal labour market.

Given the youthful demographics of sub-Saharan Africa and the persistence of high fertility rates, this is a recipe for economic and political ruin—especially as young people are more prone to participate in oppositional protests and disruption, dynamics that are seemingly exacerbated by the proliferation of mobile digital technologies (Honwana, 2012). This speaks to the centrality of the structural transformation discourse across pan-African political, development and financing institutions. It is also a discourse that can enrol and animate the private sector and civic groups keen on fostering a politics of inclusion and voice, especially for youth. It even resonates with proponents of the informal economy because these practices are seen as evidence of a lack of structural transformation and therefore as ideal agents to be supported in order to deepen industrialisation and productivity. However, the dimension of the UNECA outlook that is most striking is the recent embracing of a spatial and territorial perspective in thinking through the governance preconditions for reorienting macroeconomic and infrastructure policies to derail the low-industrial, path-dependent track that most African countries find themselves on.

Earlier in 2017, UNECA launched its flagship annual development report, themed *Urbanization and Industrialisation*. It unpacks with refreshing candour the connections between African urbanisation and economic performance:

> African cities thus face low productivity, tepid job creation, high informality, huge infrastructure and service gaps, weak linkages with rural areas, high levels of informality, increasing inequalities, growing environmental damage and vulnerability to climate change and weak institutional systems and capacities. Unless resolved, these impediments will undermine Africa's urban potential for structural transformation. [...] The challenge

> confronting Africa is thus to accelerate structural transformation by harnessing the rapid urban transition to promote economic diversification, with a special focus on industrialization that will create jobs, enhance access to basic services and reduce inequality and poverty.
>
> UNECA, 2017, 20

The second part of this position is based on an assumption that as urbanisation intensifies the growing population represents crucial potential markets for goods, services and especially infrastructure systems that will have to conduct the generation and circulation of economic value. Thus, for UNECA, the key to structural transformation lies in territorial and infrastructure planning because global value chains have particular geographies and there is policy scope to rethink and re-engineer these geographies through thoughtful and anticipatory infrastructure planning in order to foster dynamic, interdependent and differentiated national and (subnational) regional economies. In the previous report in 2016, UNECA goes further and argues that territorial infrastructure planning can disrupt uneven development and urban primacy, as well as catalyse a simultaneous transition to a green economy in terms of the underlying technologies that will shape energy, mobility, water and ICT investments (UNECA, 2016).

Significantly, the *Urbanization and Industrialization* report goes further than infrastructure and foregrounds the problematic urban form (spatial structure) of many African cities, which not only reinforces social segregation but also represents a substantial cost for urban livelihoods and businesses. However, the report not only argues for refined macroeconomic policy but also for drastic intergovernmental institutional reconfiguration so that local actors who are most knowledgeable about local conditions can do the frontline work of detailed industrial and spatial policy design, effectively providing a renewed argument for the substantive devolution of powers, functions and financial authority. This is important because evidence from many sub-Saharan African countries demonstrates that devolution reforms have essentially become stuck for at least the past two decades, with cases of re-centralisation when opposition political parties were able to get a foothold in municipal governance (Resnick, 2012).

UNECA can be this bullish in its policy arguments because of important shifts that have taken place at the African Union level. In order to prepare for an African regional perspective on a new urban agenda deliberated at Habitat III in 2016, the African Union established a new political subcommittee on Urban Development and Human Settlements of the African Union Specialized Technical Committee on Public Service, Local Government, Urban Development and Decentralization. This technical committee was itself a novel structure when it was first convened in 2014. The work of this subcommittee culminated in the adoption of the Common African Position on the Third

United Nations Conference on Housing and Sustainable Urban Development, in February 2016. The Common Position sets out a number of approaches that set the stage for the *Africa Economic Outlook* 2016 and UNECA's publication, *Urbanization and Industrialization*. These overlapping and mutually reinforcing macro policy frameworks are indeed unprecedented and represent, if read carefully, a radically different institutional and political landscape for future governance dynamics as territorial considerations become interlinked with macroeconomic decisions and infrastructure investment regimes. In the second half of this chapter, I delineate what this political landscape contains in order to make a speculative argument for 'translational research' that can document, critique and extend multi-scalar politics.

4 Recasting the Nature of (Urban) Governance

In the wake of the SDGs, the Paris Climate Accord and the New Urban Agenda, the formal policy reference points of an ideal multilevel governance approach have shifted. It is now recognised that multilevel institutional configurations must be defined in relation to a macroeconomic policy ideal that seeks to accelerate industrialisation. This ideal is based on a locally defined set of economic strategies that seek to intervene in the value chains of key economic sectors that depend on expanding urban populations. It is further accepted that the infrastructure investments required to optimise industrialisation and urban efficiencies should be made and coordinated by local actors who understand the micro dynamics of the territorial economies that should anchor economic diversification. It is further asserted that these infrastructure investments should not only drive industrialisation but also create a platform for a transition to a low-carbon and resource-efficient economic structure that optimises labour absorption. These are significant discursive shifts that raise daunting questions about how one can change the predominant dynamics and values of pre-existing governance cultures.

Three weighty problems present themselves. First, most African countries and cities are marked by infrastructural and spatial path dependency dynamics that are notoriously difficult to change. In other words, the regimes of infrastructure technological design, operations and management are crystallised around a deeply entrenched set of vested interests. Since infrastructure investments have long lead times, what is currently on the books will remain a dominant structuring force for at least the next five to ten years. Second, technical path dependency is reinforced by an even more pernicious dynamic of institutional inertia. There is a large body of scholarship on the dysfunctional nature of public sector bureaucracies in many African countries (Rakodi, 2002;

Stren, 2014). Typically, the public sector remained cast in the mould of colonial administrations, especially in terms of hierarchical power relations embedded in command-and-control decision-making. This was a system that proved useful to entrench a new postcolonial administrative elite that was intimately entwined with the political party machines that overdetermined the economy, politics and administrative functioning. These dynamics were further entrenched and perverted when new public administration tools around privatisation, corporatisation, partnerships and performance management were overlaid in an instrumentalised fashion. Instead of promoting greater responsiveness to the needs and demands of citizens, bureaucratic power became more intensified and opaque but draped in a language of accountability and performance, fuelling deep-seated mistrust and public cynicism. Rents that politically connected actors are able to extract rely on this institutional dysfunction. Third, in most African contexts dominant ruling political parties overdetermine every aspect of public priority setting and resource allocation. This is such a pervasive fact of life that most actors and citizens simply take it as a given and this power is derived from keeping the system as is.

The culturally specific manifestation of these dynamics needs to be made legible through careful research and analysis. Three conceptual entry points are relevant for this research work: narrative, ritual and deal-making. The narrative dimension of governance refers to where dominant circulating discourses are deployed to fashion and reproduce the necessary fictions (or facts) of rule. These are large, muscular and often masculine normative frames such as patriotism, pan-Africanism, empowerment, *Ubuntu*, and the like. These narratives stabilise nation building and forge the basis of the legitimacy and authority of ruling elites. Importantly, such narratives feed off and blend in with popular cultural currents that congeal the meanings of citizenship and political attachment. It is arguable that the highly successful Pentecostal mega churches that are mushrooming across African cities in all linguistic regions manifest a similar dynamic (Adesoji, 2016; Rakodi, 2014). It is unhelpful to dismiss the popular cultural beliefs and practices of this order as false consciousness or deceit. These narratives endure and reinvent themselves because they function in highly subtle and resonant ways as public affects (Amin and Thrift, 2013; Connolly, 2014). They are best dislodged and problematised through competing narratives that have a stronger affective pull.

The ritual dimension denotes the embodied institutional scripts that flow from these narrative frames and allow for a certain kind of translation into administrative practices and effects. It is in rituals that the performative dimensions of politics come to the fore. In a context of relatively limited resources due to small tax bases and highly truncated systems of patronage, rituals are even more exaggerated and achieve a life force and dynamism of their own. Generally, political party cultures, hierarchies, decision-making systems and informal networks shape these, but they are always interwoven with formal deliberative governmental procedures in both the legislature and the executive and administrative components of the state. Arguably, party dominant bureaucracies take their cue from these ritualised practices to establish a set of administrative systems and practices that quickly manifest in unique rituals that must be mastered if one is to get anything done or enabled. These rituals can vary widely, ranging from militarist efficiency to the extravagantly baroque (Mbembe, 2001). It is not possible to move economic or political agendas forward without understanding and engaging with these performative dimensions of statehood. Furthermore, non-state cultural reference points, such as religious affiliations or hometown networks, are vital to the maintenance and reproduction of these rituals.

Deal-making is another dimension of the unravelling and remaking of multilevel governance. The understanding of framing narratives and the ritual of performative politics are helpful to decipher the profound gap between formal state rhetoric and practice, and how such practices relate back to party dynamics and elite functioning. However, they are always intertwined with a profound pragmatism to cut deals in order to navigate opaque 'rules of the game' and keep resources flowing. Deal-making happens behind the translucent screens of narrative and ritual. In other words, if actors who want to advance an alternative, more progressive politics fail to read the prevailing narratives and their functioning, along with the rituals of public administration, they will simply not be effective in shaping narratives or destabilising practices that reproduce the status quo. This brings this chapter to its penultimate thematic: what kind of politics can be imagined and institutionalised to ensure that the progressive normative ambitions of *Agenda 2063* and the trope of green structural transformation can in fact be achieved?

5 Reimagining Power Through Infrastructural Politics

The most potent politics aggregates around infrastructure (Larkin, 2013; Swilling, 2013). Since infrastructure deficits and malfunctioning constitutes the largest brake on sustained economic growth and accumulation, it attracts an inordinate amount of political and technical attention, not least from international actors on the financing side of the development industry (Pieterse and Hyman, 2014). The downstream effects of infrastructure malfunction are also most likely to trigger social dissent and protest and, in this sense, always carry a political charge. The planning and financing of infrastructure falls to the most powerful centres of the state: ministries of finance, economic development, and infrastructure, and typically the presidency.

These actors are also the primary targets of pan-African norm-setting forums and national commitment, which does, in theory, create leverage in terms of holding them accountable and advocating, at the policy narrative level, around adopted or professed norms. For example, the assertions and commitments embedded in the Common African Position on a New Urban Agenda adopted in February 2016 are highly consistent with the recommendations from UNECA's work discussed earlier. Since the senior ministries in the state are involved and a number of bold and clear policy propositions have been accepted, it is conceivable that a radical, transformative platform can be constructed to shift the trajectory of the country and the city. However, this does depend on a savvy coalition of actors from diverse sectors of civil society who are able to explicitly connect local demands for more transparent and equitable infrastructure investments and democratic decentralisation reforms with the normative imperatives of these pan-African frameworks. Increasingly, the African Union (AU) and various UN bodies that deal with these questions are creating spaces for civil society actors to engage, monitor implementation and apply pressure. If these opportunities are exploited by various civil society networks and movements that work on social justice and democratisation, this potential can be realised (Miller et al., 2006).

Significantly, infrastructure systems also reveal most clearly the co-existence of formal and informal systems of social and economic reproduction. For example, given the low levels of baseload energy infrastructure, the majority of African households are responsible for their own micro infrastructure solutions. This is typically expensive and inefficient but energy-poor households find a way (Jaglin, 2014). Similar scenarios pertain to water access, sanitation, transport, housing and so forth. A rich and helpful academic research agenda has sprung up to make legible and comprehend these hybrid sociotechnical systems that underpin the functioning of African cities and communities. In the case of energy, most urban households who live in slum conditions rely on biomass, which is not particularly efficient and often detrimental in environmental health terms. Similarly, most of the (public) transport infrastructure—minibus taxis—is privately owned and operates in a grey zone of semi-formality. Likewise, neighbourhood-based social enterprises and/or cooperatives organise waste management and sanitation disposal (Thieme, 2017). The point is that any future evolution of these hybrid infrastructures must engage with the de facto hybrid functioning of these systems and allow for a contextually defined transition to more effective, integrated and formal structures over time, with an acceptance that multiple systems with different rhythms and institutional forms will have to coexist for the foreseeable future. It is indeed these system adaptions that can undergird the green economy, as envisaged by UNECA (2016) and others (Cartwright, 2015; Hyman and Pieterse, 2017; OECD et al., 2016; Pieterse and Hyman, 2014).

Notably, the expansion of infrastructure investment and the concomitant planning of future systems that are more inclusive and adaptive will require a change to multilevel governance systems. It is in this imperative that the strongest potential for a transformative politics lies. Why? Infrastructure priorities defined in terms of the imperatives of access, green economic transitions and basic urban efficiency demand a more coordinated, sequenced and integrated approach to infrastructure planning, investment, delivery, maintenance and repair. And since any infrastructure response will have to acknowledge and incorporate de facto hybrid systems of functioning, it will also require careful and sustained engagement with informal providers and intermediaries. The imperatives of coordination and incorporation demand a localised institutional framework for infrastructure planning and management, especially as the complexity of variegated demands in major urban hubs intensifies and international investors demand localised institutional capacity and accountability. These exogenous factors conspire to create novel political openings and opportunities for progressive urban actors wishing to animate new terms of engagement and urban incorporation. However, this implies a savvy and nimble political sensibility and capacity. In order to clarify and advance what this imaginary might add up to, I explore a few conceptual diagrams that can anchor localised strategies.

6 Triangulating Dimensions of Governance, Forms of Power, and Political Settlement

Earlier in this chapter, I proposed the utility of distinguishing between three nested dimensions of contemporary governance: narrative, ritual and dealmaking. In order to get a purchase on the strategic opportunity structure for the kind of transformational infrastructure politics of green growth and livelihood enhancement, it is important to adopt a sociological analysis of power in the state and its cultural embedding in society. The applied development policy literature (Pettit, 2013) that distinguishes between visible, invisible and hidden power provides a useful prism without suggesting that it exhausts the complex flows and dynamics of power and counter-power in the heterotopic sense. If we take one step further and triangulate these two aspects with another pragmatist framework to characterise the dominant features of political economy factors that shape macro politics and its intricate folds, the work on political settlements by Kelsall (2016) represented as a 3-D space offers some useful insights. I will briefly expound on these two frameworks before making some cursory remarks on how they can enrich a transformational urban politics.

The first framework is the useful typology on visible, invisible and hidden power proposed by Pettit (2013) and Gaventa (2013). Visible power is the manifest capacity of actors in formal decision-making bodies and public spaces to present and advance their interests, (ideological) perspective and priorities. In substantially democratic institutions, these power contests are regulated by legally enshrined principles and tend to fix public attention because they embody what is deemed 'proper' politics worthy of media attention. Much government, donor and civil society energy is invested in participatory governance instruments that target formal decision-making arenas. On the urban scale, this would typically be either the municipal council or a host of ancillary participatory mechanisms that seek to effect consultation around council decisions or various kinds of municipal planning processes. The assumption is that there is a direct connection between what is being discussed in these chambers and plans, and the routine functioning of local state institutions.

By contrast, hidden power as a concept in this framework illuminates the ways in which formal political and policy deliberative processes and forums are not a level playing field—the ways in which numerous voices and interests are systematically excluded from the debate. Hidden power explains how official political and policy arenas are constructed and hemmed by specific discourses (Flyvbjerg, 2001) and associated institutional habits. These discourses incorporate assumptions about how to frame an issue, what is 'sayable' and what is politically or culturally considered taboo (Healey, 2004; Pieterse, 2005). Hidden power is effective when the media or citizens do not question the very assumptions that structure a public policy issue.

Hidden power works effectively because it is culturally underpinned by invisible power, which stems from subjectivity—or, how a person understands and enacts a sense of self as an expression of self-esteem, confidence, self-worth, dignity and corporeality. Theoretically hidden power draws on the overlapping insights of Gyatry Spivak, Michel Foucault, Paulo Freire and Steve Biko. In highly stratified, patriarchal and unequal societies, those at the bottom of the privilege pile are systematically devalued and considered inferior, in part due to their material and educational deficits and in other senses due to their membership of 'inferior' classes or castes. Thus, invisible power 'involves the ways in which awareness of one's rights and interests are hidden through the adoption of dominating ideologies, values and forms of behavior by relatively powerless groups themselves. Sometimes this is also referred to as the "internalisation of powerlessness" in a way that affects the awareness and consciousness of potential issues and conflicts, even by those directly affected' (Gaventa, 2013). In undemocratic and authoritarian societies, political elites and dominant groups actively reproduce these cultural systems of devaluation and social exclusion because they reinforce their hold on power and resources. In an era in which religious ideologies, intertwined with accumulation practices and political sway, exercise increasing influence over the affairs of the state and the economy, various cultural belief systems tend to reinforce invisible power (Naim, 2013).

Moving on from forms of power, it is instructive to consider the intervention by Kelsall (2016) who created an analytical tool to generate a more precise and contextually specific account of dynamics from a given political settlement and how it structures the opportunity space for visible and invisible power. The tool is structured along three axes to create a cube space of triangulated description (see Figure 2.2). The first axis denotes the nature of horizontal

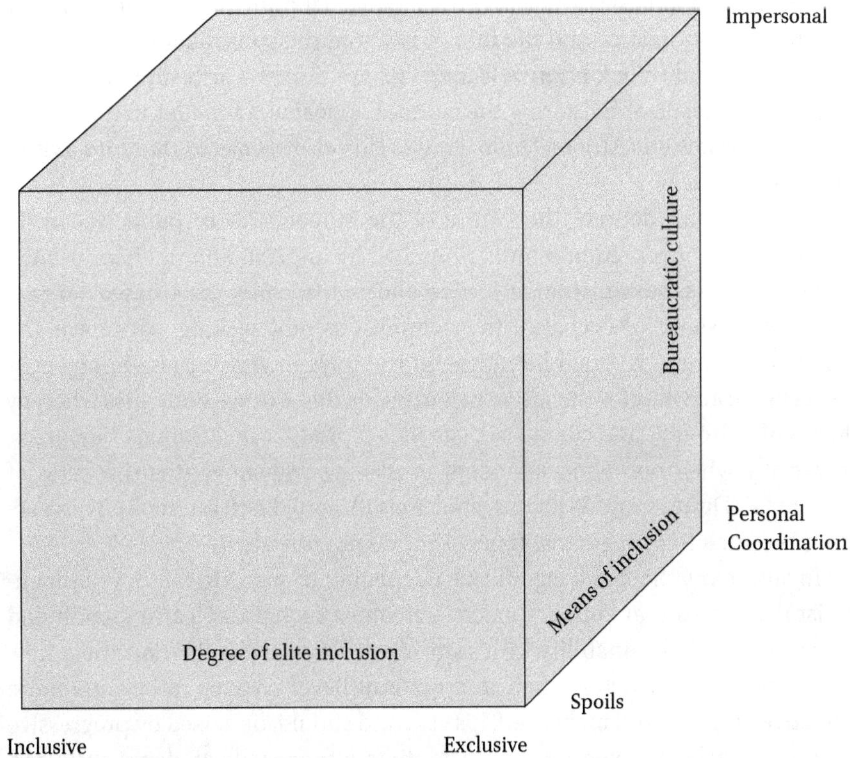

FIGURE 2.2 The political settlements 3-D space.
SOURCE: KELSALL (2016, 3)

elite incorporation. It simply addresses whether the majority of elites accept the political settlement and have given up on the option of using violence to disrupt or end it. If many elites maintain the option of violence, the axis will indicate exclusion.

The second axis addresses why elites are willing to accept the political settlement: are they 'in' because they get a share of the 'spoils' or are they persuaded by a larger common purpose that flows from a broader narrative of nation building, or developmental statehood, and so forth, which create a basis for the more inclusive structuring of institutions? Of course, in most places it would be a combination of these kinds of discourses interwoven with some measure of sharing the spoils. Returning to the earlier points about the emergence of qualitatively different developmental narratives about green industrialisation and employment being the core of the 'African Renaissance' or *Agenda 2063*, it becomes clearer how these signifiers can potentially be put to work to deepen the ideological and symbolic repertoire of local political actors who want to embrace a pan-African cosmopolitanism. I would go so far as to say that the progressive aspirations of *Agenda 2063* that pertain to the entrenching of 'democratic values, cultural practices, universal principles of human rights, gender equality, justice and the rule of law' and the consolidation of 'capable institutions and transformative leadership' are norms worth supporting with vigour as a means of bolstering the cultural appeal of a broader non-personal political aspiration (African Union, 2015). This also speaks to the third axis of the framework.

The third axis denotes the nature of the bureaucracy or public sector. In its ideal form, it is predominantly propelled by impersonal principles of rule-driven fairness, administrative justice and meritocracy, or is based on personalised systems of exchange that manifest as rent seeking, patronage and clientelism. There is a rich literature on the ways in which these lumpy concepts fail to account for the micro negotiations that can see outcomes whereby forms of patronage and clientelism can in fact produce inclusionary outcomes, especially when non-elites are adept at playing and subverting the 'rules of the game' (Duncan and Williams, 2012; Kelsall, 2016; Platteau, 2004). These accounts enrich this pragmatist frame, they do not obviate it.

In summary, there is a significant deepening of pan-African developmentalist discourses that connect macro outcomes such as inclusive growth and environmental sustainability with a stronger territorial imagination about how states need to restructure their internal multilevel systems to become more effective, popular and inclusive. This can, and should, be seized by progressive actors and scholars who wish to instantiate a more radical, democratic and inclusive urban politics. However, to be effective in this regard it is important to deploy research and analysis to build a much more rounded and fine-grained account of the status quo and why it remains stubbornly impervious to successive waves of policy reform. Such a research effort demands a more sober and direct account of the political opportunity structure if it is to progressively instantiate these emerging developmentalist discourses. This section of the chapter suggests the triangulation of three analytical prisms. This begins with a broader analysis of the nature of the political operating field through the adapted use of Kelsall's 3-D cube, which typifies elite incorporation, culture and bureaucratic disposition. The crude accounting that such a step yields can then be nuanced by isolating the ways in which overarching narratives of nationhood and state-building create a series of rationalities for specific rituals of state performance, which in turn provides a canopy for a wide range of grounded micro practices of deal-making within which ordinary people and their various intermediating social networks are always hard at work to capitalise on deals or renegotiate them. However, to establish a truly grounded reading of the cultural terms of these processes, it is necessary to overlay the analysis with an account of how visible, hidden and invisible power dynamics work in practice. This requires fine-grained and possibly 'embedded' research to account for the practices, rationalities and dynamics of public institutions charged with interpreting and enacting broader normative visions. In the last section of this chapter, by way of a conclusion, I make a case for sustained social science research to populate the triangulation imperatives with sound data and analysis. However, this is not enough; we need to think of the role of research as integral to the larger imperatives of fostering new institutional systems of governance, management and rule that strengthen national imperatives to discharge coordination and alignment. At the same time, we need to recognise that alternative local governance and policy processes cannot emerge unless they are connected to experiments, which can generate novel ways of planning, structuring, investing in and running sustainable infrastructures that contribute directly to economic empowerment and socio-spatial inclusion.

7 Fostering Exploratory Research Milieus

At the risk of frustrating the reader, I will not elaborate in any detail upon what this experimental research milieu entails but will simply deploy a diagrammatic overview of its recursive logics (Figure 2.3). The entry point is the fundamental task of academic research: critical thought. Such thought is conventionally

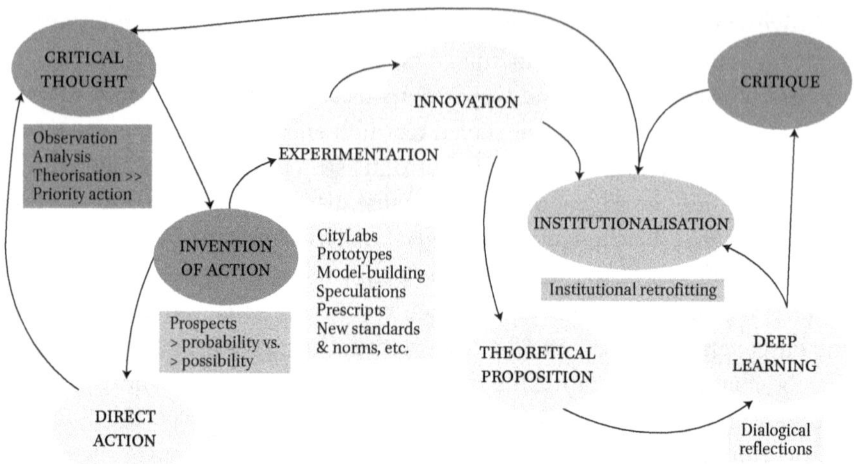

FIGURE 2.3 Dialogical experimental urban research.
SOURCE: AUTHOR

the interplay between established theoretical assumptions, a research question, which leads to a research strategy, and the eventual reporting on the outcomes of the research. Fundamentally, such work is driven by a desire to figure out what should be done to 'solve' and engage the problem at the core of the research question. However, instead of adopting muscular explanatory theories that have fixed the structural determinants of the problem, this approach is interested in foregrounding the range of possible actions with an eye to what might work in the entangled messiness of the real city.

Actions are tabulated in two columns: probable future directions versus possible future directions. Critical social scientists are very well trained in probability. We can offer long lists of why the status quo is likely to remain stubbornly in place, and the more our outlooks are shaped by structural ontologies, the more we are trapped by probable horizons. In contrast, actions in the possible futures column are adopted by actors who are willing to take a couple of leaps of faith, believers as they are in the potential of surprise, contingency and new conjunctures that trigger unexpected cultural affects. Those who struggle to leave the land of the probable tend to conclude that the only worthy next step is confrontational political action, which in turn requires more theoretical fuel to keep the critical thought project alive.

The 'romantics', on the other hand, for lack of a better term, are keen to enter experimental labs, sites and milieus with a diversity of practitioners invested in the issues at the core of the research question (Swilling et al., forthcoming). This cohort is fated to learn how to conduct translational research—a practice of intermediating between different knowledge registers in order to move between science and experience, codified knowledge and tacit understanding, abstracted ideas and experientially based insights, and so on (Parnell and Pieterse, 2016). However, to achieve genuinely novel and surprising insights, these different registers need to be animated by various learning techniques that are able to surface and articulate both reasoned and affective rationalities. If done well, if curated with care, if underpinned with rigorous scholarship and commitment to social justice, these experimental labs can produce genuine innovation with regard to how to understand specific problems and/or new ways of tackling them (Simone and Pieterse, 2017).

At all times in these experimental milieus the goal is to figure out how to institutionalise novel approaches that can have material effects that will, over time, and through learning, impact on large numbers of people. The core drive of experimental milieus is to figure out what has a chance of succeeding and how the innovation can be scaled and sustained through the routine functioning of democratic institutions. In some cases, the experiments may be too modest or narrow to translate into institutional propositions. In such instances, the search moves to theorisation—raising new questions that can challenge and stretch the theoretical accounts of what might or might not work in a given situation. Both the practice of institutionalisation across differences and theoretical spadework contribute, ultimately, to deep learning. Such learning has to be embedded in the cultural aspirations of social and knowledge actors invested in figuring out an urban politics that excites, animates and instigates transformational political acts.

8 In Conclusion

A core argument of this chapter is that we are in the midst of a number of important policy discursive shifts that will trigger the establishment of new urban governance mechanisms and processes. It is important to pay attention to these processes and not assume a priori that they are simply more of the same. Instead, we need to offer a critical perspective on why these institutional proposals are not simply about technocratic competence but rather a different kind of politics that needs researchers to identify and analyse the ways in which vested interests and hidden dynamics of power operate to frustrate infrastructural modernisation and democratisation. Thus, this is not an argument for only conducting research linked to institutional experimentation that must supplant conventional scholarship. On the contrary, we need a lot more interdisciplinary analysis of political institutions, lifeworlds and culture across the visible and hidden dimensions of politics that shape urban life and opportunity. This is especially important at a time when investments in the built environment are increasing, with profound spatial effects. However, I do think that the established academic research approaches and theoretical frameworks can be enriched and expanded if there is more articulation with localised practices of speculative research. In my reading, both traditional academic research and applied speculative exploration are essential to make sense of the new kinds of cultural–political–institutional configurations that are emerging in order to substantiate new normative commitments and aspirations. By paying attention to the multilayered nature of these contradictory processes, explicated in this chapter, we might yet have something useful to contribute to a new African urban politics and imagination.

Acknowledgements

I am grateful to the organisers of the 7th European Conference on African Studies (ECAS 2017) at the University of Basel for inviting me to present a version of this paper as a keynote address. I am also grateful for the review comments and continuous discussions with my colleagues, Sue Parnell, Anton Cartwright, Gareth Haysom, Sylvia Croese and Kim Gurney. I am solely responsible for the argument presented here. My research is supported by the National Research Foundation of South Africa.

References

Adesoji, A. (2016) 'The New Pentecostal Movement in Nigeria and the Politics of Belonging', *Journal of Asian and African Studies*, pp. 1–15, DOI: 10.1177/0021909616649209.

African Union (2015) *Agenda 2063. The Africa We Want*. Popular version, second edition. (Addis Ababa: African Union).

Amin, A. and N. Thrift (2013) *Arts of the Political: New Openings for the Left* (Durham, N.C.: Duke University Press).

Bayat, A. (2010) *Life as Politics: How Ordinary People Change the Middle East* (Stanford, CA: Stanford University Press).

Cartwright, A. (2015) *Better Growth, Better Cities. Rethinking and Redirecting Urbanisation in Africa*. (London: New Climate Economy), http://2015.newclimateeconomy.report/wp-content/uploads/2015/09/NCE-APP-final.pdf (accessed on 19 June 2016).

Castells, M. and P. Himanen (2014) *Reconceptualizing Development in the Global Information Age* (Oxford: Oxford University Press).

Connolly, W. (2014) 'Freedom, teleodynamism, creativity', *Foucault Studies*, 17, pp. 60–75.

Davis, M. (2006) *Planet of the Slums* (London: Verso).

Duncan, A. and G. Williams (2012) 'Making Development Assistance More Effective Through Using Political-economy Analysis: What Has Been Done and What Have We Learned?', *Development Policy Review*, 30, pp. 133–148, DOI: 10.1111/j.1467-7679.2012.00568.x.

Ferguson, J. (2011) 'Toward a left art of government: from "Foucauldian critique" to Foucauldian politics', *History of the Human Sciences*, 24, pp. 61–68, DOI: 10.1177/0952695111413849.

Flyvbjerg, B. (2001) *Making social science matter: Why social inquiry fails and how it can succeed again* (Cambridge: Cambridge University Press).

Gaventa, J. (2013) 'Understanding the power cube and related concepts' in *Power Pack. Understanding Power for Social Change* (Brighton: Institute of Development Studies, University of Sussex).

Harris, A. and S. Moore (2013) 'Planning Histories and Practices of Circulating Urban Knowledge', *International Journal of Urban and Regional Research*, 37(5), 1499–1510, DOI: 10.1111/1468-2427.12043.

Healey, P. (2004) 'Creativity and Urban Governance', *Policy Studies*, 25, pp. 87–102, DOI: 10.1080/0144287042000262189.

Honwana, A. (2012) *The time of youth: Work, social change and politics in Africa.* (Washington DC: Kumarian Press).

Hyman, K. and E. Pieterse (2017) 'Infrastructure deficits and potential in African Cities' in R. Burdett, and S. Hall (eds.) *The SAGE Handbook of Urban Sociology: New approaches to the twenty-first century city* (London: Sage Publishers), pp. 429–451.

Jaglin, S. (2014) 'Regulating service delivery in Southern cities: rethinking urban heterogeneity' in S. Parnell and S. Oldfied (eds.) *The Routledge Handbook on Cities of the Global South* (London and New York: Routledge), pp. 434–447.

Kelsall, T. (2016) *Thinking and working with political settlements* (London: ODI).

Larkin, B. (2013) 'The politics and poetics of infrastructure', *Annual Review of Anthropology*, 42, pp. 327–343, DOI: 10.1146/annurev-anthro-092412-155522.

Mason, P. (2015) *Postcapitalism: A Guide to our Future* (London: Penguin).

Mbembe, A. (2016) 'Africa in the new century' *Cityscapes*, 7, pp. 51–58, https://www.cityscapesdigital.net/2015/12/09/africa-new-century/ (accessed on 23 May 2018).

Mbembe, A. (2001) *On the Postcolony* (Berkeley and Los Angeles: University of California Press).

McKinsey Global Institute (2016) *Lions on the move II: Realizing the potential of Africa's economies* (New York: McKinsey & Company).

Miller, V., L. VeneKlasen, M. Reilly and C. Clark (2006) *Making change happen: Concepts for Revisioning Power for Justice, Equality and Peace*, (Washington D.C.: Just Associates).

Miraftab, F. (2004) 'Making neo-liberal governance: the disempowering work of empowerment', *International Planning Studies*, 9, pp. 239–259, DOI: 10.1080/13563470500050130.

Myers, G. (2011) *African Cities: Alternative Visions of Urban Theory and Practice* (London: Zed Books).

Naim, M. (2013) *The End of Power: From Boardrooms to Battlefields and Churches to States, Why Being In Charge Isn't What It Used To Be* (New York: Basic Books).

Obeng-Odoom, F. (2015) Africa: On the rise, but to where? *Forum for Social Economics*, 44, pp. 234–250.

OECD, AfDB and UNDP (2016) *African Economic Outlook 2016. Sustainable Cities and Structural Transformation* (Paris: OECD).

Parnell, S. (2016) 'Defining a global urban development agenda', *World Development*, 78, pp. 529–540, DOI: 10.1016/j.worlddev.2015.10.028.

Parnell, S. and E. Pieterse (2016) 'Translational global praxis—rethinking methods and modes of African urban research', *International Journal of Urban and Regional Research*, 40, pp. 236–246, DOI: 10.1111/1468-2427.12278.

Pettit, J. (2013) *Power analysis. A practical guide* (Stockholm: SIDA).

Pieterse, E. (2008) *City Futures: Confronting the Crisis of Urban Development* (London and New York: Zed Books).

Pieterse, E. (2005) 'Transgressing the Limits of Possibility: Working Notes on a Relational Model of Urban Politics' in A. Simone, and A. Abouhani, (eds.) *Urban Processes and Change in Africa* (London: Zed Books).

Pieterse, E. and K. Hyman (2014) 'Disjunctures between urban infrastructure, finance and affordability', in S. Parnell and S. Oldfield (eds.) *The Routledge Handbook on Cities of the Global South* (London: Routledge).

Pieterse, E., S. Parnell and S. Croese (2017) *The 2030 Agenda: Sustainable Urbanisation and the Research-Policy Interface—Issues for The G20* (Bonn: GIZ (Deutsche Gesellschaft für Internationale Zusammenarbeit)).

Platteau, J-P. (2004) 'Monitoring Elite Capture in Community-Driven Development', *Development and Change*, 35, pp. 223–246, DOI: 10.1111/j.1467-7660.2004.00350.x.

PwC (PricewaterhouseCoopers) (2015) *Into Africa: The continent's Cities of Opportunity* (Johannesburg: PwC).

Rakodi, C. (2002) 'Order and disorder in African cities: governance, politics, and urban land development processes', in O. Enwezor, U.M. Bauer, S. Ghez, S. Maharaj, M. Nash and O. Zaya (eds.) *Under Siege: Four African Cities. Freetown, Johannesburg, Kinshasa, Lagos* (Berlin: Hatje Cantz).

Rakodi, C. (2014) 'Religion and social life in African cities', in S. Parnell and E. Pieterse (eds.) *African's Urban Revolution* (London: Zed Books), pp. 82–109.

RSA (Republic of South Africa) (2016) *Integrated Development Urban Framework* (Pretoria: Department of Cooperative Governance and Traditional Affairs).

Resnick, D. (2012) 'Opposition Parties and the Urban Poor in African Democracies', *Comparative Political Studies*, 45(11), pp. 1351–1378, DOI: 10.1177/0010414012437166.

Roe, E. (1993) 'Against power: For the politics of complexity', *Transitions*, 62, pp. 90–104.

Scoones, I, M. Leach and P. Newell (eds) (2015) *The Politics of Green Transformations* (London: Routledge).

Simone, A.M. and E. Pieterse (2017) *New Urban Worlds. Inhabiting Dissonant Times.* (Cambridge: Polity Press).

Srnicek, N. and A. Williams (2015) *Inventing the Future: Postcapitalism and a World without Work* (London: Verso).

Stren, R. (2014) 'Urban Service Delivery in Africa and the Role of International Assistance', *Development Policy Review*, 32(S1), pp. 19–37.

Swilling, M. (2016) 'Towards Sustainable Urban Infrastructures for the Urban Anthropocene', in A. Allen, A. Lampis and M. Swilling (eds.) *Untamed Urbanism*. (London and New York: Routledge), pp. 19–32.

Swilling, M. (2013) 'Economic Crisis, Long Waves and the Sustainability Transition: An African Perspective', *Environmental Innovations and Societal Transitions*, 6, pp. 95–115, DOI: 10.1016/j.eist.2012.11.001.

Swilling, M. and E. Annecke (2012) *Just Transitions: Explorations of Sustainability in an Unfair World* (Cape Town and Tokyo: UCT Press and United Nations University Press).

Swilling, M., E. Pieterse and M. Hajer (forthcoming) 'Futuring, experimentation and transformative urban politics', in R. Poli (ed.) *Handbook of Anticipatory Systems* (New York: Springer).

Thieme, T. (2017) 'The hustle economy: Informality, uncertainty and the geographies of getting by', *Progress in Human Geography*, DOI: 10.1177/0309132517690039.

UNECA (United Nations Economic Commission for Africa) (2017) *Economic Report 2017: Urbanization and Industrialization for Africa's Transformation*, (Addis Ababa: UNECA).

UNECA (2016) *Economic Report 2016: Greening Africa's Industralization* (Addis Ababa: UNECA).

UNECA (2015) *Economic Report on Africa 2015: Industrializing Through Trade* (Addis Ababa: UNECA).

UN-Habitat (2016) *World Cities Report 2016. Urbanization and Development: Emerging Futures* (Nairobi: UN-Habitat).

UN-Habitat (2014) *State of African Cities Report 2014. Re-imagining sustainable urban transitions* (Nairobi: UN-Habitat).

UN-Habitat and UNECA (2015) *Towards an African Urban Agenda* (Nairobi: UN-Habitat).
UCLG (United Cities and Local Government) (2016) *Co-Creating the Urban Future: The Agenda of Metropolises, Cities and Territories*, Fourth Global Report on Decentralization and Local Democracy (Barcelona: UCLG).
United Nations (2015) *Transforming our world: the 2030 Agenda for Sustainable Development* (New York: UN Publications).

PART 2

Urban Governance

CHAPTER 3

Urban Governance in Africa: An Overview

Warren Smit

Abstract

Africa is urbanising rapidly and is facing enormous urban challenges, such as the growth of slums and increasing inequality. Secondary cities, with their smaller economies and less capacitated local governments compared to primary cities, face particularly severe challenges. However, responsibility for key urban governance issues is often fragmented amongst large numbers of government stakeholders with limited capacities and conflicting interests. Key urban governance stakeholders therefore need to be brought together in collaborative processes to jointly develop and implement new strategies that are based on a broader range of interests and meet a broader range of needs. In order to be able to do this, understanding actual urban governance processes, which are essentially about how different actors interact to make and operationalise decisions, is vitally important. This chapter highlights the diversity of actors involved in urban governance in Africa and the complexity of urban governance processes, with Kisumu, a secondary city in Kenya, used as an example. Key actors in urban governance in African cities include all levels of government, political parties, traditional leaders, private sector organisations and informal business organisations (such as traders' organisations), international agencies and civil society organisations. The basic objects of urban governance can include a wide range of issues, such as land use management, the provision of basic services, ensuring access/mobility and ensuring public health and safety. The diversity of governance actors and of agendas complicates addressing urban issues, but can also be seen as an opportunity for leveraging additional skills and resources through collaborative urban governance processes that bring different stakeholders together to develop and implement more holistic and inclusive strategies.

1 Introduction

Africa is the most rapidly urbanising region of the world and has immense urban challenges, such as growing slums and growing poverty and inequality, combined with weak government capacity (UN-Habitat, 2014). Urban Africa, though, also has enormous opportunities and potential for innovation. Key to effectively tackling urban challenges in Africa is an understanding of urban governance processes and how they can be enhanced and strengthened. This chapter attempts to highlight the diversity of actors involved in urban governance in African cities, and the complexity of urban governance processes.

It should be noted that Africa is a vast and diverse continent, and there are enormous international and intra-national differences in urbanisation dynamics and governance conditions. Nevertheless, there are certain key urban governance trends that are widespread in Africa. Drawing on a review of the literature on governance in Africa and on personal experience of working in a number of cities across the continent, I review some of the key issues relating to African urban governance, showing how responsibility for key urban governance issues is often fragmented amongst large numbers of government stakeholders with limited capacities and conflicting interests, and that, in order to overcome these challenges, governance stakeholders need to be brought together in collaborative processes to jointly develop and implement new strategies that are based on a broader range of interests and meet a broader range of needs. As secondary cities in Africa face particularly severe challenges—given their weaker economies and weaker local governments compared to primary cities—I particularly focus on the experiences of secondary cities, using Kisumu (the third-largest city in Kenya) as an example. This chapter is partially based on a review of 101 peer-reviewed articles relating to urban governance in Africa (see Smit, 2016) and partially on a stakeholder workshop held in Kisumu in July 2015 and the analysis of interviews with a range of governance stakeholders in Kisumu conducted in June 2016.

First, I briefly review some of the key challenges facing African cities. I then discuss different conceptions of governance and define my working definition of governance as the complex ways through which groups and individuals engage with each other to, in practice, make and operationalise decisions. Using Kisumu as an illustrative example, I then discuss the key governance actors found in most African cities and examine four particular arenas of urban governance: land use management, the provision of basic services, transport/mobility, and food safety. Although certain aspects of these governance processes function adequately, there are also many cases of fragmentation and a lack of coordination between urban governance actors. Finally, I discuss the possibility of overcoming these problems through developing collaborative governance processes that bring different stakeholders together to develop and implement more holistic and inclusive strategies.

2 Urbanisation in Africa

The urban population of Africa has been growing rapidly, from an estimated 237 million in 1995 to an estimated 472 million in 2015, an average growth rate of 3.44 per cent per year (UN-Habitat, 2016). Although megacities like Lagos dominate the literature on African cities, in fact, the fastest growing urban centres are the smaller cities with less than one million inhabitants, which accounted for 62 per cent of the urban population in Africa in 2015 (UN-Habitat, 2016).

Unlike urbanisation in many other parts of the world, urban population growth in most of Africa has generally not been accompanied by a commensurate increase in formal employment, resulting in growing urban poverty and increased urban vulnerability (Bryceson and Potts, 2006; Fox, 2012). The capacity of government bodies to plan for and manage urban growth in Africa is generally relatively weak (Myers, 2011). The net result of rapid urbanisation and inadequate capacity for planning or managing cities is the rise of inequality, the increasing prevalence of informality, and increased health risks. The growth of 'slums' is the most tangible manifestation of these issues. In 2014, an estimated 56 per cent of sub-Saharan Africa's urban population lived in informal settlements or other types of slum—that is to say, areas lacking adequate housing and services. The number of households living in slums in sub-Saharan Africa has been growing steadily—from an estimated 111 million in 1995 to 201 million in 2015 (UN-Habitat, 2016).

Secondary cities in Africa face particularly severe challenges. The concept of 'secondary cities' emerged from the concept of 'primate cities' proposed by Jefferson (1939). Whereas primate cities are the large cities that dominate the economic and political life of their countries, secondary cities are essentially non-primate cities, ranging from small cities of about 100,000 people to national second cities with populations in the millions (Rondinelli, 1983). It has recently been recognised that secondary cities play a key role in urbanisation processes (for example, Roberts, 2014). Secondary cities generally have weaker urban economies than primate cities, and thus 'suffer from weaker institutional and financial bases', but, simultaneously, 'rates of demographic growth are often higher in secondary compared with primate cities' (UN-Habitat, 2016, 172–173). The net result is that secondary cities are typically characterised by 'chronic inequality of opportunities, widespread poverty, inadequate capital investments in public goods, and lack of pro-poor social programmes' (UN-Habitat, 2016, 173). Kisumu in Kenya is a typical example of a secondary city. It was founded in 1901 by the British as a railway terminus port (Anyumba, 1995), and now is the third-largest city in Kenya, with a population of about 500,000 people, compared with more than 3 million people in Kenya's primate city, Nairobi (AFD, 2013). As with many African countries, the national economy is highly concentrated in the primate city, with few manufacturing activities in secondary cities (Otiso, 2005). The smaller revenue base means a smaller and less capacitated local government. As is typical of many secondary cities in Africa, Kisumu is strongly linked with a specific ethnic identity (Luo), whereas the primate city of Nairobi is more cosmopolitan. Intersections between ethnic identity and political parties have generally meant that parties in opposition to the national government have generally predominated in Kisumu, frequently resulting in conflict, such as was the case during the elections of October 2017 (Allison, 2017). All these factors have combined to make urban governance challenges in Kisumu particularly complex.

Urban governance is both one of the key challenges facing African cities and a potential lever for helping African cities become more equitable, with a better quality of life for residents. 'Governance' is also a contested concept that can mean many things; in the next section, I discuss the concept and what seems to be a useful definition.

3 The Concept of Governance

Governance can be defined in various ways. The term governance became widely used in the 1990s to refer to the shifting patterns of governing linked to the 'hollowing out' of the state associated with neo-liberalisation (Rhodes, 1997; Stoker, 1998). The term governance was seen as signifying 'a change in the meaning of government, referring to a new process of governing; or a changed condition of ordered rule; or the new method by which society is governed' (Rhodes, 1997, 652–653). Whereas 'government' was seen as being characterised by hierarchies and clear separations between state and society (Kjær , 2011), governance at the local level is seen as being characterised by a blurring of public–private boundaries, the rise of networks, and an increased role for actors other than the local government in the attainment of public goals (Pierre, 2005).

The term 'good governance' became especially linked with the World Bank, as a normative 'development paradigm' (Obeng-Odoom, 2017). The World Bank's first mention of 'good governance' was in the foreword to the *1989 World Bank Study Sub-Saharan Africa—from Crisis to Sustainable Growth* (World Bank, 1989), and the concept was further fleshed out in two subsequent reports, *Governance and Development* (World Bank, 1992) and *Governance, The*

World Bank's Experience (World Bank, 1994). The World Bank's conception of governance, which largely focused on efficiency and accountability, has been criticised for being 'a mainly administrative and managerialist interpretation of good governance' (UN-Habitat, 2016, 10), for being too depoliticised, and for being associated with elements of neo-liberal ideology, such as the need to promote conditions favourable for international businesses (Doornbos, 2001; Olivier de Sardan, 2011; Pearce, 2003).

United Nations (UN) agencies also instituted campaigns for good governance, but with a greater emphasis on democratic practice and human and civil rights (UN-Habitat, 2009). UNDP defined governance more broadly, as 'the mechanisms, processes and institutions through which citizens and groups articulate their interests, exercise their legal rights, meet their obligations and mediate their differences' (UNDP, 1997, 2–3). The two key aspects of this definition are as follows: 'Governance as a concept recognizes that power exists inside and outside the formal authority and institutions of government. [...] Second, governance emphasizes "process". It recognizes that decisions are made based on complex relationships between many actors with different priorities' (UN-Habitat, 2002, 12–13). Building on this, UN-Habitat launched its Global Campaign on Urban Governance (Taylor, 2000; UN-Habitat, 2002). UN-Habitat has defined urban governance as 'the sum of the many ways individuals and institutions, public and private, plan and manage the common affairs of the city [...] It includes formal institutions as well as informal arrangements' (UN-Habitat, 2002, 14). UN-Habitat's good urban governance campaign focused on the outcomes of governance, seeing good urban governance as resulting in ensuring that all residents have 'access to the necessities of urban life, including adequate shelter, security of tenure, safe water, sanitation, a clean environment, health, education and nutrition, employment and public safety and mobility' (UN-Habitat, 2002, 14).

Many scholars have used the UN conception of governance, or similar definitions, in an analytical way, to understand actual processes of governing and the complex ways in which different governance actors engage with each other (through formal and informal processes and in relationships ranging from co-operation to deep conflict) to make and operationalise decisions (for example, Bakker et al., 2008; Smit, 2016). In reality, non-government stakeholders have always played a key role in governing, and using governance as an analytical concept can help shed light on how decisions are actually made and implemented and can assist in identifying opportunities for intervention. As Koechlin (2016, 7) notes, using the concept of governance in this non-normative way 'opens up a window to identify and understand complex forms of interaction and co-ordination between different actors'.

One of the key characteristics of using a governance lens is the recognition that there is a wide range of actors involved in governance, such as various government organisations, civil society organisations—for example, non-governmental organisations (NGOs) and community groups—and the private sector (Devas, 2001). Using a governance lens is essentially about understanding these actors and the relationships between them. Inextricably intertwined with these processes are power and politics. Power can be conceived of as being distributed amongst these different actors and 'exercised from innumerable points' (Foucault, 1998 [1976], 94) by individuals such as planners, policy analysts and researchers, and politicians (Richardson, 1996). Power is not evenly distributed, however, as there are particular 'centres' or 'nodes' with concentrations of power (Lindell, 2008). These 'governance nodes' are groups of decision makers where knowledge, capacity and resources are mobilised to manage the course of events (Johnston and Shearing, 2003; Shearing and Wood, 2003). As Watson (2009) notes, different nodes can have very different ways of viewing the world, or 'conflicting rationalities', which can make engagement extremely difficult. In particular, there is a vast divide between an 'increasingly informalised and marginalised population and techno-managerial and marketised systems of government' (Watson, 2009, 2272).

These governance nodes impact on cities and towns through a range of 'formal' and 'informal' decision-making and regulatory processes.[1] As Devas (2004b) notes, informal governance processes are, in practice, often more important than formal governance processes. Closely linked to these governance processes, of course, is politics; as Rakodi (2001, 216) notes, these issues of power, resources, accountability and legitimacy are 'the stuff of politics'.

4 Urban Governance Actors in African Cities

The essence of using a governance lens is recognising that there is a wide range of actors involved in urban governance, with very different interests and agendas. Below, I discuss the main types of urban governance actors in African cities: government, traditional leaders, the private sector, international agencies, and civil society.

1 As discussed in the introduction to this special issue, formality/informality should be regarded as a continuum rather than a dichotomy, but I use the terms to refer to the respective ends of the continuum.

4.1 *Government*

All levels of government can play an important role in governing urban areas. Policymaking and the division of national revenue typically occur at a national level, and subnational levels of governments (states, provinces, counties or districts) often also perform key functions. Although the allocation of functions between different levels of government can vary enormously from country to country, local government bodies generally play a key role in urban governance.

Much of Africa did not have a tradition of strong local government in the colonial or early post-independence eras. However, from the 1980s onwards there was a shift towards decentralisation in Africa as governments and international agencies decided that improved urban management, decentralisation, and local democracy were interlinked (most notably, in the World Bank's 'good governance' agenda). The implementation of decentralisation in Africa has, however, been very uneven and partial, and has in some cases been reversed (Andrews and Schroeder, 2003; Smit and Pieterse, 2014; UN-Habitat, 2008). Although there are potentially advantages to decentralisation if it is undertaken carefully (with capacity development and resource allocation accompanying the transferral of responsibilities to lower levels of government), it has been argued by some scholars that the rushed and partial decentralisation of public authority in Africa has often resulted in local governments that are 'weak, disorganized, inadequately trained and staffed, and often underresourced relative to the new range of responsibilities they are expected to take on' (Meagher, 2011, 51). In addition, the role of local government is often further complicated by the key position it plays in the patronage system of political parties (Obeng-Odoom, 2017) and by the widespread phenomenon of African cities often being the bases of political parties in opposition to national governments led by parties with a largely rural support base (Resnick, 2011).

Simultaneously with increased decentralisation (and also linked to the 'good governance' agenda of the World Bank), there has been a shift in recent decades in the way local governments in Africa operate, towards privatisation and partnerships (Myers, 2005; Nunan and Satterthwaite, 2001; Olivier de Sardan, 2011). Privatisation of service delivery often disadvantages the urban poor, who are unable to pay for adequate levels of service provision. This is exacerbated by local governments usually having 'inherited a collection of repressive bylaws, and planning and building standards, which are unsuited to the needs and ability to pay of the poor' (Devas, 2001, 404).

The case of Kisumu reflects the typical complexity found in urban governance in Africa. Kisumu Municipal Council used to be a relatively autonomous local government body, located within Nyanza Province. Subsequent to the 2010 Constitution of Kenya, there was major restructuring of subnational government in Kenya, resulting in counties becoming the main subnational level of government. There is still a municipal administration (Kisumu City), but although it is meant to have a Municipal Board (according to the 2011 Urban Areas and Cities Act) the Governor of Kisumu County has not officially established this board (as is generally also the case in other counties in Kenya). Kisumu City essentially functions as an agency of Kisumu County, with all Kisumu City officials employed by Kisumu County. There are also a number of independent agencies that operate in the area, such as the Kisumu Water and Sewerage Company (KIWASCO). In addition, many national ministries also play a direct role in Kisumu; for example, the National Ministry of Land and Housing allocates land within the city area.

Closely intertwined with these various levels of government are political parties. Although there has been a rapid spread of multiparty democracy in Africa in recent decades, the political landscape tends to be dominated by clientelist political parties (i.e. those which focus on providing benefits to their constituents), which analysis suggests are less likely to improve the quality of public services than are programmatic political parties (parties with coherent and consistent positions on policy issues) (World Bank, 2017). As is very common in African cities, Kisumu is (and has almost always been since independence) the base of a political party in opposition to the ruling party at the national level—the Orange Democratic Movement (ODM) party, which became part of the Coalition for Reforms and Democracy (CORD). Members of this party hold most elected positions in the Kisumu area, including that of county governor and those of members of parliament and members of the county assembly. There has been frequent violent political conflict in Kisumu, most notably the violence following the 2007 General Election (for example, see Harneit-Sievers and Peters, 2008).

4.2 *Traditional Leaders*

A typical characteristic of urban governance in Africa is that traditional leaders often play an important role in governance—for example, with regard to land allocation in peri-urban areas. Traditional leaders can be more accessible to residents than elected politicians are, although they can also be 'unresponsive, corrupt and interested mainly in maintaining power and patronage' (Devas, 2004a, 118). Olivier de Sardan (2011) notes that their only real accountability is to higher levels of government.

In Kisumu, outside of the historical core of the city, traditional leaders play an officially recognised role in governance. 'Locations' are headed by Chiefs, 'sub-locations' are headed by Assistant Chiefs and 'sub-units' are headed by one or two village elders (Omedo et al., 2014). Chiefs, Assistant Chiefs and village elders all play an important role in the governance of Kisumu—for example, in government health-promotion campaigns (Omedo et al., 2014).

4.3 *Private Sector*

Large private sector organisations, such as property development or food production companies, can play an important role in urban governance in African cities. In some cases, 'their actions can be damaging to the poor, forcing them off land they occupy and preventing informal traders from operating' (Devas, 2001, 400). Informal business organisations can also play an important role in urban governance, governing marketplaces for example, but they usually have less influence on government decision-making than do big, private sector companies (Brown et al., 2010). For example, a study of informal business organisations in Nigeria highlights their limitations in affecting formal decision-making, noting that 'small entrepreneurs pay their local government taxes and even some state-level taxes, but they continue to receive little in the way of basic services in return' (Meagher, 2011, 68).

In Kisumu, big property development companies are playing a major role in the urban transformation of the city, through investment in a number of large development projects, mainly shopping malls. One company, which is investing in a mixed-use project linked to a shopping mall, has the stated ambition of turning Kisumu into another Dubai, for the East Africa region (Matete, 2016). The Chamber of Commerce also plays a prominent role in Kisumu, leading, for example, attempts to relocate street traders away from the main shopping street of the city. Informal trader organisations play an important role in managing all the marketplaces in Kisumu (for example, by ensuring that these markets are cleaned).

4.4 *International Agencies*

Multilateral agencies, development banks, and international donor agencies play a large and important role in African cities. Most global aid and loans to Africa are linked to the 'good governance' agenda and the promotion of decentralisation and democratisation (Dietrich and Wright, 2015). In Kisumu, the World Bank and the Agence Française de Développement (AFD) are particularly active funders and have invested vast amounts in infrastructure, including in the new motorway system that encircles the city. Particularly notable is the Integrated Strategic Urban Development Plan (ISUD-Plan), which is funded by AFD and has a budget of 40 million euros. It seeks to prepare for the city's future through a range of strategies, including planning Kisumu's expansion, upgrading informal settlements, refurbishing and building new markets, and by developing strategies for capital investment in the city (AFD, 2013). There are also a number of international NGOs active in Kisumu on a range of issues, such as Plan International (which works on children's rights).

4.5 *Civil Society*

There is a vast range of civil society associations who, in practice, play a key role in urban governance in Africa. These include ethnicity-based networks, home-town associations, youth associations, savings groups, and funeral groups (Devas, 2001; Olivier de Sardan, 2011; Tostensen et al., 2001). These organisations often, in practice, perform roles undertaken by the state in cities in the global North, such as providing basic services, allocating land, ensuring safety, providing social security nets, and so on. In addition, many Western-style community associations have been set up by international development agencies, often with a focus on 'wells, grain mills, credit, seeds, market gardening, etc.' (Olivier de Sardan, 2011, 25). Various types of religious associations (for example, charismatic movements and Islamic brotherhoods) also play an important role in urban governance in Africa, particularly with regards to humanitarian interventions such as providing food (Olivier de Sardan, 2011). NGOs can also be important 'in enabling communities to organize and articulate demands' (Devas, 2001, 401).

As is the case with most African cities, Kisumu has a large number of civil society organisations, most of which belong to a federation called the Civil Society Organisation Network. There is a particular concentration of NGOs in Kisumu, with an estimated 900 based in the city—this figure includes a number of international NGOs, but mainly consists of local organisations (Prince, 2013). There are a large number of HIV/AIDS organisations with offices in Kisumu, as the surrounding region has an HIV prevalence rate that is double the national average (Camlin et al., 2013).

5 The Objects of Governance

Governance does not occur for its own sake; there are particular objects, tangible or intangible, that are governed. Governance can be considered as 'collective practices addressing societal problems' (Förster, 2016, 211). In an urban context these 'problems' are the collective issues that have always impacted on the lives of residents whenever large groups of people live in close proximity to each other, and include how to govern who can do what where, how to ensure access to water and sanitation and solid waste disposal, and how to ensure there is a well-functioning transport system. The most basic object of urban governance is land allocation and land use management, which essentially is about who can do what where. The second most basic object of urban governance is the provision and management of basic infrastructure/services, such as water, sanitation, and waste management. A third key object of governance can be considered as the movement/accessibility system, which is essentially about how people and goods can get around from one part of the settlement to another—at its most basic, this will consist of footpaths and roads, while at a higher level there would be buses, trains, and so on. In most settlements there are formal or informal organisations that attempt to govern these issues; for example, in informal settlements there are typically residents' associations that allocate land and ensure some basic level of service provision and maintenance of footpaths (Smit, 2006).

Beyond these basic and widespread objects of urban governance, found in most contexts, there are also many other possible objects of urban governance, such as ensuring good health and well-being, ensuring safety from crime and violence, disaster risk management, education, social/cultural development, economic development, environmental management, and so on. In this chapter, I discuss the three basic objects of urban governance, and also look at food safety as an example of another object of urban governance.

5.1 *Land Use Management*

African countries generally have multiple land administration systems: formal systems of deed registries with freehold and leasehold title; officially recognised customary tenure systems; and informal, extra-legal tenure in informal settlements. Areas with formal tenure generally have zoning schemes and building regulations enforced by the state, whereas these are generally not enforced in customary or informal tenure areas. African cities are often characterised by 'unregulated peri-urban land development' (Kombe, 2005, 113). The ability of local government to control such sprawl is often limited by peri-urban areas being in customary ownership and under the authority of traditional leaders (for example, Gough, 1999).

A major land use management issue in many African cities is urban agriculture. While some scholars see urban agriculture as having an important role to play in poverty reduction and food security (e.g. Lee-Smith, 2010), most African national and local governments are intolerant of urban agriculture, seeing it as incompatible with their 'modernist' visions of what cities should look like (Kuusaana and Eledi, 2015; Simatele and Binns, 2008; Tong, 2010), viewing it as a rural activity 'whose practice within the city boundaries is inappropriate and detracts from the modern image of the city' (Simatele and Binns, 2008, 2). In African cities experiencing steep economic decline, however, there has been a rapid increase in levels of participation in urban agriculture, and organisations of urban farmers can play an important role in promoting and supporting urban agriculture (Schmidt et al., 2015). In Dar es Salaam for example, the activities of urban farmers' associations include 'joint production on communally held property and serving as a loan or finance agency for their members' (Schmidt et al., 2015, 158).

Another important aspect of land use management is the governance of retail, which essentially is about who can sell what where (and when). Much of the retail sector in most African cities can be classified as being at the 'informal' end of the formality/informality continuum. There are usually a wide variety of different types of informal food retail outlets, such as large, traditional marketplaces (which might have thousands of traders), various types of informal shops and kiosks, and street traders. Urban governance can impact on informal traders in various ways, including through processes for allocating trading space and through the provision of infrastructure and services, such as water, electricity and refuse removal.

Marketplaces are a particularly important element of urban food systems in Africa and are an important site of urban governance. Market associations generally play an important role in managing marketplaces in Africa (King, 2006; Lyon, 2003; Porter et al., 2007). In Maputo, for example, 'the market committees provide infrastructure (water, toilets, etc.), maintenance and security services, and organise cleaning in their respective markets [...] The committees also act as the principal regulators in the markets' (Lindell, 2008, 1889). Trader associations govern marketplaces using a range of techniques—such as surveillance, peer pressure and control of physical space (Lyon, 2003)—and can sometimes also influence the plans of local government (King, 2006). Local governments also usually play a role in managing marketplaces, partially because trader fees can be a significant source of local government revenue (King, 2006). As most local governments lack adequate power to plan, regulate and provide infrastructure and services, this role is often limited to collecting fees (Meagher, 2011). Whereas traders in marketplaces have some protection as a result of the large number of traders and some form of official recognition, street traders are much more vulnerable. There are frequently waves of evictions of street traders to 'clear the streets'—for example, when there is a change of political power or when a major event is about to take place (Devas, 2001; Hansen, 2004; King, 2006).

Over time, the nature of food retail in African cities has been changing, with increased growth in 'formal' retail outlets. In the past two decades there has been rapid growth in supermarkets in Africa, with largely negative impacts on the food security of the urban poor (Crush and Frayne, 2011; Reardon et al., 2003, 2004, 2007; Weatherspoon and Reardon, 2003). For example, between 1995 and 2012, Shoprite Checkers, a South African supermarket chain, opened 131 supermarkets in 16 different African countries outside of South Africa (Battersby and Peyton, 2014). Currently, the roll-out of supermarkets is being driven by the private sector; Crush and Frayne (2011, 806) note that there is an 'absence of regulatory controls on supermarket expansion in urban markets' in Africa (for example, as to where they are located, how big they are, whether they are accessible to pedestrians, whether they offer trading space for informal traders, and so on).

Kisumu is typical of African cities in that it has a low-density, 'formal' historic core (mainly consisting of land leased from the state on 99-year leaseholds), where building and regulations are quite tightly enforced, surrounded by a zone of dense, informal areas (many of which are been upgraded) and 'ancestral land' areas (now technically under freehold ownership) where planning and building regulations are much less enforced (Anyumba, 1995). Kisumu is also typical of state views of urban agriculture in African cities. An estimated 50 per cent of Kisumu's residents are engaged in urban/peri-urban agriculture, even though it was, until recently, technically illegal in terms of public health and water legislation. With the introduction of the Urban Areas and Cities Act of 2011 urban agriculture became legal. In terms of retail, Kisumu has 30 marketplaces, with Kibuye market being the biggest. Kisumu City collects fees from these traders on a daily or monthly basis—at the Jubilee Market, for example, the fee is 30 Kenyan Shillings per day for traders outside the market (collected every day) and 350–600 Kenyan Shillings per month for stalls inside the market (paid monthly to the City)—but provides little in return. Market associations play an important role in managing marketplaces. In some markets, such as Jubilee market, traders' associations collect additional fees to provide services, including sanitation and cleaning. A number of markets are scheduled for redevelopment (through the provision of new multi-storey buildings) as part of the Kisumu Urban Project, but all these projects have been delayed. In Kisumu, street traders are in a precarious position. For example, the street traders who occupy the pavements of Jaramogi Oginga Odinga Avenue (the main street of Kisumu) are constantly at risk of being relocated due to perceptions that they obstruct the pavements and negatively impact on formal businesses along the street. In the past two decades the number of supermarkets in Kisumu has grown to 20, many of them the anchor tenants of shopping malls. There has been virtually no local government control over the location/design of supermarkets or what they sell.

5.2 *Provision and Management of Basic Infrastructure/Services*

Providing basic services such as water, sanitation and waste management is usually a key purpose of urban governance. In most cases, this is the main official role of local government, but in general only a small proportion of African urban residents are served by state-provided services—as noted earlier, 56 per cent of Africa's urban population live in unserviced areas (UN-Habitat. 2016), and even many serviced areas have stand-alone infrastructure such as VIP toilets and boreholes rather than networked infrastructure. This gap in infrastructure provision has (partially) been filled by the provision of services in particular areas by community groups and NGOs.

Kisumu reflects the typical complexity of service provision in African cities, particularly water provision. The Kisumu Water and Sewerage Company (KIWASCO) is a privatised utility company that was set up in 2003 to replace the water and sewerage department of the former Kisumu Municipal Council. It is supervised by Lake Victoria South Water Services Board, one of seven regional water boards in Kenya. As the formal water and sewerage network was limited to only the area of the former colonial town, in order to roll out water provision to peri-urban areas KIWASCO has relied upon a network of subcontractors who in turn sell water to connected customers and to water kiosk operators, the latter selling on to unconnected customers (Schwartz and Sanga, 2010). Although this approach has been successful in extending the provision of water supply, the net result is a very uneven pattern of access to water, with the extent of piped, private connections and yard taps ranging from 97.6 per cent of households in a high-income area (Milimani) to only 2.8 per cent in Migosi Estate (Wagah et al., 2010).

Solid waste management is a particular area of concern, with the Kachok dumpsite in the centre of Kisumu unable to cope with all the waste generated (Munala and Moirongo, 2011; Sibanda et al., 2017). City officials estimate that only between 20 per cent and 35 per cent of solid waste is collected (either directly by the City or by private collectors who sell their services to companies and institutions), leaving about 65–80 per cent (of which most is organic waste) uncollected (Sibanda et al., 2017). There are a number of informal waste pickers in Kisumu, who play an important role in the recycling of waste.

A number of NGOs and community groups are actively involved in the provision of water, sanitation, energy and solid waste management (e.g. Practical Action and SANA International), but these are generally small, ad hoc projects.

5.3 *Urban Transport Systems*

The key elements of urban transport systems are the provision and maintenance of roads, managing traffic, and ensuring the roadworthiness of vehicles.

In general, urban transport infrastructure in African cities is inadequate. A study of 14 cities in Africa found that 'to a greater or lesser extent in each of the cities, the networks of paved roads and associated traffic control facilities are deficient' (Kumar and Barrett, 2008, 37). The stock of vehicles is also largely inadequate: 'widespread dilapidation is apparent, as basic safety standards with regard to lighting, tires, and brakes are openly flouted. Systems and procedures for routine vehicle inspections are clearly failing, while petty corruption among police officers means that no action is taken on the road' (Kumar and Barrett, 2008, 37). The net result is that many African cities are choked with traffic congestion.

Kisumu used to be a rail centre and important harbour, but now its main transport links are roads. A number of agencies are involved in providing and maintaining roads in Kisumu (Kenya National Highways Authority, Kenya Urban Roads Authority, Kenya Rural Roads Authority, etc.), with lots of overlap and duplication. It is estimated that only about 30 per cent of the existing road network is being maintained. Although not very pedestrian friendly, Kisumu's transport system generally works well, with a wide range of affordable transport options, such as minibus taxis, *tuk-tuks*, *boda-bodas* (motorcycle taxis) and bicycle taxis. A Bus Rapid Transit (BRT) system is planned for Kisumu, even though evidence suggests that BRT systems are only feasible in larger cities (Hidalgo and Gutiérrez, 2013).

5.4 *Food Safety*

The main determinants of food safety are 'the procedures and standards and regulations (or lack of) for food production, processing, and packaging' (Ericksen, 2008, 240). Many food-safety regulations need to be enforced at a national level, but at the city scale there needs to be local-level enforcement—for example, in the form of regular visits by health inspectors. While regulating and enforcing food production, processing, distribution and retail in the formal sector can be relatively straightforward if there is sufficient capacity in place, addressing food safety in the informal sector is probably the main food-safety challenge faced at the local level (Cambaza dos Muchangos et al., 2015).

Street foods are a particular concern. Numerous studies have confirmed that street food can have a high risk of contamination (for example, Roesel and Grace, 2015). Typical issues include inadequate access to water and sanitation, inadequate refuse removal, and exposure to flies, which can all result in the contamination of food.

Some, but not all, local governments are involved in enforcing standards of hygiene amongst informal traders (Muyanja et al., 2011). Even where local government does attempt to enforce health standards, this enforcement is often only partial. For example, in Abeokuta, Nigeria, food vendors are required to obtain an annual certificate from health authorities, but a survey found that only 31 per cent of vendors had these (Omemu and Aderoju, 2008).

The Kisumu City Health Department is meant to ensure food safety, but is understaffed (they say they ideally need 30 health inspectors, but only have 14). The department runs a clinic for food handlers, carrying out screening and vaccinations for typhoid, hepatitis B and TB. The health inspectors check 'hot spots' once per week, but there is a lack of equipment with which to undertake proper tests (such as testing milk).

6 Conclusion

The net result of the wide range of governance actors with very different agendas found in urban governance processes in Africa is that, as Lindell (2008, 1896) notes with regard to the governance of marketplaces in Maputo, 'governance appears to lack any semblance of coherence and to be fragmented, disjointed and split by deep antagonisms. The key actors continuously challenge each other's legitimacy to "govern"'. The governance of most issues is characterised by fragmentation and a lack of coordination between governance actors; in the case of government actors, the ability to enforce regulations is usually quite limited. Skills and resources seem to be more thinly spread and diffused than is the case than in the global North, meaning that one or two urban governance actors acting in isolation on their own are seldom able to address many key urban challenges. As a result, key problems such as inadequate infrastructure in marketplaces, traffic congestion and inadequate waste disposal systems are not addressed, and the problems persist and grow over time.

Although this diversity of actors can be seen as a problem, it can, however, also be seen as an opportunity for mobilising additional skills and resources with which to address challenges in African cities. Following this view, there have been repeated calls for collaborative governance—bringing 'multiple stakeholders together in common forums with public agencies to engage in consensus-orientated decision-making' (Ansell and Gash, 2008, 543)—and for the 'co-production' of contextually appropriate projects and policies by a range of urban governance actors (Polk, 2015). In the words of Harrison (2006, 320), we need to recognise the existence of multiple rationalities and search for 'the in-between spaces, the interstices, where different conceptions of the city, and of planning and rationality, have intermingled and have produced hybrid logics and practices'.

There have been some attempts at this in Kisumu, initially through the multi-stakeholder Kisumu Action Team (KAT). KAT initially only represented a narrow range of interests, but subsequently included broader representation—for example, of the informal traders in Kisumu (Onyango and Obera, 2015). KAT used 'interdisciplinary, cross-sector and policy approaches [...] to solve some of the urban planning and development issues in the city, drawing on inputs from various stakeholders' (Onyango and Obera, 2015, 93). This was a conflict-ridden process, but resulted in the raising of substantial funds for an ambitious range of physical upgrading projects in Kisumu, such as the redevelopment of the marketplaces. KAT then transformed into the Kisumu Local Interaction Platform (KLIP), a consortium of Kisumu City, Kisumu County, the Civil Society Coalition, the Chamber of Commerce and the two local universities (Maseno University and the Jaramogi Oginga Odinga University of Science and Technology) that undertakes collaborative research and implementation to develop Kisumu (Polk, 2016). In this way, the limited skills and resources available for dealing with urban problems in a secondary city like Kisumu have been pooled together and used to leverage more resources, and different interests have been brought together to develop strategies that are more holistic, inclusive and sustainable.

Access to information and data is crucial for effective collaborative governance. Although many governments are wary of making data accessible to the public (World Bank, 2017), this is an essential precondition for civil society and other stakeholders to engage with government bodies in collaborative governance.

In order to be able to collaboratively design and implement interventions to improve the quality of life of urban residents, we need to better understand existing, complex urban governance processes and the competing interests of urban governance actors. Through establishing multi-stakeholder forums such as KAT and KLIP, and through ensuring that all stakeholders have access to information and relevant data, different interest groups can be brought together to successfully collaborate on planning for and managing cities, and more appropriate local strategies and projects can be developed and implemented. Collaborative governance can be messy and conflictual, but only through facilitating engagement and collaboration between different urban governance actors can urban challenges in Africa be effectively addressed.

References

AFD (Agence Français de Développement) (2013) *Kisumu: ISUD-Plan: Part 1. Integrated Strategic Urban Development Plan: Understanding Kisumu,* (Kisumu: AFD).

Allison, S. (2017) 'Kisumu Boycotted the Kenyan Elections, Though They Didn't Have Much Choice', *Mail and Guardian,* 26 October, https://mg.co.za/article/2017-10-26-in-kisumu-the-election-that-wasnt (accessed on 20 April 2018).

Andrews, M. and L. Schroeder (2003) 'Sectoral Decentralisation and Intergovernmental Arrangements in Africa', *Public Administration and Development,* 23(1), pp. 29–40, DOI: 10.1002/pad.257.

Ansell, C. and A. Gash (2008) 'Collaborative Governance in Theory and Practice', *Journal of Public Administration Research and Theory,* 18(4), pp. 543–571, DOI: 10.1093/jopart/mum032

Anyumba, G. (1995) *Kisumu Town: History of the Built Form, Planning and Environment: 1890–1990* (Delft: Delft University Press).

Bakker, K., M. Kooy, N.E. Shofiani and E.-J. Martijn (2008) 'Governance Failure: Rethinking the Institutional Dimensions of Urban Water Supply to Poor Households', *World Development,* 36(10), pp. 1891–1915, DOI: 10.1016/j.worlddev.2007.09.015.

Battersby, J. and S. Peyton (2014) 'The Geography of Supermarkets in Cape Town: Supermarket Expansion and Food Access', *Urban Forum,* 25(2), pp. 153–164, DOI: 10.1007/s12132-014-9217-5.

Brown, A., M. Lyons and I. Dankoco (2010) 'Street Traders and the Emerging Spaces for Urban Voice and Citizenship in African Cities', *Urban Studies,* 47(3), pp. 666–683, DOI: 10.1177/0042098009351187.

Bryceson, D. and D. Potts (eds.) (2006) *African Urban Economies: Viability, Vitality or Vitiation?* (London: Palgrave Macmillan).

Cambaza dos Muchangos, A.B., K. Roesel, C. McCrindle, H. Matusse, S. Hendrickx, K. Makita and D. Grace (2015) 'Informal markets in Mozambique Risky for Local Chicken', in K. Roesel and D. Grace (eds.), *Food Safety and Informal Markets: Animal Products in Sub-Saharan Africa* (Abingdon: Routledge), pp. 197–200.

Camlin, C.S., Z.A. Kwena and S.L. Dworkin (2013) '*Jaboya vs. Jakambi:* Status, Negotiation, and HIV Risks among Female Migrants in "the Sex for Fish" Economy in Nyanza Province, Kenya', *AIDS Education and Prevention,* 25(3), pp. 216–231, DOI: 10.1521/aeap.2013.25.3.216.

Crush, J. and B. Frayne (2011) 'Supermarket Expansion and the Informal Food Economy in Southern African Cities: Implications for Urban Food Security', *Journal of Southern African Studies,* 37(4), pp. 781–807, DOI: 10.1080/03057070.2011.617532.

Devas, N. (2004a) 'Urban Government: Capacity, Resources and Responsiveness' in N. Devas (ed.), *Urban Governance, Voice and Poverty in the Developing world* (London: Earthscan), pp. 95–122.

Devas, N. (2004b) 'Urban Poverty and Governance in an Era of Globalization, Decentralization and Democratization' in N. Devas (ed.), *Urban Governance, Voice and Poverty in the Developing World* (London: Earthscan), pp. 15–36.

Devas, N. (2001) 'Does City Governance Matter for the Urban Poor?' *International Planning Studies,* 6(4), pp. 393–408, DOI: 10.1080/13563470120092395.

Dietrich, S. and J. Wright (2015) 'Foreign Aid Allocation Tactics and Democratic Change in Africa', *The Journal of Politics,* 77(1), pp. 216–234, DOI: 10.1086/678976.

Doornbos, M. (2001) 'Good Governance: The Rise and Decline of a Policy Metaphor?' *The Journal of Development Studies,* 37(6), pp. 93–108, DOI: 10.1080/713601084.

Ericksen, P.J. (2008) 'Conceptualizing Food Systems for Global Environmental Change Research', *Global Environmental Change,* 18(1), pp. 234–245, DOI: 10.1016/j.gloenvcha.2007.09.002.

Förster, T. (2016) 'The Formation of Governance: The Politics of Governance and Their Theoretical Dimensions', in L. Koechlin and T. Förster (eds.), *The Politics of Governance: Actors and Articulations in Africa and Beyond* (New York: Routledge), pp. 197–218.

Fox, S. (2012) 'Urbanization as a Global Historical Process: Theory and Evidence from sub-Saharan Africa', *Population and Development Review,* 38(2), pp. 285–310, DOI: 10.1111/j.1728-4457.2012.00493.x.

Foucault, M. (1998 [1976]) *The Will to Knowledge: The History of Sexuality Volume 1,* Translated by R. Hurley (London: Penguin).

Gough, K. (1999) 'The Changing Nature of Urban Governance in Peri-urban Accra, Ghana', *Third World Planning Review,* 21(4), pp. 393–410.

Hansen, K.T. (2004) 'Who Rules the Streets? The Politics of Vending Space in Lusaka' in K.T. Hansen and M. Vaa (eds.), *Reconsidering Informality: Perspectives from Urban Africa* (Uppsala: Nordic Africa Institute).

Harrison, P. (2006) 'On the Edge of Reason: Planning and Urban Futures in Africa', *Urban Studies,* 43(2), pp. 319–335, DOI: 10.1080/00420980500418368.

Harneit-Sievers, A. and R.-M. Peters (2008) 'Kenya's 2007 General Election and Its Aftershocks', *Afrika Spectrum,* 43(1), pp. 133–144, http://nbn-resolving.de/urn:nbn:de:0168-ssoar-353260 (accessed on 20 April 2018).

Hidalgo, D. and L. Gutiérrez (2013) 'BRT and BHLS around the World: Explosive Growth, Large Positive Impacts and Many Issues Outstanding', *Research in Transportation Economics,* 39(1), pp. 8–13, DOI: 10.1016/j.retrec.2012.05.018.

Jefferson, M. (1939) 'The Law of the Primate City', *Geographical Review,* 29(2), pp. 226–232. DOI: 10.2307/215528.

Johnston, L. and C. Shearing (2003) *Governing Security: Explorations in Policing and Justice* (London: Routledge).

King, R. (2006) 'Fulcrum of the Urban Economy: Governance and Street Livelihoods in Kumasi, Ghana' in A. Brown (ed.), *Contested Space: Street Trading, Public Space, and Livelihoods in Developing Cities* (Rugby: ITDG Publishing), pp. 100–118.

Kjær, A.M. (2011) 'Rhodes' Contribution to Governance Theory: Praise, Criticism and the Future Governance Debate', *Public Administration,* 89(1), pp. 101–113. DOI: 10.1111/j.1467-9299.2011.01903.x.

Koechlin, L. (2016) 'Introduction: The conceptual polysemy of governance', in L. Koechlin and T. Förster (eds.), *The Politics of Governance: Actors and Articulations in Africa and Beyond* (paperback edition; New York: Routledge), pp. 1–22.

Kombe, W.J. (2005) 'Land Use dynamics in Peri-urban areas and Their Implications on the Urban Growth and Form: The Case of Dar es Salaam, Tanzania', *Habitat International*, 29(1), pp. 113–135. DOI: 10.1016/S0197-3975(03)00076-6.

Kumar, A. and F. Barrett (2008) *Stuck in Traffic: Urban Transport in Africa* (Washington, DC: World Bank).

Kuusaana, E.D. and J.A. Eledi (2015) 'As the City Grows, Where do the Farmers go? Understanding Peri-urbanization and Food Systems in Ghana—Evidence from the Tamale Metropolis', *Urban Forum*, 26(4), pp. 443–465. DOI: 10.1007/s12132-015-9260-x.

Lee-Smith, D. (2010) 'Cities Feeding People: An Update on Urban Agriculture in Equatorial Africa', *Environment and Urbanization*, 22(2), pp. 483–499, DOI: 10.1177/0956247810377383.

Lindell, I. (2008) 'The Multiple Sites of Urban Governance: Insights from an African City', *Urban Studies*, 45(9), pp. 1879–1901, DOI: 10.1177/0042098008093382.

Lyon, F. (2003) 'Trader Associations and Urban Food Systems in Ghana: Institutionalist Approaches to Understanding Urban Collective Action', *International Journal of Urban and Regional Research*, 27(1), pp. 11–23. DOI: 10.1111/1468-2427.00428.

Matete, F. (2016) 'Mega City to Make Kisumu "like Dubai"', The Star, 10 February, https://www.the-star.co.ke/news/2016/02/10/mega-city-to-make-kisumu-like-dubai_c1291774 (accessed on 16 September 2017).

Meagher, K. (2011) 'Informal Economies and Urban Governance in Nigeria: Popular Empowerment or Political Exclusion?', *African Studies Review*, 54(2), pp. 47–72, DOI:10.1353/arw.2011.0026.

Munala, G. and B.O. Moirongo (2011) 'The Need for an Integrated Solid Waste Management in Kisumu, Kenya', *Journal of Agriculture Science and Technology*, 13(1), pp. 65–78.

Muyanja, C., L. Nayiga, N. Brenda and G. Nasinyama (2011) 'Practices, Knowledge and Risk Factors of Street Food Vendors in Uganda', *Food Control*, 22(10), pp. 1551–1558. DOI: 10.1016/j.foodcont.2011.01.016.

Myers, G.A. (2011) *African Cities: Alternative Visions of Urban Theory and Practice* (London: Zed Books).

Myers, G.A. (2005) *Disposable Cities: Garbage, Governance and Sustainable Development in Urban Africa* (Aldershot: Ashgate).

Nunan, F. and D. Satterthwaite (2001) 'The Influence of Governance on the Provision of Urban Environmental Infrastructure and Services for Low-income Groups', *International Planning Studies*, 6(4), pp. 409–426, DOI: 10.1080/13563470120103365.

Obeng-Odoom, F. (2017) 'Urban Governance in Africa Today: Reframing, Experiences, and Lessons', *Growth and Change*, 48(1), pp. 4–21, DOI:10.1111/grow.12164.

Olivier de Sardan, J.-P. (2011) 'The Eight Modes of Local Governance in West Africa'. *IDS Bulletin*, 42(2), pp. 22–31, DOI: 10.1111/j.1759-5436.2011.00208.x.

Omedo, M., M. Ogutu, A. Awiti, R. Musuva, G. Muchiri, S.P. Montgomery, W.E. Secor and P. Mwinzi. (2014) 'The Effect of a Health Communication Campaign on Compliance with Mass Drug Administration for Schistosomiasis Control in Western Kenya—The SCORE Project', *American Journal of Tropical Medicine and Hygiene*, 91(5), pp. 982–988, DOI: 10.4269/ajtmh.14-0136.

Omemu, A.M. and S.T. Aderoju (2008) 'Food Safety Knowledge and Practices of Street Food Vendors in the City of Abeokuta, Nigeria', *Food Control*, 19(4), pp. 396–402. DOI: 10.1016/j.foodcont.2007.04.021.

Onyango, G.M. and B.O. Obera (2015) 'Tracing Kisumu's Path in the Co-production of Knowledge for Urban Development', in M. Polk (ed.), *Co-producing Knowledge for Sustainable Cities: Joining Forces for Change* (Abingdon: Routledge), pp. 73–97.

Otiso, K.M. (2005) 'Kenya's Secondary Cities Growth Strategy at a Crossroads: Which Way Forward?' *GeoJournal*, 62(1), pp. 117–128. DOI: 10.1007/s10708-005-8180-z.

Pearce, K.C. (2003) 'Democracy and Development as Contested Terrain: The Discourse of the 'Good Governance' Agenda in Africa', *Review of Communication*, 3(1), pp. 28–30, DOI: 10.1080/1835859032000084151.

Pierre, J. (2005) 'Comparative Urban Governance: Uncovering Complex Causalities', *Urban Affairs Review*, 40(4), pp. 446–462, DOI: 10.1177/1078087404273442.

Polk, M (2016) 'How to manage Complexity: Co-producing Knowledge for Urban Change', in *Co-production in Action: Towards Realising Just Cities* (Gothenburg: Mistra Urban Futures), pp. 32–45.

Polk, M. (ed.) (2015) *Co-producing Knowledge for Sustainable Cities: Joining Forces for Change* (Abingdon: Routledge).

Porter, G., F. Lyon and D. Potts (2007) 'Market Institutions and Urban Food Supply in West and Southern Africa: A Review', *Progress in Development Studies*, 7(2), pp. 115–134, DOI: 10.1177/146499340600700203.

Prince, R. (2013) '"Tarmacking" in the Millennium City: Spatial and Temporal Trajectories of Empowerment and Development in Kisumu, Kenya', *Africa*, 83(4), pp. 582–605, DOI: 10.1017/S0001972013000478.

Rakodi, C. (2001). 'Forget Planning, Put Politics First? Priorities for Urban Management in Developing Countries', *International Journal of Applied Earth Observation and Geoinformation*, 3(3), pp. 209–223, DOI:10.1016/S0303-2434(01)85029-7.

Reardon, T., C.P. Timmer, C.B. Barrett and J. Berdegúe (2003) 'The Rise of Supermarkets in Africa, Asia, and Latin America', *American Journal of Agricultural Economics*, 85(5), pp. 1143–1146. DOI: 10.1111/j.0092-5853.2003.00520.x.

Reardon, T., P. Timmer and J. Berdegue (2004) 'The Rapid Rise of Supermarkets in Developing Countries: Induced Organizational, Institutional, and Technological

Change in Agrifood Systems', *Electronic Journal of Agricultural and Development Economics*, 1(2), pp. 168–183.

Reardon, T., S. Henson and J. Berdegúe (2007) 'Proactive Fast-tracking' Diffusion of Supermarkets in Developing Countries: Implications for Market Institutions and Trade', *Journal of Economic Geography*, 7(4), pp. 399–431, DOI: 10.1093/jeg/lbm007.

Resnick, D. (2011) 'In the Shadow of the City: Africa's Urban Poor in Opposition Strongholds', *The Journal of Modern African Studies*, 49(1), pp. 141–166. DOI: 10.1017/S0022278X10000686.

Rhodes, R.A.W. (1997) *Understanding Governance: Policy Networks, Governance, Reflexivity and Accountability* (Buckingham: Open University Press).

Richardson, T. (1996) 'Foucauldian Discourse: Power and Truth in Urban and Regional Policy Making', *European Planning Studies*, 4(3), pp. 279–292, DOI: 10.1080/09654319608720346.

Roberts, B.H. (2014) *Managing Systems of Secondary Cities: Policy Responses in International Development* (Brussels: Cities Alliance/UNOPS).

Roesel, K. and D. Grace (eds.) (2015) *Food Safety and Informal Markets: Animal Products in Sub-Saharan Africa* (Abingdon: Routledge).

Rondinelli, D.A. (1983) 'Dynamics of Growth of Secondary Cities in Developing Countries', *Geographical Review*, 73(1), pp. 42–57. DOI: 10.2307/214394.

Schmidt, S., W. Magigi and B. Godfrey (2015) 'The Organization of Urban Agriculture: Farmer Associations and Urbanization in Tanzania', *Cities*, 42(Part B), pp. 153–159. DOI:10.1016/j.cities.2014.05.013.

Schwartz, K. and A. Sanga (2010) 'Partnerships between Utilities and Small-scale Providers: Delegated Management in Kisumu, Kenya', *Physics and Chemistry of the Earth, Parts A/B/C*, 35(13), pp. 765–771, DOI: 10.1016/j.pce.2010.07.003.

Shearing, C. and J. Wood (2003) 'Nodal Governance, Democracy, and the New "Denizens"', *Journal of Law and Society*, 30(3), pp. 400–419, DOI: 10.2307/1410537.

Sibanda, L.K., N. Obange and F.O. Awuor (2017) 'Challenges of Solid Waste Management in Kisumu, Kenya', *Urban Forum*, 28(4), pp. 387–402. DOI: 10.1007/s12132-017-9316-1.

Simatele, D.M. and T. Binns (2008) 'Motivation and Marginalization in African Urban Agriculture: The Case of Lusaka, Zambia', *Urban Forum*, 19(1), pp. 1–21, DOI: 10.1007/s12132-008-9021-1.

Smit, W. (2016) 'Urban Governance and Urban Food Systems in Africa: Examining the Linkages', *Cities*, 58, pp. 80–86, DOI: 10.1016/j.cities.2016.05.001.

Smit, W. (2006) 'Understanding the Complexities of Informal Settlements: Insights from Cape Town', in M. Huchzermeyer and A. Karam (eds.), *Informal Settlements: A Perpetual Challenge?* (Cape Town: Juta), pp. 103–125.

Smit, W. and E. Pieterse (2014) 'Decentralisation and Institutional Reconfiguration in Urban Africa' in S. Parnell and E. Pieterse (eds.), *Africa's Urban Revolution: Policy Pressures* (London: Zed Books), pp. 148–166.

Stoker, G. (1998) 'Governance as Theory: Five Propositions', *International Social Science Journal*, 50(155), pp. 17–28, DOI: 10.1111/1468-2451.00106.

Taylor, P. (2000) 'Institutional Profile: UNCHS (Habitat)—The Global Campaign for Good Urban Governance'. *Environment and Urbanization*, 12(1), pp. 197–202. DOI: 10.1177/095624780001200114.

Tong, T. (2010) 'From Colonialism to Modernism to Postcolonialism: The Case of Urban Agriculture in Lusaka, Zambia', *Undercurrent: The Canadian Undergraduate Journal of Development Studies*, 7(3), pp. 36–43.

Tostensen, A., I. Tvedten and M. Vaa (eds.) (2001) *Associational Life in African Cities: Popular Responses to the Urban Crisis* (Uppsala: Nordiska Afrikainstitutet).

UNDP (United Nations Development Programme) (1997) *Governance for Sustainable Human Development* (New York: UNDP).

UN-Habitat (United Nations Human Settlements Programme) (2016) *Urbanization and Development: Emerging Futures. World Cities Report 2016* (Nairobi: UN-Habitat).

UN-Habitat (2014) *The State of African Cities 2014: Re-imagining Sustainable Urban Transitions* (Nairobi: UN-Habitat).

UN-Habitat (2009) *Global Report on Human Settlements 2009: Planning Sustainable Cities* (London, UK: Earthscan).

UN-Habitat (2008) *The State of African Cities 2008: A Framework for Addressing Urban Challenges in Africa* (Nairobi: UN-Habitat).

UN-Habitat (2002) *Global Campaign on Urban Governance: Concept Paper* (2nd edition; Nairobi: UN-Habitat).

Wagah, G.G., G.M. Onyango and J.K. Kibwage (2010) 'Accessibility of Water Services in Kisumu Municipality, Kenya', *Journal of Geography and Regional Planning*, 2(5), pp. 114–125, http://www.academicjournals.org/journal/JGRP/article-abstract/E9F373C39648 (accessed on 20 April 2018).

Watson, V. (2009) 'Seeing from the South: Refocusing Urban Planning on the Globe's Central Urban Issues'. *Urban Studies*, 46(11), pp. 2259–2275, DOI: 10.1177/0042098009342598.

Weatherspoon, D.D. and T. Reardon (2003) 'The Rise of Supermarkets in Africa: Implications for Agrifood Systems and the Rural Poor', *Development Policy Review*, 21(3), pp. 333–355, DOI:10.1111/1467-7679.00214.

World Bank (2017) *World Development Report 2017: Governance and the Law* (Washington, DC: The World Bank), DOI: 10.1596/978-1-4648-0950-7.

World Bank (1994). *Governance, The World Bank's Experience* (Washington, DC: The World Bank).

World Bank (1992) *Governance and Development* (Washington, DC: The World Bank).

World Bank (1989) *Sub-Saharan Africa, From Crisis to Sustainable Growth, A Long Term Perspective Study* (Washington, DC: The World Bank).

CHAPTER 4

Informal Governance: Comparative Perspectives on Co-optation, Control and Camouflage in Rwanda, Tanzania and Uganda

Claudia Baez Camargo and Lucy Koechlin

Abstract

This article applies a novel conceptual framework to characterise and assess the repertoire of practices used by informal networks to redistribute power and access to resources. These distinct norms and practices are typologised as co-optation, control, and camouflage. Co-optation involves recruitment into the network by means of the reciprocal exchange of favours. Control is about ensuring discipline amongst network members by means of shaming and social isolation. Camouflage refers to the formal facades behind which informality hides and is about protecting and legitimising the network. All three are relevant to a more fine-grained understanding of corruption and its underpinnings. Findings from our comparative research in three East African countries (Rwanda, Tanzania and Uganda) suggest that these informal practices are relevant to an understanding of the choices and attitudes of providers and users of public services at the local level. Adopting this analytical lens helps to explain the limited impact of conventional anti-corruption prescriptions and provides a basis to develop alternative strategies that harness the potential of social network dynamics to promote positive anti-corruption outcomes.

1 Introduction

The literature dealing with corruption has typically based its analysis on a principal–agent model of decision-making, which assumes corruption happens as the result of flawed incentives on the part of the agent and weak monitoring capacity of the principal (Klitgaard, 1988; Rose-Ackerman, 1999). Policy solutions based on this conceptualisation prescribe measures such as a tougher criminalisation of corruption and stronger monitoring mechanisms in the public sector. The lack of success of conventional anti-corruption measures in many countries, including in sub-Saharan Africa, has subsequently led other scholars to conceptualise corruption as a collective action problem (Persson et al.,

 DOI:10.1163/9789004387942_005

2013; Marquette and Peiffer, 2015), which although providing a compelling framework to explain the unyielding persistence of high levels of corruption has nonetheless failed to provide alternative policy solutions. While the conceptual debate on this topic continues (Heywood, 2017; Mungiu-Pippidi, 2017), a growing consensus points to the need to collect empirical evidence in order to better understand the practices underpinning corruption, which evidently persist despite structural and institutional reform (Baez-Camargo and Passas, 2017).

Regarding African countries, the lack of a context-sensitive approach to anti-corruption measures is not due to a lack of data. In fact, a vast body of literature on Africa has illustrated extensively particular features characterising African political regimes (Bayart, 1993; Bratton and Van de Walle, 1994; Chabal and Daloz, 1999) as well as particular social norms and practices among citizens that in one way or the other are associated with the prevalence of high levels of corruption (Hyden, 1980; Olivier de Sardan, 1999; Blundo and Olivier de Sardan, 2006). It would therefore be useful to work towards developing better systematic approaches linking the evidence on local drivers of corruption to the wider debate on anti-corruption. Such approaches should avoid a purely relativistic perspective while ensuring that generalizable dimensions are well specified and allow for contextual variation.

Relevant questions to be asked include: How are the decisions and practices of key national and subnational actors shaped? What are the practices that individuals find useful in addressing their problems and needs? What are the networks linking up different actors, and how are they articulated? How do these networks and their practices underpin corruption?

In this chapter we present empirical evidence[1] aimed at identifying those practices and norms that inform the agency of local actors, whether they be political and business elites, bureaucrats and providers of public services, or citizens, in three East African countries: Rwanda, Tanzania and Uganda.

1 Empirical evidence presented in this paper stems from the findings from two research projects of the Basel Institute's Public Governance Division. The first project, entitled 'Informal Governance and Corruption—Transcending the Principal-Agent and Collective Action Paradigms', is funded by the joint UK Department for International Development (DFID) and British Academy Anti-Corruption Evidence (ACE) programme. For more information about the ACE programme and the project please visit http://www.britac.ac.uk/anti-corruption and http://www.britac.ac.uk/node/4660. The second project is entitled 'Corruption, Social Norms and Behaviours in East Africa' and is funded by the East Africa Research Fund (EARF) of DFID. For more information about EARF and the project please visit http://www.earesearchfund.org/ and http://www.earesearchfund.org/research-corruption-social-norms-and-behaviors-east-africa (accessed on 2 May 2018).

In the analysis of the empirical evidence from the case study countries we favour an approach to the characterisation of local governance processes that moves attention away from conventional categories and dichotomies (such as state vs. non-state actors, public vs. private, or sector-based assessments), shifting our analytical attention to the socially grounded practices that transcend the public sector.[2] That notwithstanding, we make use of the term 'informal governance' because, although it reproduces dichotomies that are empirically and conceptually debatable, it connects closely to the manner in which corruption is problematised among international development practitioners, who constitute a key audience for our research. In this sense, our use of 'informal' does not imply a fundamental divide between different spheres, but signifies the wide and contingent range of repertoires that actors have at their disposal, which transcend and straddle essentialist distinctions between 'the public' and 'the private'.

In this chapter, we build on the evidence emerging from the ongoing research projects, discussing data collected from focus group discussions (FGDs) and interviews conducted across the three countries—namely, Tanzania, Uganda and Rwanda.[3] The data strongly indicates the importance of social networks linking up actors that shape and are shaped by particular patterns of informal governance. Thus, social networks emerged inductively as heuristic entry points for a better understanding of prevalent practices and norms as well as lines of inclusion and exclusion of actors.[4] Throughout the chapter we pay particular attention to the role of social networks as articulations through which social norms are enacted and reiterated. Through this analytical lens

2 For a discussion of a non-normative, inductive approach to governance see Blundo and Le Meur (2008), Bevir (2013) or Koechlin (2015).

3 The projects used qualitative data collection methods with the support of a team of local researchers. The data presented in this paper was collected during research activities conducted between January 2016 and August 2017, activities that involved focus group discussions (FGDs) at two sites (one urban and one rural area) in each country. In the FGDs we used the health sector as an indicative entry point to study the interface where corruption risks arise. The participant profiles of the focus groups were a) community members, b) providers of health services, and c) managers of health facilities. A total of 18 FGDs were conducted. The local researchers are Prof. Tharcisse Gatwa and Mr Abel Dufitumukiza of the Protestant University of Rwanda, Dr Richard Sambaiga and Mr Egidius Kamanyi of the University of Dar es Salaam, Prof. Paul Bukuluki of Makerere University and Mr Robert Lugolobi, independent anti-corruption consultant in Uganda.

4 The concept of social networks is sociologically highly loaded—for a critique of social network analysis see (Emirbayer and Goodwin, 1994); for the seminal contribution to the actor–network approach see (Latour, 2005). Here, the significance of social networks as a frame of reference emerged inductively from the data, and still needs to be theorised adequately, although our interpretations are closer to the constructivist approach of actor–network theory.

we seek to gain a better understanding of 'real' governance processes[5] and the ways in which they underpin or reproduce corruption.

The chapter is organised as follows: Section 2 provides general background information about the prevailing conditions across the three countries with regard to the fight against corruption. Section 3 outlines the conceptual approach used for uncovering locally determined drivers of corruption and the general traits characterising social networks in the three countries. Next, we describe how networks utilise the practices of co-optation (Section 4), control (Section 5) and camouflage (Section 6). Finally, in Section 7 we reflect on the implications of our findings.

2 Background Information on Corruption in Rwanda, Tanzania and Uganda

East Africa presents excellent opportunities to explore what may be important factors impinging on the effectiveness of anti-corruption efforts. Regional trends point to sharp differences in performance that are reflected in the three cases included in our research.

At one extreme, Uganda represents a modal pattern in the region, involving endemic corruption in spite of extensive reforms and anti-corruption interventions implemented by the government of President Yoweri Museveni. Instances of bribery, favouritism, absenteeism and gift-giving are widespread, with significant negative impacts on the provision of basic public services. The situation is confirmed by research findings in which Ugandan participants corroborate the perception that corruption is rampant and has become a normalised feature of daily life.

In Rwanda, the government led by President Paul Kagame is considered to have achieved significant success in controlling corruption by means of radical public sector reform, enforcement of traditional accountability mechanisms, and the introduction of locally designed governance tools (Golooba-Mutebi and Booth, 2013; Bozzini, 2014). Strong political commitment is operationalised in a 'zero-tolerance' approach to corruption based on harsh punishments and their strict enforcement, coupled with mass campaigns sensitising the public about the value of anti-corruption measures and integrity, which have resulted in Rwanda being categorised among the least corrupt countries in Africa.

In the case of Tanzania, high levels of corruption have pervaded all aspects of public administration for decades, becoming a constant feature in the

5 See Olivier de Sardan (2008), who coined the expression 'real' governance.

experience of citizens in their interactions with the state, especially when it comes to the delivery of public services. However, since the 2015 election, the government led by President John Magufuli has vowed to renew anti-corruption efforts, and has taken significantly bold actions to punish and prevent illicit behaviours. Although some of the measures undertaken by the current administration have generated national and international criticism on the grounds of being perceived as detrimental to essential democratic rights and civil liberties, it is nonetheless remarkable that President Magufuli's promise to fight corruption has received overwhelming support from Tanzanian citizens.[6]

These three distinct anti-corruption outcomes are consistent with the recent East African Bribery Index (EABI), which found that 81 per cent of respondents in Uganda describe the level of corruption in their country as high, whereas in Tanzania 44 per cent of respondents describe levels of corruption in their country as medium. A majority of Rwandan respondents—61 per cent—describe corruption in their country as low. Furthermore, the EABI also indicates that Ugandans share a grim assessment of past and future performance, as 59 per cent of respondents believe that corruption has increased in comparison to the previous year and will continue to increase during the following 12 months. In contrast, a positive outlook was shared among a majority of Tanzanian and Rwandan respondents (70 per cent and 61 per cent, respectively), who believe that corruption has decreased in comparison to the previous year and will continue to decrease in the subsequent 12 months (70 per cent of respondents in each country) (Transparency International, 2017).

3 Conceptual Approach to Social Networks: Solidarity, Lock-in and Protection

Research findings from the three countries confirm a vast body of literature regarding the role of social networks in East Africa and beyond: strong personal connections constitute an effective mechanism with which to pool scarce resources and provide access to goods, services, resources and even career opportunities in contexts of resource scarcity and weak state performance (Jauregui, 2014; Ruud, 2000; Chang et al., 2001; Grodeland et al., 1998; Ledeneva,

6 A citizens' assessment and expectations survey published in September 2016 reported that '96 per cent of Tanzanians approve or strongly approve of President Magufuli's performance since taking office' (Twaweza East Africa, 2016). Numerous local and international media have also reported on the popularity of President Magufuli. See for example the BBC's profile of the president (Nesoba, 2015) and the *New African*'s analysis of 'John Magufuli: Tanzania's rising star' (*New African Magazine*, 2017).

1997; Sneath, 2002). The findings concerning social networks deserve to be further emphasised in the context of the present chapter because they provide valuable insights about local social practices that are linked to the prevalence of corruption but are nevertheless not normally taken into consideration in conventional anti-corruption programming.

Whereas it is clear that individuals belong to multiple, overlapping networks anywhere, the type of networks that are most relevant for this research are those to which the individual feels bound by obligations that are enforced and sanctioned by stringent social controls. Such networks are the social equivalent of what political science refers to as the leader's 'winning coalition' (Mesquita et al., 2005), meaning those constituencies whose support is most essential for maintaining support and legitimacy in the case of the political leader, and status and social recognition within the community in the case of the individual. They are the core networks, or reference groups (Koni-Hoffmann and Navanit-Patel, 2017), in which strict social norms are enforced and the individuals feel obliged to satisfy the expectations of the group.

Indeed, our data shows how informal social networks generate strong moral imperatives, including a sense of obligation to provide mutual assistance and reciprocity for favours given, which go above and beyond any respect for the formal legal framework. Individuals are thus expected to share with their next of kin, who in turn feel strongly entitled to a share of the wealth. Obligations vis-à-vis networks outside the family are based on strong norms of reciprocity. Thus, social networks rely on a transactional logic characterised by the exchange of a gift and then a counter-gift, sequentially. These imperatives translate, in practice, in that an individual who has a position in the public sector has the duty to utilise that position for the benefit of his or her network and that the economy of favours penetrates the public arena at the point of service provision in the form of practices of bribing, gift-giving and favouritism.

Significantly, the research suggests that inclusion criteria for entry into the core networks may be fluid and instrumentally constructed. This means that networks are sometimes expanded in a deliberate manner to link up individuals increasingly far removed from each other on the basis of pragmatic considerations. As one Tanzanian research participant remarked, 'when you have a problem and you do not have people to help you with it, then you go ahead and build the network to the person who can help you'. Thus, we find that the size of the core networks varies considerably across the three cases and this variation appears to be related to state effectiveness in terms of accessibility to essential public services and enforcement of the rule of law.

Thus, the research findings suggest that extensive social networks are more prevalent in Uganda and Tanzania, where formal rights and entitlements are seen as having little bearing on the actual provision of essential services such as healthcare and where there is a perception that law enforcement is weak. Contrarily, core networks appear to be much smaller in Rwanda, where the perception is that services are provided according to the formal legal stipulations and that detection of corrupt actions is effective and followed by sanction enforcement.

In the subsequent sections of this chapter we zoom into the practices of the social networks in Rwanda, Tanzania and Uganda through the analytical lens of three distinct patterns of governance practices, which we have previously identified (Baez-Camargo and Ledeneva, 2017) and by means of which political, business and social networks pursue their goals, whether these be to stay in power, maximise financial gains, access resources and services or simply 'get things done'. In this chapter we discuss these informal practices—which we have termed co-optation, control and camouflage—and argue that they are associated with high levels of corruption because they ultimately enact an informal redistribution of power and resources.

- *Co-optation* is associated with recruitment or strategic appointments into public office of allies and potential adversaries, who are granted impunity in exploiting the power and resources associated with public office in exchange for mobilising support and maintaining loyalty to the regime.
- *Control* mechanisms are instrumental to the management of clashes of hidden interests, to ensuring elite cohesion and to enforcing discipline among allies, which is why the unwritten rules of co-optation depend on the existence of such informal control practices. Common examples involve the selective enforcement of anti-corruption laws against opponents or renegades, underscoring the validity of the saying attributed to former Brazilian dictator Getulio Vargas: 'For my friends everything, and for my enemies the law'.
- *Camouflage* refers to the manner in which the realities of political co-optation and control are hidden underneath institutional facades and policies consistent with a commitment to good governance and democratic accountability. Thus, punishment of a detractor may be presented as evidence of the leaders' commitment to anti-corruption.

4 Co-optation

The first of the informal practices we have identified is *co-optation*, which is the means by which recruitment into the network takes place. A key feature of co-optation is that it is transactional; it involves establishing a relationship that is based on strong bonds of trust, reciprocity and loyalty, which enable and sustain a system of mutually beneficial exchanges. Thus, a gift, an appointment, a bribe or a favour are used to establish a relationship, which generates indebtedness on the part of the accepting party and a gift economy arises. The balance of indebtedness never gets settled; otherwise there would be no relationship. Practices of co-optation happen in a top-down, horizontal, or bottom-up fashion.

Co-optation can occur in a *top-down* fashion, initiated by higher-level officials (e.g. at the Ministry or District Council level) or mid-level service managers (for example, hospital accountants) and targeting lower-level staff and service providers (for example, nurses and teachers). Top-down, actors engage in co-optation in order to promote and consolidate their own positions. They do so by rewarding supporters and by neutralising opposition through a discretionary allocation of opportunities and resources, thus nurturing and expanding the networks that ensure support. In turn, the beneficiaries can typically extract rents in return for their unconditional support. Top-down co-optation can extend to the grassroots level incorporating important social groups into the ruling coalition, and is observed in the prevalence of patronage and clientelistic networks.

Practices of top-down co-optation in the public sector result in situations where service providers are confronted with the demands of hierarchical networks in the workplace in addition to their formal work responsibilities and the demands and expectations of family, friends and acquaintances. According to our research findings, vertical networks can be found in the Tanzanian and Ugandan health sectors as the result of corruption in the recruiting process. Research participants from both countries indicated that employment is often obtained through network connections where a relative, friend or other social acquaintance of the appointing official recommends a particular individual for a position. Under those circumstances, it is understood that the job giver is granting a favour to the recipient, who thereafter enters the workplace with an unwritten, but well understood, indebtedness vis-à-vis the sponsor. Corruption in recruitment also happens when substantial sums are paid to secure a position. In such cases the debt is both a moral one (for being considered for the position, for which the bribe is just the precondition) as well as a real one (as invariably one will have to raise money with family and friends to generate enough funds to pay for such a position).

In such contexts, where employment is obtained not by virtue of skills and professional qualifications, but rather as a personalised transaction cemented by social connections and/or money, loyalty tends to be much more valued than on the job performance when it comes to being eligible for promotion or other benefits. The research data further suggests that vertical networks are conducive to collusive behaviours in which corrupt service providers enjoy, if not the full support and complicity, at least passive concealment on the part of their colleagues.

Co-optation can also be exercised *horizontally* when two or more networks engage in practices that serve the mutual benefit of all those involved. Thus, political elites frequently not only obtain the support of key non-state actors but also become recruited into exercising public authority to inordinately favour particular interests. For example, powerful business interests may be co-opted into supporting the interests of the political elites (e.g. financing electoral campaigns), receiving in exchange substantial benefits (e.g. large government contracts). Horizontal co-optation also happens when public officials use their decision-making authority over the provision of services, access to opportunities or distribution of resources instrumentally to grow their own networks. In Uganda, head teachers or principals at prestigious schools have been known to informally earmark some slots in the enrolment process in order to please higher ranking public figures or wealthy families whose children would not otherwise be accepted on the basis of their grades alone. Other accounts from Tanzania indicate that health staff may choose to provide preferential treatment strategically to particular patients, say a teacher, with a view to receiving a favour in return through help with a child's enrolment in the future.

Bottom-up co-optation is associated with informal networks at the community level, where membership of particular social groups binds individuals through ties of reciprocity and moral obligation into supporting each other and pooling resources. Co-optation practices at this level are associated with corruption because when a member gets a position in public office then the network expects this person to extract rents for the benefit of the group. In Uganda and Tanzania, like in many other African countries, a fair amount of social pressure is exerted on individuals who are formally employed or somehow perceived to be relatively affluent, pushing them to acquire resources for the benefit of their group—thereby legitimising certain corrupt acts and practices for the sake of the community, family and kin.

Social pressures may also be associated with more extortive modalities of bribing and even embezzlement. This can happen when the opportunities for material redistribution that a provider's salary allows do not adequately meet the expectations of the networks. This was vividly narrated in an interview with a medical doctor in Tanzania, who explained that the prevalent socially constructed preconception is that holding a medical degree is associated with a high salary, which is drastically contradicted by the reality of prevailing wages in the public health sector.

The research data from Tanzania and Uganda shows that social networks tend to be extensive and fluid. In this regard, exchanging favours is a key practice conducive to expanding social connections, which works to both initiate and corroborate co-optation into the network. 'There is a reciprocal relationship, meaning today you have helped me, tomorrow I must find a way to return the favour', as one Tanzanian Focus Group Discussion participant described it. Thus, building a network involves evolving relationships on the basis of a reciprocal exchange of favours, goods and resources. These hinge on the mutually reinforcing conditions of indebtedness on the part of the recipient of the favour and entitlement on the part of the giving party. These practices are observed in the case of the delivery of public health services in that patients actively seek to co-opt health workers into their networks based on the belief that otherwise it will not be possible to obtain the medical treatment required. This is one reason why patients often bring unsolicited gifts of different kinds to their appointments at the health facility with the expectation that by doing so they can create a privileged relationship with the provider.

In Uganda, service providers estimated that in about half of the interactions concerned users offer unsolicited 'gifts' to providers. Tanzanian service providers mentioned that they are used to receiving gifts from people in the form of material goods, such as maize, rice, goats, beans or through a credit transfer via mobile phone. Due to the ambivalent nature of the gift, one service provider stated that one has to try to figure out what the gift means in the current context and if it would create an environment in which one is suddenly indebted—when the motive of the gift was a form of co-optation—which raises the question, as one participant asked: 'How do you deal with such matters, when you have already eaten the fish he bought?' Further examples of the different types of co-optation are described below (Table 4.1).

The case of Rwanda provides both contrast to and confirmation of the practices described above. According to evidence from our research, in Rwanda favouritism is the modality of petty corruption that is still most prevalent in the health sector, where preferential (faster) treatment is given to family and friends of service providers. However, the instrumental use of gift-giving or bribing to build useful networks appears to be less utilised in Rwanda. Whereas this certainly has to do with the potential risk of detection and punishment that accompany such activities (discussed in the following section), an important element to underscore is that the Rwandan regime, by significantly improving the quality and accessibility of public services, has made the functionality of network building for the most part redundant, in the sense that no informal strategy such as gift-giving or appealing to social connections is needed in order to receive adequate treatment.

TABLE 4.1 Types of co-optation

	National level	Workplace (service provision)	Community level
Top-down co-optation	Political appointments of supporters and opponents	Recruitment and promotion practices	Patronage and clientelistic networks
Horizontal co-optation	Symbiotic relationships between political elites and business interests	Collusive behaviours in the work place/use of public office to build networks	Instrumental construction of networks
Bottom-up co-optation	Expectations of voters about leaders' duty to provide particularistic benefits to their groups	Favouritism in service provision and embezzlement/abuse of office to favour network	Proactive gift-giving to build networks in order to include useful individuals

SOURCE: COMPILED BY CLAUDIA BAEZ-CAMARGO

The generalised experiences among Rwandan research participants indicate that for the most part service provision is delivered as stipulated by formal rules and entitlements.[7] In other words, one of the drivers for the growth and and nourishment of social networks identified in Tanzania and Uganda—that is, overcoming the challenges associated with the poor quality and accessibility of essential services—is mitigated in Rwanda with improved public services.

5 Control

The second pattern of informality is *control*, which relates to how informal networks enforce discipline among their members. This can happen by means of the selective enforcement of formal rules (e.g. anti-corruption laws) or informally (e.g. by means of veiled threats or exclusion from the network).

7 These rules emanate from *Ubudehe*, a home-grown solution and poverty-reduction initiative and one of the country's core development programmes. *Ubudehe* involves a system of categorisation of all households according to income level, which forms the basis on which entitlements are determined and subsidies allocated.

Interestingly, informal control also occurs bottom-up, whereby powerful actors are locked into the system and expected to tend to the demands and expectations of their networks, otherwise risking negative consequences ranging from social shaming to even violence.

There are several kinds of sanctions that can be expected if one does not adhere to the norms of the networks. Practices of control among hierarchical networks in the workplace were illustrated by two Ugandan rural health workers, according to whom people not only become corrupt to get better positions, but also because those not participating in the prescribed corruption schemes or those who denounce incidences of corruption may face serious repercussions. As one health worker experienced: 'If you refuse, you miss the job [opportunity] or your name will not appear on the payroll'. Therefore, fear over losing one's job or being bullied can translate into a 'don't ask, don't tell' policy, as explained by a nurse who had witnessed incidences of corruption involving fellow health workers: 'Although you know what is happening, you stay quiet because it's beyond your understanding'.

As previously mentioned, the effectiveness of social networks is related to the manner in which they embody deeply ingrained values of reciprocity, solidarity and moral obligation towards one's group. Based on these values, certain behaviours are expected. Concretely, when it comes to the family, the entitlement to partake of the gains of one's next of kin is an essential, unquestionable premise of social life in the three countries. Consequently, one of the worst transgressions occurs when an individual is seen to turn his or her back on a family member. This can result in social isolation and shaming, although in some contexts the consequences might be more extreme as explained by a service user in Kampala: 'If my brother earns 15 million and I ask him to help me pay twenty thousand shillings for my son to register for exams and he tells me about his cow, which is sick, and that he needs 100,000 for it to get treated yet he can't help me with only twenty thousand shillings, then what do I need from him apart from beating him to death?'

Outside the family, social networks rely on an expectation of reciprocity in the ongoing exchange of favours and gifts. Service providers recounted the difficulties they face rejecting unsolicited gifts from users; because the act of presenting and receiving a gift is socioculturally anchored, rejecting a gift can be interpreted as disrespectful.

The significance of the control that can be exercised by social networks is underscored by the notable extent to which fulfilling one's duties and obligations vis-à-vis the network is closely linked to social status. In the FGDs participants were asked about the actions that gain individuals respect and good social standing in their communities versus those that cause a person shame

TABLE 4.2 Actions conducive to gaining and losing status

Uganda	Tanzania	Rwanda
Actions/conditions conducive to gaining status/respect		
– Help the group – Get jobs – Solve problems – Steal from others to share with group – Being wealthy	– You do everything to help relatives or friends – High income/education (being called 'professor')/ appearance	– Use the office to enrich him/herself to help his associates – Helping relatives settle financial obligations and other problems
Actions/conditions conducive to shame/falling into disgrace		
– Discriminate against members of the group – Losing an influential position – Applying the law – Being poor (esp. after having had money) – Demanding excessive bribes	– Failing to help your relatives or friends	– Not helping to meet the family's needs – Being caught in an act of corruption

SOURCE: COMPILED BY CLAUDIA BAEZ-CAMARGO

and to fall into disgrace. Some of the FGD responses to this question are summarised above (Table 4.2).

In Tanzania and Uganda, the expectation of help and a contribution to the network's welfare described above influences the behaviours of service providers profoundly. For example, if a service provider does not favour a relative in service provision or rejects a small bribe or a gift, the perception among research participants was that this person's adherence to formal rules destroys his or her trust-based relationships, and such a person might be ultimately abandoned by the community. The infringement of socially embedded norms is therefore seen as affecting the moral economy of the community, because it threatens the socially constituted values and practices of economic redistribution that are critical to meeting essential needs.

The responses from Rwanda are particularly interesting as they suggest the tensions generated by a context in which there are strict constraints in place inhibiting service providers from engaging in those practices that are nonetheless still regarded as the gateway to social status and respect. Rwandan service providers can therefore be characterised as being subject to bottom-up control in a similar manner as their Tanzanian and Ugandan counterparts, as attested by the following statement from a Rwandan health worker: 'Actually, when you refuse to render the service, people you are associated with will say that "having him is like not having someone". The effect of this is that the worker is put aside and is looked upon as a bad person, even losing friends or the appreciation of their extended family'.

However, social pressures exist in significant tension with formal control mechanisms in Rwanda, which because of its enforcement of a zero-tolerance approach to corruption has distinguished itself significantly from Tanzania (at least until recently) and Uganda. In Rwanda, instances of petty corruption involving bribing or favouritism are harshly sanctioned, including by means of a policy of naming and shaming whereby individuals guilty of corruption are publicly identified in published lists that not only bear their names but also those of their parents and community. Our research indeed suggests that, because the sanctions against cases of corruption are widely perceived to be extremely harsh and effectively enforced, compliance is commonly associated with fear with regard to the possible reporting of negative performance or to legal repercussions.

Our research also shed light on creative solutions by means of which health workers in Rwanda negotiate the tensions that exist between the formal and the informal norms they must abide by. In particular, health workers gave account of receiving family members for treatment outside the opening hours of the health facility to avoid openly disrupting the first come, first served rules of service provision. Rwandan FGD participants also expressed that bribery still can occur but requires intricate arrangements to avoid disclosure and may only be arranged with people who are well known and trusted by the service provider for fear of being denounced to the law-enforcement authorities.

For those reasons, Rwandan health providers concluded that corruption has increasingly become a private affair, meaning that it is restricted to the innermost circle of the informal network, due to the harsh costs associated with detection and the risk of being shamed extending to the whole family. Consequently, the strong enforcement of anti-corruption laws in Rwanda appears to be resulting in a situation where core networks are shrinking.

Interestingly, the research findings from Tanzania suggest how the incentives of service providers are being reshaped with increased enforcement of sanctions against corrupt behaviours under the current regime. As in Rwanda, this exacerbates the tensions between the demands of the formal and informal normative frameworks to which the service providers are expected to respond. One participant in the service providers' FGD explained that they 'only employ you as an individual and not as a family. However, they [the family] do not understand such a thing [...] they do not know the regulations the employed have to follow'.

Thus, the perception that anti-corruption enforcement is tightening means that the opportunity space to engage in practices of petty corruption is shrinking. Interestingly, service providers are now developing a new language to convey the situation. According to anecdotal evidence, public officials who cannot grant a favour or provide the amounts expected by their networks resort to simply stating 'Magufuli' to communicate the idea that under the current president things have changed.

6 Camouflage

The third informal pattern is *camouflage*, which refers to how informal practices of co-optation and control take place beneath a facade of commitment to formal procedures, such as the rule of law, anti-corruption measures or democratic accountability. Camouflage also takes place under the guise of respecting 'traditional values'. Practices of camouflage protect the network from external scrutiny by external actors and play on the coexistence of multiple normative frameworks (Olivier de Sardan, 1999; Blundo et al., 2006).

Thus, informality becomes difficult to grasp to an outsider precisely because it makes use of the formal order (whether based on legal or traditional norms) in order to pursue hidden agendas. For example, camouflage is routinely used by corrupt political regimes to create a smooth facade that legitimates them not only vis-à-vis donors and the international community but also with domestic audiences. Seemingly upholding certain pledges with regard, for example, to elections or legal reform, de facto the reforms are undertaken to facilitate relations with external actors, often succeeding in hiding 'real' processes, practices and power from closer scrutiny.

Whereas camouflage is normally seen to be a practice exercised from the top down, evidence suggests that it might also be practiced from the bottom up. For instance, lowly public officials may use 'correct' (i.e. formalised) procedures to hide malfeasance and extraction from the law enforcement authorities or citizens may convey bribing as an expression of the gift-giving customs cherished by society.

In our research data one of the most conspicuous forms of camouflage relates to the ambivalent nature of gift-giving. FGD participants elaborated on how although a gift can be offered simply as a gift, the expectation of a counter-gift—in the form of a service or a favour—is inherent, understood by all parties involved although it may never be explicitly articulated. Thus the act of gift-giving is intrinsically ambivalent and a bribe can always be disguised as a gift. Rwandan FGD participants explained that a gift is perceived as part of the social routine, an inherent social practice, and as such is described as a public rather than a private transaction. A bribe, in contrast, is an essentially private transaction. Therefore, it comes as no surprise that if the bribe becomes exposed (taken out from the private into the public realm), it should immediately morph into a gift.

Kampala health facility staff agreed that there is nothing wrong with giving preferential treatment to family members—'Your relative must be given priority; if there is not an emergency, my mother, father, son or daughter come first'—because this is the way things should proceed 'according to culture'. In this context the same health staff gave other examples of practices of camouflage that make use of social norms to cover up illicit activities. Some research participants recounted how support staff at the health facility often ask them to treat their family members, when in reality they are soliciting bribes from health facility users in order to pose as a relative and thus get them expedited treatment. There were stories told of support staff that sometimes requested speedy treatment for up to five sick relatives in one day. This practice is referred to as 'clan soccer', and according to the FGD participants it takes advantage of the fluid manner in which the terms 'brother' and 'sister' are used in Uganda.

Camouflage is also proactively used in other ways in order to get access to a network. Participants of FGDs in Tanzania and Uganda described how service providers often assess the situation to determine whether it is worth co-opting the service seeker into their network. Thus, service seekers recount how they prepare before going to the facility; strategies include dressing up in order to give the impression that they have resources that will make them attractive, or—conversely—dressing down and bringing small children along to encourage feelings of compassion on the part of the provider. On their part, FGD participants from Rwanda acknowledged that in order to get away with bribing one needs to carefully plan in order to mask the bribe as a gift, or make sure the exchange never happens directly but rather through a mutual and trusted acquaintance, because one cannot even try to engage in any remotely suspicious activity with strangers out of fear of being denounced.

An interesting example of camouflage among public officials in Rwanda occurs when they resort to a practice known as 'techniquer'. In Rwanda, to 'techniquer' a report (*'gutekinika Raporo'*) or statistics mean to falsify or present false reports or figures to one's superiors (Baez Camargo and Gatwa, 2018). In a first instance, resorting to 'techniquer' may be used to hide corruption favouring individuals or percolating up (or down) the network. However, that may not be the only use of this practice as Baez Camargo and Gatwa found that public officials may also use such practices pre-emptively when they have not been successful in meeting their professional performance targets and fear tough sanctions from above. Therefore, what is particularly interesting in the case of Rwanda is that these practices are not condoned by or led from the top, as is the case in the other East African countries. Rather, camouflage is used to hide such practices from the top leadership.

7 Concluding Remarks

In this chapter, we have sought to outline the patterns shaping social networks in three East African countries. Evidence from two related research projects shows that governance processes are informed by the norms and practices through which social networks are configured. The findings confirm that there are certain patterns that can be identified, each with a distinct set of practices and norms. Co-optation, camouflage, and control are all practised both to secure the moral economy from which the network draws its legitimacy and to enable the extraction of concrete material gains for individual members. These practices are 'star-shaped', so to speak, in that they radiate in all directions: bottom-up, horizontally, as well as top-down. The distinction between 'formal' and 'informal' governance becomes obsolete, as these practices draw on a diverse and contingent range of norms. Whereas certain practices may be more iterative and habitual, others emerge from calculated judgements of particular situations and contexts.

Some of the most interesting findings are emerging from 'liminal' contexts, where established patterns of locking into and reproducing networks are breaking down and new ones remain in the making. Such open-ended transformations are likely present in all countries, even though in some contexts they may be happening within more circumscribed spaces than in others. Our findings suggest that these transformations are the result of changes of political regimes—particularly in the case of Rwanda under Paul Kagame, where social networks have had to reconfigure and react to top-down sanctions against corruption in the public sector. Whereas in Tanzania and Uganda the networks are more fluid and are built instrumentally, in Rwanda there seems to be a trend whereby people are trimming rather than expanding their networks as formal rules and procedures are being vigorously enforced by the regime. Thus, while health workers continue to be subject to their networks' expectations of preferential treatment, these are increasingly restricted to encompass only family and close friends.

Tanzania is also an important case to follow up on given that similar top-down approaches to anti-corruption are being favoured by the government of John Magufuli, the president—for example—using personal discretion and presidential authority to short-circuit 'official' procedures, albeit to sanction corrupt senior officials. In these cases, although at first glance it may seem as if the regime is imposing 'official' norms, the picture on the ground is somewhat messier. Although our findings may not be sufficient to make a strong argument, it seems as if new forms of camouflage are emerging that are not top-down (as in the case of Uganda, for instance), but bottom-up. This could also be observed in Rwanda, where camouflage practices are being used to hide both inefficiencies and failures to achieve the centrally determined performance targets from the feared eye of the government. This raises important questions as to shifts in informal patterns: whether a unilinear move from greater trust in informality networks to formal rules and institutions is really underway in Rwanda, or whether the transformation process is more complicated, with new and different forms of informal practices emerging—one being new practices of camouflage. Our findings also highlight some significant side effects of enforcing anti-corruption measures in a strictly top-down manner, whereby social networks based on values of solidarity and reciprocity break down, the wider consequences of which in the long run are not yet clear.

From a political economy perspective, it is conventionally argued that the eradication of corruption hinges not merely on institutional reform, but on the political will to change norms and practices. However, our findings suggest a far more contextualised and complicated relationship. Firstly, leadership indeed matters. Ugandans refer to the scandalous behaviour of political leaders to justify their own acts of corruption. In Tanzania, on the other hand, Magufuli sacked his close associates, even some who were known to be close friends of his. Shared images and ideas about social roles—including what constitutes being a 'good' politician, service provider and public official—influence how people come to expect themselves and others to behave in different situations (Kotzian, 2011). However, the evidence from our research projects suggests very strongly that leaders, even those at the very top, are not as autonomous and powerful as they are sometimes portrayed in the literature. Our focus on social networks carves out the many ways in which they are locked into configurations from which they cannot easily or readily break away. All members of a network, *including* powerful actors, are tied into relations of reciprocal exchange through co-optation and control. These practices are all the stronger as they are frequently underpinned by social norms and values that are used to legitimise extraction and redistribution (Olivier de Sardan, 1999).

Furthermore, as indicated above, even in the cases where to all intents and purposes the strong political will of a president exists to enforce official norms and procedures, the effects on the actual patterns of governance are empirical questions. Whether and where new forms of 'gaming the system' emerge, or indeed a Weberian public ethos is nurtured, is subject to specific contexts and networks. These effects are highly contingent upon the structuring of the society in question, the patterns of the networks and the practices of governance (Koechlin 2013). These need to be understood in more detail if we are to shed light on the transformations effected by political will. In what way urbanisation and the transformation of urban spaces affect such processes is a further pertinent topic of future research.

What do our findings imply for anti-corruption policies? We join the large choir of scholars and practitioners who call for more nuanced and evidence-based approaches to the anti-corruption field. Although our findings are still emerging, there are some pointers that can be drawn from the two research projects.

Social norms and values matter—and they can and do change. The patterning of networks is not just imposed by structures or by calculated self-interest; our findings show how actors orient themselves and their practices explicitly (i.e. not merely habitually) along particular norms and values, and seek to create moral coherence by drawing on specific norms and values when legitimising or underpinning their practices. 'Being part of a family', 'being one of us' or 'looking after each other' are frequent expressions that are employed by actors when they explain why and how they interact within social networks. In this sense, they are evidently also used to legitimise 'corrupt' practices, by drawing on alternative normative repertoires that emphasise reciprocity or social obligations.

However, it is absolutely central to underline that these norms and values themselves are contingent upon context. Of course all actors draw on multiple repertoires that speak to different normative frameworks—we speak and act differently depending on the role we are playing and the situation we are in. But more pertinently for anti-corruption policies, the key point emerging from our research is that societal norms and values can and do change in interaction with changes in the political and economic environment.

Our research findings underline that these changes need to be understood far better than has been the case to date. In Rwanda, for instance, such change is being effected by the regime, and enforced rigorously throughout the state and society. The effects may not be as coherent and consistent as some authors portray them—that is to say, as marching towards a rule-and-procedure-based state. But there is no doubt that actors are evaluating their practices in the light of these changes and that certain norms and values may indeed be changing fundamentally, the ultimate outcome of which remains to be seen. Also, the jury is still out with regard to the current situation in Tanzania; the effects of Magufuli's very top-down and personal anti-corruption battle are yet to be fully ascertained. One interesting insight is that, much like in Rwanda, new practices of camouflage seem to be emerging bottom-up.

To conclude, the three governance patterns identified in this chapter—namely, control, co-optation, and camouflage, all play with the ambivalence of 'formal' or 'official' norms, on the one hand, and 'informal' or 'traditional' norms, on the other, depending on the context and the most promising strategy for the intended purpose. In practice they cannot be separated, but are part and parcel of a range of repertoires at the disposal of the actors to address specific problems and pursue specific interests. At the same time, our findings underline that ingrained expectations and social sanctions can lead to a situation in which actors are 'locked' into particular patterns. However, governance patterns are changing all the time, sometimes as a result of changing political regimes. The many ambivalences characterising these patterns and their dynamics may represent potential entry points to promoting positive behavioural changes and advancing anti-corruption agendas if understood in-depth and by working closely with the social actors concerned.

Acknowledgements

The research projects discussed in this paper are funded by UK aid from the UK government. However, the views expressed do not necessarily reflect the UK government's official policies.

References

Baez-Camargo, C. and T. Gatwa (2018) *Rwanda Country Report*, Research report on behalf of research project 'Informal Governance and Corruption: Transcending the Principal-Agent and Collective Action Paradigms', (Basel: Basel Institute on Governance), http://informalgovernance.baselgovernance.org/sites/default/files/2018-07/Rwanda.InformalGovernance.Country%20Report.pdf (accessed on 30 August, 2018).

Baez-Camargo, C. and A. Ledeneva (2017) 'Where Does Informality Stop and Corruption Begin? Informal Governance and the Public/Private Crossover in Mexico, Russia and Tanzania', *The Slavonic and East European Review*, 95(1), pp. 49–75, DOI: 10.5699/slaveasteurorev2.95.1.0049.

Baez-Camargo, C. and N. Passas (2017) 'Hidden Agendas, Social Norms and Why We Need to Re-Think Anti-Corruption' (OECD/ 2017 OECD Global Anti-Corruption &

Integrity Forum), https://www.oecd.org/cleangovbiz/2017-integrity-forum-research-posters.htm. (accessed on 17 October, 2017).

Bayart, J.F. (1993) *The State in Africa: The Politics of the Belly* (New York: Longman).

Bevir, M. (2013) *A Theory of Governance* (Berkeley:University of California Press).

Blundo, G. and P.-Y. Le Meur (eds) (2008) *The Governance of Daily Life in Africa: Ethnographic Explorations of Public and Collective Services* (Leiden and Boston: Brill Academic Publishers).

Blundo, G. and J.-P. Olivier de Sardan (2006) *Everyday Corruption and the State: Citizens and Public Officials in Africa* (London and New York: Zed Books).

Blundo, G., J.-P. Olivier de Sardan, N.B. Arifari and M.T. Alou (2006) *Everyday Corruption and the State: Citizens and Public Officials in Africa* (Cape Town: Zed Books).

Bozzini, A. (2014) 'Fighting Corruption While Undermining Accountability: The Case of Rwanda' Working Paper (Hamburg: German Institute of Global and Area Studies), http://anticorrp.eu/wp-content/uploads/2014/03/Rwanda-Background-Report_final.pdf (accessed on 24 September, 2017).

Bratton, M. and N. Van de Walle (1994) 'Neopatrimonial Regimes and Political Transitions in Africa', *World Politics*, 46(4), pp. 453–489, DOI: 10.2307/2950715.

Chabal, P. and J.-P. Daloz (1999) *Africa Works: Disorder as Political Instrument* (Indiana: Indiana University Press).

Chang, C.S., N.J. Chang and B.T. Freese (2001) 'Offering Gifts or Offering Bribes? Code of Ethics in South Korea', *Journal of Third World Studies*, 18(1), pp. 125–139, https://trove.nla.gov.au/version/72287458 (accessed on 2 May 2018).

Emirbayer, M. and J. Goodwin (1994) 'Network Analysis, Culture, and the Problem of Agency', *American Journal of Sociology*, 99(6), pp. 1411–1454, DOI: 10.1086/230450.

Golooba-Mutebi, F. and D. Booth (2013) *Bilateral Cooperation and Local Power Dynamics: The Case of Rwanda*, ODI Research Reports and Studies, (London: Overseas Development Institute), https://www.odi.org/publications/7888-bilateral-cooperation-and-local-power-dynamics-case-rwanda (accessed on 2 May 2018).

Grodeland, A.B., T.Y. Koshechkina and W.L. Miller (1998) '"Foolish to Give and Yet More Foolish Not to Take". In-Depth Interviews with Post-Communist Citizens on Their Everyday Use of Bribes and Contacts', *Europe-Asia Studies*, 50(4), pp. 651–677, http://www.jstor.org/stable/153781.

Heywood, P.M. (2017) 'Rethinking Corruption: Hocus-Pocus, Locus and Focus', The Slavonic and East European Review, 95(1), pp. 21–48, DOI: 10.5699/slaveasteurorev2.95.1.0021.

Hyden, G. (1980) *Beyond Ujamaa in Tanzania: Underdevelopment and an Uncaptured Peasantry* (Berkeley and Los Angeles: University of California Press).

Jauregui, B. (2014) 'Provisional Agency in India: Jugaad and Legitimation of Corruption', *American Ethnologist*, 41(1), pp. 76–91, DOI: 10.1111/amet.12061.

Klitgaard, R. (1988) *Controlling Corruption* (Berkeley, Los Angeles and London: University of California Press).

Koechlin, L. (2015) 'The Conceptual Polysemy of Governance', in L. Koechlin and T. Förster (eds) *The Politics of Governance: Actors and Articulations in Africa and Beyond* (New York: Routledge).

Koechlin, L. (2013) *Corruption as an Empty Signifier: Politics and Political Order in Africa* (Leiden: Brill).

Koni-Hoffmann, L. and R. Navanit-Patel (2017) *Collective Action on Corruption in Nigeria: A Social Norms Approach to Connecting Society and Institutions* (London: Chatham House—The Royal Institute of International Affairs), https://www.chathamhouse.org//node/29640 (accessed on 7 August 2017).

Kotzian, P. (2011) 'Cosi Fan Tutte: Information, Beliefs, and Compliance with Norms', *Zeitschrift Für Soziologie*, 40(4), pp. 158–173. DOI: 10.2139/ssrn.1497922.

Latour, B. (2005) *Reassembling the Social: An Introduction to Actor-Network-Theory* (Oxford: Oxford University Press).

Ledeneva, A.V. (1997) 'Practices of Exchange and Networking in Russia', *Soziale Welt*, 48(2), pp. 151–170.

Marquette, H. and C. Peiffer (2015) *Corruption and Collective Action*, Research Paper 32, Developmental Leadership Program and U4 Anti-Corruption Resource Centre, (Birmingham: University of Birmingham), http://publications.dlprog.org/CorruptionandCollectiveAction.pdf (accessed on 5 January 2017).

de Mesquita, B.B., A. Smith, R.M. Siverson and J.D. Morrow (2005) *The Logic of Political Survival* (Cambridge and London: MIT Press).

Mungiu-Pippidi, A. (2017) *Corruption as Social Order*, World Development Report Background Paper (Washington D.C.: World Bank), https://openknowledge.worldbank.org/handle/10986/27046 (accessed on 16 January 2018).

Nesoba, R. (2015) 'Tanzania's John Magufuli in Profile', BBC *News*, 24 November, http://www.bbc.com/news/world-africa-34670983 (accessed on 30 October 2017).

New African Magazine (2017) 'John Magufuli: Tanzania's Rising Star', 8 June, http://newafricanmagazine.com/john-magufuli-tanzanias-rising-star/ (accessed on 30 October 2017).

Olivier de Sardan, J.-P. (2008) *Researching the Practical Norms of Real Governance in Africa*, APPP Discussion Paper No. 5 (London: Department for International Development), https://www.gov.uk/dfid-research-outputs/appp-discussion-paper-no-5-researching-the-practical-norms-of-real-governance-in-africa (accessed on 30 October 2017).

Olivier de Sardan, J.P. (1999) 'A Moral Economy of Corruption in Africa?', The Journal of *Modern African Studies*, 37(01), pp. 25–52.

Persson, A., B. Rothstein and J. Teorell (2013) 'Why Anticorruption Reforms Fail—Systemic Corruption as a Collective Action Problem', *Governance*, 26(3), pp. 449–471, DOI: 10.1111/j.1468-0491.2012.01604.x.

Rose-Ackerman, S. (1999) *Corruption and Government* (New York and Cambridge: Cambridge University Press).

Ruud, A.E. (2000) 'Corruption as Everyday Practice. The Public—Private Divide in Local Indian Society', *Forum for Development Studies*, 27(2), pp. 271–294, DOI: 10.1080/08039410.2000.9666142.

Sneath, D. (2002) 'Reciprocity and Notions of Corruption in Contemporary Mongolia', *Mongolian Studies*, 25, pp. 85–99.

Transparency International (2017) *The East African Bribery Index 2017* (Nairobi: Transparency International), https://actionfortransparency.org/view/accountability/the-east-african-bribery-index-2017/ (accessed on 19 September 2017).

Twaweza East Africa (2016) *The People's President? Citizens' Assessment and Expectations of the Fifth Phase Government*, Sauti Za Wananchi Brief No. 35 (Dar es Salaam: Twaweza East Africa), http://twaweza.org/uploads/files/PeoplesPresident-EN-FINAL-A4.pdf (accessed on 9 February 2017).

CHAPTER 5

Why is Co-management of Parks Not Working in Johannesburg?

The Difficult Reframing of State Mandate and Practices in the Post-Apartheid Era

Claire Bénit-Gbaffou

Abstract

Johannesburg City Parks and Zoo (JCPZ) has affirmed its strong redistributive objective in post-apartheid Johannesburg, with the rapid development of new urban parks in former black townships. However, its operational budgets have remained limited in the face of the many pressing housing and infrastructural needs. Many park users, especially in formerly white (and still middle-class) suburbs, have resorted to forms of neighbourhood or community management to compensate for JCPZ's absence. JCPZ is attempting to rebuild its mandate with regards to these public spaces, developing various policy instruments in response to the involvement of park users in the management of urban parks, but also to formalise that involvement. This chapter traces the genealogy of these policy instruments in the making, caught between multiple logics where neo-liberal pressures and models, regular engagements with park users marked by contested legitimacies and racial tensions, and the broader municipal redistributive agenda shape the way in which the post-apartheid state redefines its mandate. The chapter argues that the specific social and racial configurations in which these partnerships are framed on the ground are used by municipal officials to resist transforming their own practices towards more participatory and democratic processes of co-production of parks. The chapter reflects on shifting state mandates in urban governance in contemporary cities of the South and analyses policy instruments crafted for the complex task of formalising and regulating state–society co-production of urban services in the field of park management.

1 Preamble—A (Usual) Scene in a Nature Reserve Joint-Management Forum in Post-apartheid Johannesburg

In April 2017, I attended (as I have been doing for about one year) the monthly Klipriviersberg Nature Reserve Forum meeting in Johannesburg, which brings

DOI:10.1163/9789004387942_006

together representatives of the several civil society organisations (CSOs) interested in the reserve and the one City Park official in charge of nature reserves in Johannesburg[1]. The meeting's agenda seemed innocuous, with classic items (approval of minutes and management and security issues); there was a relatively low attendance: about ten members of civil society (a majority of old, white, middle-class males, with a passion for and an interest in the environment and the reserve) and one (black, younger, male) City Parks' official. Tensions had been ongoing for several years between these CSO members and City Parks (Baloyi et al., 2015; Mokgere, 2016), which had led to the establishment of the Forum—an exception in the management of parks and nature reserves as City Parks does not have the resources to commit its officials to monthly meetings with park users for the 2,500-odd parks and reserves falling under its responsibility.

The meeting turned aggressive, with members of the Forum pointing fingers at the City official and publicly humiliating him with explicit accusations of dishonesty and lies. The conflict crystallised around two issues. The first was the presence of horses and their stables in the reserve. The stables had been informally accepted by CSOs and City Parks a decade before, on the understanding that the horse owner would patrol the reserve and contribute to its maintenance in exchange for being hosted on site and allowed to offer horse riding in the reserve. This agreement was now contested by the CSOs as the previous owner had stopped patrolling the park and had sold his horses to a new owner. The official, however, showed reluctance to terminate the agreement, and was accused of delaying the eviction process. The second issue was around the opening of a coffee shop at the main entrance of the reserve, in a City Parks' facility that had so far been made available free of charge for CSOs' meetings. The CSO members accused the official of commodifying the park, and of acting by stealth as the matter had not been discussed within the Forum.

The official's own view was that a coffee shop was important to render the facility more user-friendly, and to garner resources for the park's management. He confided (to me) that several user groups had been selling drinks informally to visitors coming for guided tours and that he had approached each of them to ask if anyone was interested in manning the shop; so, in his view, everyone was

1 This research is part of a broader research programme on 'Practices of the State in Urban Governance', funded by the South African National Research Foundation. It involves individual research (interviews, participant observation in meetings, research-action through the facilitation of workshops with park user groups and City parks officials), as well as collective research (facilitating class projects, mentoring postgraduate research reports: these are referenced in the text), on the governance and management of parks in Johannesburg.

aware of the move. Similarly, for him the horse riding activities were welcome in the reserve, making it more attractive and potentially generating income whilst opening access to a wider range of environmentally oriented activities. But the City Parks' official never stated his opinions in the meeting. Rather, in the face of these accusations he remained silent, did not defend his views publicly, and appeared to agree with all what was 'suggested' (that he was to write a letter in order to evict the horse owner and that the process of renting the space in question to an entrepreneur was to be revisited). After the meeting, though, he confided to me that he would do nothing of the sort. He would continue formalising agreements with the horse owner and the coffee shop owner as this was best for the reserve. When I asked him why he had not defended his views in the meeting and why he had not discussed these developments in the Forum, he replied that he was tired of seeing all his initiatives being blocked or torn down in these meetings. He would continue regardless, as he was confident he had the mandate and power to do so.

Throughout this meeting I felt deeply embarrassed by the public humiliation I was witnessing—no matter how right the park users' representatives were about incorrect process and lack of dialogue. The tone of the accusations, the configuration of the argument (one single black man alone against a resourced white collective), the finger pointing, the loss of face—all were almost unbearable, perhaps more especially in a post-apartheid context. I was also puzzled about the function of the meeting: the forum had become a space for 'problem-making' rather than a problem-solving arena. Like the official, I saw the two contested initiatives as potentially beneficial to the reserve (if properly managed), and therefore potentially able to achieve consensus within the Forum. It did not seem impossible to formalise horse riding activities and a coffee shop to service an underused reserve and to negotiate their contribution to the maintenance of an undermanned reserve—especially as underuse and lack of management resources are constraints that the Forum acknowledges and struggles with. So, how was this joint management forum leading to the growth and consolidation of contention and the blocking of any initiative or development, instead of collectively building on activities that could easily be framed as beneficial additions to the reserve?

The history of this conflict, the involvement of individuals from both sides in what have become personalised attacks, and the micropolitics of this forum (including deeply entrenched and tacit racial tensions that perhaps limit the ability to find a common language), have been documented elsewhere (Baloyi et al., 2015; Mokgere, 2016). Beyond the specifics of this case, I wondered why the official did not feel an interest, the need, or an institutional motive to solve the issue, rather than leave the conflict to inflate, explode and ultimately destroy the forum. Why did he use an 'exit' rather than a 'voice' strategy (Hirshman, 1970)? Why did he act on his own, by stealth, rather than confronting the group and confidently asserting City Parks' mandate: mobilising resources and increasing and diversifying access and use? I therefore sought to analyse the policy instruments guiding the practice of joint park management, and the resources officials could garner to respond to mobilised, and at times demanding, park user groups.

More broadly, this chapter aims at assessing to what extent state practices are challenged and reframed through interaction with civil society in the provision of public services, in a context where parks and their management are given low political and budgetary priority at the municipal level. Through an interrogation with regard to how community engagement is framed as a municipal objective within City Parks, and how tools for guiding these engagements are crafted, I wish to interrogate how the state's mandate is redefined in contemporary cities of the South. I will reflect on the challenges the state faces in its attempt to regulate what is by definition highly informal and unstable: community engagement in park management. The chapter's ambition is therefore both theoretical and empirical—contributing to understanding contemporary statecraft (through the lens of officials' practices in the joint management of urban parks), debating the challenges of governing public spaces in contemporary cities, and reflecting on the meaning of 'post-apartheid' today.

The first section of the chapter borrows from different theoretical fields (participation, neo-liberalisation and coproduction) to conceptualise how the study of the joint management of parks can lead to an understanding of the dynamics of statecraft. The second section reviews the policy instruments developed by City Parks to frame community engagement around park management and reflects on the conflicting state rationalities they embody and they construct, in the context of post-apartheid Johannesburg.

2 Co-production of Park Management—Between Neo-liberalisation, Democratisation and Pragmatic Service Delivery in Cities of the South

This section considers a variety of theoretical approaches in order to make sense of the joint management of parks, as public spaces, in contemporary cities. It discusses the relevance and limitations of theories around community participation, neo-liberalisation, and co-production of urban services in cities of the global South.

2.1 *Joint Management of Parks as Community Participation—Empowerment or Exploitation?*

The involvement of park user groups in the shaping of public or collective urban spaces has long been studied and understood under the framework of community participation, as a right embedded in conceptions of urban citizenship, empowerment, and local democracy, where the public at large is legitimately expected to be able to influence the design and management of the urban spaces it uses. This literature has for some time debated whether participation was a tool of empowerment and democratisation emerging from below, that should be advocated and nurtured, or a tool of oppression and manipulation in the hands of public authorities, that should be distrusted and rejected (Cooke and Kothari, 2001; Williams, 2004). This dichotomy has somehow been overcome, with attention paid to the multiple facets of participation (contrasting invented with invited spaces of participation: Miraftab, 2004), an emphasis on the unpredictability of outcomes (Cornwall, 2008), analytical tools for analysing the micropolitics of public meetings (Cornwall, 2007; Bénit-Gbaffou and Mkwanazi, 2012) and an exploration of conditions for empowerment even in the most institutionalised participatory platforms (Williams, 2004). A second debate marks this field of the literature, one perhaps less visible and resolved: how to measure the degree and nature of community participation? Several tools have been developed, the most famous being Arnstein's 'ladder of participation' (1969), focusing on the degree of power vested in the citizens, starting from lower degrees (tokenism) and going towards higher degrees (full control) of citizen's empowerment. But these tools mostly focus on processes of decision-making and are of lesser relevance when it comes to assessing the outcomes of community participation and the difference that it makes with regard to the actual content of the policy, form of the urban space, or outcome of the project built.[2] Besides, by normatively affirming the primacy of 'citizens' control', the ladder is implicitly assuming the illegitimacy of the state's vision, adopting a suspicious take on the State typical of the postmodern and postcolonial era. It is *a contrario* celebrating the legitimacy and intrinsic progressiveness of community views. This posture has been criticised theoretically and practically, in contexts where participation spaces are appropriated exclusively by middle-class groups to further their already existing privileges (Bénit-Gbaffou, 2007), where mass movements adopt exclusionary and violent behaviour against local social groups defined as 'outsiders' (Glaser, 2015), or

2 This interrogation on outcomes is shared by social movement studies (Giugni, 1998), but it has possibly not led either to significant analytical progress, theoretically or methodologically.

even more generally where a complex politics of scale opposes legitimate but narrow local claims to looser but broader public benefits (Purcell, 2006).

Coming back to the state's assumed illegitimacy, participatory literature is generally entrenching a deep suspicion around public intervention. This suspicion stems from the postmodern critique of the state, assumed (or at least likely) to be oppressive; the united and obvious 'antagonist' or 'enemy' in urban governance that needs to be constantly checked, tracked, resisted or challenged; or the machinery incapable of grasping the complexity and fluidity of society, especially when it is developing multiple strategies of resistance (Scott, 1985). Participation theories are therefore often ill-equipped to unpack state practices. They fail to see the state not only as a heterogeneous and complex organisation (Gupta, 2012), but also as a potentially developmental agent, with legitimacy not only in partnering but sometimes also in countering, or at least reshaping, claims emerging from not always progressive or visionary, at times parochial and conservative, local civil societies. However, this view of the state as potentially sinister in its agenda and control apparatus is starting to be challenged, especially from intermediary countries, such as Brazil, India and South Africa—where states affirm, and resource with some capacity, strong redistributive agendas in highly unequal urban societies.

Some theoretical tools are more balanced in their understanding of civil society's versus the state's different objectives and rationalities when embarking on community participation. Pretty's typology (1995, adapted in Cornwall, 2008) usefully places participation in a continuum between a managerial objective (facilitating project implementation and public-space maintenance through community buy-in) and an empowerment objective (resourcing civil society to shape urban spaces and partake in decisions that affect its environment). Both objectives are legitimately shaping actual processes of participation, in a constant negotiation and balancing act. This approach can be found, usefully for our object of research, in Jones' (2002) model of cycles of engagement between municipal officials and user groups, expressed in his case study of joint park management in the UK. Jones writes from a policy context where British municipalities are required to partner with civil society organisations to lead projects and manage public assets (due to shrinking public funding and as a condition for accessing public grants). Based on observation of interactions between officials and park user groups ('Friends of the Park'), Jones investigates what is required from officials to support both successful joint management of parks and interaction with those groups. He suggests different skills, resources and objectives in what he analyses as different steps in the relationship (from complaints and distrust, to constructive relationships around small practical objectives, to enhancing autonomy and the 'responsibilisation' of park user groups). The limit of his approach is that he does not unpack the state much—it is represented and encapsulated by one single municipal official in charge of community engagement, without placing this official in a set of policies, budgets, official norms and rules, specific policy instruments and their politics.

Beyond the field of participation studies, other layers of critique, stemming from similar conceptions of the state as potentially driven by a sinister and oppressive agenda, and of the state as relatively unitary, have developed in the vast array of theories critiquing processes of neo-liberalisation. This literature, inspired either by Foucauldian or by neo-Marxist analyses, helps 'complexifying' the theorisation of the state in ways that are useful for our purpose.

2.2 *Critical Theories of Neo-liberalisation—Joint Park Management as 'Rolled-Out' State or as 'Realist "Governmentality"'*

Foucauldian-inspired analyses of neo-liberal governmentalities see participation as a relatively recent *dispositif* of power leading participants to internalise and naturalise the policy choices driven by other interests, and partly overlapping with theirs (Roy, 2009; Morange, 2015; Rosol, 2015). Rosol (2015) however departs from an assumed suspicion of the state, unpacking the recourse to participatory tools as a state strategy for overcoming residents' opposition to its spatial planning objectives (densification and compaction of the city in Vancouver), without assuming these state objectives are illegitimate. The state's intervention and use of *dispositifs* of governmentality (though sets and techniques of participatory engagements), she argues, have on the contrary assisted in overcoming and reshaping civil society's conservatism and parochialism. She usefully proposes the concept of 'realist governmentality' mingling deep participatory processes (where residents' concerns are considered and answered, if reframed) with forms of neo-liberal governmentality (where residents are confronted with existing budgetary constraints and required to make choices in such contexts). Her focus on participation as a tool of government intervention, analysed as realist governmentality, is helpful for our unpacking of state practices of community engagement in parks.

Going further in unpacking policy instruments, MacKinnon analyses the effect of key performance indicators (KPIs) on officials' practices in the provision of public service (MacKinnon, 2000). He argues that while the KPIs are an efficient tool of administrative control (in particular the control of the local level by the central level of the state), officials often retain a degree of agency and choice. This agency leads either to 'colonisation' (the reshaping of sets of practices alongside the KPIs) or to 'decoupling' (the development of two parallel sets of practices as resistance to control) in organisational responses to this neo-liberal management tool. Hibou (2012) is more pessimistic, showing how 'public goods' typically cannot easily be quantified, and how the control of officials' practices, through a quantitative measurement of their outputs, essentially marginalises and destroys the very spirit of public service.

Neo-Marxist analyses also interrogate state restructuring in several ways. They analyse the 'rescaling' of the state and the 'geographies of actually existing neoliberalism' in various parts of the world (Brenner and Theodore, 2002). They thereby enrich analyses of the state as a multi-layered, multi-scalar organisation with potentially competing agendas and dynamics that are locally embedded. These studies also nuance the hypothesis of the state's 'roll-back' (withdrawal from certain functions and mandates that used to be public) with explorations of state 'roll-out' dynamics—where it delegates some of its functions to non-state agents, through a variety of agreements, to provide public service (see also Hibou, 1999). Research directions stemming from this approach are multiple. Some critically analyse partnerships, unpacking the effects of the privatisation of service provision on social and spatial equity for instance (Graham and Marvin, 2001). Others examine the blind spots of neo-Marxist and Foucauldian perspectives on state practices, interrogating the circulation of policy ideas across scales of the state and between state and society (Uitermark, 2005). Others interrogate service providers' working conditions, rendered precarious under a multiplicity of scattered and temporary service provision schemes (Miraftab, 2004; Krinsky and Simonet, 2017).

Krinsky and Simonet, in particular, examine the question of 'who cleans your park' in contemporary New York. Through an ethnography of the various agreements with an array of temporary workers, social programmes, volunteers and interest group and NGO members, they show how these fragmented resources have come to replace the coordinated municipal service that used to manage public parks, to the detriment of service provision, workers' rights and spatial equity. Rosol (2010, 2012) looks, rather, at the social dynamics leading to the consolidation of user groups for the management of neighbourhood parks ('community gardens') in Berlin. Coming back to classic debates within the participation literature on whether citizens' involvement in the management of parks is the expression of alternative urban citizenry or the ultimate neo-liberal tool with which the state withdraws from its responsibilities, she concludes that both dynamics shape the new way in which neighbourhood parks are managed. She argues that temporary and locally constructed arrangements emerge as forms of citizens' mobilisation, and then tend to become institutionalised thanks to the broader (neo-liberal) acceptance that the state needs to delegate tasks of service provision to non-state agents (Rosol, 2012). She advises (Rosol, 2010), usefully for this chapter, that the fluid and ad hoc nature of these local arrangements require careful examination and tracking, and calls for suspending the strong normative assumptions attached to both participation and neo-liberalisation theoretical approaches (the former being seen as progressive and desirable, the second as regressive and to be avoided). However, this tracking focuses more on community dynamics, their links to social movements and their forms of institutionalisation than it equips us with conceptual tools with which to unpack state practices and the state's changing mandate.

2.3 *Joint Park Management as Co-production: Shifting State and Citizens' Mandates through the Co-Production Process?*

Understanding the shifting definition of statehood could be argued to be the focus, although often implicit and intuitive, of the literature on the co-production of public services. This concept stems from experiences of service delivery in developing cities in the 1970s (Ostrom, 1996; Turner, 1976) and is re-emerging in contemporary debates attempting precisely to suspend for one moment the normative assumptions attached to notions such as partnerships, seen through the critical lens of neo-liberalisation theory. Ostrom (1996) interestingly conceptualises co-production as a process of joint production of public infrastructures or services, by state and non-state[3] stakeholders. What is interesting in the cases she describes is the way in which both citizens and state officials transform their practices in the process of the production of services. Both adapt their practices in order to coordinate with and complement the others' in intertwined processes. Differently from the concept of partnerships (where each partner is generally defined with set resources and actions that they will bring to the deal), the notion of co-production emphasises the process of the joint and mutual redefinition of mandates. It allows for an open and dynamic definition of needs, claims and preferences (Stone, 2006), but also of skills, priorities, types of intervention and modes of action.

Joshi and Moore (2004), discussing Ostrom (1996) from the explicit perspective of the global South, interrogate the state more centrally. They argue that co-production, as 'unorthodox public service delivery in challenging environments', is the norm in most countries and cities of the global South. But, unlike Turner (1976), who contrasts self-help housing provision with state responsibilities, they unpack the interactions between state and non-state agents engaging in service provision. Doing so, they avoid taking normative positions—in terms of governmentality (often seen as the manipulation and disguised oppression of society by the state) or in terms of neo-liberalisation (in terms of the subjugation of society to the logics of economic profit alone).

3 She considers civil society as the main non-state co-producer in her paper.

The authors argue that both framings are partly ill-fitting in Southern contexts, where the state actually never provided any services in certain areas or sectors of society. Therefore co-production is rather seen as an extension, not as a shrinking, of the state's intervention in society (Hibou, 1999; Jaglin, 2008). This is particularly relevant for this chapter, as the state never provided for urban parks in most of the urban areas (e.g. the black portion of South African cities—the majority of its population) and the post-apartheid regime led to an extension of the scope and scale of state intervention. Co-production is also seen as the process of constructing practical and largely context-dependent collective solutions: not necessarily as driven or controlled by the state, at least not as an assumption, leaving some of the process open. This too seems relevant for the purposes of this chapter, where—rather than a situation of state roll-back or even roll-out—the current situation would be more adequately described as the expansion of state authority. In Johannesburg, park users in middle-class areas in particular have taken over the actual management of parks since the turn of the millennium, and City Parks is looking for ways to re-establish its mandate with regard to public-space management—with limited financial and human resources—and simultaneously attempting to capitalise on the mobilisation of civil society resources.

The benefit of this approach is double: it interrogates the shifting, contested and redefined mandates for the state in state–society relations understood as dynamic. And it analyses how these processes impact on the actual provision of services and production of spaces in the city, through an attention to the technicalities involved in the provision of services and their negotiation (Watson 2014). In this way, it links the materiality of instruments (in their own, sector-specific, technical logics, responding to practical challenges but also caught in their own functional dynamics) to state rationalities and the state's shifting, unstable and contested mandates. Focusing on the process of defining such instruments, as lenses illuminating both internal and external contestations contributing to redefining the state (Uitermark, 2005), it borrows from a Foucauldian approach (Lascoumes and Le Galès, 2007). But it also attempts to respond to frustrations with Foucauldian approaches by interrogating the effect of these techniques on the production of the city itself, the way they affect the making of urban services and spaces (here urban parks and their actual management) through their own functional and technical logics. This is in line with Stone's suggestion (2006) to look at 'power to' (shape the city and produce urban spaces, along a vision that is built and shared by coalitions of actors mobilising resources for its implementation) rather than only at 'power over' (questioning forms and processes of influence and domination). In this respect, the co-production approach might assist in rejuvenating our thinking about the state, its practices and its mandate in the contemporary city of the

South. It helps us interrogate actual processes of production in relation to shifting mandates by twinning the study of technical instruments (that are sector-bound and produce specific effects on the city) and the analysis of the processes of state-making.

The risk with approaches in terms of co-production—and their suspension of the normative judgements brought about by the neo-liberalisation critique or the governmentality approach—is the marginalisation of the critical interrogation of social and spatial inequality, on the one hand, and of power dynamics on the other (Watson 2014). Arguably however, adopting the lens of co-production does not prohibit an interrogation of inequality, nor an analysis in terms of power dynamics. The redefinition of state-versus-society mandates and prerogatives is a deeply political and contentious process in which these issues actually come to the forefront. As for urban parks in Johannesburg, the question of transformation (addressing past and present inequalities, especially in their socio-racial dimension) is at the forefront of City officials' mandates, discourses and preoccupations; the contestations in the processes of co-production are testimony to the deep political nature of these engagements.

The analysis of which rules are negotiated to regulate public spaces (parks in this case) and how they redefine the boundaries of the state remains underdeveloped. Ostrom (1996) interrogates explicitly, analytically and normatively the rules to regulate 'the commons' (based on observations of a multiplicity of case studies), but she steers away from analysing the respective and shifting mandates of society and state, focusing predominantly on rules negotiated within civil society to establish systems of self-regulation (less central to our objective here). We are still to theorise on how forms of the co-production of public services (rather than autonomous, citizen- or private-led provision) affect, challenge and shift the practices, the mandate and the nature of the state in contemporary cities of the South.

3 Unpacking the Objectives of 'the State' through Policy Instruments for the Management of Parks: Rise or Marginality of Co-production as Form of Service Delivery?

This section interrogates the state's practices and objectives through the lens of co-production in order to investigate why practices of the joint management of parks fail to work in post-apartheid Johannesburg, in spite of what could be considered favourable conditions for their emergence and consolidation. These favourable conditions are: firstly, the existence of park user groups with some experience in park management, at least in middle-class areas; and secondly, a policy framework for City Parks that seeks improved relationships with users to address the negative image marking the municipal agency, and that aims at mobilising complementary human and financial resources in the context of scarce public funding for parks.

Through the analysis of various policy instruments, it is argued that genuine engagement with communities to deepen the accountability and responsiveness of the state is not a priority objective for City Parks compared to the need to garner financial resources. Secondly, the mandate and responsibility to engage with communities is actually scattered across the agency and contested between different units and officials, with a gap between those actually on the ground and confronted by user groups and those officially in charge of community engagement. Thirdly, developing actual partnership guidelines that foster the co-management of parks is seen as a challenge by City Parks' officials—both technically and politically. It seems much easier to delegate the management task to non-state institutions or to build partnerships with the corporate sector, where the terms of exchange are simpler and clearer (for instance, where the corporate sponsor is branded, in exchange for its financial contribution); avoiding the legal and political issues of joint fundraising or staff management. These guidelines are all the more difficult to imagine and develop, given that where joint management forums do exist (and could provide an opportunity to experiment) they are mostly found in former white, middle-class suburbs without the political legitimacy necessary to act as real 'partners' for the City. In these joint management forums, contentious and vocal user groups are easily ignored by City Parks, which often considers them to be inspired by parochial attempts to reproduce racial and social privilege, in the (middle-class, suburban) areas that are not its priority.

3.1 *Community Engagement—Framed Mostly in Neo-liberal Terms in Policy Instruments*

The 2013 institutional restructuring of City Parks, a municipal agency reframed as Johannesburg City Parks and Zoo (merging a deficit-prone entity, City Parks, with a profit-generating one, Johannesburg Zoo), was also the occasion to align the agency with new public management principles. This alignment (see Figure 5.1) illustrates the importance of auditing processes emphasising cost-effectiveness and financial monitoring; it created a legal and contract management arm, and multiplied dedicated units aside from service delivery (still defined as 'core business'): marketing, public relations, and new business development inter alia.

Looking at community engagement within this organogram reveals how scattered the agency is (Bosaka, 2015; Bénit-Gbaffou, forthcoming). The official task of liaising with communities lies with Stakeholder Liaison Officers (SLOs) working in Stakeholder and Public Relations Management—and their main

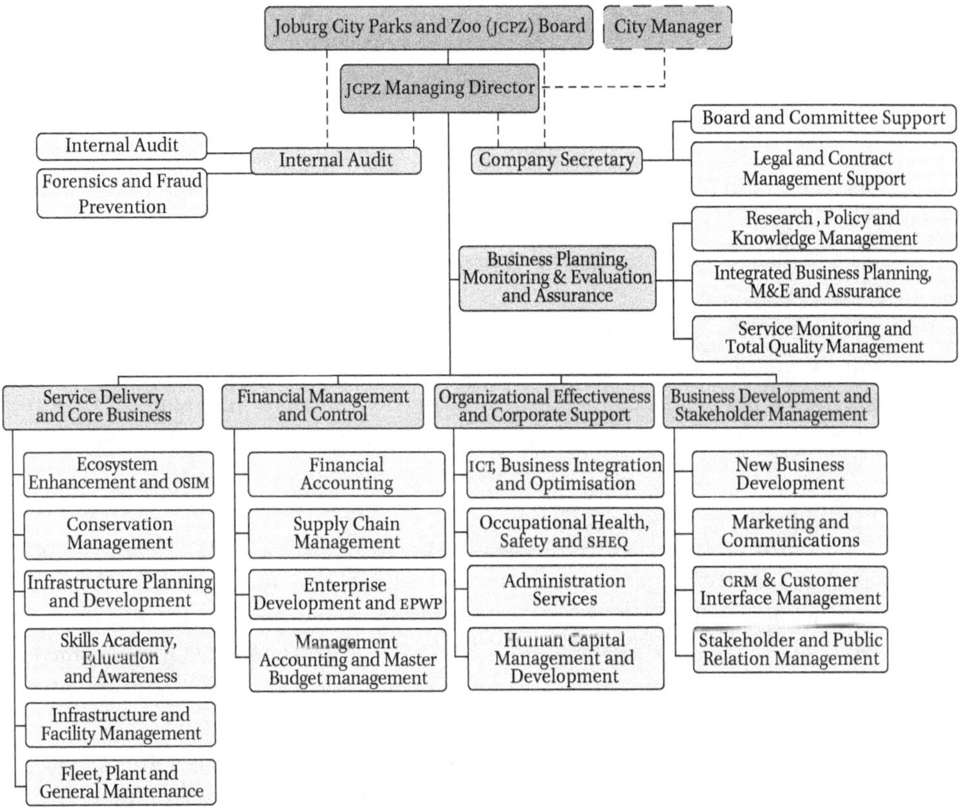

FIGURE 5.1 JCPZ organogram, 2013. Recommended level 3 positional structure.
SOURCE: JCPZ (2013A)

objective is to defend and protect City Parks' reputation and avoid conflict, bad publicity and reputational damage. The function of Customer Interface Management was never consolidated in a department; rather, it has been tasked to the regional managers (under Service Delivery and Core Business), whose Key Performance Indicators include measurement of users' complaints and the rapidity of their responses to these complaints. Other officials in charge of community engagement are situated under New Business Development, which is about fundraising for the City or the agency through events organised in parks[4] and partnerships established with donors, mostly from the corporate sector. A third type of community engagement is effected by officials in charge of Education and Awareness, who develop educational campaigns and partnerships with township schools in particular, with regards to behaviour

4 Which City Parks actually does not benefit from, as the event fee goes into City of Johannesburg coffers.

management (respect for public assets and the park) but also to introducing environmental education to groups that have been deprived of access to green open spaces. The fourth type of engagement with the public falls under the management of outsourced services and the distribution of minor jobs (Supply Chain Management, Enterprise Development, and EPWP[5]). The latter programme in particular (EPWP) constitutes a key element of the interaction between JCPZ and residents in townships and informal settlements, as it is used to distribute piece jobs and stipends to the unemployed in disadvantaged areas and groups.

Community engagement, or rather 'Stakeholder Management' is therefore mostly seen as a branding and marketing, public relations exercise—responding to crises when organised user groups become too vocal or threatening, but not addressing the fundamental causes of complaint: insufficient operational budgets and human resources to cater for the 2,500-odd open spaces that JCPZ is responsible for. The objective of mobilising resources is framed mostly in terms of garnering financial contributions from the private sector (rather than seeing community involvement in park management as a 'resource') and developing new business opportunities. This is done through big corporates branding themselves in exchange for financial contributions to events, infrastructure, or management, or through small emerging black enterprises and cooperatives given short-term contracts by City Parks. These contracts are actually a way for JCPZ to mobilise financial resources from other branches of the state—the national state through EPWP, or the municipality at large through Jozi@work programmes.[6]

This framing—which could be termed neo-liberal—however coexists with a strong redistributive discourse (JCPZ, 2013a) focusing on opening new parks in disadvantaged areas (former black townships and informal settlements) and bridging the 'green divide' between the 'leafy suburbs' to the 'dusty townships'. This discourse is not mere rhetoric and is matched by important capital budgets that go each year to marginalised areas and the active development of new parks—with no increase, however, in operational budgets for the management of the agency's growing assets and only low levels of community engagement

5 The Expanded Public Works Programme (EPWP) consists of stipends given to disadvantaged individuals for community work for a short period of time (one to three months). The programme is funded by the national government and in Johannesburg is used mostly by municipal entities such as City Parks and Pikitup (waste management). Based on a critique of the limited developmental impacts of EPWP, Johannesburg Mayor Parks Tau developed a City-funded programme, Jozi@work, that organised service delivery contracts between municipal entities and cooperatives (contracts for a period of three years, including training by the municipal entity contracting the cooperative)—distributing more stable employment on more collective terms. However, the programme was terminated during the tenure of Democratic Alliance Mayor Herman Mashaba in 2017.

6 See previous footnote.

in contexts where there has been limited historical opportunity for the consolidation of local park user groups. The emphasis on the capital budget also means that funding for the outsourcing of various tasks (including management ones) is easier to mobilise than that for hiring supplementary staff, for which operational budget is direly lacking in the agency.

Community engagement, even in its many ambiguous meanings and dimensions, is therefore a rather marginal and certainly quite implicit policy objective, as illustrated by the ten strategic Key Performance Areas for the agency (see Table 5.1). However, it is also clear that the neo-liberal framings (lack of

TABLE 5.1 Ten strategic Key Performance Indicators for JCPZ

Ten Strategic Key Performance Areas	Key Performance Indicators
1. Financial balance	Value (rands) of external funding collected
2. Food security	Number of community gardens created
3. Active citizenship	Number of public workshops in environmental education
4. Sustainable city	Number of projects linked to 'Corridors of Freedom'*
5. Partnerships with external stakeholders	Number of service level agreements signed with external partners (other municipalities, universities, sponsors)
6. Small Micro and Medium Enterprises (SMMEs)	Number of training workshops for SMMEs
7. Small Micro and Medium Enterprises (SMMEs)	Number of EPWP jobs created
8. Small Micro and Medium Enterprises (SMMEs)	Number of cooperatives created
9. Small Micro and Medium Enterprises (SMMEs)	Number of cooperatives trained
10. Green space development	Number of hectares of green space created

* The 'Corridors of Freedom' is a mayoral flagship programme that identifies four 'corridors' in the city where transport infrastructure and other public and private investments are to be concentrated in order to 're-stitch' the post-apartheid city.

SOURCE: JCPZ, 2014.

human and financial resources to manage parks) and discourse (increasingly pressing requirement to raise complementary resources to manage parks) also open opportunities for various forms of community involvement in the management of parks—not principally through fundraising (although this is one dimension in the wealthier neighbourhoods), but mostly through human resources: voluntary work, individual or collective, addressing the everyday issues of park management in the absence of dedicated municipal staff for each park. Indeed, each park manager has under his or her responsibility up to 70 public open spaces (developed parks, undeveloped parks, conservancies, and nature reserves) for which he or she manages small teams of between 15 and 30 horticulturists, rotating them between parks according to a tight service roster.[7]

3.2 *Engaging with Communities: Competing and Contested Mandates for Street-Level Officials*

Park managers, as the only City officials regularly (if insufficiently) 'on the ground', serve as the de facto liaison between the agency and park users: everyday operational challenges require a degree of interaction with surrounding communities and being onsite makes them the complaint desks for local users. How to have the team of horticulturists cut the grass in the park, when it has two hours to do so before moving to the next park, if there is litter on the grass that has not been collected by the municipal agency in charge of litter collection (Pikitup), or when that litter is regularly deposited by anonymous users in sections of the park that could be described as 'border vacuums' (Jacobs, 1961)? What to do when groups of homeless people sleep and live in the park, sorting out the waste they want to recycle and sell and leaving litter in the park, when residents complain, and when police evictions only lead to these homeless groups coming back a few days later? Park managers, in practice, engage regularly with users and user groups, but they have no mandate to do so, generally no professional training for such interactions (although they often have learnt by doing), and limited resources and back up with regard to the solving of issues. In the Klipriviersberg Nature Reserve Forum, for instance, the official sitting in the meeting is the Head of Conservation; he has environmental training and a passion for birds, and expresses an explicit dislike for the politics of community engagement.

Park managers report directly to regional managers, whose Key Performance Areas (KPAs) relate—to a significant extent (45 per cent)—to the number and importance of park users' complaints within their administrative region, as

7 Parks get serviced between once a week and once a month depending on their status, size, and use, but also their spatial and political visibility.

well as to the rapidity with which they solve the issues that led to the complaints. However, the other KPAs and the bulk of park managers' job is to manage the scarce staff rotating between parks, track their movements and the time spent in each park, tick their scorecards and manage staff scarcity (Table 5.2). This leaves limited time to engage in solving the issues that lead to complaints, which generally have complex and structural causes and require long-term engagement with users and local contexts rather than quick fixes.

Those with an official mandate, the Stakeholder Liaison Officers (SLOs), do not attend any user group, residents' association or civil society organisation meetings, even if City Parks is officially invited to these meeting and its presence is crucial to respond to users' issues. It is only when there are major crises, such as the one in Klipriviersberg Nature Reserve (involving the media and the

TABLE 5.2 Summary of Key Performance Indicators for JCPZ Regional Managers, 2017

Key Performance Area (KPA), park regional managers (2017)	Key Performance Indicator (KPI)
1. Financial sustainability and resilience (20%)	Percentage of General Auditor's findings responded toPercentage of operational budget spent Number of EPWP and Jozi@work jobs created Number of cooperatives and SMMEs engaged in programmes (Jozi@work)
2. Customer perspective (45%)	Annual Customer Satisfaction IndexPercentage of resolution of customer complaints Number of complaints received over 30 days Targeted turnaround time per maintenance cycle, for various types of parks (flagship, developed, undeveloped parks, etc.)
3. Internal business processes (23%)	Number of mature trees actively maintainedNumber of trees planted and maintained Turnaround time of fallen tree removal
4. Learning and growth (12%)	Quarterly performance assessment conducted for all direct reports Number of innovation initiatives

SOURCE: AUTHOR'S OWN ANALYSIS, FROM JCPZ DOCUMENTS, 2017A, 2017B AND 2017C.

possibility of litigation) that they intervene with user groups. Their Key Performance Indicators (Table 5.3) are actually framed around engagement not with user groups, but with ward councillors, as the sole legitimate representatives of civil society at the local level.[8]

TABLE 5.3 Summary of Key Performance Indicators for Stakeholder Liaison Officers, 2015

Key Performance Area (KPA), Stakeholder Liaison Officers	Key Performance Indicator (KPI)
1. Internal business process	Internal engagement with other JCPZ departments and number of meetings attendedInternal coordination and facilitation of departmental programmes such as environmental education, operations, and recruitment of community liaison officers (CLO) Monthly reports, responses to councillor queries
2. External stakeholder perspective	Number of engagements with councillorsNumber of engagements and joint programmes and campaigns with city, provincial, and national government Number of participants in engagement with organs of civil society, concerned residents, and political parties regarding service delivery challenges Attendance at quarterly Councillor forum Attendance at regional service delivery, Joint Organisation Committee, or Section 79 meetings
3. Learning and development	Training and development programmes including workshops—one per financial year

SOURCE: AFTER BOSAKA (2015), FROM JCPZ DOCUMENTS, 2015A AND 2015B.

8 A ward represents around 20,000 registered voters, which could indicate between 60,000 and 100,000 residents, depending on the ward.

The narrow definition of 'stakeholder engagement' (defined as engagement with councillors as local brokers with communities) is explained first by the extreme lack of resourcing of the unit: only four SLOs for the whole metropolitan area and 2,500 open spaces (not all of them having user groups[9]). There is no way such a limited staff can attend extremely demanding community meetings, often occurring once a month at late hours and in generally remote and suburban locations where public transport is scarce and dangerous. The narrowness of SLOs' mandate is also linked to the resistance of elected ward councillors, who protect and defend their prerogative as the only legitimate mediators between the City and residents—all the more so because the national legislation on municipal structure has deprived them of any real institutional power, out of fear of fostering racial fragmentation and predatory or violent clientelism (Bénit-Gbaffou, 2008). SLOs therefore complain that they are prohibited from calling any public meeting without recourse to the mediation of ward councillors, whose mobilisation and interest is uneven across the city.

Beyond those street level officials, another area of contestation arises between the official heading the 'Stakeholder Management' unit and the one in charge of 'New Business Development'—the latter theoretically focusing on engagements and partnerships that involve financial transactions (sponsorship or event organisation). However, in practice the lines are blurred, as financial contributions often require a prior process of informal engagement and the building of a relationship of trust, while engagement with communities might lead to fundraising initiatives that financially benefit the park. This institutional blurriness is aggravated by the different professional skills and trajectories of the two officials. The former is a loyal and long-standing parks official defending the image of the agency and its traditional mandate, and seeing communities mostly as a nuisance, a risk, or a challenge; the latter, meanwhile, coming from Johannesburg Zoo, is far more socially aware, builds networks, and is entrepreneurial in spirit.

Whilst there is merit in community engagement not being confined to one single unit or official and being mainstreamed in the institution where various forms of engagement with individual or collective users are acknowledged or encouraged, there is also a lack of clarity regarding roles and mandates on the ground as well as at the high bureaucratic level. This lack of clarity also leads to a lack of proper resourcing, both of those officially in charge of Stakeholder

9 City Parks officials were unable to provide us with a number for (formal or informal) user groups, and had no consolidated list of such groups, dealing with them on an ad hoc basis depending on how vocal they were in their claims, and at times more regularly where user groups were more consolidated.

Management and of those practically confronted by users and user groups on a daily basis. This might reflect the fundamental ambiguities of City Parks' position on community engagement—a neo-liberal frame confronted with potentially democratising practices that have not been explicitly or actively embraced. The concept of co-production and the changing state practices it entails is still foreign to City Parks officials' conceptions of themselves and their institution, even if co-production practices are developing on the ground.

3.3 *Uncertainty Regarding How to Define and Consolidate the Rules of Co-management*

This gap is visible in City Parks' attempts to formalise partnerships between itself, as the agency mandated for park management by the City of Johannesburg, and park user groups actually involved in the management of specific parks. These attempts are studied through the development process of partnership guidelines as well as formal documents establishing different types of agreements and signed by City Parks and specific non-state agents.

The first document, initiated in 2013, is entitled 'Framework on Stakeholder Partnership Agreement for Joint Natural Resources Management of Natural Areas' and is being developed by the New Business Development unit (JCPZ, 2013b). It attempts to provide generic guidelines for the establishment of joint management committees, bringing together City park officials and park user groups to manage nature reserves—areas larger than parks, less used, and more difficult to maintain due to the specific environmental conservation requirements that the status of nature reserve entails.[10] This document is currently only a draft, and has not been finalised, consolidated or adopted four years after its drafting—neither has this draft been discussed with stakeholders; it remains blocked due to legal concerns. The first of these concerns is financial. Whilst the partnership is explicitly geared towards mobilising complementary resources for the management of nature reserves, and in particular financial resources, City Parks as a municipal agency is uncertain if it is entitled to engage in fundraising activities jointly with park user groups. In particular, it invokes the 2013 Municipal Finances Management Act as an important obstacle to the possibility of ring-fencing funding raised by the City for a specific park. This Act has been framed explicitly to avoid the local ring-fencing of financial resources for a specific space or territory, in response to the apartheid-era local government structure, which separated resourced and tax-endowed white local authorities from impoverished and tax-deprived black local authorities.

10 In particular, the legal obligation (not followed in parks) to regularly and repeatedly destroy 'invasive alien vegetation', which is seen as a threat to water reserves and to indigenous species—work that is very costly in terms of human resources.

The Act aligns with the construction of metropolitan institutions to govern cities, inspired by the political slogan popular in the 1980s—'one city, one tax base', rejecting the institutional fragmentation and resource ring-fencing that were central to the reproduction of racial and social segregation. South African municipalities therefore have recourse to various forms of delegated ring-fencing—as mechanisms for raising supplementary resources affected to specific territories—such as City Improvement Districts, or here, park user groups. This delegation, however, means a loss of power for municipal institutions, which have no grasp of the amounts of resources actually collected by those groups, and no influence over how this funding is used. This is the case with park user groups, some of which have been able to garner a substantial amount of funds for the parks in question (through events or campaigns) and have used these funds without necessarily informing or obtaining formal agreement from City Parks to upgrade or develop park facilities.[11]

The development of a *joint* management committee in the draft framework, therefore, prevents such a committee from actually leveraging funding for the reserve—a major impediment to the consolidation of such joint management in the draft framework. A possible technical solution could be to task the partnering stakeholders to fundraise and report to the joint management committee. But this would entail a degree of trust (that currently does not exist), of reciprocity in disclosing resources available for the park (which grounded officials currently have no mandate for), and also a form of delineation of each partner's mandate and role—currently not developed in the framework. This issue is arguably, although less visibly, the second major obstacle to the consolidation of the framework: uncertainty regarding the definition of the respective roles and mandates of each partner. City Parks indeed appears, in its practices of engagement with park user groups, extremely reluctant to give up sections of its mandate and share decision-making authority on issues affecting the park. How temporary staff (EPWP and Jozi@work) are deployed and coordinated, what events are organised in the park and when, when public interventions are planned, and what budget is allocated for the year are areas of great contention between City Parks and park users, the latter complaining that they are never consulted on nor even informed of these matters, even though they affect the everyday management of the park that they themselves are driving.

11 This has been the case in Zoo Lake, where the user committee has unilaterally revamped a sports field. City Parks has strongly criticised this initiative and frozen the committee for a few years, before the committee was revived with a less autonomous stance (Hadebe, 2015).

A similar uncertainty is to be found in another, more ad hoc document, a Memorandum of Agreement (MoA) jointly signed by one user group—the Friends of Kloofendal (FroK)—and City Parks (JCPZ, 2015b, 2017c). Interestingly, the document was framed based on an existing interaction between the user group and the Education and Awareness unit. FroK accepted to participate in City Parks' programmes of environmental education for township school children (in the form of ten tours they would provide free of charge annually for about 60 learners each) in exchange for the free use of a City Parks office on site. This agreement, supervised by City Parks' legal department, is however silent on the subject of other management partnerships, in particular everyday practices of the conservation manager and the user group—in terms of invasive alien plant destruction, the training and coordination of outsourced staff, the organisation of tours and events, etc. Although the conservation manager is on site, no provision is made for regular meetings between the two parties; nothing in the MoA alludes to a division of labour or the coordination of tasks—something FroK is complaining bitterly about while the everyday relationship has soured and this tension has challenged the continuation of the agreement in 2017.

The distrust embedded in some sections of City Parks with regard to users and community engagement is visible in another document, drafted by the Stakeholder Management unit. The *Volunteers Policy* (JCPZ, 2015a), which guides the way in which volunteers from civil society can apply for the status that enables them to assist City Parks in maintaining parks and open spaces. The policy not only makes it clear that volunteers are to fit within City Parks' (undisclosed) existing needs, it also displays a high level of distrust of volunteers, required them to sign (three times throughout the agreement form) a commitment to the non-disclosure of any internal information on JCPZ that they might be exposed to during their volunteer work. This policy clearly does not constitute co-production, rather reaffirming City Parks' traditional mandate and dominance in what is not conceived as a 'partnership'. It is City Parks using a voluntary workforce to complement its staff in pre-existing programmes or interventions—at its discretion, and accompanied by a degree of fear of indiscretion on the part of any outsider exposed to its inner workings.

In parallel, the New Business Development unit has developed ad hoc agreements (more or less formal—letters of adoption with user groups and residents' associations; Memorandum of Agreement with the corporate sector) to formalise partnerships for the management of parks (Table 5.4). Contrasting with the complex and protracted processes of engaging with user groups around the joint management of nature reserves, the formalisation of partnerships with civil society organisations (homeowners', community,

TABLE 5.4 Types of formal agreements developed by City Parks to engage with user groups and property owners: from co-production to delegation

Year	Type of agreement	Stakeholders involved	Type of park	Sharing responsibilities—role of each party	Provision for coordination	Duration	Examples	Type of partnership (analysis)
2013	Framework for Stakeholders Partnership Agreement—draft	City Parks and various user groups	Template for all nature reserves	Not specified. The management committee is expected to engage in fundraising.	Establishment of a management committee with representatives of all parties, a contitution, a business plan, and a quarterly progress report.	N/A	JCPZ 2013	Co-production—vision, development plan and fund raising oriented.
2015	Volunteer Policy	City Parks and individual 'volunteer'	Guidelines and contract	Volunteer to provide time/work on a volunteer basis to City Parks. City Parks to host the volunteer, allocate tasks, provide uniform and integrate volunteer into its staff.	Each volunteer to be assigned to a supervisor in the host unit. Each host unit to report to Stakeholders and Management unit in City Parks.	ad hoc	JCPZ 2015	Volunteer work for City Parks.
2015, 2016, 2017 (draft)	Memorandum of Agreement (MoA)	City Parks and Friends of Kloofendal (FroK)	One nature reserve	FroK to provide environmental educational tours for children from disadvantaged schools (10 groups per annum) , and in exchange be granted full access and use of the on-site community centre. FroK to assist when possible in invasive alien plant removal.	Since 2017: Each party to appoint one representative and to meet "as often as deemed necessary". Minutes to be recorded and archived. FroK must provide JCPZ with "tangible proof" of funds used for and in the reserve.	1 year	JCPZ 2015b, 2017c	Co-production—provision of environmental education/ access to City Parks premises.

TABLE 5.4 Types of formal agreements developed by City Parks to engage with user groups and property owners: from co-production to delegation (*cont.*)

Year	Type of agreement	Stakeholders involved	Type of park	Sharing responsibilities—role of each party	Provision for coordination	Duration	Examples	Type of partnership (analysis)
2016	N/A	City Parks and Klipriviersberg user groups	One nature reserve	Not specified.	Monthly meetings in Kilpriviersberg Nature Reserve (Head of conservation plus user groups members).	N/A	N/A	Co-production—problem-solving oriented.
2016, 2017	Letter of Adoption	City Parks and residents' associations	One neighbourhood park	Ad hoc residents' offers—varying between park maintenance (grass cutting, tree pruning etc), infrastructure maintenance (repainting, fixing or replacing facilities), park development (tree planting, new infrastructure, art pieces, landscaping, fencing). City Parks to try and provide extra-maintenance "if ressources allow".	Residents' association to "maintain a close working relationship and consult from time to time to make sure interventions are environmentally compliant" with the regional manager.	3 years	JCPZ 2016a, b & c	Delegation—mobilisation of community resources: maintenance oriented.
2016	MoA	City Parks and single property owner	Inner city parks (neighbourhood)	Property owner to take full management responsibility for the park (cutting grass, cleaning, emptying dustbins, opening and locking gates, providing security). City Parks to remain responsible for maintaining and fixing park equipment and facilities.	Property owner to submit written reports to City Parks "when required" on services rendered, security statistics, security roster, etc.	5 years	JCPZ 2016d	Delegation—mobilising property owners' resources: security and maintenance.

Year	Type of agreement	Stakeholders involved	Type of park	Sharing responsibilities—role of each party	Provision for coordination	Duration	Examples	Type of partnership (analysis)
2017	Memorandum of Understanding (MoU)—draft	City Parks, Johannesburg Development Agency (JDA) and City Improvement District (CID)	Inner city parks (neighbourhood)	JDA to upgrade the park and fund management (cleaning security and maintenance) for the park for a "handover management period" (2 years). City Parks to oversee the handover management period and take responsibility post-handover for park and facilities maintenance. CID to fund park security guards (Park Safety Patrols), maintain the park (grass cutting, cleaning, emptying dustbins) and activate the park (event organisation).	Not specified in the draft agreement. Two representatives from each party to meet once a quarter to finalise the MoU.	Not specified (handover management period = 2 years)	JCPZ 2017b	Delegation—mobilisation of CID resources: security, maintenance, community building.
2017	Service Level Agreement (SLA)	City Parks, private security companies and residents association	All parks in the area (Blairgowry)—unspecified	Private security patrolling the parks, working with park rangers and Johannesburg Metropolitan Police Dept.	Monthly security reports on incidents from security companies to City Parks. Creation of a steering committee, meeting monthly (2 representatives of City Parks, 2 representatives of association and security companies).	3 years	JCPZ 2017a	Between co-production and delegation—mobilisation of community's resources: security oriented with strong anti-homeless stance.

SOURCE: AUTHOR'S ANALYSIS, 2017.

or ratepayers' associations) for neighbourhood parks' management has been straightforward. It has taken the form of 'letters of adoption' delegating tasks defined on an ad hoc basis, depending on what community organisations are willing to offer (JCPZ, 2016a, 2016b). Communities 'adopting' a specific park do so for a period of five years, and provide services from everyday park management (cleaning and grass cutting) to equipment maintenance (fixing and replacing facilities; repaving paths) to park development (new playground and security equipment, landscaping, tree planting, and the purchase of artwork).

Other, more elaborate partnerships have been developed with building owners or coalitions of property owners (in particular when they are working within City Improvement Districts) in inner city neighbourhoods as more formal Memorandums of Agreement (MoAs). In these MoAs, specific services are provided by non-state partners: park security first and foremost (and the funding of permanent security guards in the park through the CID) (JCPZ, 2017a), but also park maintenance (cleaning and grass cutting) and even at times community-building through the organisation of events (JCPZ, 2016d, 2017b).

Formal agreements are not, however, limited to the corporate sector, and letters of adoption are not always restricted to civil society organisations. For instance, a suburban residential complex has also 'adopted' a park through a letter of adoption (JCPZ, 2016c). More interestingly, a Service Level Agreement has been signed between City Parks and Blairgowrie Community Association, as well as the two main security companies patrolling the neighbourhood, to expand their security patrols to the park and regularly report to City Parks (JCPZ, 2017a). City Parks has agreed to have monthly meetings with the security company and the residents' association regarding these reports, therefore going beyond a simple delegation of security services and towards what might involve co-production. In practice, many residents' associations have negotiated with local security companies to expand their services to neighbourhood parks, but few have actually formalised this arrangement with City Parks, and most therefore do not benefit from institutionalised or regular engagement with the agency.

This set of documents consolidates various kinds of partnerships. These range from what can be seen as co-production (entailing regular meetings to 'co-decide' and co-manage, which can be understood as changing the state's practices towards accountability and problem-solving in conjunction with the partner, community, or corporate) to what constitutes degrees of delegation (where non-state agents provide a service that is not provided by City Parks, in a semi-autonomous mode with some level of reporting to City Parks but no regular meeting or joint decision-making). What the chronology and diversification of formal partnership agreements show is a rise in partnerships with the corporate sector (building owners and City Improvement Districts), especially in the inner city (the locus of mayoral regeneration efforts); and a shift away from complex and resource-hungry co-production towards more straightforward delegation.

The limits of the delegation model, however, are twofold. It effectively privatises park management, and does have social exclusionary effects, especially towards the more marginalised park users (Matubatuba et al., 2018). The most formal partnerships (SLAs and MoAs) have an explicit objective to evict the homeless from public parks, stating, for instance:

> Unmanaged public space in Johannesburg inner city parks and open spaces makes them a haven for vagrants [sic], unemployed youth and criminals whose unlawful activities and anti-social behaviour render the essential and valuable recreational spaces in high-rise residential areas inaccessible for general public use – social, sporting, recreational.
>
> JCPZ, 2017b, 4

> JCPZ shall observe and be responsible for the following: [...] To ensure illegal street vendors and vagrancy issues when reported by any of the parties will be addressed within a reasonable time-frame as required, depending on the levels of urgency indicated.
>
> JCPZ, 2017a

A second limitation is that these partnerships can only involve financially resourced partners, such as CIDs, building owners or middle-class residents' associations, which are able to fundraise. Less well-endowed communities, more fragmented ones, are unable to find the financial resources to sustain park management in the long run, but also therefore to demand accountability and service delivery from City Parks, unlike more resourced communities. The coordination of multiple but informal community contributions to the park, as they happen in less-structured communities, does require regular engagement with City Parks' officials, and forms of co-production, not delegation, of the management of public space.

3.4 *City Parks' Resistance to Co-production*

What explains the relative failure of co-production arrangements and their formalisation in Johannesburg? The existing, informal processes of co-production, in nature reserves in particular, have proven complex and often conflict-ridden (Mokgere, 2016). This has led City Parks to tentatively reconfigure the platform for engagement. An example of this is Klipriviersberg nature reserve, where the Forum was created in 2016 to avoid the further mediatisation of issues by very vocal associations; the Forum was, however, disbanded in mid-2017, soon after the meeting reported above. The configuration of these platforms makes them highly unequal, and renders debates implicitly racialised (Mokgere, 2016), with often one black, low-income City official confronted by groups of white, middle-class local leaders. The mutual and self-perpetuating racial prejudice present in these meetings has been used by some higher-placed City Parks officials to discard the issues raised by park users on this platform, and to delegitimise them as partners as only being interested in reproducing their own (white) privilege.

What this understanding does not answer to is the issue of the capacitation of park managers (here the head conservationist) to engage with and be resourced to respond to users' claims, and to drive their collective and joint framing (Jones, 2002). Granted, putting more public resources into already privileged suburban spaces (capacitating municipal staff to efficiently engage in the co-production process requires resources) is clearly politically illegitimate in post-apartheid South Africa. As the issue of co-production is framed in racial terms, and as existing practices have developed mostly in former white and middle-class areas, City Parks' internal processes of reflecting on the conditions for co-production and its institutionalisation, on changing the state's practices and mode of provision of services in conditions of scarcity, have been effectively frozen. To some extent therefore, the racialisation of social relations between City officials and existing park user groups, prevents City Parks from learning lessons from these experimental and informal practices of co-production. The political delegitimisation of (white and middle-class) park user groups, and the reluctance of City Parks to share state power with and dedicate resources to groups with perceived structural (class, racial and spatial) privilege, leads City Parks (and some officials) to block needed reflection on the transformation of its own practices.

This is ultimately damaging both for service delivery and for City Parks' key strategic objective—redressing the wrongs of the past, bridging the green divide, and developing universal access to and enjoyment of urban parks and the environment. Indeed, the absence of templates for agreements and tools for the co-management of parks, and the lack of reform of City Parks' institutions and practices, is also and perhaps even more detrimental to lower-income communities: in townships, informal settlements, and the inner city. There, partnerships with City Parks (in the form of delegation, the partnership that is the most formalised and the easiest) are unlikely, as local communities have not organised around parks. They have not done so for a multiplicity of reasons: because parks are a scarce or new urban asset, or are not seen as the most crucial issue for collective mobilisation; because residents have got used to open spaces being hazards rather than assets (see Hadebe, 2015; Mcetywa et al., 2015); or because there is limited capacity or opportunity for fundraising. In these lower-income or less-organised areas, co-production championed by City Parks might be the only way to mobilise local residents, and garner local resources that might exist locally in the form of multiple uses and investment in the park, but remain fragmented and isolated.

Co-production remains a theoretical and practical frontier, worth analysing beyond radical critiques of neo-liberalising or 'governmentalising' partnerships. Much work remains to be done to unpack the technical, existential and political challenges entailed by processes of framing new rules, institutions and practices if one wants to go beyond informal pilots that are flexible but under-resourced and under-recognised, yet mobilise needed resources and provide forms of public goods in challenging environments. The question of the uneven capacity for co-production, across segregated spaces and unequal communities, remains; but co-production in this respect might be a lesser evil than delegation—practically efficient in selected spaces and with resourced partners, but more directly reproducing metropolitan inequalities and local exclusions.

Co-production involves both an existential and a technical reflection within the state. An existential reflection on the definition of the state's mandate and the selection of what it can delegate versus what needs to remain core; on the nature of City Parks' social and public objectives, and how they can be delivered, possibly by non-state agents, without compromising these objectives; on the trade-offs between sharing power and control. A technical reflection on the tools—their legality and practicality; their cost and their benefits—needed to set up and institutionalise the space for co-production. Here, the current proliferation of formats of agreement (MoAs, MoUs, SLAs, letters of adoption…) shows innovation and experiment in framing locally adapted partnerships in the absence of a broader template to guide them—an effort that City Parks has at least temporarily set aside. However, in these experiments, the temptation is to go for the simplest tools—delegation rather than co-production (which would imply not only resourcing from City Parks but also a change in practice, a prioritisation of engagement and community facilitation that has not (yet?) been adopted as a strategic priority by City Parks). As Stone (2006) suggests, it is probably much easier for the state to establish and monitor market-based exchanges than it is to frame and guide the blurred, shifting, complex and personalised relationships involved in community engagement—even if delegation, far more than co-production, consolidates inequality of public provision between resourced and un-resourced communities and spaces.

4 Conclusion

Why is the co-management of parks not working in Johannesburg? A number of elements explain this challenge. Contextual elements—as City Parks has not prioritised community engagement in its strategic objectives and has framed it in confused and often exclusively neo-liberal ways: as damage control, as income-generating, or as precarious job distribution. Organisational elements—as the mandate for community engagement lies in diverse, overlapping and competing administrative units marked by various professional and bureaucratic cultures that sometimes are resistant to change, still considering City Parks as the sole provider of services in line with its traditional public mandate, and in denial when it comes to its incapacity to deliver services on its own. But also, it needs to be acknowledged that the institutionalisation of co-production is extraordinarily complex—technically and politically—and that this complexity fuels the conservative forces within the state. It seems much easier for City Parks to delegate park management to resourced partners (at no direct cost to City Parks, and involving little change in its practices, tools and self-representation) than to put City Parks resources and energies into engaging in regular forums or committees of co-production, inventing new instruments and reshaping its own mandate, accepting the power trade-offs and skill reshuffling requested by such partnerships. These complex but productive (and possibly ultimately more efficient) paths are being experimented in Johannesburg nature reserves; but they are being blocked by a degree of racialisation of state-user groups' engagements that makes them easy to discard, and limits City Parks' ability to learn from them, refine, and institutionalise them.

The reconfiguration of this section of the state (a municipal agency that is marginalised in strategic and budgetary terms in the Johannesburg City Council) can therefore be understood as being reshaped by diverse and overlapping rationalities. The first is neo-liberal rationality and its solution set (external fundraising, use of temporary and volunteer workers, emphasis on partnerships, and protection of the brand) and modalities of bureaucratic control (quantitative KPIs). But it would not on its own suffice to explain City Parks' practices and their shift. There is secondly a degree of pragmatic rationality. Delegating park management to resourced user groups or corporates is an efficient and immediate response to a funding, staff, and skills shortage, and to the legal incapacity of the municipality to ring-fence locally raised funding (which is partly overcome through the recourse to such user groups' initiatives). It can be done simply through ready-made contracts, more readily available than complex, negotiated community agreements requiring regular interaction, legal innovation and joint problem-solving. Thirdly, besides the neo-liberal and pragmatic rationalities, there is still a powerful rationality constructed around the notion of 'transformation'—actively addressing the racial and social inequalities inherited from the past. This post-apartheid rationality drives budgetary choices (the emphasis on the distribution of small service contracts to individuals and collectives), but also forms of delegitimisation of existing user groups: good enough to be delegated park management in some cases, but not deemed worthy of setting up deep engagement and cooperation with, which would entail increasing, or at least restructuring (Ostrom, 1996), the state's human resources. Explicit redistributive mandates necessitating forms of centralised governance, together with racialised experiences of community engagements, therefore still strongly shape City Parks' practices and policy instruments, in resistance to the potential dynamics of co-production. Together with the neo-liberal and pragmatic rationalities, they lead, however, to the delegated management of well-resourced parks to the private sector, on the one hand, and to the limited mobilisation of state as well as non-state resources to manage parks in less-resourced areas, on the other, therefore paradoxically reproducing forms of separate and unequal management in the post apartheid city.

References

Arnstein, S. (1969) 'A Ladder of Citizen Participation', *Journal of the American Planning Association*, 35(4), pp. 216–224, DOI: 10.1080/01944366908977225.

Baloyi, L., M. Hunter and S. Ntombela (2015) *Community engagement with the state: deciphering resident associations' influence on park management, development and conservation in the Klipriviersberg Nature Reserve*, unpublished students report (Johannesburg: School of Architecture and Planning, Wits University).

Bénit-Gbaffou, C. (forthcoming) 'La participation au cœur de la gestion des parcs urbains ? Le cas de City Park à Johannesburg', submitted to *Revue Internationale de Politique Comparée*, August 2017.

Bénit-Gbaffou, C. (2008) 'Practices of local participation in Johannesburg—side-lining the institutional participatory channels?', *Transformation: critical perspectives on Southern Africa*, 66–67, pp. 1–34, DOI: https://doi.org/10.1353/trn.0.0003.

Bénit-Gbaffou, C. (2007) 'On conservative participation. Discussion on S. Tawa Lama-Rewal and M.H. Zerah's "middle class" mobilisation in Delhi and Mumbai', paper presented to the intenational seminar India's democratic renewal in question, Centre des Sciences Humaines, New Delhi, 9–10 July, http://hdl.handle.net/20.500.11910/5950.

Bénit-Gbaffou, C. and E. Mkwanazi (2012) 'Expressions de la xénophobie en réunion publique et construction d'une identité de quartier: le cas de Yeoville, Johannesburg', *Politique Africaine*, 127, pp. 109–134. DOI: 10.3917/polaf.127.0109.

Bosaka, P. (2015) *Changing practices of the state: Johannesburg City Parks and Zoo officials' views on opportunities and challenges of community engagement*, unpublished Honours report (Johannesburg: School of Architecture and Planning, Wits University).

Brenner, N. and N. Theodore (2002). 'Cities and the Geographies of "Actually Existing Neoliberalism"', *Antipode*, 34(3), pp. 349–379. DOI: 10.1111/1467-8330.00246.

Cooke, B. and U. Kothari (eds) (2001) *Participation, the New Tyranny?* (Chicago: University of Chicago Press).

Cornwall, A. (2008) 'Unpacking Participation: models, meanings and practices', *Community Development Journal*, 43(3), pp. 269–283, DOI: 10.1093/cdj/bsn010.

Cornwall, A. (2007) *Deliberating Democracy: Scenes from a Brazilian Municipal Health Council* IDS working paper No. 292 (Brighton: Institute for Development Studies).

Glaser, D. (2015) 'Uncooperative masses as a problem for substantive and participatory theories of democracy: The cases of 'people's power' (1984–6) and the 'xenophobia' (2008) in South Africa', in C. Bénit-Gbaffou (ed.) *Popular Politics in South African cities. Unpacking community participation*, (Cape Town: HSRC Press), pp. 139–170.

Giugni, M. (1998) 'Was It Worth the Effort? The Outcomes and Consequences of Social Movements', *Annual Review of Sociology*, 24, pp. 371–393, http://www.jstor.org/stable/223486.

Graham, S. and S. Marvin (2001) *Splintering Urbanism. Networked Infrastructures, Technological Mobilities and the Urban Condition.* (London: Routledge).

Gupta, A. (2012) *Red Tape: Bureaucracy, Structural Violence, and Poverty in India* (Durham: Duke University Press).

Hadebe, S. (2015) *Learning from communities' involvement in the management of park. The case of Zoo Lake and Thokoza Park, Johannesburg*, unpublished Honours report (Johannesburg: School of Architecture and Planning, Wits University).

Hibou, B. (2012) *La bureaucratisation du monde à l'ère néolibérale* (Paris: La découverte).

Hibou, B. (1999) La « décharge », nouvel interventionnisme. *Politique africaine* 1(73), 6–15. DOI: 10.3917/polaf.073.0006.

Hirshman, A. (1970) *Exit, Voice and Loyalty. Responses to Decline in Firms, Organisations and the State* (Cambridge: Harvard University Press).

Jacobs, J. (1961) *The Death and Life of Great American Cities* (New York: Random House).

Jaglin, S. (2008) 'Differentiating networked services in Cape Town: Echoes of splintering urbanism?', *Geoforum*, 39(6), pp. 1897–1906, DOI: 10.1016/j.geoforum.2008.04.010.

Jones, R. (2002) 'Partnerships in action: strategies for the development of voluntary community groups in urban parks', *Leisure Studies*, 21 (3–4), pp. 305–325, DOI: 10.1080/0261436022000030623.

Joshi, A. and M. Moore (2004) 'Institutionalised coproduction: Unorthodox public service delivery in challenging environments', *The Journal of Development Studies*, 40(4), pp. 31–49, DOI: 10.1080/00220380410001673184.

Krinsky, J. and M. Simonet (2017) *Who cleans your park? Public work and urban governance in New York City* (Chicago: University of Chicago Press).

Lascoumes, P. and P. Le Galès (2007) 'Introduction: Understanding Public Policy through Its Instruments—From the Nature of Instruments to the Sociology of Public Policy Instrumentation', *Governance: An International Journal of Policy, Administration, and Institutions*, 20(1), pp. 1–21, DOI: 10.1111/j.1468-0491.2007.00342.x.

MacKinnon, D. (2000) 'Managerialism, governmentality and the state: a neo-Foucauldian approach to local economic governance', *Political Geography*, 19(3), pp. 293–314, DOI: 10.1016/S0962-6298(99)00086-4.

Matubatuba, T., S. Ndlela and C. Bénit-Gbaffou (2018) *Safe but exclusive, exclusive but safe? The management of Ekhaya park by a City Improvement District in Hillbrow, Johannesburg*. CUBES report (Johannesburg: School of Architecture and Planning, Wits University).

Mcetywa, N., L. Molema, T. Thaver and X. Zondo (2015) *A Golf Course or an Eco Park in Mshenguville, Soweto? Exploring the extent of community influence in the park development process*, unpublished students' report (Johannesburg: School of Architecture and Planning, Wits University).

Miraftab, F. (2004) 'Making Neo-liberal Governance: The Disempowering Work of Empowerment', *International Planning Studies*, 9(4), pp. 239–259, DOI: 10.1080/13563470500050130.

Morange, M. (2015) 'Participation, neoliberal control and the voice of street traders in Cape Town—a Foucauldian perspective on "invited spaces"', in C. Bénit-Gbaffou (ed.), *Popular Politics in South African cities. Unpacking community participation* (Cape Town: HSRC Press), pp. 171–195.

Mokgere, T. (2016). *Constructing a joint vision for Johannesburg nature reserves: City Parks and users' committee engagements in Melville Koppies, Klipriviersberg and Kloofendal nature reserves*, unpublished Honours research report (Johannesburg: School of Architecture and Planning, Wits University).

Ostrom, E. (1996) 'Crossing the great divide: Coproduction, synergy, and development', *World Development*, 24(6), pp.1073–1087, DOI: 10.1016/0305-750X(96)00023-X.

Purcell, M. (2006) 'Urban Democracy and the Local Trap', *Urban Studies*, 43(11), pp. 1921–1941, DOI: 10.1080/00420980600897826.

Rosol, M. (2015) 'Governing cities through participation—a Foucauldian analysis of CityPlan Vancouver', *Urban Geography*, 36(2), pp. 256–276, DOI: 10.1080/02723638.2014.952542.

Rosol, M. (2012) 'Community Volunteering as Neoliberal Strategy? Green Space Production in Berlin', *Antipode*, 44(1), pp 239–257, DOI: 10.1111/j.1467-8330.2011.00861.x.

Rosol, M. (2010) 'Public Participation in Post-Fordist Urban Green Space Governance: The Case of Community Gardens in Berlin', *International Journal of Urban and Regional Research*, 34(3), pp. 548–563. DOI: 10.1111/j.1468-2427.2010.00968.x.

Roy, A. (2009) 'Civic Governmentality: The Politics of Inclusion in Beirut and Mumbai', *Antipode*, 41(1), pp. 159–179, DOI: 10.1111/j.1467-8330.2008.00660.x.

Scott, J. (1985) *Weapons of the Weak: Everyday Forms of Peasant Resistance* (New Haven: Yale University Press).

Stone, C. (2006) 'Power, Reform, and Urban Regime Analysis', *City & Community*, 5(1), pp. 23–38, DOI: 10.1111/j.1540-6040.2006.00151.x.

Turner, J. (1976) *Housing by People: Towards Autonomy in Building Environments* (London: Marion Boyars).

Uitermark, J. (2005) 'The genesis and evolution of urban policy: a confrontation of regulationist and governmentality approaches', *Political Geography*, 24, pp. 137–163, DOI: 10.1016/j.polgeo.2004.07.009.

Watson, V. (2014) 'Co-production and collaboration in planning—the difference', *Planning Theory and Practice*, 15(1), pp. 62–76, DOI: 10.1080/14649357.2013.866266.

Williams, G. (2004) 'Evaluating participatory development: tyranny, power and (re) politicisation', *Third World Quarterly*, 25(3), pp 557–578, DOI: 10.1080/0143659042000191436.

Documents

JCPZ (Johannesburg City Parks and Zoo) (2017a) *Service Level Agreement (SLA) between Johannesburg City Parks and ADT Security and CSS Tactical and Blairgowry Community Association*, September (Johannesburg: JCPZ).

JCPZ (2017b) *Memorandum of Agreement between the Johannesburg Development Agency, the Johannesburg City Parks, and Legae La Rona & eKhaya City Improvement Districts*, draft version 1.2., 27 January (Johannesburg: JCPZ).

JCPZ (2017c) *Memorandum of Agreement between Johannesburg City Parks and Zoo (JCPZ) and Friends of Kloofendaal (FrOK)*, September (Johannesburg: JCPZ).

JCPZ (2016a) *Letter to the Blairgowrie Community Association (BCA), re: their offer to adopt the Rose Garden Park in Blairgowrie*, 3 Feb (Johannesburg: JCPZ).

JCPZ (2016b) *Letter to the Cresta Ext 1 and Darrenwood Ext 2 Ratepayers Association (CDRA), re their Offer to adopt the Gilla Drive Park in Cresta*, 2 June (Johannesburg: JCPZ).

JCPZ (2016c) *Letter to the Gaylin Estate manager, re his Offer to adopt the Rose Garden in Northcliff*, 27 January (Johannesburg: JCPZ).

JCPZ (2016d) *Memorandum of Agreement between Johannesburg City Parks and AFHCO Holdings (Pty) Ltd*, 8 July (Johannesburg: JCPZ).

JCPZ (2015a) *Volunteer Policy* (Johannesburg: JCPZ).

JCPZ (2015b) *Memorandum of Agreement between Johannesburg City Parks and Zoo (JCPZ) and Friends of Kloofendaal (FrOK)*, October (Johannesburg: JCPZ).

JCPZ (2014) *2013–2014 Annual Report* (Johannesburg: JCPZ).

JCPZ (2013a) *Corporate Strategic Plan, 2013–2018.* (Johannesburg: JCPZ).

JCPZ (2013b) *Framework on Stakeholder Partnership Agreement (SPA) for Joint Natural Resources Management of Natural Areas.* Draft policy document (Johannesburg: JCPZ).

PART 3

Planning, Politics and the Urban Grey Zone

CHAPTER 6

Online Representation of Sustainable City Initiatives in Africa: How Inclusive?

Ton Dietz

Abstract

Africa's rapid population growth, and even more rapid urbanisation, creates serious sustainability challenges. Like many cities in other parts of the world, African cities try to become 'green', and promote change in urban design and lifestyles to encourage more sustainable living. Many of these initiatives are supported by international agencies and illustrated on agency websites. Studying these websites, we try to answer three related questions dealing with the inclusivity of those initiatives: the geographical coverage (which cities?), the thematic coverage (how 'holistic'?) and the social inclusivity (how inclusive in terms of social focus?). Both scholars and practitioners should become more inclusive in their approaches to sustainable cities in Africa.

> 'The challenge of achieving sustainable urban development will be particularly formidable in Africa.'
>
> COHEN 2006, 63

1 Africa's Urbanisation

Many scholars still regard Africa as a rural continent, with few and relatively unimportant megacities, compared to Asia, the Americas and Europe. In the world's leading textbooks on urban geography, Africa has received very limited attention so far (e.g. Kaplan and Holloway, 2014; Knox and McCarthy, 2012; Hall and Barrett, 2012; Pacione, 2009). Things are changing, though, because Africa is changing, and it is changing rapidly, even if its demographic transition lags behind compared to all other continents. The lowering of Africa's fertility levels started only in the 1980s and demographers expect that Africa will have completed its demographic transition only in 2100. In the meantime, Africa's population has grown from 300 million in 1960 to more than 1.2 billion in 2015, while it is expected to grow to between 3.3 and 5.6 billion in 2100 (with 4.4

 | DOI:10.1163/9789004387942_007

billion given as the median figure). High fertility levels play a major role here, but improved health care, food availability and hygiene, which together result in much higher life expectancy figures, play a role as well. A rapidly growing, relatively very young and possibly very vibrant urban African population will become a major demographic factor in the world. The demographic expectation is that Africa will have close to 40 per cent of the world's population by 2100, probably more than Asia, and more than five times the figure for Europe (see Heilig's website www.demographics.at).

Also in global terms Africa's cities are becoming relatively more important. In a comparative study, Barney Cohen (Cohen, 2006), the former Chief of the Population Studies Branch of the United Nations in New York, presents interesting data, which we summarise in Table 6.1.

Cohen noted with concern that around the year 2000 many urban Africans lacked piped water, flush toilets and electricity in their urban homes, particularly in the smaller urban centres: in sub-Saharan Africa 50 per cent of the urban households lacked these amenities in cities with fewer than 100,000 inhabitants, 40 per cent in cities of between 100,000 and 500,000 inhabitants, 35 per cent in cities of half a million to a million inhabitants, and 22 per cent in cities of more than one million inhabitants, unlike for instance North Africa (where these figures were only 5, 2, 4 and 6 per cent, respectively) or all other parts of the world (including Asia), where these figures were all much lower than in Africa. Cohen writes (2006, 75 and 77): 'There is an urgent need to build and support the capacity of local governments to manage the environmental and social service problems that accompany rapid urban growth'. He adds: 'An

TABLE 6.1 Africa's cities in world perspective

	No. of cities >1 million in Africa	**Total urban population in Africa**	**African urban population as % of world urban population**	**% of African population in cities**
1950	2	33	5	15
1975	8	103	7	25
2000	35	295	10	37
2015	*61*	*481*	*12*	*41*
2030 (pred.)		748	15	54

SOURCES: COHEN (2006); DATA FOR 1950, 1975, 2000 AND 2030 PREDICTION: PP. 70, 71 AND 75. FOR 2015: CALCULATED FROM WORLD BANK DATA AND *STATISTICS TIMES*

essential feature of current African urbanisation, is that unlike cities in much of Asia and Latin America, urbanization appears to have become decoupled from economic development. The vast majority of African cities are economically marginalized in the new global economy and most African cities are growing despite poor macroeconomic performance and without significant direct foreign investment'. This was written in the middle of that first decade of the new millennium, and based on statistics from around 2000, when it was not yet clear that Africa was about to enter an era of rapid economic growth that would last until 2015 and during which African cities (although not all) *did* become engines of rapid economic growth, and of social vitality. But it is obviously true, and it will remain true for many decades, that managing African cities, also in terms of sustainability, will be one of the major challenges of the twenty-first century.

In 2012, the African Studies Centre in Leiden produced a thematic map of 'Africa: From a Continent of States to a Continent of Cities' (Dietz et al., 2012). Table 6.2 provides an update of this thematic map for all urban agglomerations with currently more than two million inhabitants, based on data from the website citypopulation.de.[1] Other sources use other definitions of urban areas or cities, and arrive at different, often lower figures. The most important of these are the statistical sections in the UN-Habitat 'State of the African City' Reports (e.g. the one for 2014) and the World Bank data on urbanisation, the annual World Urbanization Prospect reports (United Nations Department of Economic and Social Affairs, 2014). For the thematic map, and for Table 6.2 of this chapter, we used the agglomeration assessments, because they give a more useful indication of built-up areas.

In total, Africa in early 2016 had 32 urban agglomerations with more than two million inhabitants. Of Africa's current 54 states, 36 have, today, at least one urban agglomeration with more than one million inhabitants, and the total number of African multi-million urban areas is 61. More than 150 million of Africa's 1.2 billion people now live in these multi-million agglomerations, and soon there will be many more.

2 Online Representation of Sustainable City Initiatives in Africa

Urban areas in Africa have different political and economic functions (e.g. as capital cities or harbour cities) and their locational characteristics also differ: coastal or inland; in dry lands or more humid climatological conditions.

1 More particularly the page 'Major Agglomerations of the World', http://www.citypopulation.de/world/Agglomerations.html (*see Brinkhoff's website*).

TABLE 6.2 Africa's major urban agglomerations in 2016[a]

Urban agglomeration	Country	Population in millions (1.1.2016)
Lagos	Nigeria	17.1
Cairo	Egypt	16.8
Johannesburg	South Africa	13.4
Kinshasa	DR Congo	10.6
Luanda	Angola	6.8
Khartoum	Sudan	5.6
Dar es Salaam	Tanzania	5.3
Nairobi	Kenya	5.2
Alexandria	Egypt	5.2
Abidjan	Côte d'Ivoire	5.1
Accra	Ghana	4.6
Casablanca	Morocco	4.2
Cape Town	South Africa	4.1
Kano	Nigeria	4.1
Algiers	Algeria	3.7
Addis Ababa	Ethiopia	3.5
Dakar	Senegal	3.3
Durban	South Africa	3.2
Ibadan	Nigeria	3.2
Kampala	Uganda	3.0
Bamako	Mali	3.0
Abuja	Nigeria	2.8
Douala	Cameroon	2.8
Yaoundé	Cameroon	2.7
Kumasi	Ghana	2.7
Tunis	Tunisia	2.5

Urban agglomeration	Country	Population in millions (1.1.2016)
Harare	Zimbabwe	2.3
Lusaka	Zambia	2.3
Antananarivo	Madagascar	2.2
Conakry	Guinea	2.2
Maputo	Mozambique	2.2
Ouagadougou	Burkina Faso	2.1
Port Harcourt	Nigeria	2.1

a According to Brinkhoff's website, 'Urban agglomerations include a central city and neighboring places mostly linked by (more or less) continuously built-up areas. Some agglomerations have more than one central city'. Compared to the 2012 data from the same source, two towns in Somalia (Mogadishu and Hargeisa) dropped below the two million threshold used here, while Pretoria had become part of Greater Johannesburg. Bamako, Maputo, Antananarivo, Lusaka, Yaoundé, Ouagadougou, Conakry and Port Harcourt had all crossed the two million threshold in those few years.

SOURCE: BRINKHOFF T., HTTP://WWW.CITYPOPULATION.DE/WORLD/AGGLOMERATIONS.HTML

Environmental conditions may determine perceptions of sustainability: coastal areas are prone to storms, flooding and sea level rise (UN-Habitat, 2014), while dry lands can face droughts and water stress. Political and economic conditions may determine the urge of national governments to deal with popular concerns, including living conditions, some of which are related to sustainability issues. So it is wise to look at the characteristics of cities if one wants to get an idea of their environmental challenges, and if one wants to understand the diversity of sustainable city initiatives. In this second part of the chapter we will present various representations of Africa's sustainability experiences on relevant Internet sites. We will look at these representations, and ask ourselves three related questions, all dealing with the inclusiveness of sustainability: (1) what is the geographical coverage of these sustainable city initiatives (which cities are the 'favourites' of the various 'African sustainable cities' websites, and which ones are not?), (2) what is the thematic coverage? (how 'holistic' is the representation; what themes get most attention?), and (3) how do these websites present the social inclusiveness of 'their' sustainable city initiatives?

3 The EIU/Siemens Project: African Green City Index

One of the most informative overviews of sustainable city initiatives in Africa is given in a report by The Economist Intelligence Unit (EIU) (supported by Siemens) in 2010, the African Green City Index. Following comparable assessments of cities in Europe, Latin America, Asia, the USA and Canada, the Unit carried out an extensive survey of 15 major African cities, and tried to apply eight different main assessment criteria together with 25 sub-criteria (EIU, 2011, 31; Table 6.3 of this chapter presents the results). Some cities could not be included because of a lack of data; for example, Kinshasa, Khartoum and Algiers were explicitly mentioned and data availability and reliability was a major problem in almost all other cities as well.

For the fifteen major African cities selected by The Economist Intelligence Unit, the results of the assessment of environmental performance show major differences. The assessment was based on a combination of EIU judgements, Siemens judgements, and judgements made by a panel of six external, independent experts, the last of which, however, did not include a single African (see EIU, 2011, 4). Table 6.4 gives the details, combining scores on a five-point scale (from ++ to --) with major and minor highlights mentioned in the text (H and h). Highlights show the most important recent initiatives (that is, before 2010) undertaken by city governments in any of the eight categories of 'major issues'.

Three South African cities lead the assessment, and they share eight of the 24 highlighted examples among them, including attention to Cape Town's energy policy, Durban's overall environmental governance, and Johannesburg's efforts to improve the city's land use in a sustainable way. Two North African cities (Casablanca and Tunis) follow, as does Accra in Ghana, which gets a major highlight for its water and sanitation approaches, and a minor one for environmental governance. These six cities get a positive overall assessment. Five African cities receive an average judgement: one in West Africa (Lagos, with a special highlight for its waste management approaches), two in Egypt (Cairo, with a special highlight for its transport approach and Alexandria, with a special highlight for water and sanitation policies), one in the Horn of Africa (Addis Ababa) and one in South Africa (Pretoria/Tshwane). Four cities get an overall negative assessment (Nairobi and Luanda) or even an overall very negative assessment (Dar es Salaam and Maputo). For Luanda, Nairobi and Maputo the report highlights some attempts to develop better environmental governance and for Dar es Salaam and Maputo minor highlights are presented regarding water and sanitation initiatives.

The scores on energy and CO2 reflect the major differences in energy consumption and energy composition on the continent, on the one hand, with

TABLE 6.3 EIU criteria for the African Green City Index

Issues (main criteria)	Sub-criteria
Energy and CO_2	Percentage of households with access to electricity. Electricity consumption per capita CO_2 emissions from electricity Measure of a city's efforts to reduce carbon emissions
Land Use	Population density Percentage of population living in informal settlements Green spaces per capita (sum of all public parks, recreation areas and 'greenways') Land use policy
Transport	Public transport network: length of superior transport network (bus rapid transit, trams, light rail and 'subway'), and length of mass transport network Urban mass transport policy Congestion reduction policy
Waste	Total annual volume of waste generated by the city Waste collection and disposal policy Waste recycling and reuse policy
Water	Access to potable waterWater consumption per capita Water system leakages Water quality policy Water sustainability policy
Sanitation	Population with access to improved sanitation (share of the total population either with sanitation connections to sewerage or access to on-site sources) Sanitation policy: measure of a city's efforts to reduce pollution associated with inadequate sanitation
Air Quality	Clean air policy: measure of a city's efforts to reduce air pollution
Environmental Governance	Environmental management: measure of the extensiveness of environmental management undertaken by the city Environmental monitoring: measure of the city's efforts to monitor its environmental performance Public participation: measure of the city's efforts to involve the public in environmental decision-making.

SOURCE: EIU (2011, 31)

TABLE 6.4 Assessment of environmental performance in 15 major African cities

City	Energy and CO2	Land use	Transport	Waste	Water	Sanitation	Air quality	Environmental governance	Total
Cape Town	-H	++	+	+h	+h	o	+	+	+/6
Durban	-	+	+	+h	+h	+	+	+H	+/6
Johannesburg	+	+H	+h	o	o	o	+	+	+/5
Casablanca	+	+h	o	o	+	+	+	o	+/5
Accra	+h	o	-	o	oH	+	+	++h	+/4
Tunis	-	oh	+h	+	o	+	+	o	+/3
Lagos	++h	-	oh	+H	o	o	o	o	o/2
Addis Ababa	++	+h	-	o	+	o	-	-	o/1
Alexandria	o	-	o	++h	-H	o	o	o	o/o
Cairo	o	o	+H	-	oh	o	o	o	o/o
Pretoria	-h	o	+h	--	o	-	+	+	o/-1
Nairobi	-	oh	-	o	o	o	-	-h	-/-4
Dar es Salaam	o	-h	-	--	oH	--	-	-	--/-8
Maputo	-	-	-	oh	-H	--	-	-h	--/-8
Luanda	o	--	--	o	--	o	-	--h	-/-9
Average	+1	o	-1	+1	o	-1	+2	o	o/+2

SOURCE: BASED ON EIU (2011, 31). THE LAST COLUMN GIVES THE ASSESSMENT BY EIU/SIEMENS (++ TO --) AND MY OWN CALCULATION OF THE NUMBER OF PLUSSES AND MINUSES GIVEN; THE CITIES APPEAR IN ORDER OF BEST OVERALL PERFORMANCE

South African cities surpassing all other cities by far (although mainly based on coal), but on the other hand also reflects efforts to address the so-called carbon footprint, where Cape Town is the continent's pioneer, but examples given for Pretoria, Accra and Lagos (see LASEPA website) also show that there are serious attempts to develop solar and wind energy sources, as well as to use the opportunities that carbon credit schemes give to lower carbon emissions. As the first African metropolis, Cape Town launched its Integrated Environmental Policy in 2003 and this was followed by a climate change strategy in 2006, while the Cape Town Energy and Climate Change Plan was launched in 2011 (City of

Cape Town, 2011). The city also took an initiating role in bringing African cities into the 'Compact of Mayors' that was launched in June 2016 (See Global Covenant of Mayors for Climate & Energy website).

For land use, the main example that was highlighted dealt with the impressive attempts of the Johannesburg Development Agency (which started in 2001) to combine urban renewal, inner-city regeneration, transport improvements and better security. These have attracted many private investors and led to the launch of a large number of initiatives in the form of public–private collaborations (See Johannesburg Development Agency's website). Other examples of land use improvement given are a major reforestation effort around Addis Ababa as well as the renewal of the city's parks, urban agriculture initiatives in Casablanca, the green line project to establish a perimeter forest around the Nairobi National Park and attempts to revitalise Swahili building styles in Dar es Salaam.

For transport issues, Cairo was chosen to highlight a combination of efforts to deal with heavy congestion problems on the city's roads. This combines a major extension of the metro system, changing buses to ones that use compressed natural gas, and a carbon finance vehicle scrapping and recycling project to replace old taxis. Additional smaller highlights were given regarding the Johannesburg–Pretoria high-speed rail link, the light rail project in Tunis, together with the creation of rapid bus corridors, and finally Lagos's public–private partnership to develop rapid transit buses.

Waste management gets considerable attention. The major highlight is the way Lagos changed a very dilapidated system to a much more effective approach, through the creation of a new Lagos Waste Management Authority and its 'waste-to-wealth programme' (see the LAWMA website). With regard to Cape Town the report shows the importance of waste separation initiatives, an integrated waste exchange website, and the city's *Smart Living Handbook*. For Maputo it shows the way that the city has introduced waste management into its informal settlements, for Alexandria a new mercury waste processing plant, and for Durban the way that the city has started to support informal waste pickers.

Water and sanitation issues were separately judged, but the highlights combined them. Seven approaches were highlighted. Accra, with its strategic planning for urban water management and its 2030 vision for improved sanitation, Alexandria with its attempts to reduce water intake from the River Nile ('Switch urban water'), Dar es Salaam with its campaign for water education and Maputo for its city-wide sanitation strategy got the most attention. But Cairo's rehabilitation project for water and sanitation in the old city, Casablanca's private contractor to manage the city's water and sanitation, and Durban's sewage education programme were also mentioned.

Air pollution received some attention in the scores: in five of the 15 African cities that were compared, air quality was below world average levels, despite the fact that the major reason for bad air quality—industrial pollution and vehicle emissions—is (still) a less prominent problem in Africa than elsewhere in the world.

Finally, the issue of environmental governance received (very) positive scores in Accra and in the three South African cities that were part of the comparison. Major highlights were given for Durban and a minor one for Accra, but also for three cities with (very) negative overall assessments and also with negative assessments for environmental governance (Luanda, Maputo and Nairobi), probably to show that not all is lost. Durban's case is the most interesting one. The city introduced its comprehensive 'Imagine Durban' approach,[2] with a lot of involvement from civil society and citizen organisations. It also formulated goals to become a zero-waste city in 2020 and a carbon neutral city by 2050. For Accra the report mentions the greenhouse gas emission identification efforts made in order to prepare for a climate change mitigation policy. Despite its negative position on the overall assessment scores, Luanda was highlighted as an example due to the establishment of an environmental database focusing on the city (supported by the African Development Bank)[3], as was Maputo for its environmental education programme in schools (with emphases on tree planting and beach cleaning approaches), and finally Nairobi, where the government was working on an online approach to enable citizens to monitor their water and energy consumption (see for example, World Bank, 2015).

4 Institutional Landscape of (Online) Sustainable City Collaborations/Networks with African Participation

The institutional 'landscape' for sustainable city collaboration in Africa, and with other parts of the world, is quite complicated. One organisation that has been active since 1990 is ICLEI, the International Council for Local Environmental Initiatives. Since 2012 it has had a separate Africa ICLEI Committee and

2 See ASSAF's website: http://www.assaf.org.za/files/2010/04/Imagine-Durban-LTDF-2009.pdf

3 See EIU (2011), and more particularly the Green City Index on Luanda: https://www.siemens.com/entry/cc/features/greencityindex_international/all/en/pdf/luanda.pdf (accessed on 3 May 2018).

there is also an African office in Cape Town (the organisation's World Secretariat is in Bonn). According to the Council's website, 74 municipalities in Africa from a total of 18 African countries have joined, and 19 of these are 'profiled members' (plus two local government associations) from a total of 12 African countries[4]. South Africa is by far the most active country in this network, with eight cities participating as profiled members, including Johannesburg, Durban and Pretoria. Of the other megacities in Africa (> two million inhabitants, see Table 2) Dakar and Addis Ababa are 'profiled members' and Cape Town, Dar es Salaam, Kampala, Lagos and Port Elizabeth/Nelson Mandela Bay are ordinary members.

Another relevant global network is UCLG Africa (United Cities and Local Governments, Africa Section) with its headquarters in Dakar.[5] Together with ICLEI it partnered with UN-Habitat to produce the 'State of the African City' report of 2014 (UN-Habitat, 2014). The organisation's website gives access to all relevant national associations of local government, including the important South African Association of Local Government Authorities[6] and the Association des Maires du Sénégal (AMS).[7] Its focus on sustainability is rather limited, though, with the exception of the attention paid to informal settlements, and their environmental problems, in the 'Know Your City' programme, with a special focus on Ouagadougou and Lusaka.

A third network is Rockefeller Foundation's 100 Resilient Cities (http://www.100resilientcities.org), with eleven participants from Africa, including a few surprising ones: Accra, Addis Ababa, Cape Town, Dakar, Durban, Enugu (in Nigeria), Kigali, Lagos, Luxor, Nairobi and Paynesville (in Liberia). On its website, the Rockefeller project states: 'As of May 2016, the 100 Resilient Cities network has reached 100 members. The new group of cities spans five continents and is diverse in both its makeup and the challenges the cities face. The 100 Resilient Cities Challenge is the application process by which cities join our network. 100RC selected a first group of 32 cities in December 2013, a second group of 35 in 2014, and its final round of winners in May 2016 [including six new 'winners' from Africa]. Members of the 100 Resilient Cities team and a panel of expert judges reviewed over 1,000 applications from prospective cities. The judges looked for innovative mayors, a recent catalyst for change, a history of building partnerships, and an ability to work with a wide range

4 See ICLEI's African Secretariat website: http://africa.iclei.org.
5 See UCLG Africa website: http://www.uclga.org.
6 See SALGA's website: http://www.salga.org.za.
7 See UCLG Africa website: http://www.afriquelocale.org/fr/ams.

of stakeholders'. Africa is relatively well represented now, after North America (with 31 member cities), Asia (with 20) and Europe (with 17).

A fourth network, also with a major input from the USA (funded by three philanthropic organisations), but with offices in New York, London and Rio de Janeiro, is C40 (http://c40.org), for so-called climate action cities. It is connected to the Clinton Climate Initiative. Nine African megacities are part of this network, and there is a separate directorate for Africa within C40, directed by economist and 'environmental diplomat' Hastings Chikoko, from Malawi. The participating African cities (so far) are Cairo, Accra, Lagos, Addis Ababa, Nairobi, Dar es Salaam, Johannesburg, Durban and Cape Town. Johannesburg plays a key role.

Canada has launched its own support programme for sustainable cities (http://sustainablecities.net/), based in Vancouver. It has three African partner cities: Dakar in Senegal, with three projects, Dar es Salaam with two projects, and Durban in South Africa, also with two projects. These are all part of the so-called PLUS network for sustainability learning.

The Fondation Africaine pour la Gestion Urbaine, a network that started in Senegal and that was based at the Institut Africain de Gestion Urbaine (IAGU) in Dakar (IAGU, 2008), mainly deals with cities in French-speaking Africa, with projects in Dakar, Thiès and Pikine in Senegal, but also (with an emphasis on urban agriculture) in Burkina Faso (Bobo Dioulasso), Benin (Porto Novo), Rwanda (Kigali) and Mauritania (Nouakchott). With the exception of Dakar, no other African megacity (defined as having agglomerations of more than two million inhabitants) participates.

In preparation for the climate conference in Paris in 2015 a lot of effort was mobilised to stimulate debates about Africa's sustainability issues,[8] and part of it was focused on issues of urban sustainability (see Dago, 2014). To create *villes durables* (sustainable cities) the focus should be on six elements, according to this approach: connect health and the environment, stimulate resilience, emphasise popular participation (through *sensibilisation* (sensitization)), diversify finances to fund green initiatives, create stakeholder platforms (*cerveaux collectifs*), and adapt and readjust for every city, connecting environmental, social, economic and cultural specificities.

In 2016, partly as a response to the climate conference in Paris, many mayors of the world formed the Compact of Mayors (see Global Covenant of Mayors for Climate & Energy website). For all participating cities, the organisation's website shows a map of the city, the name of the current mayor, mostly the current population figure, and what the city has done in terms of commitment,

8 See the AfriqueCroissanceVerte website: https://afriquecroissanceverte.com/.

inventory, target formulation and planning for climate mitigation and adaptation. It is the intention to also add data about greenhouse gas emissions and sectoral composition for each city. Almost all African cities are still in the 'commitment phase', but Cape Town and Durban have completed all phases, and one can download the climate adaptation and climate action plans for these cities. The Compact of Mayors has so far managed to connect to 18 of Africa's multi-million agglomerations and to 32 other African cities.

With growing privatisation and many public–private partnerships in environmental management it is also relevant to mention a site that provides a global overview of environmental companies, including of more than 1,500 companies working in Africa: Environmental XPRT.[9] The large majority of these companies have their headquarters elsewhere in the world, but they also have an office, or are distributors, in Africa, and particularly in South Africa. But there are also African companies and NGOs on the list (like the Water and Sewerage Company in Nairobi, and the Waste Management Society of Nigeria, based in Port Harcourt).

If we look at all those initiatives and focus on Africa's multi-million agglomerations it is obvious that some of those urban areas are leading in many initiatives, and others are invisible (see Table 6.5).

TABLE 6.5 Summary of online networks/assessments of participating African megacities

Urban agglomeration	EIU	C40	Rockefeller	SSnet	ICLEI [/UCLG]	Compact
Lagos	+	+	+		+	+
Cairo	+	+				
Johannesburg/ Pretoria	++	+			+	+
Kinshasa						+
Luanda	+					
Khartoum						
Dar es Salaam	+	+		+	+	
Nairobi	+	+	+			+
Alexandria	+					

9 See Environmental XPRT, *Environmental Industry Companies in Africa* webpage : https://www.environmental-expert.com/companies/location-africa (accessed on 3 May 2018).

TABLE 6.5 Summary of online networks/assessments of participating African megacities (*cont.*)

<table>
<tr><th>Urban agglomeration</th><th>EIU</th><th>C40</th><th>Rockefeller</th><th>SSnet</th><th>ICLEI [/UCLG]</th><th>Compact</th></tr>
<tr><td>Abidjan</td><td></td><td></td><td></td><td></td><td></td><td>+</td></tr>
<tr><td>Accra</td><td>+</td><td>+</td><td>+</td><td></td><td></td><td>+</td></tr>
<tr><td>Casablanca</td><td>+</td><td></td><td></td><td></td><td></td><td></td></tr>
<tr><td>Cape Town</td><td>+</td><td>+</td><td>+</td><td></td><td>+</td><td>+</td></tr>
<tr><td>Kano</td><td></td><td></td><td></td><td></td><td></td><td></td></tr>
<tr><td>Algiers</td><td></td><td></td><td></td><td></td><td></td><td></td></tr>
<tr><td>Addis Ababa</td><td>+</td><td>+</td><td></td><td></td><td>+</td><td>+</td></tr>
<tr><td>Dakar</td><td></td><td></td><td>+</td><td>+</td><td>+</td><td>+</td></tr>
<tr><td>Durban</td><td>+</td><td>|</td><td>+</td><td>+</td><td>+</td><td>+</td></tr>
<tr><td>Ibadan</td><td></td><td></td><td></td><td></td><td></td><td></td></tr>
<tr><td>Kampala</td><td></td><td></td><td></td><td></td><td>+</td><td>+</td></tr>
<tr><td>Bamako</td><td></td><td></td><td></td><td></td><td></td><td></td></tr>
<tr><td>Abuja</td><td></td><td></td><td></td><td></td><td></td><td></td></tr>
<tr><td>Douala</td><td></td><td></td><td></td><td></td><td></td><td></td></tr>
<tr><td>Yaoundé</td><td></td><td></td><td></td><td></td><td></td><td>+</td></tr>
<tr><td>Kumasi</td><td></td><td></td><td></td><td></td><td></td><td></td></tr>
<tr><td>Tunis</td><td>+</td><td></td><td></td><td></td><td></td><td></td></tr>
<tr><td>Harare</td><td></td><td></td><td></td><td></td><td></td><td>+</td></tr>
<tr><td>Lusaka</td><td></td><td></td><td></td><td></td><td>[+]</td><td></td></tr>
<tr><td>Antananarivo</td><td></td><td></td><td></td><td></td><td></td><td></td></tr>
<tr><td>Conakry</td><td></td><td></td><td></td><td></td><td></td><td></td></tr>
<tr><td>Maputo</td><td>+</td><td></td><td></td><td></td><td></td><td></td></tr>
<tr><td>Ouagadougou</td><td></td><td></td><td></td><td></td><td>[+]</td><td></td></tr>
<tr><td>Port Harcourt</td><td></td><td></td><td></td><td></td><td></td><td></td></tr>
</table>

SOURCE: AUTHOR'S OWN ANALYSIS OF THE VARIOUS WEBSITES MENTIONED IN THE TEXT. CITIES ARE LISTED IN DESCENDING ORDER OF NUMBER OF INHABITANTS, FOLLOWING THE ORDER USED IN TABLE 6.2

5 UN-Habitat's State of African Cities

UN-Habitat is the institutional flagship organisation within the UN system dealing with urban issues. It is based in Nairobi and can be expected to pay special attention to Africa. Since 2008 it has published three overviews of the state of Africa's cities (UN-Habitat 2008, 2010 and 2014). In 2008, the report was published together with the United Nations Commission for Africa (UNECA), the United Nations Environmental Programme (UNEP) and the International Development Research Centre (IDRC) in Canada. In 2010 only UNEP stayed as a partner, and in 2014 the partnership changed to include both ICLEI and UCLG. In 2008, urban environmental challenges were one of six major themes. In 2010, the report had a very geographical set up: with sections on the social geography of urbanisation, the economic geography of cities, the geography of urban land markets and the geography of climate change. The report published in 2014 explicitly deals with urban sustainability in its sections on social and environmental challenges. In these reports UN-Habitat's strongly geographical outlook means a strong emphasis on broad geographical and thematic inclusiveness, and a growing emphasis on the combination of sustainability issues and social inclusion issues, particularly in sections regarding vulnerability to climate change and in those dealing with the health risks of pollution and waste management. In the UN-Habitat 2014 publication there are many references to the recent wave of 'climate change and cities' publications, including Rosenzweig et al. (2011). Another work referred to is the ICLEI study authored by Kemp et al. (2011): *Sub-Saharan African Cities: A Five-City Network to Pioneer Climate Adaptation Through Participatory Research & Local Action*. These authors (some of them biologists) were based in Cape Town when they carried out the study. Cartwright et al. (2012) published another relevant study about Cape Town itself in 2012. One of its authors is a leading urban geographer in South Africa, Sue Parnell. Some of these studies connect issues of climate change with urban food security, as does the work of Frayne et al. (2013). Bruce Frayne and Gina Ziervogel are geographers, connected to the University of Cape Town. Sustainable city initiatives in South Africa have become an important, if not dominant, element in Africa's sustainability efforts, and we will therefore continue with a brief focus on South Africa.

6 The South African Cities Network

In South Africa, the South African Cities Network started in 2002, and has so far published four reports about 'the state of South African cities' (SACN). On its website, the Network states: 'The South African Cities Network (SACN) is an established network of South African cities and partners that encourages the exchange of information, experience and best practices on urban development and city management. As both a research source and a catalyst for debate, the SACN covers the full scope of the urban management process, under the following thematic areas: city development, inclusive cities, sustainable cities, well-governed cities and productive cities'. And under the heading of 'sustainable cities' there are four major topics: sustainable energy, improving waste management, improving water management, and mitigating climate change effects. To date, there have been four 'state of South African cities' reports (see SACN, 2004, 2006, 2011 and 2016). From the start 'sustainable cities' was a major and recurrent theme. In 2016, there was also a 'People's Guide'.

The chapter about sustainable cities in the 2016 SACN document about South African Cities (SACN, 2016) was written by Sandiswa Tshaka, an energy and climate change expert who previously worked for the Danish Embassy, and by Gillian Maree, who had professional training as a spatial planner in the Netherlands and who has worked to support spatial economic policy and strategic environmental planning in South Africa. The key messages in this chapter come very close to a fully holistic approach: 'The typical South African city is growing in a resource-intensive way and suffers from inefficiencies across all sectors (energy, food, water, waste and transport). The current silo approach to planning and delivery is inefficient and increases risks of exclusion. Cities should pursue spatial transformation, which encourages compact cities and sustainable neighbourhoods that value natural and open spaces. Sustainability and growth are interdependent, and so sustainability must be fundamentally embedded in a city's development paradigm, and not just in its long-term visions and strategies. Cities need to tackle resource efficiency aggressively' (SACN, 2016, 12).

One of the leading think tanks addressing Africa's urban and urban environmental issues is firmly connected to geography and urban planning: the University of Cape Town's African Centre for Cities (ACC). Many of its research projects and publications deal with Cape Town itself, but there is also a growing connection to other cities in southern Africa, cities in Africa more generally, and cities elsewhere, with a major attempt to connect African and Asian experiences. The ACC is a central player in major academic and think tank networks concerned with sustainable cities with a focus on Africa: UrbanAfrica.net ('communicating about African cities'), the Association of African Planning Schools,[10]

10 See the Association of African Planning Schools (AAPS) website: http://www.africanplanningschools.org.za/.

the African Urban Research Initiative[11] and the African Food Security Network.[12] The ACC's director, Edgar Pieterse (with a PhD from the London School of Economics) holds the South African Research Chair in Urban Policy at UCT, but is also one of four African members of the Sustainable Development Solutions Network[13] (SDSN; based in Paris and New York as the UN's think tank for sustainable cities).[14] Among Pieterse's most influential publications are *City futures: Confronting the crisis of urban development* (Pieterse, 2008) and 'The "right to the city": institutional imperatives of a developmental state' (Parnell and Pieterse, 2010). A more recent work by Parnell and Pieterse is concerned with Africa's urban revolution (Parnell and Pieterse, 2014). South Africa's leading role in Africa's sustainable cities 'movement' is very much assisted by the important role think tanks such as the AAC play, but also by the way metropolitan governments in South Africa use information databases to make informed choices on where to prioritise investments in better environmental services (see Sutherland et al. 2015).

7 Online Sustainability Representations and Social Inclusion

Looking at the various Internet representations of sustainable cities initiatives in Africa presented in this chapter one cannot escape the impression that most focus on well-to-do neighbourhoods that are part of planned city expansions or those developed by city development or housing companies. Also, demands for 'better environmental care' often come from middle-class (or upper-class) activists, with limited attention paid to the living conditions and major environmental issues in shanty towns and among the urban poor. As there is a

11 More information on the African Urban Research Initiative (AURI) on http://www.africancentreforcities.net/programme/knowledge-networks/african-urban-research-initiative.

12 See the African Food Security Urban Network (AFSUN) website: http://www.afsun.org.

13 Other African members of the SDSN Network are Martin Oteng-Ababio, geographer at the University of Ghana at Legon, climate change expert Debra Roberts of the Ethekwini Municipality (Durban), and urban planner Rafael Tuts of UN-Habitat (with a degree as an architectural engineer from the University of Leuven, Belgium). The UN started this initiative in 2012 with a goal to "mobilize global scientific and technological expertise to promote practical problem solving for sustainable development, including the design and implementation of the Sustainable Development Goals (SDGs)" (see the SDSN website, i.e. http://unsdsn.org/about-us/vision-and-organization/). Martin Oteng-Ababio's most cited work is about waste management in Accra; see Grant and Oteng-Ababio (2012); Oteng-Ababio et al. (2013).

14 See the Thematic Network 'Sustainable Cities: Inclusive, Resilient, and Connected': http://unsdsn.org/what-we-do/thematic-networks/sustainable-cities-inclusive-resilient-and-connected (accessed on 3 May 2018).

clear tendency for the urban poor to live in the most risky and vulnerable areas (in particular, marshy and flood-prone areas near coasts are noteworthy: areas where ever more urban poor start their urban lives), attention to urban sustainability should highlight these areas and people, but this often does not happen, and is not the highest priority for eager city planners and city administrators who want their cities to shine on prestigious websites. . The growing attention being paid to climate change (Bicknell et al., 2009; Carmin et al., 2012; Simon, 2013; Dodman et al., 2015; Wisner et al., 2015) and the inclusion of 'sustainable cities and communities' as Goal 11 of the Sustainable Development Goals might change that bias: the highest social vulnerability to the effects of climate change can be found in the neighbourhoods with the most problematic environmental conditions. Particularly in coastal cities many informal settlements can be found in high-risk locations with regard to storms, floods and disease outbreaks. Cities like Durban and Cape Town can probably be seen as useful and early cases of experimentation where a holistic approach to sustainability has been combined with sincere attention to social inclusiveness from scholars and in some cases also from urban planners, although a lot more could have been done and could be done (see, e.g., Roberts and Nicci (2002); Sutherland et al. (2015) for Durban, and Cartwright et al. (2012) for Cape Town).

8 Conclusion

Although recently many initiatives have attempted to stimulate African cities to develop policies for more sustainable urban development, the geographical coverage of those initiatives is by no means complete, and websites devoted to these 'sustainable city initiatives' in Africa show a very unbalanced picture, with some South African and some North African cities getting a lot of attention, together with cities like Accra, Lagos and Nairobi, but with other cities enjoying much less, particularly those outside anglophone countries. In terms of thematic coverage for African cities as a whole, the websites show that all major aspects are covered, with particular attention given to waste management and water management. However, for almost all individual cities (except for Cape Town and Durban), there is no 'holistic approach', and the institutional set-up of most metropolitan regions does not stimulate a holistic approach to integrated environmental management. And if we look at the third aspect of 'inclusion', social inclusiveness, the Internet representation of successful urban sustainability projects seems to favour well-to-do neighbourhoods and new neighbourhoods. We recommend that policymakers become more inclusive, and that scholars—as well as scholarly informed international agencies working to stimulate urban sustainability in Africa—become more focused on the three types of inclusion outlined in this chapter: wider geographical coverage, a more holistic approach, and attention given to the social inclusiveness of approaches and effects. We also recommend much more active participation by the urban poor, and their organisations where those exist. To enable such an approach, urban planners, environmental scientists and urban geographers should devote more energy to liaising with urban anthropologists, and others for whom participatory observation, and long-term involvement with and among the urban poor, is a more natural habitus than for many current urban sustainability experts.

Acknowledgements

An earlier version of this chapter was published as a working paper on the website of the African Studies Centre Leiden (www.ascleiden.nl) as 'Sustainable City initiatives in Africa and comparison with the OURSUS approach'. An outline was presented at the IGU Congress in Beijing, on 22 August 2016, and benefited from comments by Qiu Li and Brij Maharaj, as well as other people participating at the conference. Additional discussions took place during the annual conference of the Netherlands Association of African Studies, in 2017, and during the 7th European Conference on African Studies (ECAS) in Basel in 2017.

References

Bicknell, J., D. Dodman and D. Satterthwaite, eds. (2009) *Adapting Cities to Climate Change: Understanding and addressing the development challenges* (London: Earthscan).

Carmin, J., I. Anguelovski and D. Roberts (2012) 'Urban climate adaptation in the global south planning in an emerging policy domain' *Journal of Planning Education and Research* 32(1), pp. 18–32, DOI: 10.1177/0739456X11430951.

Cartwright, A., S. Parnell, G. Oelofse and S. Ward (eds.) (2012) *Climate change at the city scale: Impacts, mitigation and adaptation in Cape Town* (London, New York: Routledge).

City of Cape Town (2011) *Moving Mountains. Cape Town's Action Plan for Energy and Climate Change.* (City of Cape Town: Cape Town) http://resource.capetown.gov.za/documentcentre/Documents/Graphics%20and%20educational%20material/Moving_Mountains_Energy+CC_booklet_2011-11.pdf (accessed on 3 May 2018).

Cohen, B. (2006) 'Urbanization in developing countries: current trends, future projections and key challenges for sustainability', *Technology in Society* 28(1), pp. 63–80, DOI: 10.1016/j.techsoc.2005.10.005.

Dago, S. (2014) '7 exigences pour les villes durables en Afrique de l'Ouest', *Afriquecroissance-verte*, https://afriquecroissanceverte.com/2014/10/02/villes-durables-en-afrique-de-louest-7-exigences-pour-en-faire-une-realite/ (accessed on 3 May 2018).

Dietz, T., D. Foeken, S. Soeters and N. de Vink (2012) *Africa: from a continent of states to a continent of cities* (Leiden: African Studies Centre), http://hdl.handle.net/1887/20017.

Dodman, D., K. Soltesova, D. Satterthwaite and C. Tacoli (2015) *Understanding the Assessment and Reduction of Vulnerability to Climate Change in African Cities: A Focus on Low-Income and Informal Settlements*, Série grise (Paris: Agence Française de Développement), https://www.afd.fr/en/understanding-assessment-and-reduction-vulnerability-climate-change-african-cities-focus-low-income-and-informal-settlements (accessed on 3 May 2018).

EIU (Economist Intelligence Unit) (2011) *African Green City Index. Assessing the environmental performance of Africa's major cities.* (München: Siemens A.G.), https://www.siemens.com/entry/cc/features/greencityindex_international/all/en/pdf/report_africa_en.pdf (accessed on 3 May 2018).

Frayne, B., C. Moser and G. Ziervogel (eds.) (2013) *Climate change, assets and food security in Southern African cities* (London, New York: Routledge).

Grant, R., and M. Oteng-Ababio (2012) 'Mapping the invisible and real "African" economy: urban e-waste circuitry' *Urban Geography* 33(1), pp. 1–21, DOI: 10.2747/0272-3638.33.1.1.

Hall, T., and H. Barrett (2012) *Urban Geography*, 4th ed. (London & New York: Routledge).

Institut Africain de Gestion Urbaine (IAGU) (2008) *2004–2007 Partenariats pour des villes durables* (Dakar: IAGU), http://www.iagu.org/ (accessed on 3 May 2018).

Kaplan, D.H. and S. Holloway (2014) *Urban Geography* (New York: Wiley Global Education).

Kemp, L., L. Fairhurst, P. Rowswell and T. Quayle (2011) *Sub-Saharan African Cities: A Five-City Network to Pioneer Climate Adaptation Through Participatory Research & Local Action.* (Local Governments for Sustainability ICLEI: Cape Town), http://resilient-cities.iclei.org/fileadmin/sites/resilient-cities/files/Images_and_logos/Resilience_Resource_Point/ICLEI_Africa_5_City_Adaptation_Network_Workshop_Report_Final4_web_size.pdf (accessed on 3 May 2018).

Knox, P.L. and L. McCarthy (2012) *Urbanization: an introduction to urban geography.* (Boston: Pearson).

Oteng-Ababio, M., J.E. Melara Arguello and O. Gabbay (2013) 'Solid waste management in African cities: Sorting the facts from the fads in Accra, Ghana', *Habitat International* 39, pp. 96–104, DOI: 10.1016/j.habitatint.2012.10.010.

Pacione, M. (2009) *Urban geography, a global perspective*, 3[d] ed., (London, New York: Routledge).

Parnell, S., and E.A. Pieterse. (2014) *Africa's urban revolution* (London: Zed Press).

Parnell, S. and E.A. Pieterse (2010) 'The 'Right to the City': Institutional Imperatives of a Developmental State', *International journal of urban and regional research*, 34(1), pp. 146–162, DOI: 10.1111/j.1468-2427.2010.00954.x.

Pieterse, E.A. (2008) *City futures: Confronting the crisis of urban development* (London: Zed Books).

Roberts, D. and D. Nicci (2002) 'Durban's Local Agenda 21 Programme: Tackling Sustainable Development in a Post-Apartheid City', *Environment and Urbanization*, 14(1), pp.189–201, DOI: 10.1177/095624780201400116.

Rosenzweig, C., W. Solecki, S Hammer and S. Mehrotra (eds.) (2011) *Climate Change and Cities: First Assessment Report of the Urban Climate Change Research Network* (Cambridge: Cambridge University Press).

SACN (South African Cities Network) (2016) *State of African Cities Report 2016* (Braamfontein: SACN), http://www.sacities.net/state-of-cities-reporting/socr-2016 (accessed on 3 May 2018).

SACN (2011) *State of African Cities Report 2011* (Braamfontein: SACN), http://www.sacities.net/state-of-cities-reporting/45 (accessed on 3 May 2018).

SACN (2006) *State of African Cities Report 2006* (Braamfontein: SACN), http://www.sacities.net/state-of-cities-reporting/44 (accessed on 3 May 2018).

SACN (2004) *State of African Cities Report 2004* (Braamfontein: SACN), http://www.sacities.net/state-of-cities-reporting/43 (accessed on 3 May 2018).

Simon, D. (2013) 'Climate and environmental change and the potential for greening African cities', *Local Economy*, 28(2), pp. 203–217, DOI: 10.1177/0269094212463674.

Sutherland, C., D. Scott and M. Hordijk (2015) 'Urban Water Governance for More Inclusive Development: A Reflection on the "Waterscapes" of Durban', *South Africa European Journal of Development Research*, 27(4), pp. 488–504, http://hdl.handle.net/11245/1.487646.

UN-Habitat (United Nations Human Settlements Programme) (2014) *The State of African Cities 2014. Reimagining Sustainable Urban Transitions* (Nairobi: UN-Habitat), http://unhabitat.org/books/state-of-african-cities-2014-re-imagining-sustainable-urban-transitions/ (accessed on 3 May 2018).

United Nations Department of Economic and Social Affairs (2014) *World Urbanization Prospects (Revision)* (New York: United Nations), https://esa.un.org/unpd/wup/ (accessed on 3 May 2018)

UN-Habitat (2010) *The State of African Cities 2010. Governance, Inequality and Urban Land Markets* (Nairobi: UN-Habitat), https://www.citiesalliance.org/sites/citiesalliance.org/files/UNH_StateofAfricanCities_2010.pdf (accessed on 3 March 2018).

UN-Habitat (2008) *The State of African Cities 2008. A framework for addressing urban challenges in Africa* (Nairobi: UN-Habitat), http://unhabitat.org/books/the-state-of-the-african-cities-report-2008/ (accessed on 3 March 2018).

Wisner, B., M. Pelling, A. Mascarenhas, A. Holloway, B. Ndong, P. Faye, J. Ribot and D. Simon (2015) 'Small Cities and Towns in Africa: Insights into Adaptation Challenges and Potentials', in S. Pauleit, G. Jorgensen, S. Kabisch, P. Gasparini, S. Fohlmeister, I. Simonis, K. Yeshitela, A. Coly, S. Lindley, W.J. Kombe (Eds) *Urban Vulnerability and Climate Change in Africa, a multidisciplinary approach* (Dordrecht: Springer), pp. 153–196, DOI: 10.1007/978-3-319-03982-4_5.

World Bank (2015) *Open Energy Data Assessment Nairobi, Kenya* (Washington D.C.: World Bank), http://opendatatoolkit.worldbank.org/docs/odra/odra_energy-nairobi.pdf (accessed on 3 May 2018).

Webpages

ASSAF (Academy of Science of South Africa), http://www.assaf.org.za/files/2010/04/Imagine-Durban-LTDF-2009.pdf (accessed on 29 May 2018).

AAPS (Association of African Planning Schools), http://www.africanplanningschools.org.za (accessed on 3 May 2018).

ACC (African Centre for Cities), https://www.africancentreforcities.net (accessed on 3 May 2018).

AfriqueCroissanceVerte, https://afriquecroissanceverte.com (accessed on 3 May 2018).

AFSUN (African Food Security Urban Network), http://www.afsun.org (accessed on 3 May 2018).

Brinkhoff T., *Major Agglomerations of the World,* http://www.citypopulation.de (accessed on 3 May 2018).

C40 cities, http://www.c40.org (accessed on 3 May 2018).

Global Covenant of Mayors for Climate & Energy, http://www.compactofmayors.org/cities/ (accessed on 3 May 2018).

Heilig, K, http://www.demographics.at (accessed on 3 May 2018).

ICLEI (International Council for Local Environmental Initiatives), http://www.iclei.org/ (accessed on 3 May 2018).

JDA (Johannesburg Development Agency), http://www.jda.org.za (accessed on 3 May 2018).

LASEPA (Lagos State Environmental Protection Agency), http://lasepa.gov.ng/, (accessed on 3 May 2018).

LAWMA (Lagos Waste Management Authority), http://www.lawma.gov.ng, (accessed on 3 May 2018).

Rockefeller Foundation, *100 Resilient Cities*, http://www.100resilientcities.org.

SALGA (South African Local Government Association), http://www.salga.org.za (accessed on 3 May 2018).

SDSN (UN Sustainable Development Solutions Network), http://unsdsn.org (accessed on 3 May 2018).

Statistics Times (2015), *List of Countries by Population,* http://statisticstimes.com/population/countries-by-population.php (accessed on 3 May 2018).

Sustainable Cities International (SCI), http://sustainablecities.net (accessed on 3 May 2018).

United Cities and Local Governments, Africa Section, http://www.uclga.org (accessed on 3 May 2018).

UrbanAfrica.net, http://www.urbanafrica.net (accessed on 3 May 2018).

World Bank Data, *Urban Population,* https://data.worldbank.org/indicator/SP.URB.TOTL.IN.ZS (accessed on 3 May 2018).

World Bank Data, *Sub-Saharan Africa regional aggregate,* https://data.worldbank.org/region/sub-saharan-africa (accessed on 3 May 2018).

CHAPTER 7

Incremental Dependencies: Politics and Ethics of Claim-making at the Fringes of Windhoek, Namibia

Lalli Metsola

Abstract

On the basis of a case study of informal residents' claims over land, housing and basic amenities in Windhoek, Namibia, this chapter seeks to contribute to debates on the broad sociopolitical implications of claim-making dynamics between residents and public authorities. In contrast with antagonistic readings of such situations that focus on resistance, autonomy and rights, the chapter finds that both residents' strategies and policies outline incremental paths of betterment and intersect in multiple ways. It ponders whether and how such incrementality produces institutionalised forms of relations between citizens and authorities, and calls attention to the principle of mutual dependencies as a key aspect in them.

1 African Urbanities, Claim-making and Citizenship

Urbanisation is repeatedly identified as one of the key stories of our time. We have rapidly moved from a predominantly agrarian world into one where the majority of people live in cities and towns.[1] It is common to associate this change with the grand teleological narrative of industrial development. However, anxieties related to perceived changes in the global economic structure and empirical observations of urbanisation without industrialisation in many Southern contexts, particularly in Africa, question this story. Rapid urbanisation thus appears both as a great promise, an incubator of creativity and new economic and social forms, and as a threat (Bekker and Fourchard, 2013). On the one hand, there are visions of 'world-class cities' that are affluent, efficient and sustainable—these embody dreams of technologically and socially advanced, sustainable, clean and orderly futures. On the other hand, there are dystopian vistas of social and ecological decay, growing disorder and

1 World Bank, https://data.worldbank.org/indicator/SP.URB.TOTL.IN.ZS (accessed on 13 November 2017).

DOI:10.1163/9789004387942_008

unequal cities divided into gated communities and proliferating slums (e.g. UN-Habitat, 2008). While mainstream planning perspectives on urbanism see the latter as problems to be managed through social, administrative and technological reforms and innovations in order to create sustainable, resilient and inclusive cities (UN-Habitat, 2016; Mitlin, 2014), critical urban theory sees them as more profoundly anchored in the very structures of the global political economy (e.g. Brenner, 2009; Marcuse, 2010). These tropes of promise and threat are particularly pronounced in the case of debates and studies on 'world cities' (Robinson, 2015) or 'global cities' (Sassen, 2005).

These perspectives are largely devoid of historical, cultural or political specificity. In contrast to such approaches, this chapter suggests that it is fruitful both to question the instrumental focus of planning perspectives and not to take it as given that urbanity everywhere converges toward similar forms and outcomes. It calls attention to the historical formation of particular African urbanities and the city as a lived space versus a planned space, and to what practices bridge the gap between planning ideals and the realities of simultaneous growth and shortage in Southern cities. In this perspective, the workings and failures of formal institutions of government, what kinds of plans they make, and how these are implemented are not all there is to governance. Equally important are the constant work towards survival and betterment by ordinary residents as well as the multiple mediations, negotiations and struggles between residents, governmental agencies and various other collective bodies, such as neighbourhood associations, social movements, companies, churches or informal networks. Everyday governance grows out of this meeting and negotiation of different interests, ideals and aspirations, often involving provisional accommodations and solutions in both formal and informal spheres (Blundo and Le Meur, 2008; Cornea et al., 2017).[2]

In many postcolonial contexts, including Africa, modern institutions of governance were initially built upon the colonial principles of exclusion and selective recognition (Mbembe, 2001; Mamdani, 2007; Hansen and Stepputat, 2005). With transitions to independence, emergent states increasingly framed the people living in their territories as citizens instead of subjects (see e.g. Hindess, 2005; cf. Mamdani, 1996), but the extent to which people can transform their legal citizenship into tangible political and economic rights and benefits has remained uncertain and contested. Hence citizenship is better approached as a claim instead of a mere ascribed status (Das, 2011). In trying to make a living,

2 This approach is closely related to the literature that focuses on state formation and statehood as a process of institutional centralisation and potential fragmentation; see Metsola, 2015, 35–51; Steinmetz, 1999; Mitchell, 1999; Clapham, 1998; Das and Poole, 2004.

enjoy basic security and gain social acceptance, people seek to be recognised as deserving claimants vis-à-vis various authorities (Fraser and Honneth, 2003; Taylor, 1994; Englund, 2004; Metsola, 2015, 75–78) by resorting to the various material resources, social relations and discursive registers to which they have access (Hagmann and Péclard, 2010). Claims can take multiple forms including protests, polite requests, formal applications, accusations of corruption, court cases or acts of occupation. This process is relational; making claims to another party, whether a political office holder, state agency, traditional leader, local Big Man, land board or a neighbourhood association implies (even if provisionally) the recognition of their authority to grant what has been demanded (Lund, 2006; Lund and Boone, 2013). African claim-making environments are often institutionally plural, which means that claimants have to assess which authorities they can or should turn to. In turn, authorities may compete over who has jurisdiction to respond to claims, seeking out claimants in their bid for legitimacy. Because of this, claim and response dynamics are well suited for exploring the development of public authority, citizenship and institutions of governance.

One relatively common response to the uncertainties of belonging in contemporary Africa has been for claimants to try to ground entitlement in identity and seek to narrow down the circle of those sharing that identity and hence entitled to a slice of the cake. This is what the politics of autochthony, ethnonationalism and other exclusivist reformulations of belonging familiar from many current or recent African citizenship struggles and conflicts try to do (e.g. Dorman et al., 2007; Geschiere, 2011; Nyamnjoh and Brudvig, 2014). While these cases are significant and attract a lot of attention, they do not offer the full picture of contemporary African claim-making. In many cases, particularly in contexts with relatively well-functioning set-ups of centralised institutions—in other words, stronger states—claims may also take the form of negotiating vis-à-vis the existing regime without reference to supposedly primordial identities.

While claim-making can pivot around multiple objects, land is often prominent due to its importance for many different purposes: for agriculture, residence, as a commercial asset and, often, as a symbolically charged entity (for example as a burial ground or a place of worship). The significance of access to land, the overlapping claims related to it and the multiple institutions regulating it have often been noted as a major issue in African politics and development, particularly in rural contexts (e.g. Lund, 2011; Berry, 2009; Boone, 1998). With rapid urbanisation, urban spaces are becoming more pronounced as arenas for the articulation of various, criss-crossing claims over land (Koechlin 2017, 3). Claims are made by national and transnational capital, by the elites, but also by the vast number of people living in various degrees of precarious existence—the so-called informals, squatters, or subalterns. Additionally, various authorities at different levels and agencies of government, and in traditional or religious institutions, mediate the claims of others but also of each other.

Based on a case study of informal residents' claims over land, housing and basic amenities in Windhoek, Namibia, this chapter seeks to contribute to debates on the broad sociopolitical implications of claim-making dynamics between residents and public authorities. Through a critical conversation with the literature on urban claim-making in Africa and beyond, the chapter discusses incrementality as a characteristic of both residents' strategies and policies, and the interplay between the two. Contrary to both the policy-oriented, top-down accounts of African social problems and their governmental solutions, and antagonistic accounts of claim-making dynamics, this chapter explicitly connects the study of claim-making dynamics with the themes of institutionalisation, negotiated statehood and everyday governance, with particular attention to the principle of mutual dependencies as a key ingredient in the relations between residents and authorities. The chapter provides an overview of the interplay between residents' demands and official responses in Windhoek without going deep into the details of the different positions and actions of various kinds of residents, or into discussing the various other actors involved such as the central government, the Shack Dwellers Federation, the Affirmative Repositioning movement, or entrepreneurs. These will be the subject of future work.[3]

In what follows, I will first outline some influential ways in which urban claim-making has been previously discussed. In particular, I make a distinction between antagonistic and mutualistic readings, as well as between perspectives that emphasise claimants' efforts towards political autonomy and rights and those that stress relations of mutual dependence between claimants and authorities. I will then move on to present the case of claims and responses in the informal settlements of Windhoek, before returning to broader analytical

3 The fieldwork on which this case study is based took place from June to August 2016. Field activities consisted of interviews and conversations with ordinary residents and ground-level community leaders. The author also interviewed officials from the City of Windhoek, members of local and regional government, ministry personnel, representatives of organisations working on housing and squatters' issues, and academics, and organised a focus group discussion with youth leaders. He also attended a number of relevant events, including a meeting between the municipality's representatives and community leaders in one informal settlement, a community information meeting in another, and an Affirmative Repositioning book launch. These sources are complemented by grey literature and media stories.

discussion in which I focus on distinctions between instrumental clientelism and a more general ethos of mutual dependence, and on the developmental implications of such mutualities.

2 Perspectives on Urban Claim-making

In the literature on claim-making, there is a divide between what can be called antagonistic and mutualistic perspectives on relations between citizens and authorities. Antagonistic readings operate through a focus on social movements, struggles, resistance and 'the right to the city' and tend to pit the interests of the rulers and the ruled against each other. In this view, claims result from and make visible the lines between the powerful and the powerless, the rich and the poor, the privileged ones and the disenfranchised. David Harvey (2008, 37) provides a good example of writing in this vein: 'Signs of rebellion are everywhere: the unrest in China and India is chronic, civil wars rage in Africa, Latin America is in ferment. Any of these revolts could become contagious.' What should happen, he continues, is for social movements to focus on demanding 'greater democratic control over the production and utilization of the surplus' in 'a global struggle, predominantly with finance capital' (Harvey, 2008, 37; see also Sassen, 2010).

Not all accounts of the urban condition and resistance within it are as grandiose. Mike Davis (2006), for one, is sceptical about such grand narratives. For him, '[p]ortentous post-Marxist speculations, like those of Negri and Hardt, about a new politics of "multitudes" in the "rhizomatic spaces" of globalisation remain ungrounded in any real political sociology. Even within a single city, slum populations can support a bewildering variety of responses to structural neglect and deprivation, ranging from charismatic churches and prophetic cults to ethnic militias, street gangs, neoliberal NGOs, and revolutionary social movements.' (Davis, 2006, 201–202.) Yet he still frames the responses of the urban 'poor' or 'informals' exclusively in terms of resistance to global capitalism: 'But if there is no monolithic subject or unilateral trend in the global slum, there are nonetheless myriad acts of resistance. Indeed, the future of human solidarity depends upon the militant refusal of the new urban poor to accept their terminal marginality within global capitalism.' (Davis, 2006, 202.)

While this perspective captures a significant aspect of claim-making and response dynamics, many such interactions are not captured by its interpretive lens. A more ethnographically oriented body of scholarship has moved beyond the focus on explicit (and globally oriented) resistance and added nuance to our understanding of the political agency of informals (Das and Randeria, 2015;

Simone, 2013; Bayat, 2010; Holston, 2008). A number of important points from this literature could be raised, but as there is no room for extensive discussion I will highlight two that are most important for my purposes. First, many of the actions of informal urban residents do not take the form of conscious, collective political action but occur in the form of disconnected, mundane actions that have practical aims. Second, they are not necessarily antagonistic, but involve significant degrees of reciprocity, mutuality and negotiation. For example, through studies on the daily realities of 'urban poor' in Egypt and Iran, Asef Bayat (2000, 2010, 2015) points out the shortcomings of perspectives that see the poor as merely surviving instead of having long-term dreams, plans and strategies, as well as of perspectives that tend to focus excessively on their organised collective action through the prism of resistance. Instead, Bayat highlights what he refers to as 'quiet encroachment', the multiple ways in which squatters engage in clandestine, piecemeal actions primarily aimed towards individual, family or other immediate group betterment, and how this may have systematic, unintended, collective—and hence political—outcomes. James Holston (2008), in turn, has focused on how poor urbanites in Brazil have staked claims through land occupation, auto-construction and legal action, in the process gaining increasing traction as a political force and realising their citizen rights. However, later studies have observed that the movements that initially spoke about 'rights to the city' and took an antagonistic stance towards public authorities have since been demobilised as their demands for recognition and participation, and to some extent their agency, was co-opted into official doctrines and practices (Caldeira, 2015).

While both Bayat and Holston have produced richly contextualised reconceptualisations of precarious existence in Southern settings, they retain the antagonistic focus that juxtaposes residents and state power and portrays increasing autonomy and citizen rights as the eventual objective of the former. In contrast, this chapter suggests that there may be a significant degree of mutuality in the claim and response dynamics involving informal urban dwellers.

3 Claiming Residence, Welfare and Security at the Fringes of Windhoek

In Namibia, urbanisation is proceeding rapidly, both through population growth occurring in the city and continuous in-migration propelled by persistent rural poverty and hopes of better opportunities. This strains the capacities of city and town administrations. Coupled with pervasive unemployment and rising land prices and housing costs, this has resulted in widespread precarity among urban dwellers. At the same time, the country's stability and relatively high administrative capacity and economic performance facilitate the pooling of resources and significant redistributive mechanisms through state coffers. Together, these conditions help generate popular demands for translating the political inclusion of legal citizenship into social and economic inclusion through the provision of opportunities, jobs, health, education, housing and basic amenities.

3.1 *Informal Settlements and Their Residents*

Before Namibian independence, migration was severely restricted and 'illegal' settlement not tolerated. Independence set in motion a heavy influx of people from rural areas to cities and towns. Windhoek has grown from a city of under 150,000 inhabitants at independence to one with over 400,000 now. High demand for residential land and housing, together with a complicated and costly process of surveying, demarcating and servicing has pushed the prices of houses as well as rents beyond what most urban residents are able to pay. Therefore, most urban population growth occurs in informal settlements on municipal land in the north-western and western fringes of the city, mostly in the constituencies of Moses Garoeb, Tobias Hainyeko, Samora Machel and Khomasdal North.

There are many kinds of informality. In the extreme outskirts of the city, new, relatively sparsely populated and completely unserviced areas constantly spring up with more land becoming occupied. Older informal settlements have gradually become congested but have often been provided with basic services like public prepaid water taps, communal toilets, and some paved streets and street lights. Yet other areas are still predominantly filled with *kambashus* (shacks) but have already been demarcated into individual plots that are usually fenced. Additionally, there are small tracts of informal residence in open areas within established townships, as well as shacks in people's backyards, used for renting out. Many of the research participants had at some point moved from one informal area to another due to various reasons, including less noise and congestion, better location, available services, cheaper living expenses, security considerations, avoiding problematic relations with relatives, or acquiring more space in a newer area.

Likewise, the people who live in informal areas or conditions should not be seen as a single group of 'squatters'. They consist of employed, partially employed, unemployed, students and pensioners; people with different levels of income, different social connections and at different stages of their life cycles. The sizes of their homes, mostly built of corrugated iron, as well as the amenities in them vary considerably. Some only consist of one room with next to nothing inside, while at the other end of the spectrum there are homes with multiple rooms, electricity (either tapped illicitly from permanent houses nearby or powered by solar panels or a generator), fridges, stoves, windows and quite a lot of furniture, even inside toilets. These have often been built incrementally over time, as resources permit. While people strive towards better life through degrees of formalisation, changes can occur in the opposite direction too, with informalisation—moving to a shack—providing an outlet in a situation in which formal accommodation has become financially unsustainable. In some cases, living informally is a choice that facilitates saving a larger portion of one's incomes for other, longer-term purposes, such as purchasing land or investing in property in rural areas (see also Niikondo, 2010; Kamminga, 2000, 51). Indeed, many research participants referred to existing links to their places of origin and to their wish to retire there. Furthermore, not all shacks are for residence—some are also for business; people may own more than one and rent them out, or use them as *shebeens* (informal bars).

3.2 *Actors and Policies*

Numerous actors populate the organisational landscape related to the issues of land, housing and services in Windhoek. These include the City, the central government, savings groups and their umbrella organisation the Shack Dwellers Federation, and—more recently—the Affirmative Repositioning movement (AR). I will provide a brief overview of this landscape before moving on to discuss the interplay between residential claims and the City.

The Shack Dwellers Federation is 'a network of 605 saving schemes with 20400 members throughout the country'.[4] Savings groups, either independent ones or those belonging to the Federation, purchase or lease plots that the City then provides with a basic level of services on a collective basis. The groups subdivide the plot among members and each of them can develop their share incrementally (City of Windhoek, 1999; City of Windhoek, n.d. b). This model is not without its problems, for example related to the management of funds and collective services, but it has provided a significant avenue for many poor residents to achieve different degrees of improvements, including access to formal housing and basic services.

While the achievements of the Shack Dwellers Federation and independent savings groups are considerable, only a minority of informal residents have benefited from them. The persistent and growing land and housing shortage led to the emergence of a new militant movement called Affirmative

4 Shack Dwellers Federation of Namibia, http://sdfn.weebly.com/ (accessed on 14 September 2017).

Repositioning in 2014. Led by prominent young political figures with a history in the SWAPO Youth League, it started a high-profile campaign regarding urban land availability. Its rhetoric has been openly hostile to the established political elite, with a mixture of radical socialist and Pan-African themes (AR book launch, 4.8.2016). In response to the pressure from the AR, the central government revitalised some previously problematic and hence inactive housing programmes. These include the Build Together Programme, originally started in 1992 and meant to provide housing loans for low- and middle-income households, and the Mass Housing Programme that provides subsidised ready units. Additionally, the government started a Mass Urban Land Servicing Project with the promise of delivering 200,000 plots countrywide for residential purposes. So far, progress in delivering these has been slow.

Neither of the abovementioned organisations is a mass-based popular squatters' movement like for example Abahlali baseMjondolo in neighbouring South Africa. The Shack Dwellers Federation has considerable real presence on the ground, particularly among women, but has not adopted similar antagonistic rhetoric and broadly political objectives as Abahlali base Mjondolo. Instead, it focuses on more immediate practical questions of housing and often cooperates with public agencies. Affirmative Repositioning, in turn, does speak a militant language that situates the issues of urban land, housing and services in the context of broader injustices. However, on the basis of my observations and discussions with Windhoekers of various walks of life it seems to draw much of its support from among the young middle-class and to not have an equally strong support base among informal residents.

While the above policies and organisations play a significant role, the interaction between informal residents and the municipality through immediate or low-level official channels is the primal node in the claim and response dynamics in Windhoek. This is, first, because informal settlements have mostly grown on municipal land, and second, because the City has considerable autonomy over the generation of its own revenue and budget but is also expected to cater for its expenses without central government subvention, apart from specific, earmarked capital expenditures. Hence, my primary focus here is with the claims and responses between residents in various informal settlements and the City.

In day-to-day practice, the City is not a unitary actor and the approach of different agencies, or the line taken in regulating the use of municipal land, may vary at different moments and in different situations. Sometimes those working in the City structures stress that 'we cannot condone illegal settlement' (as one of my City civil servant interviewees put it, and the Head of the City Police confirmed) while others accept the reality of rapid urban growth and try to think of practical ways to address the situation. However, many City employees dealing with 'informals' argued that they are 'fighting a losing battle'. In practice, informal residence has been mostly tolerated since independence and as I shall demonstrate below, the City has, in principle, accepted that the problem should be addressed through constructive engagement rather than through harsh control.

The first response by the City to the heavy influx of squatters in the early 1990s was to establish three 'reception areas' where new residents were given rental plots with rudimentary services. It was assumed that once the new residents had established themselves they would be able to find formal accommodation and move out. This did not happen. (City of Windhoek, n.d. a; World Bank, 2002, 17–18.) As the spread of low-income informal areas continued, the City outlined a new housing policy (City of Windhoek, 2000) and a concomitant development and upgrading strategy (City of Windhoek, 1999). Drawing from such international precedents as Mexico and Botswana, as well as World Bank guidelines (City of Windhoek, n.d. a), these documents advocated a transition from seeing informal residents as lawbreakers and a mere problem into a participatory approach that sees them as active agents trying to improve their lives. As put in the City's guidelines on informal settlements in the mid-1990s, '[t]his should not be seen as yet another project to mend squatter problems in Windhoek, but rather a process proposed to positively accommodate and manage informal settlements in the City. In addition it must be realised that, in order for this process to succeed, traditional views (confine people to a specific area to exercise control over them) on informal settlement shall have to be discarded' (City of Windhoek, n.d. a, 6).

The development and upgrading strategy combines in situ upgrading of existing settlements with establishing new residential areas under the sites-and-services model (City of Windhoek, 1999; World Bank, 2002, 9). The strategy outlines seven development levels of upgrading that differ from each other in terms of resident income, tenure arrangements, service levels and payments (City of Windhoek, 1999, 4; World Bank, 2002, 10). Levels 0–3 consist of 'ultra-low income' areas with gradually increasing levels of communal services. Tenure at levels 1–2 is primarily lease-based (City of Windhoek, 1999: Annexure A). For most of the people (over 80 per cent in the early years of the new millennium) this was the only affordable level of officially recognised tenure (de Kock, 2006, 28–29; City of Windhoek, 2000, 4). Block layout at level 1 remains informal, while levels 2 and 3 consist of demarcated *erven* (plots) that the residents lease or purchase. Levels 4–6 refer to low- and middle-income areas, with individually owned plots and individual service connections (City of Windhoek, 1999: Annexure A).

The areas selected for upgrading tend to be heavily congested. This leads to the requirement that some move out to make way for the upgrading and new subdivision of plots. Who can stay is primarily decided on a first come, first served basis, with those who have arrived in the area first getting to stay. For this purpose, the City registers residents on a waiting list and numbers their shacks. In practice, most communities currently remain at the lowest three levels. Upgrading is slow and the situation of partial informality and partial formality may become a relatively lasting state. City officials and other observers give multiple reasons for this state of affairs. City representatives argue that they will not be able to solve the problem without central government subventions. Other crucial resources noted as often lacking are land for resettlement, time, will and capacity.

3.3 *Residents' Claims and Their Negotiation*

Participation and incremental upgrading have been the official policy for over 15 years. The approach has permeated the lived experience and colonised the claim-making processes of informal urban dwellers to a considerable extent, so that their claims largely mirror the incremental upgrading strategy. In part, such residents always have to frame their demands in a way that is intelligible to those in a position to respond. However, the doctrine of incremental upgrading also offers a possibility to gradually transform non-tolerated practices into tolerated ones, illicitness into licitness, and informality into formality. It offers the residents a stepping stone via which to start actively working towards a more secure existence in the city.

Among my research participants, water and sanitation were usually the primary needs expressed, followed by electricity, and then paved roads and street lights. Additionally, a concern over security is a recurring theme. Finally, after these basic needs, having one's own house under a secure tenure arrangement of some kind represents the eventual ideal. These aspirations seem to form a partially overlapping series, in which the focus of needs and demands would shift as the situation of provision changed. Claim-making over these needs has taken many forms: petitioning the authorities in public meetings or through community leaders and councillors, writing letters to officials, sending SMSs to newspapers, and in some rare cases, protests against evictions.

There are two kinds of community leaders. The first one includes a tier system based on areas of residence that extends from the level of the regional councillor responsible for a constituency through community chairpersons responsible for different settlements within the constituency and consisting of a few hundred households, to block leaders responsible for about 20–30 households each (City of Windhoek, 1999, 13–14; City of Windhoek, 2011).

This is in accordance with the City's Development and Upgrading Strategy, which states that '[i]n Development Levels 1–3 [...] or any other situation where a community has access to communal services [...] [t]he community (20 to 30 households sharing the same toilet block) must democratically elect a constituted formal neighbourhood committee and a chairperson [...] The aim of such neighbourhood committees will be [...] [t]o act as communication channel with Council [...]; To empower the communities to run their own organisation, finances, maintenance, cleaning of services and problem solving; To lessen the burden on Council in terms of resources needed for community liaison, administration, credit control, maintenance, etc.; To facilitate a structure through which saving and self-help actions may be promoted; To create a structure through which education, training and capacity building may be effectively carried over to individual households' (City of Windhoek, 1999, 13).

The other kind consists of constituency development committees. Each constituency has one of them and their membership is drawn from people who reside in the constituency and represent different walks of life. For example, in Moses Garoeb constituency in Northwestern Windhoek, the CDC members are classified as representing the following categories: community, youth, traditional authority, the Ministry of Veterans Affairs, City of Windhoek, Family of Hope Services (an NGO assisting orphaned and vulnerable children), Youth Forum, businesses, The Evangelic Lutheran Church in Namibia, the Ministry of Defence and the Ministry of Agriculture (information obtained from the Moses Garoeb constituency office, August 2016; see also Republic of Namibia 1998, Appendix II).

These two kinds of leaders occupy a key position between informal residents and higher levels of authority. They live in the areas that they represent and are usually the first layer of administration to hear the residents' concerns and are entrusted to campaign for them with regard to the City and other authorities. At the same time, they are the main channel of news and directives in the other direction, from higher administrative levels to the communities. They also regulate land use and mediate disputes; they do not have any official policing or judicial capacity but are recognised as arbiters of less serious cases of disagreement or misbehaviour. Grass-roots local leaders are not remunerated for their services but in practice such positions might offer them leverage with which to advance their own agendas of betterment, as some of them openly admitted, for example by enabling them to be among the first in line when improvements occur. In many respects, their role resembles that of a traditional headman, and indeed their blocks were often referred to as 'villages'.

To give an example of the interactions between such leaders and higher administrative tiers, in one old informal settlement in Tobias Hainyeko constituency, the community leaders had long been sending letters to the City, and the Mayor in particular, requesting that the latter meet them and address their concerns. During my fieldwork, they eventually got their wish and a meeting between the Mayor, City officials, City councillors, the Regional Councillor and the community leaders from various informal settlements in that constituency was held. In the meeting, the community leaders were given room to air their concerns. These were primarily of a practical nature, focusing on the provision and maintenance of services as well as the desired allocation of *erven*. However, there were also more general, and critical, interventions, focusing on what was perceived as a lack of will or capacity of those responsible for delivering land and services. For example, an old man who was a member of the elders' council in his area quite straightforwardly pointed out what he saw as the discrepancy between promises and actual delivery, stating that 'promises made ten years ago hurt us. Why do you run when people in other areas ask you to come? Why are services not given here like in town?' As the questions and comments were collected, there was no direct answer to these questions. In their responses to all the queries and pleas that were heard, the CEO of the City and the Mayor referred to their responsibility to cater for the needs of the whole city with limited funds. While basic services were a human right, said the Mayor, changes could not happen overnight. The Mayor and City representatives further pointed out that more efficient implementation aided by community involvement and sharing of information would be key to making the most of available resources. In general, the principles of affordability and cost recuperation recurred in my interviews with City representatives. From the perspective of informal residents such principles might be a bitter pill to swallow, as they seem to embody new arrangements of privilege that perpetuate the stark inequalities inherited from the racial hierarchy of settler colonialism.

The leadership structure described above is formally geared towards developmental aims (upgrading and services) but it has significant political effects. In principle, the structures of community leadership are administrative, not political positions—as one of the leaders firmly asserted to me and as the City's guidelines also stipulate (City of Windhoek, 2011, 4). In practice, however, SWAPO structures and government structures often overlap at the grass-roots level through the persons holding positions in them. While I did not systematically chart this issue, at least in the areas where I worked most of the leaders I met had previously been active in party structures or continued to be so (see also Kamminga 2000, 50–51). Furthermore, they closely cooperate with regional and City councillors, which are politically elected positions. In Windhoek, all of the regional councillors for constituencies where there are informal settlements belong to SWAPO and 12 out of 15 City councillors represent the ruling party. In the eyes of such elected officials, issues of welfare provision are of high political significance: 'they elect us', as one regional councillor put it.

Notably, in the context of Namibian urban residential politics, people are striving to become visible and recognised through various forms of claim-making. They want to be registered and have their details recorded instead of resorting to tactics of invisibility or exit. This is because they mostly do not see the political and administrative authorities of regional and local government as a threat but rather as key in controlling access to secure residence in the city. Hence acceptance of their bureaucratic requirements is a precondition for becoming a beneficiary. Hence, they do not resist becoming subjects of the data generation exercises of the City but are, on the contrary, trying hard to enter its surveys, waiting lists and classifications; measures that constitute an integral part of biopolitical 'legibility' and control of contemporary postcolonial states (Das and Poole, 2004).

The above point should be qualified by noting a key moment when residents' strategies concerning visibility change. In the past, the City used to remove at will 'illegal' squatters from sites designated for development. However, a few years ago, a group of squatters, assisted by the public law firm Legal Assistance Centre, challenged this practice in court. Eventually, the Supreme Court ruled that the sections of the Squatters Proclamation of 1985[5] that authorise the demolition of squatters' shacks are unconstitutional (Ellinger, 2015, 10–11). Since then, squatters cannot be removed without a court order and them being provided with an alternative place to settle. This has led to a game of cat and mouse in which the City Police tries to prevent people from establishing their presence in an area in the first place while the aspirant residents try again, often during the night, until they succeed. After this, they cannot be evicted and can start their incremental struggle towards formalisation. Obviously, the issue of whether one can be considered to already reside in a structure or not is not straightforward to assess and may lead to contested evictions.[6]

3.4 *Summing Up the Situation in Windhoek*

The antagonistic forms of claim-making, such as AR campaigning or sporadic movements to oppose evictions, have received the most media attention and are therefore visible to broader publics. Nevertheless, most claims over urban

5 Proclamation AG 21; *Official Gazette Extraordinary of South West Africa* No. 5047, 7–17.

6 See the High Court case of Junias vs. The Municipal Council of the Municipality of Windhoek (A 35/2014) for an illustrative discussion of such assessment.

land, services and housing have long taken the form of residents' everyday tactics to try to incrementally gain a foothold to reside securely in the city. They have combined this with campaigning towards the City and 'the government' through community leaders and councillors. These claims mirror a policy of participatory incrementality in the informal settlement upgrading strategy of the City of Windhoek, and resonate with the operating logic of the Shack Dwellers Federation as well as the provisions of the recent Flexible Land Tenure Act. The slow rate of delivery has made room for land occupations that can be transformed into open claims after establishing oneself on a site.

Significantly, it is not one, straightforward demand that is made and responded to in this arena, but rather a shifting front line that moves from one aspiration to another through a series of claims and responses. In the process, residents' strategies and official responses have increasingly converged. The former have gradually sought to improve their access to land, housing and services, as well as their legal standing and security, while the latter have sought to transform informality into formality through step-by-step increases in tenure security, incremental provision of housing and services and the mobilisation of 'self-help' to facilitate such improvements.

Even though such incrementality works on practical questions it also produces relations of citizenship and authority. To give an example, let me refer to the requirement of the City, discussed above, for the residents of informal settlements to elect leaders to represent them vis-à-vis the authorities. While this arises from the practical needs related to communal service provision, it leads to residents of such areas having to align their interests and form organised communities—at least to some extent—instead of advancing their lot through disconnected strategies. At the same time, it leads the residents to invest their trust in and channel their aspirations through the agencies administering their affairs, thus reinforcing the authority of such agencies.

Contrary to what the proponents of formalisation through titling (most notably de Soto, 2000) propose, formality and informality in such a context are not necessarily clear-cut, either/or conditions. Rather, through the emergence of informal markets in land and housing, gradual official accommodation through enumeration, service provision and upgrading policies, court decisions against eviction, participation in savings groups and legislative instruments that outline a gradual path towards formalisation,[7] residents who start

7 Namibia has recently passed the Flexible Land Tenure Act, which provides for a formalisation path that recognises the slow and incremental nature of informal settlement upgrading. It consists of a step-by-step model of tenure, with different grades of title schemes; see Republic of Namibia (2016).

out in a condition of nearly absolute informality may move towards formality as their claims are increasingly recognised. In the process the land that they occupy and the structures they erect on it increasingly gain the characteristics of property.[8] However, the process also involves a simultaneous informalisation of formal regulations through repeated practical and tactical negotiations of rules of entitlement and precedence.

Importantly, such processes have been taking place at the fringes of Windhoek for sufficiently long to have become incorporated in the tacit practical knowledge of the residents and hence to inform their actions. Thus, while the slow rate of improvement causes impatience, the prospects of gradual betterment and the public authorities' significant role in facilitating it translate dissatisfaction into recurrent claims through officially accepted channels rather than into more antagonistic forms of activism. In other words, they serve the ends of stabilisation and pacification instead of immediate transformation.

4 The Logic of Mutuality

What kinds of insights does the above case of residential claims on the fringes of Windhoek offer for diversifying and clarifying the analytical vocabulary of claim-making dynamics? While the above observations concur with some of Bayat's (2000, 2010, 2015) and Holston's (2008) points on quiet encroachment and insurgent citizenship, there are also important differences. This is possibly in part because of the dissimilarities between Namibia and, on the one hand, the more purely authoritarian settings of Egypt and Iran, and on the other, the firmer tradition of articulate social movements in Brazil. The relations between 'the state' (and 'the City') and the 'informals' in Namibia are not necessarily separate and opposite but may permeate each other, leading to co-optation and collusion. Informal residents in Windhoek do not always acquire what they need clandestinely, nor do they necessarily seek autonomy and legal rights. They often tap into formal political channels and processes to make claims to increased residential security and welfare through a combination of persuasion, pressure and cooperation in the form of requests, seeking media attention, threatening to withdraw their political allegiance from the ruling party, and the officially endorsed policy of participation.

At first glance, such relations would seem to fit the picture of clientelism as they mobilise vertical loyalties between particular local and regional government representatives, community leaders and groups of residents, and involve

8 For a closely related argument in the context of Indonesia, see Nurman and Lund (2016).

the exchange of material and legal improvement for the informal residents to their compliance. In this sense, these relations reproduce the party–state at ground level and also involve the possibility of partial inclusions and exclusions (see also, e.g., Patel, 2016; Hammett, 2017, 5). Indeed, clientelism is the explanatory model suggested by some authors for understanding urban African claim-making dynamics (see e.g. Bénit-Gbaffou and Oldfield, 2014; Mitlin, 2014). While the above relations are very real and important to note, my analysis suggests that the notion of clientelism might be inadequate for understanding the dependencies involved. This is because of, first, its instrumentalism and insufficiently theorised agency, and second, the tendency of clientelist explanations to associate mutual dependencies with inefficiency and stagnancy.

While the play of claims and responses in Windhoek may involve a considerable amount of tactical consideration out of personal or partisan interests, these are not the only set of rules that enter the game. Beyond their own immediate needs, the claims and statements of the residents repeatedly imagine a shared political community where everyone is entitled to basic welfare—housing, water, sanitation, electricity and basic security. There is a widely shared and firm belief that 'the government' should help those in need and that this is possible because of abundant national resources and a small population. Residents often told me that they will find a way to pay their bills and build their houses little by little if the government 'meets them halfway' with land, services and public assistance. Explanations for why this is not happening enough included the lack of funds and capacity within the structures of the City, but also lack of political will. High-ranking politicians and civil servants are said to be involved in urban land speculation, benefiting from inflated house and rental prices. Contractors and their frontmen (referred to as 'tenderpreneurs') are said to utilise their networks to gain tenders at well above reasonable prices. Provision of affordable housing on a large scale would cut into these sources of income. In other words, the residents criticise particular leaders, but their criticism does not amount to questioning the relationship of mutual dependence as much as claiming that that relationship is not sufficiently honoured. This ethos provides a ground for assessing the performance of leaders—whether they care sufficiently or not—and the leaders know this. In this context, the knowledge production related to upgrading, including surveys, the enumeration of shacks, waiting lists, and meetings to share information, serve as forms of impatience management and respond to the regularly expressed need of the residents to be heard by the authorities.

While the gradual, multiform negotiation between rulers and their subjects has been identified as crucial for the formation of 'social contracts' and institutions of governance (Hickey, 2010; Nugent, 2010), such negotiations do not always occur in the same ways and yield similar results. Settings where the ethos of mutual dependence enjoys broad acceptance seem fundamentally different from contracts supposedly resulting from Hobbesian self-interest but also from the more procedural individualism of social liberalism (most notably Rawls (1971)). However, strategic bartering in which favours are exchanged for adherence might not offer a fully satisfactory explanation either. Rather, ideas of reciprocal, yet hierarchical dependence with an imperative of sharing have been identified as a significant component of the constitution of many southern African societies (see Ferguson, 2013, 2015; Englund, 2015; Friedman, 2011; Gulbrandsen, 2012).[9] They construct an ethos of a political community whose sociality precedes and is more fundamental than the individual aspirations of its members. The exact origins of this moral universe may be multiple, and their extensive discussion is beyond the scope of this chapter. What seems likely, however, is that the particular form that African state formation took during the colonial and early postcolonial periods may have played no small part in contributing towards the centrality of such forms of authority and deference. It formed a key part of what Mbembe (2001, 45) has called 'the trinity of violence, allocations and transfers' that combined coercion with the strategic recognition of key segments of the population and reciprocal chains of distribution and loyalty (see also Englebert, 2009; Bayart, 2000). Ideas of mutual dependence become embedded in subjectivities due to their long histories and social prevalence. Hence, they are ontological rather than purely ethical principles. Furthermore, such dispositions may have a significant aesthetic component in addition to the ethical one, directing assessments of what are intelligible and acceptable forms of making claims. Hence, for example, the ire that the rhetoric of Affirmative Repositioning has raised among those in power. Quite often, their angry reactions have related less to the content of AR's demands and more to their form, which allegedly demonstrates a lack of respect towards figures of authority. Critical comments by ordinary informal residents almost invariably focused on the same issue, while they tended to agree with the expressed objectives of the AR. For them, the preference of AR leaders for antagonistic expression seemed to amount to a denial of the asymmetrical, para-familial relationship of loyalty and care.

The other problem with clientelist (and more broadly, neo-patrimonialist) readings of African contexts is their association of mutualist politics with inefficiency and stagnancy. This overlooks the potential, unforeseen long-term

9 As Ferguson (2013) points out, an Afrobarometer survey found that 'a solid majority (60 per cent) of Africans see their government as a parent who ought to take care of them' (*Afrobarometer*, 2009, 4–5).

consequences of processes of mutual negotiation and recognition, possibly including prospects for social inclusion, material improvements and political participation. Claims of recognition and dependence are intimately related to resource politics. They may take the form of including some in, and excluding some from, resources and welfare through group-based criteria of merit. More positively, they may contribute to the reproduction of and reliance on the relatively immediate socialities of kinship, friendship, neighbourhood or religious community. However, it seems that they may also give rise to the institutionalisation of broader, even universalist politics of distribution and welfare in contexts where the economic and administrative base permits this. For Kelsall (2013), 'developmental patrimonialism' refers to settings of successful institutionalisation based on entrenching patrimonial authority in structures broader and more durable than the reign of any particular ruler, for example those of the ruling party or the bureaucracy. What is significant is that in such a perspective the logic of mutuality is not necessarily opposite to, but is possibly compatible with development. Kelsall's focus is on the agency of the elites, but gains added resonance when the implicit 'social contract' expressed in the ideal of mutuality and the demands it places on rulers are taken into account. From this perspective, could the growing urban settlements with their constantly moving, negotiated frontier of claims and responses over time provide a laboratory for the development of novel institutional arrangements?

Such cities do not seem to be incubators of the same kind of individuation that Weber wrote about in *The City* (Weber, 1978, 1212–1372). What we see in them, rather, is the increasing unmooring of distinct identities, but not necessarily of the logic of mutual dependence. The latter may actually gain further impetus from the erosion of economic mediation through wage labour in Africa. For sure, this mediation never was as pervasive there as in Northern industrial societies. Still, it offered a significant organising principle in postcolonial societies, particularly when linked to the loyalties and obligations of redistribution through kin networks through which salaries lubricated welfare and social reproduction beyond their immediate recipients (Mbembe, 2001; Roitman, 2007). This is no longer the case, as changes in production technologies, coupled with the erosion of debt-driven development, austerity measures of structural adjustment, and the end of the Cold War support chains have ushered in what many authors have identified as an era of jobless growth (Li, 2013; Ferguson, 2015; Englund, 2015). Such southern African states as South Africa, Botswana and Namibia are heavily reliant on the capital-intensive extraction of minerals and a large part of their populations remain superfluous to the formal economy. In spite of this, they remain relatively stable and their economies and administrative institutions function relatively well. They do have highly unequal patterns of income and wealth but have still taken significant steps in tackling poverty and improving the welfare of their citizens. This has involved extensions in social policy, including broad-based cash grant schemes such as universal, non-contributory old-age pension disability grants, child support grants, war veteran benefits, and even experiments in basic income grants (Ferguson, 2015; Metsola, 2015; Devereux, 2013; Stewart and Yermo, 2009; Pelham, 2007).

5 Conclusion

Through a case of study of incremental and mutually constitutive claims and responses by Namibian residents of informal settlements and public authorities, this chapter has questioned the general applicability of such interpretations of claim-making dynamics that focus on resistance, autonomy or instrumental clientelism. In the Namibian context, claims rather tend to reflect and construct a relational ethics of mutual dependence. This highlights the importance of contextual specificity. Claim-making processes tend to be simultaneously about concrete goods, resources or benefits and about inclusion. However, to understand the kind of political subjectivity and socio-political relationships imagined by this demand—for example, whether it is about being recognised as rights-bearing individual citizens or as 'children' under the custody of the state—requires careful, context-specific exploration. Furthermore, it requires taking people's dispositions and beliefs seriously instead of deciding their veracity or value on their behalf.

Residents' claim-making in Namibia does not represent an extension of rights or democratising politics directly. Rather, its modus operandi reconstructs relations of reciprocal dependence. However, this negotiation does represent deep-seated desires for social and economic justice and inclusion in the national body politic. While the real advances related to residents' claim-making and responses are limited and their durability is not certain, the policies and practices of participatory incrementality reflect and help reconstruct an ideal of responsive public authority that goes beyond immediate instrumental utility. Over time, this negotiation may offer a basis for enduring institutional responses that generate broad-based legitimacy and stability. However, this is far from a self-evident outcome, as dependencies can be used strategically, in a measured way, to appease and pacify. The question, then, is whether the gradual responses necessary for tempering popular claims eventually make room for and encourage such forms of political consciousness and organisation that are more difficult to harness.

Acknowledgements

I express my sincere gratitude to all research participants for generously sharing their views and experiences, my research assistants Kaarina Matti and Lukas Nangolo and the personnel of the Department of Sociology at the University of Namibia. I also thank Till Förster, Carole Ammann, Claire Bénit-Gbaffou, Jeremy Gould and the anonymous reviewers for their comments on the manuscript or earlier versions of this text. The Academy of Finland (grants 288998 and 318762) provided the funding that made this research possible.

References

Afrobarometer (2009) *Are Democratic Citizens Emerging in Africa? Evidence from the Afrobarometer*, Afrobarometer briefing paper 70, http://afrobarometer.org/sites/default/files/publications/Briefing%20paper/AfrobriefNo70.pdf (accessed on 9 May 2018).

Bayart, J.-F. (2000) 'Africa in the World: A History of Extraversion', *African Affairs*, 99, pp. 217-267, DOI: 10.1093/afraf/99.395.217.

Bayat, A. (2015) 'Plebeians of the Arab Spring', *Current Anthropology*, 56 (supplement 11 S33–S43, DOI: 10.1086/681523.

Bayat, A. (2010) *Life as Politics: How Ordinary People Change the Middle East* (Amsterdam: Amsterdam University Press).

Bayat, A. (2000) 'From "Dangerous Classes" to "Quiet Rebels": Politics of the urban subalterns in the Global South', *International Sociology*, 15(3), pp. 533-557, DOI: 10.1177/0268580000015003005.

Bekker, S. and L. Fourchard (2013) 'Introduction', in S. Bekker and L. Fourchard (eds) *Governing Cities in Africa: Politics and Policies* (Cape Town: HSRC Press), pp. 1-12.

Bénit-Gbaffou, C. and S. Oldfield (2014) 'Claiming "Rights" in the African City: Popular Mobilization and the Politics of Informality', in S. Parnell and S. Oldfield (eds) *The Routledge Handbook of Cities in the Global South* (London and New York: Routledge), pp. 281-295.

Berry, S. (2009) 'Property, Authority and Citizenship: Land Claims, Politics and the Dynamics of Social Division in West Africa', *Development and Change*, 40(1), pp. 23-45, DOI: 10.1111/j.1467-7660.2009.01504.x.

Blundo, G. and P.-Y. Le Meur (2008) 'Introduction. An Anthropology of Everyday Governance: Collective Service Delivery and Subject-Making', in G. Blundo and P.-Y. Le Meur (eds) *The Governance of Daily Life in Africa: Ethnographic Explorations of Public and Collective Services* (Leiden and Boston: Brill), pp. 1–38.

Boone, C. (1998) 'State Building in the African Countryside: Structure and Politics at the Grassroots', *Journal of Development Studies*, 34(4), pp. 1–31, DOI: 10.1080/00220389808422527.

Brenner, N. (2009) 'What Is Critical Urban Theory?' *City* 13(2–3), pp. 198–207, DOI: 10.1080/13604810902996466.

Caldeira, T.P.R. (2015) 'Social Movements, Cultural Production, and Protests: São Paulo's Shifting Political Landscape', *Current Anthropology*, 56(supplement 11), pp. S126–136, DOI: 10.1086/681927.

City of Windhoek (2011) *Community Leaders' Roles and Responsibilities*, Community Development Division, June.

City of Windhoek (2000) *Access to Land and Housing Policy*, January.

City of Windhoek (1999) *Development and Upgrading Strategy*, August.

City of Windhoek (n.d. a) *Guidelines on Informal Settlements in Windhoek*.

City of Windhoek (n.d. b) *Administration of Housing Group Applications*.

Clapham, C. (1998) 'Degrees of Statehood', *Review of International Studies*, 24, pp. 143–157.

Cornea, N.L., R. Véron and A. Zimmer (2017) 'Everyday Governance and Urban Environments: Towards a More Interdisciplinary Urban Ecology', *Geography Compass*, 11(4), DOI: 10.1111/gec3.12310.

Das, V. (2011) 'State, Citizenship, and the Urban Poor', *Citizenship Studies*, 15(3–4), pp. 319–333, DOI: 10.1080/13621025.2011.564781.

Das, V. and D. Poole (2004) 'State and Its Margins: Comparative Ethnographies', in V. Das and D. Poole (eds) *Anthropology in the Margins of the State* (Santa Fe and Oxford: School of American Research Press and James Currey), pp. 3–34.

Das, V. and S. Randeria (2015) 'Politics of the Urban Poor: Aesthetics, Ethics, Volatility, Precarity', *Current Anthropology*, 56(Supplement 11), pp. S3-S14, DOI: 10.1086/682353.

Davis, M. (2006) *Planet of Slums* (London and New York: Verso).

Devereux, S. (2013) 'Trajectories of Social Protection in Africa', *Development Southern Africa* 30(1), pp. 13–23, DOI: 10.1080/0376835X.2013.755871.

Dorman, S., D. Hammett and P. Nugent (2007) 'Introduction: Citizenship and Its Casualties in Africa', in S. Dorman, D. Hammett and P. Nugent (eds) *Making Nations, Creating Strangers* (Leiden: Brill), pp. 1–26.

Ellinger, I. in cooperation with W. Odendaal and L. von Carlowitz (2015) *Adequate Housing and Eviction: A Brief Overview of Namibian and South African (Case) Law in the Context of Informal Settlements* (Windhoek: GIZ Support to Land Reform Programme and Legal Assistance Centre).

Englebert, P. (2009) *Africa: Unity, Sovereignty, and Sorrow* (Boulder and London: Lynne Rienner).

Englund, H. (2015) 'Forget the Poor: Radio Kinship and Exploited Labor in Zambia', *Current Anthropology*, 56(supplement 11), pp. S137-S145, https://www.journals.uchicago.edu/doi/full/10.1086/682059 (accessed on 9 May 2018).

Englund, H. (2004) 'Introduction: Recognizing Identities, Imagining Alternatives', in H. Englund and F. Nyamnjoh (eds) *Rights and the Politics of Recognition in Africa* (London: Zed), pp. 1–29.

Ferguson, J. (2015) *Give a Man a Fish: Reflections on the New Politics of Distribution* (Durham and London: Duke University Press).

Ferguson, J. (2013) 'Declarations of Dependence: Labour, Personhood and Welfare in Southern Africa', *Journal of the Royal Anthropological Institute*, 19(2), pp. 223–242, DOI: 10.1111/1467-9655.12023.

Fraser, N. and A. Honneth (2003) *Redistribution Or Recognition? A Political-philosophical Exchange* (London and New York: Verso).

Friedman, J. (2011) *Imagining the Post-apartheid State: An Ethnographic Account of Namibia* (New York and Oxford: Berghahn).

Geschiere, P. (2011) 'Autochthony, Citizenship, and Exclusion—Paradoxes in the Politics of Belonging in Africa and Europe', *Indiana Journal of Global Legal Studies*, 18(1), pp. 321–339, http://www.repository.law.indiana.edu/ijgls/vol18/iss1/14.

Gulbrandsen, Ø. (2012) *The State and the Social: State Formation in Botswana and Its Pre-colonial and Colonial Genealogies* (New York and Oxford: Berghahn).

Hagmann, T. and D. Péclard (2010) 'Negotiating Statehood: Dynamics of Power and Domination in Africa', *Development and Change*, 41(4), pp. 539–562, DOI: 10.1111/j.1467-7660.2010.01656.x.

Hammett, D. (2017) 'Introduction: Exploring the Contested Terrain of Urban Citizenship', *International Development Planning Review* 39(1), pp. 1–13, DOI: 10.3828/idpr.2017.1.

Hansen, T.B. and F. Stepputat (2005) 'Introduction', in T.B. Hansen, and F. Stepputat (eds) *Sovereign Bodies: Citizens, Migrants, and States in the Postcolonial World* (Princeton and Oxford: Princeton University Press), pp. 1–36.

Harvey, D. (2008) 'The Right to the City', *New Left Review*, 53, pp. 23–40, https://newleftreview.org/II/53/david-harvey-the-right-to-the-city (accessed on 9 May 2018).

Hickey, S. (2010) 'The Politics of Social Protection: What Do We Get From a "Social Contract" Approach', *Canadian Journal of Development Studies*, 32(4), pp. 426–438, DOI: 10.1080/02255189.2011.647447.

Hindess, B. (2005) 'Citizenship and Empire', in T.B. Hansen and F. Stepputat (eds) *Sovereign Bodies: Citizens, Migrants, and States in the Postcolonial World* (Princeton, NJ: Princeton University Press), pp. 241–256.

Holston, J. (2008) *Insurgent Citizenship: Disjunctions of Democracy and Modernity in Brazil* (Princeton and Oxford: Princeton University Press).

Kamminga, E. (2000) *Herero and Owambo Collective Decision-making Mechanisms and the Implications for Children's Rights Realization in Namibia*, final report submitted to UNICEF.

Kelsall, T. (2013) *Economic Growth and Political Succession: A Study of Two Regions*, DRA working paper 1 (London: Overseas Development Institute).

de Kock, J.S. (2006) *Security of Land Tenure: Meeting Expectations Through a Community-driven Process (A City of Windhoek Perspective)*, a paper for the Decision Makers Meeting: Good Administration of Lands, Land Administration for Poverty Reduction and Economic Growth, Windhoek, 7–8 December 2006.

Koechlin, L. (2017) 'Introduction: Urban Land, Politics and Agency in East and West Africa', in L. Koechlin, A. Sanogo, M. Badoux and T. Förster, *African Cities, By Comparison: Urban Land, Politics and Agency in East and West Africa*, Basel Papers on Political Transformations (Basel: Institute of Social Anthropology, University of Basel), pp. 3–6.

Li, T.M. (2013) 'Jobless Growth and Relative Surplus Populations', *Anthropology Today*, 29(3), pp. 1–2, DOI: 10.1111/1467-8322.12026.

Lund, C. (2011) *Land Rights and Citizenship in Africa*, discussion paper 65 (Uppsala: Nordiska Afrikainstitutet).

Lund, C. (2006) 'Twilight Institutions: Public Authority and Local Politics in Africa', *Development and Change*, 37(4), pp. 685–705, DOI: 10.1111/j.1467-7660.2006.00497.x.

Lund, C. and C. Boone (2013) 'Introduction: Land Politics in Africa—Constituting Authority over Territory, Property and Persons', *Africa*, 83(1), pp. 1–13, DOI: 10.1017/S000197201200068X.

Mamdani, M. (2007) *Political Violence and State Formation in Post-Colonial Africa*, working paper 1 (UK: International Development Centre, Open University).

Mamdani, M. (1996) *Citizen and Subject: Contemporary Africa and the Legacy of Late Colonialism* (Princeton, NJ: Princeton University Press).

Marcuse, P. (2010) 'From Critical Urban Theory to the Right to the City', *City*, 13(2–3), pp. 185–197, DOI: 10.1080/13604810902982177.

Mbembe, A. (2001) *On the Postcolony* (Berkeley, Los Angeles and London: University of California Press).

Metsola, L. (2015) *Reintegration as Recognition: Ex-combatant and Veteran Politics in Namibia* (Helsinki: University of Helsinki), http://urn.fi/URN:ISBN:978-952-10-9158-2.

Mitchell, T. (1999) 'Society, Economy, and the State Effect,' in G. Steinmetz (ed.) *State/Culture: State-Formation after the Cultural Turn* (Ithaca, NY and London: Cornell University Press), pp. 76–97.

Mitlin, D. (2014) *Politics, Informality and Clientelism: Exploring a Pro-poor Urban Politics*, ESID working paper 34 (Manchester: University of Manchester), https://www.gov.uk/dfid-research-outputs/politics-informality-and-clientelism-exploring-a-pro-poor-urban-politics (accessed on 9 May 2018).

Niikondo, A. (2010) *Migrants to Cities and Towns in Namibia: What Their Interests Are?*, http://ir.polytechnic.edu.na/handle/10628/249 (accessed on 13 November 2017).

Nugent, P. (2010) 'States and Social Contracts in Africa', *New Left Review*, No. 63, pp. 35–68.

Nurman, A. and C. Lund (2016) 'On Track: Spontaneous Privatization of Public Urban Land in Bandung, Indonesia', *South East Asia Research*, 24(1), pp. 41–60, DOI: 10.5367/sear.2016.0296.

Nyamnjoh, F.B. and I. Brudvig (2014) 'Conviviality and the Boundaries of Citizenship in Urban Africa', in S. Parnell and S. Oldfield (eds) *The Routledge Handbook of Cities in the Global South* (London and New York: Routledge), pp. 341–355.

Patel, K. (2016) 'Sowing the Seeds of Conflict? Low Income Housing Delivery, Community Participation and Inclusive Citizenship in South Africa', *Urban Studies* 53(13), pp. 2738–2757, DOI: 10.1177/0042098015572090.

Pelham, L. (2007) *The Politics behind the Non-contributory Old Age Social Pensions in Lesotho, Namibia and South Africa*, CPRC working paper 83 (Chronic Poverty Research Centre), http://www.chronicpoverty.org/publications/details/the-politics-behind-the-non-contributory-old-age-social-pensions-in-lesotho-namibia-and-south-africa/ss (accessed on 9 May 2018).

Rawls, J. (1971) *A Theory of Justice* (Cambridge, MA and London: Harvard University Press).

Republic of Namibia (2016) *Guide to Namibia's Flexible Land Tenure Act (Act No. 4 of 2012)* (Windhoek: Ministry of Land Reform, Directorate of Land Reform and Resettlement).

Republic of Namibia (1998) *Decentralization in Namibia: The Policy, Its Development and Implementation* (Windhoek: Ministry of Regional and Local Government and Housing).

Robinson, J. (2015) 'World Cities, or a World of Ordinary Cities?', in F. Miraftab, and N. Kudva (eds) *Cities of the Global South Reader* (London and New York: Routledge), pp. 66–72.

Roitman, J. (2007) 'The Right to Tax: Economic Citizenship in the Chad Basin', *Citizenship Studies*, 11(2), pp. 187–209, DOI: 10.1080/13621020701262636.

Sassen, S. (2010) 'The City: Its Return as a Lens for Social Theory', *City, Culture and Society*, 1, pp. 3–11.

Sassen, S. (2005) 'The Global City: Introducing a Concept', *Brown Journal of World Affairs* XI(2), pp. 27–43.

Simone, A. (2013) 'Cities of Uncertainty: Jakarta, the Urban Majority, and Inventive Political Technologies', *Theory, Culture and Society*, 30(7–8), pp. 243–263, DOI: 10.1177/0263276413501872.

de Soto, H. (2000) *The Mystery of Capital: Why Capitalism Triumphs in the West and Fails Everywhere Else* (New York: Basic Books).

Steinmetz, G. (1999) 'Introduction: Culture and the State', in G. Steinmetz (ed.) *State/Culture: State-Formation after the Cultural Turn* (Ithaca, NY and London: Cornell University Press), pp. 1–49.

Stewart, F. and J. Yermo (2009) *Pensions in Africa*, OECD Working Papers on Insurance and Private Pensions 30 (Paris: OECD).

Taylor, C. (1994) 'The Politics of Recognition', in A. Gutmann (ed.) *Multiculturalism: Examining the Politics of Recognition* (Princeton, NJ: Princeton University Press), pp. 25–73.

UN-Habitat (2016) *Urbanization and Development: Emerging Futures—World Cities Report 2016* (Nairobi: UN Habitat).

UN-Habitat (2008) *State of the World's Cities 2010/11: Bridging the Urban Divide* (London: Earthscan).

Weber, M. (1978 [1922]) *Economy and Society: An Outline of Interpretive Sociology* (Berkeley, Los Angeles and London: University of California Press).

World Bank (2002) *Upgrading Low Income Urban Settlements: Country Assessment Report—Namibia* (Washington D.C.: The World Bank, AFTU 1 & 2).

CHAPTER 8

Towards an Integrative Approach to Spatial Transformation

Addressing Contextual and Spatial Indifference in Design, Urban Planning and International Cooperation: A Case Study from Addis Ababa

Sascha Delz

Abstract

This chapter draws from the author's research on recent urbanisation processes in Ethiopia's capital, Addis Ababa, and its hinterland. It addresses two aspects that are often neglected but crucial when discussing how to adequately address urbanisation along economic development and structural transformation lines: the importance of contextual differences, and the impact of spatial formation. Along these lines, two observations are highlighted: first, that there is an obvious need for new concepts of urbanisation that are driven by, and appropriate for, African contexts; and second, that it is fundamental to reconsider the role of space for economic development and structural change. Addressing these issues, the author argues for a move away from simplistic and abstract models of transition—which have substantially influenced the outcomes of development policies, international development cooperation and spatial practices—and for the exploration of more integrative, contextually informed models of transformation. Using an example of road construction in Ethiopia's capital Addis Ababa, the chapter firstly addresses particular issues related to policies of transition, and secondly, outlines an alternative approach that could address the complex challenges of economic, social and spatial transformation in a more integrative, contextually relevant manner. Suggesting a more open, spatially conscious stance (i.e. dialogic design and planning) and a more collectively conceived planning process (i.e. collective ground), the chapter thus advocates that when dealing with the complex challenges of everyday spaces for urban dwellers, future urban development policies should rather enable a multitude of contextually adequate and integrative proposals than promote a restrained catalogue of universally applied solutions.

 | DOI:10.1163/9789004387942_009

"Transition" implies a transformation between known points in time, "transformation" a structural change into something yet unknown.

HETTNE, 2009, 30

1 Introduction

1.1 *Contextual and Spatial Blind Spots in Urban Development and International Cooperation*

As so many sectors within the so-called global South, urban development, urban planning and urban design have been strongly intertwined with the global North's interventions through colonisation, and, since World War II, through the international frameworks of technical assistance and development cooperation. It is thus of no surprise that within the urban realm most of the concepts and methods for addressing urbanisation processes—in all involved disciplines—have been dominated by approaches developed in and for Western cities (Okpala, 1990; Healey, 2010; Ward, 2010). Furthermore, despite the emerging spatial turn within the academic fields of (mainly) the social sciences and the humanities starting in the 1970s (Low, 2014, 19–21), many development cooperation policies and projects appear to have repeatedly neglected such new perspectives and have thus maintained blind spots for the spatial realm in general, and the related effects on the built environment in particular. Intrinsically linked to the physical world however, urban configurations shaped by both imported concepts and spatially indifferent development policies have determined urban spaces of the everyday lives of urban citizens for better or—too often—worse. Thus, the general failure to genuinely accept locally evolved categories and criteria that could more suitably describe processes on the ground has been one of the key omissions with regard to adequately engaging with the challenges of structural and urban transformation in the respective contexts.

Addressing these issues within the context of African urbanisation, as well as from a perspective of spatial design, urban design and spatial planning, this chapter will briefly introduce the so-called Ring Road project that has been implemented through a collaboration involving Chinese actors and British engineers in Ethiopia's capital Addis Ababa. The Ring Road is one of the subjects of the author's recently finished dissertation, which follows an empirical bottom-up exploration structured along a methodological framework that combines case study research—as defined by Robert K. Yin—with a narrative inquiry as described within the methodology of phronetic planning research by Bent Flyvbjerg (Yin, 2003; Flyvbjerg, 2004).[1] Within this set-up, the chosen bottom-up trajectory has been a key method with regard to how to conduct the overall research: rather than beginning with the related theoretical frameworks of political, spatial and economic perspectives, each case study's starting point was an analysis of its physical manifestation. Following and unveiling the respective underlying processes that influenced these spatial results allowed a more precise introduction of the relevant theoretical, political and historical frameworks along the way. In summary—and as in the words of James Duminy, Nancy Odendaal and Vanessa Watson—applying a case study approach to the issues at hand is seen as a crucial methodology with regard to how to produce 'data and knowledge on African urbanisation, [...] [because it] allows the interweaving of qualitative and quantitative data in order to present nuanced explanations of how planning interventions intersect with everyday practices' (Duminy et al., 2014, 197–198). It is clear that within the limits of this chapter it is impossible to trace the complete process of the applied bottom-up trajectory or recapitulate the entire case study. Rather, the presented argument directly starts with some aspects of the dissertation's conclusion, shows parts of the empirical findings related to the respective case study, and ends with remarks that draw from—and extend—the original research's closing arguments. Reflecting on the results of the author's dissertation, and in accordance with the related introductory statements, the chapter will address following three aspects: a) the necessity of revisiting the underlying mechanisms of established conceptions of development cooperation, urbanisation and spatial planning; b) the importance of highlighting and re-conceptualizing the significance of the built environment and its physical impact on everyday lives; and c) a proposition towards more pluralistic, context-based practices that allow spatial and structural change to be shaped in a more integrative and adequate manner.

1.2 *Thinking in Transitions and Dialectic Thinking*

At the core of the following discussion on why things happen the way they do, and how they could be changed for that matter, lies the crucial distinction between transition and transformation as phrased by Björn Hettne in the introductory quote. The prospect of linear progress has not only substantially formed general discourse on development, it has also enduringly influenced the simultaneously established, official frameworks of development

1 The author's dissertation investigates three different projects of international development cooperation within and around Ethiopia's capital Addis Ababa. Including various global actors (German, Chinese and Dutch), and covering the sectors of housing, road construction and export agriculture, the research critically analyses the interrelation between underlying cooperation approaches, the applied financial models, and the resulting spatial impacts on the ground.

aid, assistance and cooperation (Martinussen, 1997). Indeed, looking at the origins of development thinking as framed by the establishment of the Bretton Woods institutions, a great majority of the introduced frameworks have been construed, planned and implemented rather through a perception of a transition 'between known points in time' than along a transformation that results in 'structural change into something yet unknown' (Hettne, 2009, 30). This focus can be mainly attributed to the influential modernisation theories that more broadly entered mainstream policies during the 1940s and 1950s (Martinussen, 1997, 38-39). Presuming '[d]evelopment [...] [to be] the process of transition from one situation to the other', modernisation—through its main motor of economic growth and development—was seen as 'a continuum stretching from poor to rich countries, which would allow for the replication in the poor countries of those conditions characteristic of mature capitalist ones'—such as 'industrialization, urbanization, agricultural modernization, infrastructure, increased provision of social services, and high levels of literacy' (Escobar, 1995, 38). Thus, the idea of development was clearly linked to a notion of a controllable, progressive transition from one stage to another.

On a more abstract level, the notion of a transition from A to B can be directly related to dialectic thinking, where a polar construct sets up a directional path for both problem definition, and problem-solving. As Richard Sennett eloquently summarises this well-established approach, 'in dialectic, as we learned in school, the verbal play of opposites should gradually build up to a synthesis [...]; the aim is to come eventually to a common understanding', and thus reveal 'what might establish that common ground' (Sennett, 2012, 18–19). In other words, dialectic reasoning is driven by an iterative but ultimately linear trajectory that converges oppositional suggestions into a synthesis, compromise or common understanding. Since dialectic problem-solving has been a dominant conceptual framework within Western culture, it has been fairly typical within development discourse to review the status of, and define engagement with low-income environments through opposing constructs as well. It is here where the aspiration to encourage development as a transition from A to B usually converges with dialectic reasoning: using real or constructed counterparts has served as the basis for envisioning developmental processes along linear paths. Harold Brookfield (1975), for instance, identifies major dichotomies, such as development and underdevelopment or tradition and modernity, as a crucial part of general development thinking. In his understanding, 'dichotomies, or polarized constructs, are basic to the simplest structuring of human perception into comprehensible order', and '[i]nevitably [...] grow into stereotypes' where '[...] argument often turns to the simpler method—"as if" there were only two classes' (Brookfield, 1975, 53). According to this statement, general thought often remains in simplistic, dual categories. Likewise, and particularly focusing on the African context during the early 1980s, geographer Anthony O'Connor detects similar tendencies to use 'crude dichotomies' such as 'developed v. less-developed', 'indigenous v. colonial cities', 'formal v. informal sectors within cities', or 'urban v. rural' when trying to both comprehend African cities and to find solutions to identified challenges (O'Connor, 1983, 21–22). Comparing such statements from the 1970s and 1980s to the contemporary critical accounts of, for instance, Jennifer Robinson, Filip de Boeck, Edgar Pieterse or Garth Myers highlights how persistent the cultural paradigm of polar and dichotomic thinking has been throughout time, disciplines, and geographies (Robinson, 2006; de Boeck and Plissart, 2004; Myers, 2011).

Thus, while dichotomic set-ups and their methodological twin of dialectic thinking might satisfy specific arenas of logical and academic analysis, they are rather prone to providing simplistic approaches when it comes to formulating and implementing policies within the complexities of a specific context—even more so if the target of analysis involves a foreign environment. While this presumably leads to set-ups that 'crudely impose or emulate an idea or practice promoted as some kind of "universal" solution', it also has an impact on how to engage with the physical environment (Healey, 2010, 6). As Brookfield further states, although many such 'dichotomies [...] are not conceived or elaborated in any spatial context, [...] they certainly have spatial implications' (Brookfield, 1975, 53). In other words, the abstract nature of dialectic reasoning, dichotomic set-ups and linear transitional thinking very likely leads to a disconnect between analytical thinking and its ramifications for physical environments, and thus ultimately incites a culture of contextual and spatial indifferences.

2 Contextual and Spatial Indifference

2.1 *Shaping Addis Ababa's Ring Road with Universal Planning and Design Principles*

The following brief portrayal of the Ring Road project in Addis Ababa illustrates how simplistic, linear problem-solving leads to both contextual and spatial indifference, resulting in many challenging outcomes for the city's spatial configuration, on the one hand, and citizens' everyday physical environments, on the other. Involving state-owned Chinese financiers and contractors, local authorities, as well as designs developed by Western engineers, the Ring Road can be seen as an exemplary case study on how economic development and cooperation—within the realm of road infrastructure—is conducted in contemporary Africa (Brautigam, 2009; Foster et al., 2008, 2009). It also serves as an illustration of how the neglect of contextual specificities and spatial implications is fostered by aspirations based on supposedly controllable transitional objectives—such as moving from traditional, underdeveloped street conditions to a modern, developed network of urban roads. Whereas the construction of the 33.4 km long road project started in 1998, was assigned to the China Road and Bridge Corporation (CRBC) and was partially financed by a Chinese loan, the design, planning and tender drawings were executed in collaboration with the British planning consultant Parkman Ltd (Mo et al., 2008) (see Figure 8.1). The circular road consists of both newly built and upgraded road sectors: out of the total length of 33.4 km, 19.2 km were built from scratch, while the remaining 14.2 km were renewed and adapted according to the new Ring Road layout and standards (Mo et al., 2008). Apart from street

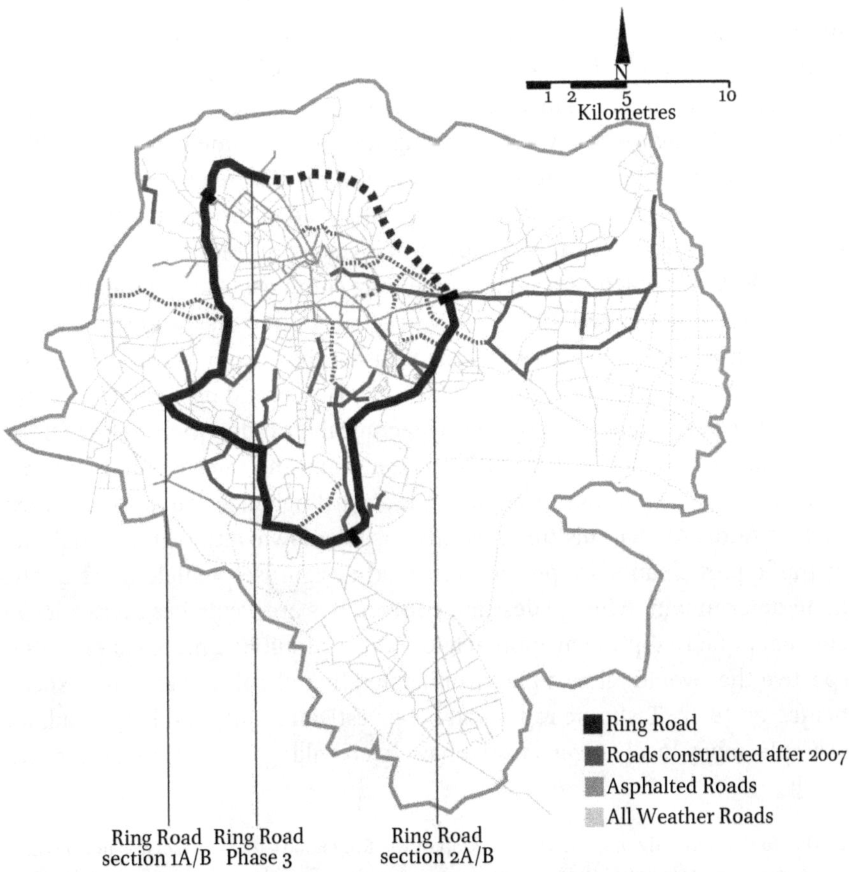

FIGURE 8.1 Ring Road sections and Addis Ababa's road network as of 2010.
SOURCE: CONSTRUCTION AHEAD, 2010 (COLOUR ADJUSTMENTS AND ANNOTATIONS BY AUTHOR)

construction work, the project features an array of supporting structures: six flyovers (bridges), 23 pedestrian bridges and 12 culverts (Mo et al., 2008).[2]

Introducing the first urban highway to Addis Ababa, the adopted approaches to the planning and design of the Ring Road have been strongly influenced by global design norms established and conceived outside of Ethiopia and Africa. Predictably, modern road and highway guidelines have been dominated by American and British standards. While one of the most representative sets of American standards—namely the design policies published by the American Association of State Highway and Transport Officials (AASHTO)—is mainly directed at the context of industrialised countries, the British Transport and Road Laboratory (TRL) has additionally produced a series of so-called Overseas Road Notes (ORNs) specifically aimed at developing countries and mainly focusing on guidelines for interurban and rural roads (TRL [1981] 2003). Accordingly, the Ethiopian Roads Authority's (ERA) guidelines on rural roads primarily use TRL codes, whereas the Addis Ababa City Roads Authority (AACRA) has compiled its Geometric Design Manual mainly along the lines of American and Australian standards (ERA, 2002; AACRA, 2003). AACRA's design manual provides an overall planning and design framework, establishing procedural guidelines regarding urban road categories, road and intersection design, landscaping, pedestrian facilities, safety measures, etc. Unsurprisingly, the combination of AACRA's adoption of American and Australian design standards, the hiring of a British engineering company, and the use of a relatively efficient set-up with Chinese finance and contractors fostered the use of global, ready-made concepts and designs rather than exploring alternative approaches derived from local circumstances, customs and necessities. This approach has been dominated by a fairly technical attitude, where vehicle flows and capacities are at the centre of considerations and the spatial or cultural-related issues of non-motorised actors are startlingly neglected. In a context such as Addis Ababa, this turns realities upside down: although the majority of traffic participants are pedestrians, road design uses vehicle flows as the main determinant, while pedestrian connections are treated as mere add-on elements. Such a top-down approach to planning inhibits a more systemic perspective that would allow a better understanding of cultural and local specificities: as Tefera Teshome reports in his investigation into the Ring Road, for example, many local citizens would have been willing to contribute their own

2 Due to the currently ongoing construction of the Ring Road's third phase, it is not possible to provide an account of the fully implemented project. Therefore, all quantitative data presented here are related to the completed, first and second stages, which represent approximately 70 per cent of the expected full contour, and were implemented from 1998 to 2004.

experiences, resources and even funding—to build bridges, for instance—to the planning process (Teshome, 2011). Ignoring such inputs from local residents, the planning actors involved opted for a rather one-sided typology comprising eight lanes on the same level, four high-speed lanes in the middle and two local feeder lanes on each side, which results in a fairly large and distinct spatial break of approx. 35 metres within the urban fabric (see Figure 8.2). Looking through the propositions of American standards with regard to how to design a street section within urban environments reveals that, indeed, the Ring Road's section design has been directly adapted from a standardised American solution (see Figure 8.3). With no further adaption, this section has been subsequently extended along the whole perimeter of the Ring Road—regardless of the variety of existing spatial conditions (see Figure 8.4).

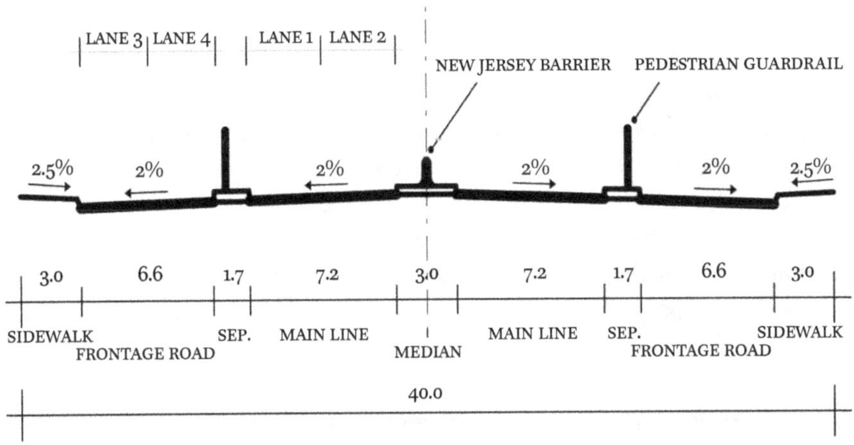

FIGURE 8.2 Schematic diagram of road cross-section geometry.
SOURCE: PARKMAN LTD. / ETHIOPIAN ASSOCIATION OF CIVIL ENGINEERS, 1998 (RETRACED BY AUTHOR)

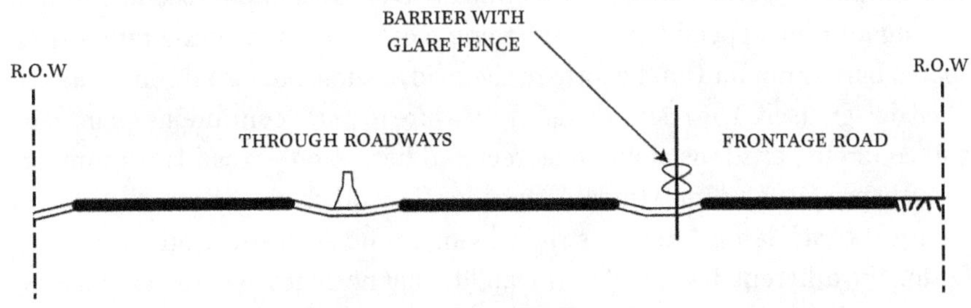

FIGURE 8.3 Restricted cross-section for ground-level freeways.
SOURCE: AASHTO, 2004 (RETRACED BY AUTHOR)

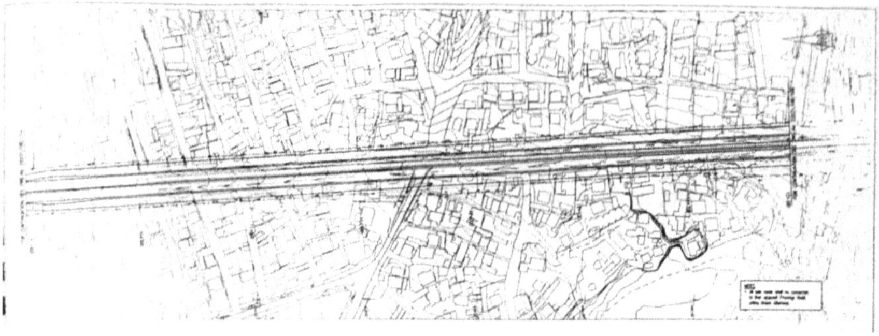

FIGURE 8.4 Ring Road tender drawings, selection of continuous road sections.
SOURCE: FDRE & PARKMAN, 1997

Using such simplified solutions has certainly been an effective method in the short term: the historically tremendous amount of road constructions (through and beyond the Ring Road) that Addis Ababa has been able to produce within a short amount of time presumably illustrates a potent transition from dusty roads towards an asphalted road network. Yet many of these projects display a clear deficit when it comes to qualitative spatial aspects that go beyond material or technical properties. In the case of the Ring Road, well-established procedural, planning, and design aspects were clearly favoured over a more qualitative, locally driven set of characteristics that could have made it possible to—at least partially—seek a new interpretation of what an urban highway could be in the particular social, economic and spatial context of Addis Ababa.

2.2 *Creating Inadvertent Spatial and Social Side Effects*

Looking at the various spatial and social effects that the design of the Ring Road has caused in Addis Ababa shows how spatially indifferent design features can produce challenging spatial set-ups beyond the abstract technicalities of site allocation, vehicle flows, curvatures and safety measures. The most influential and imminent spatial feature of the Ring Road is its schematic section design. Placing four high-speed lanes in the middle of the road creates a rather rigid spatial barrier not only in the form of the road as such, but also through the applied design itself. The resulting safety measure to place continuous guard rails and concrete partitions along the street and between the road lanes simultaneously produces an impermeable corridor for road users, and, more crucially, a critical obstacle for the pedestrians living in the adjacent neighbourhoods. Losing the different degrees of permeability that normal urban roads, and even arterial urban roads, usually offer, the Ring Road has physically segregated neighbourhoods along its whole perimeter. Closely related to this is pedestrian mobility. The planners' approach to pedestrian movement has been rather poor. Addis Ababa's high proportion of pedestrians—half of all trips within the city are made by foot; only 66 vehicles per 1,000 inhabitants—would have justified a more direct integration of pedestrian issues into the centre of design considerations (World Bank and UNECA, 2002, 105). Yet the chosen strategy of installing a series of pedestrian bridges to supposedly fix punctual connection problems reflects a predominantly technical design attitude that considers pedestrians as an abstract number, and not as actors who behave according to their human, economic and social needs. This attitude is clearly exposed through the design and distribution of these pedestrian 'supplements', which are exclusively designed along the functionalistic paradigm of safely and 'rationally' crossing a street from point A to point B.

But the Ring Road corridor not only hinders pedestrians' efforts to cross it conveniently, it also complicates vehicle drivers' lateral movements: in order to get across the Ring Road, drivers have to take a 'detour' over the roundabouts and intersections (Bekele, 2012). Furthermore, the installation of a high-speed channel, which is, for most of the time, completely separated from connecting streets, has created challenges that are directly linked to specific local conditions. Coming from a fairly Western understanding of transportation planning, such corridors are usually designed under the assumption of a steady and consistent (high-speed) traffic flow. Even small disruptions of this flow can create substantial traffic jams. Yet in the case of Addis Ababa, such consistency is hardly a given factor. To mention just some examples: the poor material condition of many heavy-load trucks or buses slows them down significantly and often results in the blockage of one lane, or sometimes both lanes (see Figure 8.5); the roundabouts, where all the local modes of transportation come together, create congestion that extends directly into the high-speed corridor; the insufficient maintenance and quality of the Ring Road generate obstacles—such as potholes or pools of water—that considerably slow down the intended consistent flow within the high-speed corridor.

Another crucial spatial effect of the Ring Road's schematic section design is caused by its rigidity. Combined with the overall planning process, the given layout seems to be fairly immune to situational adjustments that go beyond purely technical or functional means. By taking the chosen design as the given solution that accommodates the quite generally calculated capacities, even simple and minor possibilities for adjustments have not been considered. This can be shown, for instance, with the continuous implementation of the same section for the frontage roads. As it turns out, in densely populated more urban areas, these roads are often overcrowded by local vehicles, minibuses, and commercial activities. In contrast, the same layout is outsized in less populated

FIGURE 8.5 Traffic jam, Ring Road.
SOURCE: IMAGE BY AUTHOR, 2011

neighbourhoods, where all kinds of different spaces, such as agricultural land or industrial zones, adjoin the Ring Road.

Lastly, there is the issue of physical maintenance, which is related to design decisions for both road layout and materiality. On the one hand, there is the problem of property damage through both accidents and misappropriations. The instalment of relatively valuable elements, such as steel guardrails, incites many citizens to use the Ring Road as a free resource for construction materials (Teshome, 2011). On the other hand, there is a major problem with the Ring Road's drainage system, which has been designed according to British standards, but obviously (and somewhat surprisingly) did not take into account issues of local maintenance capacities, or climatic conditions, resulting in both constantly clogged and undersized drainage pipes. This repeatedly results in flooding (of the Ring Road and other newly built streets) during the rainy season (Bekele, 2012).

On an urban scale, one of the Ring Road's basic justifications was to better regulate traffic and urban growth between the city centre and its peripheries (ORAAMP et al., 2002). Through its circular set-up, the project was supposed to firstly divert through traffic from the city centre and secondly distribute both traffic and urban growth efficiently to the city's peripheries (Mo et al., 2008). Yet, looking at the changes along the project's perimeter, the Ring Road has not only served as this link between centre and periphery, but has itself become a zone for urban growth and development. Creating a first, better, or quicker access to different areas of the city, many of the plots adjacent to the Ring Road have experienced extensive spatial transformations. Rather than creating a distinction between a denser city core and dispersed expansion zones, it has accelerated the integration of remaining open territories into an ongoing pattern of suburban development (see Figure 8.6). While the general mechanism of urban development along a new or better route of access is a common result and is practically unavoidable, the specific spatial effects and formations

FIGURE 8.6 Industrial and housing development at Quarry Roundabout, 2002 (upper) / 2013 (lower).
SOURCE: GOOGLE EARTH/DIGITAL GLOBE, 2014

on the adjacent territories are often—as illustrated here—not a part of road design and road development. Performing road design from a more holistic perspective than described with the case of the Ring Road would thus implicate that designing a road means simultaneously designing a region, a city and a neighbourhood as well.

As indicated above, the most direct and challenging impacts on citizens' everyday lives caused by the Ring Road are characterised by aggravated crossing conditions. Both the Ring Road layout and the installed overpasses—rigid, ready-made structures replicated along the whole perimeter—can deliberately adapt neither to their immediate spatial surroundings nor to the existing cultural and social customs of Addis Ababa's pedestrian context. Roads as well as the overpasses are often confronted with the realities of street vending, pop-up bus stations, providing shelter, or the presence of animals (see Figure 8.7 and Figure 8.8).

The issue with animals illustrates quite specifically how both planning and design ignore the local context. Donkeys, for example, are still used as an important mode of transportation, especially within the peripheral areas and by people from the lowest income groups. The detours that the Ring Road imposes on these non-motorised participants, directly affects their daily movements, time lines and incomes. Similarly, low-income households that generated a substantial amount of their income through informal petty trade

FIGURE 8.7 Street vendors, Ring Road.
SOURCE: IMAGE BY AUTHOR, 2011

FIGURE 8.8 Animals, Ring Road.
SOURCE: IMAGE BY AUTHOR, 2011

in front of their houses thanks to walk-in customers (selling fire wood or home-made *injera* bread, for example) have experienced problems due to both relocation and spatial detachment from their immediate business environments (Teshome, 2011).[3] Apart from these specifically business-related challenges caused by impeded road crossings, different conditions can be identified under which the overpasses perform better or worse for general pedestrians. In more lively and urban surroundings, where the bridges are placed at closer intervals, they can become an almost casual part of the neighbourhoods' daily used infrastructure. Here, the density and mixed activities on both sides of the Ring Road can partially compensate for the otherwise cumbersome crossing of the highway. In areas, however, where adjacent neighbourhoods are defined by mono-functional uses such as housing, industrial production or agriculture, the bridges are usually placed further apart, creating singular bottlenecks for

3 The information compiled regarding such socio-economic issues was gathered in the form of a combination of data gained through personal observation, targeted interviews and studies produced by local researchers—such as Tefera Teshome (2011) or Gebreselassie (2012).

pedestrian crossings. While this generates an inconvenient detour for children or less agile pedestrians, many pedestrians ignore the overpasses and prefer to jaywalk than to add additional minutes or kilometres to their daily journeys (World Bank and UNECA., 2002) (see Figure 8.9).

Considering the already high number of accidents involving pedestrians in Ethiopia's cities—according to the 2002 Scoping Study on Urban Mobility from the World Bank, Ethiopia has 'one of the highest rates of road accident fatalities' with 90 per cent of fatalities being pedestrians in cities—the Ring Road's set-up clearly has not contributed to a substantial improvement (World Bank and UNECA, 2002, 40). Again, a sort of disconnection between the contextual realities and the design approach can be observed. Yet, whereas studies—such as the World Bank's—usually reveal that many of these accidents are caused by poorly defined and marked pedestrian facilities, or by pedestrians' erratic movements and behaviour in urban traffic, the proposed improvement measures mainly adhere to common notions of technical problem-solving. Apart from educational measures such as awareness campaigns, the Scoping Study on Urban Mobility, for instance, proposes the construction of additional bridges of a pedestrian-friendly design or even subways, and the installation of 'taller pedestrian barriers [...] to channel pedestrians to these facilities' (World Bank and UNECA, 2002, 41-42). However, given the local social and economic context, it is rather unlikely that the observed challenges can be resolved just by applying more technical and educational procedures—which are, once again, chiefly conveyed by an approach developed for industrialized countries and cities.

A further aspect that links spatial transformations with the socio-economic realm is signified by resettlements. In the course of implementing the Ring Road, the city government had to relocate and compensate dwellers affected by the increased spatial needs of the respective designs. Some sources, such as Mo et. al., state that 'local people forwardly assisted [the authorities] and were satisfied with the compensation for resettlements'(Mo et al., 2008, 7), while other sources report repeated challenges during these processes. According to Teshome's investigations, for instance, house owners complained that compensation for their demolished houses was too low because the applied formulaic calculations did not take replacement costs into account (Teshome, 2011). In the case of demolished Kebele housing units—the state-owned, low-end housing stock—tenants were paid ETB 1,200 (USD 146) in cash, which was supposed to cover relocation to other rental units and additional rent costs for 12 months (Gebreselassie, 2012). Within and after these 12 months, the government promised to provide alternative Kebele housing units. In view of the general housing shortage however, many inhabitants refused to take cash compensation, and demanded alternative housing units right

FIGURE 8.9 Jaywalking, Ring Road.
SOURCE: IMAGE BY AUTHOR, 2011

at the outset. The administration eventually reacted by providing low-cost housing units on the periphery of the city, often incurring higher transportation costs for residents and disconnecting the affected citizens from their communities within established neighbourhoods.[4]

3 Alternative Views on Urbanisation and Spatial Formation

3.1 *Addressing Urbanisation Through a More Ordinary and Less Ideological Mindset*

The approaches and results briefly illustrated by the examination of the Ring Road project show how rather simplistic and technocratic understandings of

4 Connected with the resettlements caused by the Ring Road, Teshome (2011) further describes an important socio-economic issue that is omnipresent in any kind of relocation of Ethiopian low-income groups: the dismantling of the so-called *iqqubs* and *iddirs*. *Iddirs* are burial associations and *iqqubs* informal savings associations, and both are strongly embedded within the social structure and spatial proximity of neighbourhoods.

urbanisation foster contextual and spatial indifference through universally applied models. This, and a de facto ignorance of the impact of such interventions on spatial formation, clearly begs a critical rethink of the underlying theoretical and practical concepts—both regarding the exploration of urban processes and the development of a spatially conscious attitude.

With regard to reframing existing concepts of urbanisation and urban processes as such, there is a series of critical, contemporary accounts that suggest a more reality-based, multifaceted, contextual attitude towards research and practice. Two important perspectives within this body of research and literature are briefly addressed here. Jennifer Robinson's book *Ordinary Cities—Between Modernity and Development* (2006) is a foundational example of this position on a global scale. Based on a postcolonial critique that during the past century dominant strands of urban research and practice were directly influenced by the overall discourse on modernisation and 'under-development', Robinson suggests an alternative vantage point when addressing cities all over the globe. Instead of ideologically labelling cities as modern and traditional, or developed and underdeveloped counterparts, Robinson demands 'that theorising about cities should be more cosmopolitan, should be resourced by a greater diversity of urban experiences', suggesting that this could ultimately lead to an understanding of every city as an ordinary entity in its own right (Robinson, 2006, 6). She further argues that this would require 'an urban theory substantially committed to comparative work', which is generally 'suspicious and cautious about deploying categories and hierarchies and eager to promote strategies for city improvements that build on their distinctive and individual creativities and resources' (Robinson, 2006, 6).

Mainly focusing on the African context, the work of urban scholar Edgar Pieterse argues along similar lines. According to Pieterse, a thorough and adequate understanding of particular urban realities and processes demands a broader base of fundamental knowledge and research: unfolding a multifaceted pool of knowledge, cultural mindsets, ideas, concepts and disciplines would ultimately lead to a deeper and more genuine understanding of what constitutes African cityness (Pieterse, 2010). To achieve this, he suggests that we 'cross-fertilise ethnographic texture, sociological patterning and topographies, spatial practices and registers and interpretive metaphors that stem from speculative philosophical enquiry and literary theory in the broad sense of the term' (Pieterse, 2010, 217). According to Pieterse, this approach would not only foster necessary, more contextual and comprehensive knowledge on African cities, it would also offer a path 'towards a more dispassionate approach' that could level out many of the extreme 'a priori moral assumptions about what is good, moral and modern, and what is not, and therefore unworthy of study, or if studied, not to be valorised' (Pieterse, 2013, 28). A dispassionate approach would therefore invest more energy in exploring 'the real city, the real economy and the real social practices and identities of the majority of urbanites who are building our cities' (Pieterse, 2013, 28). Pieterse (2013) further indicates the kind of strategy needed to perform such a research approach: converging multiple fields of expertise, such as quantitative and statistical data, literary descriptions of the urban experience, or relevant philosophical frameworks into one narrative could generate a multifaceted, reflective and critical proposition that would engage with the given urban realities, and thus would clearly move beyond contextual indifference.

3.2 *Acknowledging the Importance of Spatial Production and Spatial Agency*

While the deliberations of Robinson and Pieterse represent seminal contributions to starting re-conceptualising the study of urban issues on a methodological and theoretical level, a comprehensive inclusion of what the role—and potential—of physical space might be is still rather restrained. Yet, intrinsically linked to spatial outcomes, an exploration of new conceptions of urbanisation and urban development would have to be accompanied by investigating new notions of what the role of physical space and the built environment might be. Usually within an environment of spatial indifference, spatial formations of territory and the built environment are serving as abstract vessels that physically absorb economic progress. Territory and built structures therefore mainly represent the general, yet essential, substrate that serves to process the desired development—without consciously including the unconditional social practices that are part of everyday spatial production. Keller Easterling, for instance, convincingly describes the results of such overall processes deriving from global networks of exchange and production as spatial products that are procedural by-products of financial flows and their underlying organisational patterns rather than deliberately planned physical environments (Easterling, 2005). Under such premises, the physical environment's function is based on a sort of spatial servitude, where space, territory and the built structures are mainly conceived as the necessary material translators of political and economic activities.

Seeking to depart from such a one-sided understanding of the physical realm, the theoretical work of sociologists Henri Lefebvre and Bruno Latour offer instrumental insights and potentials. When it comes to addressing the production of social and physical urban spaces, Henri Lefebvre's writing on cities has become a well-known and widely discussed reference. This has to do not only with his framework's ability to adapt to different forms of social and political economies over time, but also with his model's set-up as a more comprehensive, interrelated model of analysis that includes political, economic, social and spatial aspects of urban formation. The analytical tool provided by Lefebvre's conceptual triad of spatial practice, representation of space, and representational space becomes particularly important within an environment of spatial indifference, since it forces one to think of spatial production as an interrelated process comprising various actors, sectors and disciplines. Lefebvre himself identifies the category representation of space—which reflects 'conceptualized space, the space of scientists, planners, urbanists, technocratic subdividers and social engineers'—as the usual 'dominant space in any society (or mode of production)' (Lefebvre, [1974] 1991, 38–39). Following Lefebvre's analysis, this dominance is the outcome of a particular political economy where 'the state and its bureaucratic and political apparatuses intervene continually in space, and make use of space in its instrumental aspect in order to intervene at all levels and through every agency of the economic realm' (Lefebvre, [1974] 1991, 378). Yet, while the analytical combinations enabled by Lefebvre's model allow us to engage with spatial production more comprehensively, it can be argued that the conceptual triad is still grounded on a certain assumption of physical spatial subordination: although social, political and cultural spaces constantly produce, reproduce and appropriate the built environment, the role of physical space is still a proxy for the portrayed mechanisms rather than a deliberately recognised, active player that is not only filled, generated and adopted, but also initiates change and actions on its own terms. Thus, when recapitulating Lefebvre's statement that space is instrumentally used—and therefore subordinated—to 'intervene at all levels' and 'through every agency of the economic realm', one would have to attribute agency to the various aspects of physical space as well (Lefebvre, [1974] 1991, 378). In other words: pursuing the idea that the physical environment can be a decisive actor on its own terms within a social environment would require introducing a concept of spatial agency.

One of the most substantial impulses that non-human objects—for example, the built environment—can participate in as actors within the social sphere derives from the so-called actor–network theory (ANT) as most prominently formulated by Bruno Latour. Latour qualifies non-human elements as determining components of society, which, indeed, can feature inherent agency as well. Given the fact that for most social models agency is directly linked to intentionality, reflexivity or meanings—a condition only humans can fulfil—Latour proposes a more abstract notion of agency that is based on the pure ability to change things as such. From this perspective, '*any thing* that does modify a state of affairs by making a difference is an actor' and therefore 'the questions to ask about any agent are simply the following: Does it make a difference in the course of some other agent's action or not?' (Latour, 2005, 71). Apart from these rather general considerations, Bruno Latour and Albena Yaneva give a brief glimpse of how the ANT's perspective could be applied to architecture—and thus to the general built environment as well. Criticising traditional architectural theory's distant way of discussing buildings as more or less neutral objects of the non-human sphere, the authors claim that—in reality—'everyone knows that a building is a contested territory and that it cannot be [only] reduced to what is and what it means' (Latour and Yavena, 2008, 86). Rather, from their perspective, a built structure should be understood in 'the way it resists attempts at transformation, allows certain visitors' actions and impedes others, bugs observers, challenges city authorities, and mobilises different communities of actors' (Latour and Yavena, 2008, 86). In this sense, a particular typology can not only be seen as the physical product of respective practices: the mere availability of a typology basically makes it an actor on its own behalf and creates a situation where a clear line between supply and demand no longer exists. Thus, if a certain typology did not exist, it would be impossible to establish this specific high-speed urban road network in such a short amount of time—or it would not even be considered in the first place. Although partially altered and adapted, the archetypes, technologies and design processes available within the global toolbox of universal solutions can be seen as active contributors to decision-making. Looking at the explored physical results and social effects of a system conceived by spatial servitude, it is, in fact, exactly along categories mentioned by Latour and Yavena (2008, 86) where the built environment could become an agent for other conceptions and attitudes: with the ability to 'resist attempts of transformation', 'challenge city authorities', or 'mobilize communities', for example, built structures and spatial formations could be more deliberately designed and organised to actively and adequately engage with respective everyday spaces, rather than being a sole accomplice of translating economic processes into space. Whether this approach would better deal with critical side effects fostered by economic agency is not entirely clear. What appears obvious though is that a more conscious attitude towards spatial agency could have the potential of introducing a crucial dimension of spatial real-life issues within economic development, development cooperation, urban planning and particular design practices.

4 Dialogic Design, Dialogic Planning and Collective Ground

4.1 *Moving Away from Linear Spatial Problem-Solving Towards More Adequate Spatial Practices*

Driven by the similar aim to dissolve the rigid structure of dialectic discourse and thinking in opposites, Richard Sennett considers an alternative and more open framework for discourse. By referring to the Russian literary critic Mikhail Bakhtin, who conceived the expression dialogic discussion, Sennett reflects on this notion 'to name a discussion which does not resolve itself by finding common ground': although, in consequence, 'no shared agreements may be reached, through the process of exchange people may become more aware of their [...] views and expand their understanding of one another' (Sennett, 2012, 19). The deliberate set-up of a dialogic discussion, where a synthetic solution 'by a play of contraries leading to agreement' is not the final objective, would allow 'bouncing off views and experiences in an open-ended way' (Sennett, 2012, 24). What if Sennett's differentiation of dialectic argument and dialogic discussion was extended to spatial planning, and design processes? A *dialogic design and planning approach*, as it were, that would automatically contest the notion of seeking transitions from A to B, or ideal, universal, and common solutions at all costs. Dialogic planning would encourage simultaneously testing different prototypes, proposals and models. In doing so, it would more adequately address the multitude of given real-life issues by contributing—in the words of Patsy Healey—to a '"pool" of knowledge' that fosters an open, diverse collection of actors, ideas and approaches within the realm of physical spatial production (Healey, 2010, 6). But a truly dialogic set-up would not only encourage a larger variety of possible ideas and solutions; it would crucially alter the way that actors from different cultural, economic, disciplinary and geographic backgrounds could cooperate with one another. Dialogic design and planning would ultimately mean that all respective stakeholders—neighbourhood representatives, local and foreign experts, local authorities, designers and NGOs—would have an equally important seat at the table from which to bring forward respective knowledge, concerns and proposals regarding how to conceive, design, implement and maintain the built environment. It would also mean that such a group would not have to agree on one or two common, overall solutions, but could negotiate, for example, a set of different approaches that were tailored for different social, economic and spatial circumstances. And finally, dialogic design and planning would inherently include the notion of spatial agency, since the produced proposals and prototypes embedded within particular built environments would induce a direct discourse on spatial impacts, challenges and performance as well.

4.2 *Using the Power of Collective Knowledge*

Although the propositions and deliberations put forward in the previous paragraph might seem diverse, they nevertheless share some mutual criteria that could, when associated with each other, offer a powerful integrative and comprehensive approach for spatial practices. Departing from abstract dialectic and transitional problem-solving, they all offer a) ways towards less universal but more reality-based solutions; b) more inclusive, open-ended planning and design processes; and c) a more comprehensive and interrelated understanding of policy and space. In contrast to an exclusive and conventional top-down arrangements of experts, models or methodologies, this approach would consist of a collective body of knowledge, evolving from a bottom-up attitude and feeding its power from truly transdisciplinary (including local residents, neighbourhood associations, industry experts, academics, public administrative staff, politicians, activists, etc.) and interdisciplinary (including actors from the fields of design, urban design, urban planning, anthropology, sociology, economics, engineering, cultural studies, etc.) set-ups.

In reference to the common ground sought by a dialectic argument, a dialogic discussion could thus aim towards a *collective ground*, where both a collection of ideas and a collective constellation of actors would aim at resolving complex urban issues with a heterogeneous, open, extendable and flexible set of different concepts, ideas and approaches. Dialogic modes of thought and exchange could eventually move away from oppositional set-ups that drive transitions towards precast solutions, and instead promote a plurality of ideas and techniques. Intentionally configured as a productive 'site of struggle' (as suggested by Patsy Healey) an approach based on a dialogic discussion would further incorporate actors and aspects that are often excluded from such processes—such as small-scale personal initiatives, cooperatively organised networks and locally-driven practices—and thus be more receptive to alternative takes, and more resilient towards unforeseen changes (Healey 2010, 6).

Based on the above-mentioned propositions, the idea of a collective ground would act as a relational network of concepts that comprises a) an ordinary and dispassionate attitude towards urban studies; b) comprehensive spatial analyses and the awareness of spatial agency; and c) an open-ended dialogic approach towards problem definition and solution finding. With regard to the presented case of urban road construction, for instance, such an approach would start the planning and design process with some essential questions to be answered by all involved stakeholders (local citizens, local and international experts from various disciplines, governmental representatives, NGOs), spurring participatory practice on a conceptional level: does Addis Ababa need an urban highway at all? If so, what is an urban highway in the context of Addis Ababa? How can a road adequately address the needs of the city's pedestrian majority? How can a road address the spatial, social and economic realities on the ground? Can a road design do more than solely accommodate calculated traffic flows? And what are the aspired spatial and economic impacts on both the affected neighbourhoods and the city as a whole?

Ultimately, allowing a flatter hierarchy and a more basic array of questions, ideas, concepts and possibilities, seeking collective ground could not only—as Garth Myers imagines—'point to the multifaceted urbanity in African contexts as a great value to global understanding of urbanism', it could also begin to dissolve the notions of opposite, transitional set-ups for urbanisation, design practices, urban planning, and economic policies as mainly defined by Western standards (Myers, 2011, 7). From this perspective, structural change into something yet unknown would literally mean opening up the way for a multitude of contextual, inclusive and innovative spatial practices that could not have been solely imagined at the desks and in the minds of established experts, administrations or remote foreign actors.

Acknowledgements

This chapter is based on the author's dissertation, which was supported by the Department of Architecture of ETH Zurich, the Future Cities Laboratory in Singapore, and the Swiss National Science Foundation (SNSF). The author would like to thank all involved reviewers for their critical and helpful input.

References

AACRA (Addis Ababa City Roads Authority) (2003) *AACRA Geometric Design Manual.* (Addis Ababa: AACRA).

Bekele, S. (2012) 'New Roads, Old Problems', *Capital*, http://capitalethiopia.com/2012/08/06/new-roads-old-problems (accessed on 1 November 2013).

Brautigam, D. (2009) *The Dragon's Gift—The Real Story of China in Africa* (Oxford: Oxford University Press).

Brookfield, H. (1975) *Interdependent Development* (London: Methuen & Co).

de Boeck, F. and M.-F. Plissart (2004) *Kinshasa—Tales of the Invisible City* (Ghent: Ludion).

Duminy, J., N. Odendaal and V. Watson (2014) 'The Education and Research Imperatives of Urban Planning Professionals in Africa' in S. Parnell and E. Pieterse (eds.) *Africa's Urban Revolution* (London and New York: Zed Books), pp. 184–199.

Easterling, K. (2005) *Enduring Innocence—Global Architecture and its Political Masquerades* (Cambridge, MA: The MIT Press).

Escobar, A. (1995) *Encountering Development: The Making and Unmaking of the Third World* (Princeton: Princeton University Press).

ERA (Ethiopian Roads Authority) (2002) *Geometric Design Manual 2002* (Addis Ababa: Ethiopian Roads Authority).

Flyvbjerg, B. (2004) 'Phronetic Planning Research: Theoretical and Methodological Reflections', *Planning Theory & Practice*, 5(3), pp. 263–306, DOI: 10.1080/1464935042000250195.

Foster, V., W. Butterfield, C. Chen and N. Pushak (2009) *Building Bridges—China's Growing Role as Infrastructure Financier for Sub-Saharan Africa* (Washington D.C.: World Bank).

Foster, V., W. Butterfield, C. Chen and N. Pushak (2008) 'China's Emerging Role in Africa—Part of the Changing Landscape of Infrastructure Finance', *Gridlines*, No. 42 (Washington D.C.: World Bank).

Gebreselassie, E. (2012) 'Addis Ababa Administration Has a Lot to Do to Make Addis Habitable', *Capital* (Online) (accessed on 1 November 2013).

Healey, P. (2010) 'The Transnational Flow of Knowledge and Expertise in the Planning Field', in P. Healey and R. Upton (eds.) *Crossing Borders—International Exchange and Planning Practices* (Oxon and New York: Routledge), pp. 1–25.

Hettne, B. (2009) *Thinking about Development* (London and New York: Zed Books).

Latour, B. (2005) *Reassembling the Social—An Introduction to Actor-Network-Theory* (New York: Oxford University Press).

Latour, B. and A. Yavena (2008) 'Give Me a Gun And I Will Make All Buildings Move—An ANT's View of Architecture', in R. Geiser (ed.) *Explorations in Architecture—Teaching, Design, Research* (Basel and Boston: Birkhäuser), pp. 80–89.

Lefebvre, H. ([1974] 1991) *The Production of Space* (Oxford and Cambridge: Blackwell).

Low, S.M. (2014) 'Spatialities: The Rebirth of Urban Anthropology through Studies of Urban Space', in D.M. Nonini (ed.) *A Companion to Urban Anthropology* (New York: John Wiley & Sons), pp. 15–27.

Martinussen, J. (1997) *Society, State and Market—A Guide to Competing Theories of Development* (London and New Jersey: Zed Books).

Mo, P., R.J. Orr and J. Lu (2008) *Addis Ababa Ring Road Project—A Case Study of a Chinese Construction Project in Ethiopia,* paper presented at the International Conference on Multi-national Construction Projects: Securing High Performance through Cultural Awareness and Dispute Avoidance, Shanghai, 21–23 November.

Myers, G.A. (2011) *African Cities—Alternative Visions of Urban Theory and Practice* (London and New York: Zed Books).

O'Connor, A. (1983) *The African City* (London: Hutchinson & Co. Publishers).

Okpala, D.C. (1990) 'The Roles and Influences of External Assistance in the Planning, Development and Management of African Human Settlement Systems', *Third World Planning Review*, 12(3), pp. 205–229, DOI: 10.3828/twpr.12.3.m26531l624816127.

ORAAMP (Office for the Revision of the Addis Ababa Master Plan), Addis Ababa City Government and Works and Urban Development Bureau (2002) *City Development Plan 2001–2010—Executive Summary* (Addis Ababa: ORAAMP).

Pieterse, E. (2013) 'Grasping the Unknowable: Coming to Grips with African Urbanisms', in E. Pieterse and A. Simone (eds.) *Rogue Urbanisms—Emergent African Cities* (Johannesburg: Jacana Media), pp. 19–37.

Pieterse, E. (2010) 'Cityness and African Urban Development', *Urban Forum*, 21(3), pp. 205–219, DOI: 10.1007/s12132-010-9092-7.

Robinson, J. (2006) *Ordinary Cities—Between Modernity and Development* (Oxon and New York: Routledge).

Sennett, R. (2012) *Together—The Rituals, Pleasures and Politics of Cooperation* (London: Allen Lane / Penguin Group).

Teshome, D. (2011) *The Effects of Urban Development in Addis Ababa—A Study of the Belt Highway Project* (Saarbrücken: VDM Verlag Dr. Müller).

TRL (Transportation Research Laboratory) ([1981] 2003) *Overseas Road Note 1—Maintenance Management for Regional and District Engineers* (Crowthorne: TRL Limited).

Ward, S.V. (2010) 'Transnational Planners in a Postcolonial World', in P. Healey and R. Upton (eds.) *Crossing Borders—International Exchange and Planning Practices* (Oxon & New York: Routledge), pp. 47–72.

World Bank and UNECA (United Nations Economic Commission for Africa) (2002) *Scoping Study: Urban Mobility in Three Cities. Addis Ababa, Dar Es Salam, Nairobi*, SSATP Working Paper No. 70 (Washington D.C.: World Bank).

Yin, R.K. (2003) *Case Study Research—Design and Methods* (London and New Dehli: Sage Publications).

CHAPTER 9

Accra's Decongestion Policy: Another Face of Urban Clearance or Bulldozing Approach?

Aba O. Crentsil and George Owusu

Abstract

Metropolitan local governments in Ghana, most especially the Accra Metropolitan Assembly (AMA), have adopted and implemented a policy of decongestion of the large metropolitan cities of Ghana in the past decades. This policy has been implemented with the explicit aim of reducing informal activities and their operators in the central business districts (CBDs) and other key areas of the cities. While the implementation of the policy in Accra, Ghana's largest metropolis, has been ad hoc in character, owing to a combination of factors such as limited public support and political liability most especially in election years, the policy in both theoretical and practical terms can be described as representing another form of the much criticised classical 'bulldozing or slum clearance' approach. Bearing in mind the backlash against the bulldozing or slum clearance approach as an unsustainable means for promoting urban development, city authorities have coined the term 'decongestion' as a simplistic approach to clearing areas of the city of Accra they perceive to be undesirable. This chapter reveals wide-ranging negative impacts of these bulldozing approaches on street traders, slum dwellers and other informal operators as well as the political liability of the policy. It also finds that the concept and practice of 'Right to the City' has, to a large extent, been 'back-burnered' as urban informal operators are regarded as not possessing any rights in public spaces, with serious implications for achieving inclusive and sustainable urban development as highlighted in the Sustainable Development Goals and the New Urban Agenda.

1 Introduction

Recent decades have witnessed a renewed interest in questions of the future of cities and the extent to which cities can shape socio-economic development in general (see UNFPA, 2007; McGranahan et al., 2001). However, nowhere have these questions received greater attention than in the global South, where rapid urbanisation has magnified the environmental impact of cities as the

DOI:10.1163/9789004387942_010

process is occurring within the context of inadequate infrastructure and services, poor planning and weak urban management and governance systems (Owusu and Oteng-Ababio, 2015). In addition, a remarkable feature of urbanisation in the global South is the widening inequalities among the population and the segregation of urban neighbourhoods along economic and income lines (Grant, 2015; Satterthwaite and Mitlin, 2014).

While the causes of these widening inequalities are not the focus of this chapter, we note that this has 'lately attracted a great deal of attention, both from academics, who have long engaged with radical urban theory, and from grassroots activists, who have been fighting on the ground for an alternative just urbanism' (Kuymulu, 2013a, 924) and a more inclusive urban development that takes account of the needs of peoples with different socio-economic backgrounds. Kuymulu (2013a) adds that the concern for inclusive urban development has also drawn considerable attention from several UN agencies, notably UN-Habitat, UNDP and UNESCO, as well as the World Bank and the International Monetary Fund (IMF), all of which have formed policy outlines to advocate for inclusive urban development. Consequently, concepts such as 'the right to the city', 'inclusive urbanisation', 'just city' and more broadly 'sustainable urbanisation' have come to dominate the policy space on urban development, which has led to fundamentally opposing institutions and ideologies (McGranahan et al., 2016; Mayer, 2012; Schmid 2012; Stanek, 2011; Fainstein, 2010; Harvey, 2008; Lefebvre, 1996 [1967]). This is because, in the view of Kuymulu (2013a, 2013b), concepts such as the right to the city are idealised political ideas with broad-based popular appeal in the face of structural urbanisation challenges and the alienation of a large section of the urban poor in respect of the benefits of urbanisation.

Ghana, a sub-Saharan African country undergoing rapid urbanisation, has largely bought into the idea of the right to the city and inclusive urbanisation, as captured in its national level policies. Indeed, Ghana's national policies such as the National Urban Policy Framework (NUPF) and Action Plan, 2012; National Housing Policy (NHP), 2015; National Spatial Development Framework (NSDF), 2015–2035; and other related national-level policies strongly emphasise urban renewal and the upgrading of slums and other informal settlements, and the promotion of the urban informal economy. However, there seems to be a policy disconnection and a contradictory policy response between the national and city levels with the introduction of a policy at the city level referred to as 'decongestion' (Awumbila et al., 2014). Decongestion policy may be defined as the removal of what city authorities perceive to be 'unwanted' activities and areas within cities in Ghana, or simply, the removal of informal settlers and street traders from public spaces in Ghanaian cities (Onuoha, 2014).

Disguised as a form of slum clearance, the policy has been implemented, particularly in the Accra metropolis, the national political and economic capital, to deal with ever-growing slums and informal economic activities, especially street trading in inner-city areas. According to Awumbila et al. (2014), growing land scarcity and high land prices have resulted in situations whereby poor, informal settlements are increasingly sited in ecologically sensitive, flood-prone areas and on vacant public lands. They further argue that these settlements develop very quickly, and only attract the attention of city authorities at a much later stage. They add that in the Accra metropolis, a special task force or unit has been established, tasked among other duties, with clearing areas of the city (including slums) that city authorities see as 'undesirable'—all under the concept of city decongestion. Yet no national-level policy, including the National Urban Policy Framework and Action Plan, 2012, advocates city decongestion. All national policies recognise and support the urban informal economy and its operators as well as the need for the upgrading and prevention of slums rather than their removal from the urban landscape.

While the concept of decongestion has been analysed by a few researchers, many of these studies have seen it as a question of the forced eviction of street traders (Broadbent, 2012; Abrokwah, 2013). For example, writing on Accra as a case study, Broadbent (2012, 1) argues that 'presented as a way of bringing order to a seemingly chaotic city centre, the mainstay of the [decongestion] policy debate surrounds the forced eviction of street hawkers from unsolicited spaces in the busiest areas of the capital'. While this assertion by Broadbent (2012) is partly true, we argue in this chapter that the decongestion policy as pursued by city authorities for the last two decades goes beyond mere forceful eviction of hawkers and street traders from central locations of the city of Accra and other major cities in Ghana. Indeed, a careful analysis of media reports, commentaries by Ghanaian urbanists as well as various media communiques of the Accra Metropolitan Assembly (AMA), the city government in charge of Accra, reveal that though pursued in an ad hoc fashion by city authorities, decongestion has been implemented for a wide variety of reasons. These include promoting the free flow of traffic and easing traffic congestion in inner-city areas, making the city fit to be a '21st Century' city under the Millennium City initiative, beautifying the city to attract tourists, businesses and investments, and making way for new flagship developments including roads and multistorey upscale market stalls/shopping malls. Other reasons cited by city authorities include dealing with perennial floods, as city authorities partly blame unauthorised structures (informal activities) for blocking waterways; reducing the growing incidence of crime, where poor, informal settlements are seen as a haven for criminals; and even, in some cases, dealing with the perceived spread of epidemics such as cholera, as was the case with the demolition—in 2014—of Mensah Guinea, a poor, informal urban community in Accra (Arku, 2014).

Targeting informal activities and blighted areas of cities in Ghana, decongestion and consequent evictions have not deterred street traders and informal economic activities nor the movement of poor migrants into poor, urban, informal settlements (Steel et al., 2014; Asiedu and Agyei-Mensah, 2008). On the contrary, informal activities (including street trading) and the proliferation of slums and informal settlements have intensified. Indeed, in 2011, the AMA and UN-Habitat identified as many as 78 settlements and pockets of slums within the Accra metropolis, with over 90 per cent of these in mature stages of development and accounting for around 38 per cent and 16 per cent of the total population and city area of Accra, respectively (AMA, 2011). While the policy of urban decongestion has been implemented for the past two decades, not enough studies have been undertaken to assess the issues of the policy responses to informality. Using the existing literature, media reports and the authors' previous, extensive study of Accra, this chapter attempts to fill this knowledge gap. It questions the policy of decongestion in both theoretical and practical terms as a means of promoting the sustainable and inclusive urban development of large Ghanaian cities such as Accra. The chapter is structured into five parts. Following the introduction, it situates urban congestion within urban theory, followed by an analysis of urban growth and the development of informality in Accra. This is followed by a discussion of the effects of decongestion, and the chapter finally concludes with the policy implications of the study, particularly with respect to the right to the city and the promotion of inclusive and sustainable development in Ghana.

2 Situating Urban Decongestion Policy within Urban Theory

The decongestion policy as defined and practiced in major Ghanaian cities, particularly Accra, is at odds with and challenges recent international slogans on promoting inclusive urban development centred on the 'right to the city' theory. This is because, as Brown (2013, 957) notes, 'the right to the city has evolved as a powerful rallying cry in the struggle against the exclusionary processes of globalisation and the commodification of urban space, and in conflicts over who has claim to the city and what kind of city it should be'. Coined by the French Marxist philosopher and sociologist Henri Lefebvre in 1967 in response to the rise of capitalist urbanisation, the theory is described as a type of human right, a collective right of all city inhabitants to participate in the use and production of urban space (Kuymulu, 2013a, 2013b; Harvey, 2008; World Social Forum, 2005). Decongestion thus represents an attempt by city authorities to hold on to the status quo and to define who has claims to the city and how it should be produced and used, and what kind of city it should be—core issues that the right to the city challenges.

Although the concept of the right to the city has also been criticised and challenged for its normative development agenda, which lacks in-depth analysis of actual political, economic, social and cultural contexts (Centner and Rojas, 2011; Jenkins et al., 2007) and overlooks underlying economic processes that perpetuate poverty and exclusion (Mayer, 2009; Fernandes, 2007), the concept has nevertheless created a vital platform for the introduction of a rights-based perspective on urban development (Brown et al., 2010). This rights-based perspective promoted by the right to the city concept holds significant implications for informal urban economies, such as street hawking, and slum developments. This is because street traders and residents of slums are highly dependent on contested urban public spaces, and their frequent dispossession through decongestion exercises carried out by city authorities in favour of other interests arguably leads to social exclusion of this section of the urban population. Huchzermeyer (2010) in employing the right to the city notion demonstrates how, in South Africa, the shack dwellers' movement Abahlali baseMjondolo in Durban invokes a Lefebvrian notion of the right to the city while embarking on rights-based action as one of several approaches it employs. Walsh (2013) also demonstrates the use of the right to the city by social movements in South Africa as having a liberalising effect as well as subverting the social antagonisms inherent in capitalism.

Some have argued that the concept of the right to the city has become intractably (and contradictorily) intertwined with the advance of the neo-liberal agenda in recent years (Brown, 2013; Harvey, 2008, 2012), with negative consequences for the urban poor. According to Harvey (2012, 13), the neo-liberal agenda has had a long-lasting and generally disastrous effect on the urban poor—the right to the city as it is now constituted is far too narrowly confined, in most cases in the hands of small political and economic elites who are in the position to shape the city more and more according to their own particular heart's desire. It is within these arguments that objectives of the decongestion policy and the right to the city concept tend to converge For example, neo-liberal policies introduced in Ghana and other sub-Saharan African countries in the 1980s as part of the World Bank/IMF's Structural Adjustment Programmes have led to increased competition for valuable and well-located land, in which the interests of affluent and powerful groups tend to prevail over those of poor communities (Grant, 2009, 2015; Fumtim, 2010; Huchzermeyer, 2010; Owusu, 2008). These policies reflect the national and city governments' desire to turn African cities into globally competitive cities. For that purpose, they tend to prioritise investments in 'world-class' infrastructure that is expected to attract foreign investors, international corporations, highly qualified professionals and tourists. These efforts to increase urban competitiveness materialise through 'urban renewal' or 'beautification' initiatives involving the demolition of informal settlements and the removal of informal street trade and unauthorised structures. Like many African capital cities, Accra has followed the same pattern by adopting an entrepreneurial approach to urban governance in which the role of the state is to facilitate private sector growth (Gillespie, 2016a; Obeng-Odoom, 2013; Grant 2009).

This view is asserted by the former mayor of Accra, Alfred Okoe Vanderpuije, who swore to transform Accra into a modern, business-friendly 'Millennium City' (Obeng-Odoom, 2013), evident from his oft-quoted catchphrase: 'eyes have not seen, neither has it entered into the ears of men, what man is about to see in Accra' (Okwuosah, 2012). Thus, in June 2009, when the AMA launched the decongestion policy to remove hawkers, illegal structures and squatter settlements from the central business district (CBD), the mayor justified the exercise with the view that 'all cities in the world are aiming at beauty and modernity so as to attract tourists, investors and other business activities' and decongestion is necessary to prevent Accra being left behind in his race for excellence (Gillespie, 2016a, 2016b). However, it needs to be stressed that most right to the city advocates condemn forced evictions and any form of criminalisation of informal settlement dwellers. Instead, they strive for recognition of urban informality, be it in the area of housing or employment and the urban economy, as the best available option for millions of people despite its obvious imperfections (Afenah, 2010, 165; Parnell and Pieterse, 2010, 153).

Again, in Ghana and elsewhere in the developing world, most urban dwellers, particularly the poor, have no legal rights in the ownership and commodification of urban spaces. The majority of them do not own land; they stay in 'encroached areas' and dwell in rented shacks. In many cases, city authorities have been repetitively unwilling to upgrade these slums, because to the authorities these urban residents are a nuisance in the urban space, and they thus deny them—especially street traders and slum dwellers—rights to space. This aligns with the Lefebvrian conception of the right to the city, wherein he argues that the right to the city is a call for the establishment of rights to include sections of the urban populace who have been denied, rather than prioritising those who already possess power, such as key political and financial interests (Marcuse, 2012; Mayer, 2012).

3 Urban Growth and the Development of Informality in Accra

A key feature of Ghana's urbanisation process to date is the unbalanced and skewed distribution of the urban population in favour of large cities that are perceived to offer a variety of livelihood opportunities (Owusu and Oteng-Ababio, 2015; Obeng-Odoom, 2013; Grant, 2009). Although Ghana had an urbanisation level of almost 51 per cent in 2010, the administrative regions of Greater Accra and Ashanti regions, have urban population levels of 90.5 per cent and 60.6 per cent, respectively. These two regions host the two largest cities in Ghana—namely, Accra and Kumasi. Accra and its metropolitan region, referred to as the Greater Accra Metropolitan Area (GAMA), was home to over 3.6 million people in 2010, representing around 15 per cent of Ghana's total population (see Table 9.1). Table 9.1 gives the impression that the Accra Metropolis is de-urbanising. However, as strongly argued in Owusu and Oteng-Ababio (2015), it has for the past two decades been fragmented into new, smaller local government areas. They add that 'this is against the backdrop of increasing land and housing prices and the process of gentrification already underway in many parts of the city— which continuously push the population to the surrounding municipalities. Under these conditions, census data are likely to give a false impression of a city undergoing depopulation' (Owusu and Oteng-Ababio, 2015, 321).

TABLE 9.1 Population of GAMA, 1970–2010

District	1970	1984		2000		2010	
	Pop.	Growth rate (%)	Pop.	Growth rate (%)	Pop.	Growth rate (%)	Pop.
Accra Metropolis	636,667	3.0	969,195	3.3	1,658,937	1.1	1,848,614
Ledzokuku-Krowor	-	-	-	-	-	-	227,932
Ga District*	66,336	4.9	132,786	8.9	550,468	5.0	908,053
Tema Metropolis	102,431	4.4	190,917	2.8	298,432	3.0	402,637
Ashaiman Municip.	22,549	5.8	50,918	6.8	150,312	2.4	190,972
Adenta Municip.	-	-	-	-	-	-	78,215
Total	827,983	3.5	1,343,816	3.9	2,501,196	3.8	3,656,423

* Includes Ga East, Ga West and Ga South Municipalities.

SOURCE: DERIVED FROM POPULATION CENSUS REPORTS 1970, 1984, 2000 AND 2010 (OWUSU, 2013)

The concentration of population in the GAMA is directly linked to migrants' strong perception that the urban centre offers better economic livelihood opportunities relative to other urban centres (Awumbila et al., 2014). Once a small coastal settlement in Ghana (then called Gold Coast), Accra became very prominent following the relocation of the national administrative capital from Cape Coast to the town in 1877 by the British colonial administrators. In the view of many analysts (Asamoah, 2001; Konadu-Agyemang, 2001; Songsore, 2009; Obeng-Odoom, 2011; Owusu and Oteng-Ababio, 2015), the relocation of the national capital to Accra, followed by significant and continuous public and private investments in its infrastructure and services throughout the colonial and postcolonial periods, has served to enhance the development of the city by attracting population, businesses and capital (including direct foreign investments).

According to Owusu and Oteng-Ababio (2015, 320), the high concentration of population in the national capital has resulted in a spillover of its population to the surrounding districts and the rapid conversion of once rural settlements into one, big, contiguous urban agglomeration referred to as the GAMA. This rapid transformation of the GAMA region has occurred with jobs and other economic opportunities such as markets and public services remaining largely within the Accra metropolis and the surrounding municipalities largely serving as dormitory centres. Consequently, there is a large demand on the services and infrastructure of the Accra metropolis, which in addition to its resident population is estimated to attract, daily, a daytime population of over 3.5 million for various socio-economic activities (Owusu, 2008). Unable to provide adequate formal housing and employment to both its permanent resident population and migrants, informality has become the order of the day for Accra. Consequently, the informal sector is the largest provider of housing, employment and other socio-economic opportunities in Accra and a critical sector for the survival of individuals and households within the city. However, the large informal sector of the city has evolved within the context of urban planning and a governance regime that are both weak, and city authorities have come to largely regard the sector as a nuisance in terms of location and operation (GoG/MLGRD, 2012). As a city, planning has failed to adequately deal with informality, and much housing and many informal businesses have tended to be haphazardly located and not in conformity with any planning regulations. This situation has largely formed the basis for the implementation of the decongestion exercises in Accra and other major cities of Ghana. Nevertheless, Accra remains the city where the decongestion policy has been widely practiced by city authorities, possibly as a result of the magnitude of urban challenges and the intense process of urbanisation (see Figure 9.1).

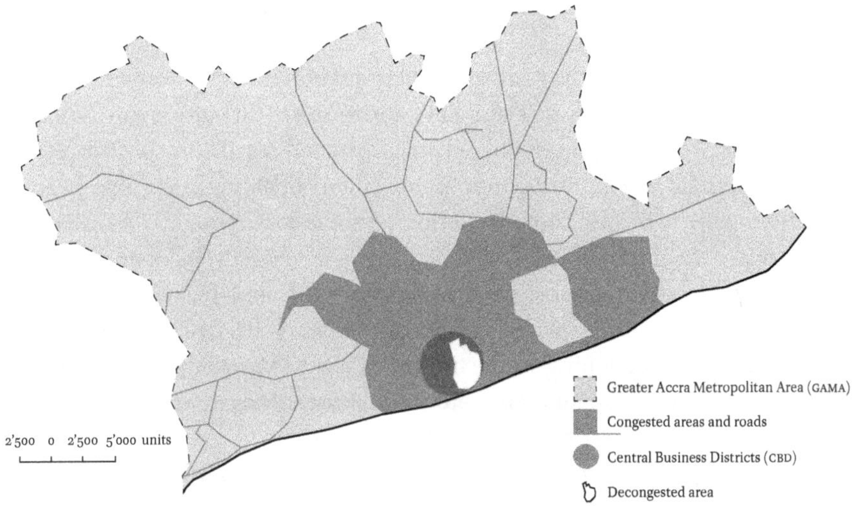

FIGURE 9.1 Map of the GAMA showing the CBD and decongested areas. (Even though decongestion occurs almost everywhere in the GAMA, we focus on areas where such activities are rampant.)
SOURCE: AUTHOR, WITH *LAND USE AND SPATIAL PLANNING AUTHORITY* DATA

4 Effects of the Urban Decongestion Policy in Accra

The implementation of the decongestion policy in Accra has taken what this chapter describes as a bulldozing approach, where a violent and impulsive stance is taken with regard to slum dwellers and workers in the informal economy, especially street hawkers. To implement the policy in 2009, the AMA passed a by-law outlawing street trading and established a Special Task Force to deal with recalcitrant street traders. The Special Task Force is also mandated to deal with all activities relating to 'illegal' occupation of space in the city. In recent years, the AMA has gone further, deploying state security agencies—especially the police—to deal with slum clearance and unauthorised occupation of public spaces (ISSER, 2014). To date, the policy of decongestion has been exercised by razing and burning unauthorised structures and chasing hawkers away from streets and sidewalks where a large number of informal economy operators eke out a living. The approach of dispossessing the informal proletariat suggests in explicit and implicit terms that certain categories of the city's workers and residents have no place in Accra to scratch out a living—an approach that advocates of the right to the city theory are very strongly critical of. For instance, stalls at the Spintex Road in Accra were set ablaze by officials from AMA as part of the city authorities' measures to beautify the city of Accra ahead of the visit in 2009 of the former US President Barrack Obama (Obeng-Odoom, 2011).

A number of researchers have also elaborated on how the implementation of the decongestion policy in Accra has been found to be tantamount to cruel, inhuman or degrading treatment, particularly when carried out with violence or with discriminatory intent (Onuoha, 2014; Steel et al., 2014; Abrokwah, 2013; Broadbent, 2012). During forced evictions, people are frequently harassed or beaten and occasionally subjected to inhumane treatment. For example, based on his interview with a street hawker, Gillespie (2016b, b974) explains how a trader's refusal to let the Special Task Force confiscate his stock resulted in his being beaten and sustaining severe injuries leading to him falling into a coma. Indeed, the Ghanaian media is replete with reports of the abuse of street traders and informal operators by the Special Task Force[1]

The decongestion of Accra's CBD also causes substantial losses for people who work in the informal economy, who usually lose goods, property, and income and suffer various inconveniences. According to Bob-Milliar and Obeng-Odoom (2011) in their study 'The informal economy is an employer, a nuisance, and a goldmine: Multiple representations of and responses to informality in Accra, Ghana', almost all traders interviewed claimed that they had lost 'something'; however, when the authors asked them to quantify their losses, they could not do so, preferring rather to stress the qualitative aspect of the loss, such as this inability to pay for their children's education. This assertion by traders of the loss of their capital and goods is thoroughly corroborated by other researchers (see Asiedu and Agyei-Mensah, 2008; Broadbent, 2012; Abrokwah, 2013; Onuoha, 2014; Steel et al., 2014) as well as media reportages.

While forced evictions have a detrimental impact on all, women often tend to be disproportionately affected and must withstand the worst of the abuse during forced evictions. This is because women tend to have a special place in the Ghanaian informal sector, a place that predates the contemporary era. According to Owusu and Lund (2004), though Ghanaian women have long been active in informal trading, the effects of economic reform programmes beginning in the mid-1980s have pushed more women into the informal sector, either as the sole providers or as supplementers of household incomes within the context of rising prices with regard to basic needs, growing unemployment

---

1 See photo archive : 'AMA used "crude tactics" to eject traders— Accra mayor', http://www.ghanaweb.com/GhanaHomePage/NewsArchive/AMA-used-crude-tactics-to-eject-traders-Accra-mayor-518311?gallery=1 and the article (2010) 'My men did not attack trader— AMA Boss', *Ghana Web*, https://www.ghanaweb.com/GhanaHomePage/NewsArchive/My-men-did-not-attack-trader-AMA-Boss-195269 (accessed on 3 September 2017).

and underemployment of male partners, declining real incomes and the growing need to meet local levies on social amenity provision in the form of user charges. Robertson (1995) adds that under these conditions, the necessity for households to have female supplementary income has become imperative and women's income-generating activities have become indispensable for family survival. This is illustrated in the work of Gillespie (2016a, 71), in the form of remarks made by one hawker, Oboye, who observed bitterly that obeying the by-law of the AMA that forbids street trading is simply not possible when one has a family to feed. Gillespie (2016a, 71) further explains that hawkers complain that the Special Task Force prevents them from making a living, vandalises their possessions, extorts bribes and sexual favours and tends to be excessively violent with traders who disobey the by-law on street trading.

Finally, the implementation of the decongestion policy has come with some political costs for both city and national leaders because of the ad hoc nature of the exercise and the lack of focus regarding the results. It is therefore no wonder that the exercise tends to be suspended during election years and only resumes after elections. In many cases, opposition parties tend to side with the informal operators while ruling national governments side with their appointed city mayors.[2] There is also evidence to show that even within the ruling party tensions tend to rise when city mayors embark on decongestion exercises. A case in point is the recent suspension of the ruling party's Member of Parliament Carlos Ahinkorah by the Tema Metropolitan Assembly following his criticism of the decongestion exercise ordered by the Assembly.[3] Similar criticisms have been levelled against former mayors of Accra, as the incumbent government sees their actions as detrimental to the election campaigns and as the potential cause of lost votes in the national polls. Within this political context, street traders and slum dwellers have mobilised against forced evictions using various strategies, including demonstrations and disobedience. For example, according to Brown et al. (2010), the Ghana trade union movement is collaborating with StreetNet International, a global network of informal workers' membership organisations, to organise traders' associations into a coordinated network that is capable of lobbying the state for the right to space in the city. These developments demonstrate how Accra's informal proletariat is taking collective action to claim its 'right to the city' (see Lefebvre

2 See the article (2009) 'Don't politicize Accra decongestion exercise—AMA boss', *Ghana Web*, https://www.ghanaweb.com/GhanaHomePage/regional/Don-t-politicize-Accra-decongestion-exercise-AMA-boss-163014 (accessed on 9 May 2018).

3 See the article (2017) 'TMA suspends Carlos Ahenkorah over alleged misbehavior', *gbcghana.com*, http://www.gbcghana.com/1.11288767 (accessed on 10 September 2017).

1996 [1967]) by defending its collective access to urban space. However, the implementation of the decongestion policy has had mixed success in keeping the informal proletariat off the streets and away from the slums. For example, the Joy FM 6 p.m. news of April 21, 2011 reported that hawkers were back on the streets doing business less than a day after a decongestion exercise was carried out. And in cases where evictions have been successful, such as the demolition of slums, evictees have moved to other squatter settlements on undeveloped land in the city. A typical case is the slum that has recently sprung up along the Accra–Tema highway—many of its inhabitants were previously residents of a section of the Old Fadama slum destroyed recently by the city authorities.

Gillespie (2016b, 989) is of the view that 'the AMA is engaging in violent processes of dispossession in order to enclose the urban commons and expel the informal proletariat'. The use of task forces in urban development exhibits a sizable level of authoritarian control in urban management as discussed above. Indeed, the use of force to dispossess the informal proletariat of urban space illustrates the influence of powerful elites in urban management, which needs to be taken into consideration in the process of urban management. We therefore are of the view that the decongestion policy in Accra is simply a disguised policy formulated and pursued by city authorities as a form of bulldozing approach of the slum clearance to undermine the presence of the poor in the city and to determine who lives and stays in the city of Accra.

5 Conclusion

Across many parts of the developing world, countries are undergoing rapid demographic transformation involving the shift of the population from rural to urban areas (Satterthwaite and Mitlin, 2014). In these countries, the pace and the recent character of the process have overwhelmed national and city governments. Consequently, in the absence of adequate preparations to cater for new and old residents of cities, individuals and households respond by addressing their needs—such as the need for housing, employment, health, education and other service delivery—by adopting a 'do-it-yourself-approach' (ISSER, 2014). However, many such approaches adopted by urban residents do not conform to city regulations and laws transplanted from the planning regulations of colonial governments, such as Ghana's antiquated Town and Country Planning Ordinance, passed in 1945, which is drawn from the pages of the British Town and Country Planning Act Ordinance of 1932 (Konadu-Agyemang, 2001, 541). This planning ordinance (CAP 84) centred around planning schemes, layouts and (more importantly) minimum plot sizes has guided the planning of Ghanaian towns for decades, and was only revised recently with the passage of the new Spatial Planning Bill in 2016.

For Accra, city authorities have conceived decongestion as a measure for addressing some of the ills of the urban development of the city. It needs to be stressed that in reality the measure is a simple attempt to conceal the inefficiencies of the city authorities as well as the poor planning and governance of the city over the years. In other words, with the probable backlash against a slum-clearance approach firmly in mind, city authorities have coined the term 'decongestion' as a simplistic approach to clearing areas of the city of Accra they perceived as undesirable. In simpler terms, there is only a rhetorical difference between a decongestion policy and slum clearance, but no difference in practical terms. Yet it is important that city authorities understand that the informal economy is not an irregularity but linked to the urban space.

In the absence of proper urban planning, largely due to weak institutions and weak enforcement of development controls, informality has come to be seen as a nuisance to urban development. Yet, this is the sector on which many urbanite Ghanaians depend for jobs, housing and other livelihood opportunities. Decongestion seems to have in some sense facilitated a hijacking of the right to the city concept by a few individuals located within the confines of the AMA who determine whose priorities and interests require attention and what the future of Accra should look like. We share the view of Brown (2013) that although the slogan 'the right to the city' seems to appeal to a broad-based constituency, transforming it into practice will remain tentative until it is embedded in the national and local systems of spatial organisation and social justice of a developing-country city such as Accra.

References

Abrokwah, S. (2013) *Decongesting the Streets of Accra: The Problems and Prospects*, unpublished MPhil dissertation (Accra: University of Ghana).

Afenah, A. (2010) 'Reclaiming Citizenship Rights in Accra, Ghana', in A. Sungranyes and C. Mathivet (eds), *Cities for All: Proposals and Experiences toward the Right to the City* (Santiago: Habitat International Coalition), pp. 155–68.

AMA (Accra Metropolitan Assembly) (2011) *Slum Situation Analysis Report Participatory Slum Upgrading and Prevention: Millennium City of Accra*, Ghana (Nairobi: UN Habitat).

Arku, J. (2014) 'AMA demolishes structures at Mensah Guinea', *Graphic Online*, http://graphic.com.gh/news/general-news/30153-ama-demolishes-structures-at-mensah-guinea.html, (Accessed on 13 August 2017).

Asamoah, A.K. (2001) *Depeasantization of Africa's Rural Economy: The Ghanaian experience* (Accra: CAF).

Asiedu, A.B. and S. Agyei-Mensah (2008) 'Traders on the Run: Activities of Street Vendors in the Accra Metropolitan Area, Ghana', *Norwegian Journal of Geography* 62(3), pp. 191–202, DOI: 10.1080/00291950802335806.

Awumbila, M., G. Owusu and J.K. Teye (2014) *Can Rural-urban Migration into Slums Reduce Poverty? Evidence from Ghana*, Migrating Out of Poverty Working Paper 13 (Brighton: University of Sussex).

Bob-Milliar, G. M. and F. Obeng-Odoom (2011) 'The Informal Economy is an Employer, a Nuisance, and a Goldmine: Multiple Representations of and Responses to Informality in Accra, Ghana', *Urban Anthropology and Studies of Cultural Systems and World Economic Development*, 40 (3-4), pp. 263-84.

Broadbent, E. (2012) *Research-based evidence in African policy debates. Case study 1. Decongestion in Accra, Ghana*, Evidence based policy development network (EBPDN), https://www.odi.org/sites/odi.org.uk/files/odi-assets/publications-opinion-files/9119.pdf (accessed on 9 May 2018).

Brown, A. (2013) 'The Right to the City: Road to Rio 2010', *International Journal of Urban and Regional Research*, 37(3), pp. 957-971, DOI: 10.1111/1468-2427.12051.

Brown, A., M. Lyons and I. Dankoco (2010) 'Street traders and the emerging spaces for urban voice and citizenship in African cities', *Urban Studies*, 47(3), pp. 666–683, DOI: 10.1177/0042098009351187.

Centner, R. and C. Rojas (2011) *Recombinant geographies of citizenship: Differentiations of the 'right to the city' in Sao Paulo, Caracas, and Buenos Aires*, Proceedings of the International RC21 Conference 2011 on: The struggle to belong; Dealing with diversity in 21st century urban settings, Amsterdam, 7-9 July 2011.

Fainstein, S.S. (2010) *The Just City* (Ithaca: Cornell University Press).

Fernandes, E. (2007) 'Constructing the Right to the City in Brazil', *Social and Legal Studies* 16(2), pp. 201-219, DOI: 10.1177/0964663907076529.

Fumtim, J. (2010) 'Building Cities for and by the People: The Right to the City in Africa', in A. Sungranyes and C. Mathivet (eds) *Cities for All: Proposals and Experiences toward the Right to the City* (Santiago: Habitat International Coalition), pp. 195–200.

Gillespie, T. (2016a) 'Accumulation by Urban Dispossession: Struggles over Urban Space in Accra, Ghana', *Transactions of the Institute of British Geographers*, 41(1), pp. 66-77, DOI: 10.1111/tran.12105.

Gillespie, T. (2016b) 'From Quiet to Bold Encroachment: Contesting Dispossession in Accra's Informal Sector', *Urban Geography*, DOI: 10.1080/02723638.2016.1191792.

Grant, R. (2015) *Africa: Geographies of Change* (Oxford: Oxford University Press).

Grant, R. (2009) *Globalizing City: The Urban and Economic Transformation of Accra, Ghana* (Syracuse, NY: Syracuse University Press).

GoG (Government of Ghana)/MLGRD (Ministry of Local Government & Rural Development) (2012) *National Urban Policy Framework and Action Plan* (Accra: MLGRD).

Harvey, D. (2012) *Rebel Cities: From the Right to the City to the Urban Revolution* (London: Verso).

Harvey, D. (2008) 'The Right to the City', *New Left Review*, 53, pp 23-40, https://newleft review.org/II/53/david-harvey-the-right-to-the-city (accessed on 9 May 2018).

Huchzermeyer, M. (2010) 'The Policy Context for Informal Settlements: Competitiveness, Slum Eradication and a Right to the City?', *Trialog*, 104(1), pp. 25–8.

ISSER (Institute of Statistical, Social and Economic Research) (2014) *Ghana Social Development Outlook*. (Accra: ISSER).

Jenkins, P., H. Smith and Y. Wang (2007) *Planning and Housing in the Rapidly Urbanising World* (Oxon: Routledge).

Konadu-Agyemang, K. (2001) *The political Economy of Housing and Urbanization in Africa: Ghana's Experience from Colonial Times to 1998* (Westport CT: Praeger).

Kuymulu, M.B. (2013a) 'The Vortex of Rights: 'Right to the City' at a Crossroads', *International Journal of Urban and Regional Research* 37(3), pp. 2013 923–40, DOI: 10.1111/1468-2427.12008.

Kuymulu, M.B. (2013b) 'Reclaiming the Right to the City: Reflections on the Urban Uprisings in Turkey',. *City*, 17(3), pp. 274–278, DOI: 10.1080/13604813.2013.815450.

Lefebvre, H. (1996 [1967]) *The Production of Space*, translated by D. Nicholson-Smith (Malden: Blackwell).

Marcuse, P. (2012) 'Whose right(s) to what city?', in N. Brenner, P. Marcuse and M. Mayer (eds) *Cities for People, Not for Profit: Critical Urban Theory and the Right to the City* (Oxon: Routledge), pp. 24-41.

Mayer, M. (2012) 'The 'Right to the City' in Urban Social Movements', in N. Brenner, P. Marcuse and M. Mayer (eds.), *Cities For People, Not for Profit: Critical Urban Theory and the Right to the City* (Oxon: Routledge), pp. 63-85.

Mayer, M. (2009) 'The 'Right to the City' in the Context of Shifting Mottos of Urban Social Movements', *City*, 13(2-3), pp. 362-374, DOI: 10.1080/13604810902982755.

McGranahan, G., D. Schensul and G. Singh (2016) 'Inclusive Urbanization: Can the 2030 Agenda be delivered without it?', *Environment and Urbanization*, 28(1), 13–34, DOI: 10.1177/0956247815627522.

McGranahan, G., P. Jacobi, J. Songsore, C. Surjadi and M. Kjellén (2001) *The Citizens At Risk: From Urban Sanitation to Sustainable Cities* (London: Earthscan).

Obeng-Odoom, F. (2013) *Governance for Pro-Poor Urban Development: Lessons from Ghana*, (Routledge, Abingdon).

Obeng-Odoom, F. (2011) 'The Informal Sector in Ghana under Siege', *Journal of Developing Societies* 27, pp. 355–92, DOI: 10.1177/0169796X1102700406.

Okwuosah, U. (2012) 'AMA is doing a good job—Accra mayor Alfred Vanderpuije', *Ghana Business & Finance*, 15, pp. 18–23.

Onuoha, D. (2014) 'Decongesting Accra', *Johannesburg Salon*, 7(1), pp. 123-130, http://jwtc.org.za/resources/docs/salon-volume-7/TheSalon_Vol7.pdf (accessed on 30 August 2017).

Owusu, G. (2013) 'Coping with Urban Sprawl: A Critical Discussion of the Urban Containment Strategy in a Developing Country City, Accra', *Planum: The Journal of Urbanism* 26(1), pp. 1-17, http://www.planum.net/planum-magazine/cities-to-be-tamed/conference-proceedings (accessed on 10 August 2017).

Owusu, G. (2008) 'Indigenes' and Migrants' Access to Land in Peri-urban areas of Accra', *International Development Planning Review*, 30, pp. 177–198, DOI: 10.3828/idpr.30.2.5.

Owusu, G. and R. Lund (2004) 'Markets and Women's Trade: Exploring their Role in District Development in Ghana', *Norwegian Journal of Geography*, 58(3), pp. 113-124, DOI: 10.1080/00291950410002313.

Owusu, G. and M. Oteng-Ababio (2015) 'Moving unruly contemporary urbanism toward sustainable urban development in Ghana by 2030', *American Behavioural Scientists (ABS)* 59(3), pp. 311–327, DOI: 10.1177/0002764214550302.

Parnell, S. and E. Pieterse (2010) 'The "Right to the City": Institutional Imperatives of a Developmental State', *International Journal of Urban and Regional Research*, 34(1), pp. 46–62, DOI: 10.1111/j.1468-2427.2010.00954.x.

Robertson, C. (1995) 'Comparative advantage: Women in trade in Accra, Ghana and Nairobi, Kenya', in B. House-Midamba and K.E. Ekechi (eds.), *African Market Women and Economic Power* (London: Greenwood Press), pp. 99-119.

Satterthwaite, D. and D. Mitlin (2014) *Reducing Urban Poverty in the Global South* (London: Routledge).

Schmid, C. (2012) 'Henri Lefebvre, the Right to the City, and the New Metropolitan Mainstream' in N. Brenner, P. Marcuse and M. Mayer (eds.) *Cities for People, Not for Profit: Critical Urban Theory and the Right To The City* (Oxon: Routledge), pp. 42-59.

Songsore, J. (2009) *The Urban Transition in Ghana: Urbanization, National Development and Poverty Reduction* (London: IIED).

Stanek, L. (2011) *Henri Lefebvre on Space: Architecture, Urban Research, and the Production of Theory*. (Minneapolis: University of Minnesota Press).

Steel, W.F., T.D. Ujoranyi and G. Owusu (2014) 'Why Evictions Do Not Deter Street Traders: Case Study in Accra, Ghana', *Ghana Social Science Journal*, 11(2), pp. 52-76.

UNFPA (United Nations Population Fund) (2007) *UNFPA State of World Population 2007: Unleashing the Potential of Urban Growth*. (New York: UNFPA).

Walsh, S. (2013) '"We won't Move": The Suburbs Take back the Center in Urban Johannesburg', *City* 17 (3), pp. 400–408, DOI: 10.1080/13604813.2013.795330.

World Social Forum (2005) *World Charter for the Right to the City*, http://www.righttothecityplatform.org.br/download/publicacoes/World%20Charter%20for%20the%20Right%20to%20the%20City.pdf (accessed on 9 May 2018).

PART 4

The Rural-Urban Continuum

CHAPTER 10

The Africa Problem of Global Urban Theory: Re-conceptualising Planetary Urbanisation

Garth Myers

Abstract

This paper works to address what I consider the enduring 'Africa problem' in global urban theory. I engage and critique selected relevant urban thought from the Globalization and World Cities research group, from Henri Lefebvre and from the new wave of urban theorisation inspired by Lefebvre's (1970) idea of 'complete, planetary urbanisation'. I argue that urbanisation in Africa, largely absent from Lefebvre's works, presents new twists that are better understood from outside a Eurocentric framework. I propose the possibilities of urban comparativism built from theories and conceptualisations that emerge from the global South and that can be utilised to compare non-Western cities' urbanisation processes. I use case studies from Dakar and Zanzibar to examine the production of what Chinese urbanists detail as a 'village' in the city, on the edge of the city, and in the suburbs over the last half-century and the complexities and comparability of urbanisation processes in these settings. I end with reflections on the implications of these cases for any claims for universalising the twenty-first century's processes of urbanisation and urbanism across the planet. My main finding for urban policy and planning practice is the documentation of the relevance and value of South–South comparisons of urbanisation processes for development.

1 Introduction

Urban theory still has an Africa problem, despite two decades of sustained critique of Euro-Americanism in theories of urbanisation. I contend that we can see this both in the work produced by the Globalization and World Cities (GaWC) research group and in ostensibly more Africa-aware work influenced by the recent push towards analysis of 'planetary urbanization'. The problem may be a different one in these two schools of thought, but it leaves us with an enduring lacuna where global South intellectual understandings and conceptualisations of urbanisation processes as they intersect with globalisation would otherwise drive scholarly analysis. My goal in this chapter is to explore an urban comparison across the global South, from southern China to two urbanisation processes in Africa (Dakar and Zanzibar), conceptualising from outside global North frameworks. I assess the utility of the intertwined Chinese ideas of a 'village-in-the-city', a 'village-on-the-edge' and a 'village-in-the-suburbs'—in scholarship analysing processes of rapid urbanisation in the Pearl River Delta over the last fifty years—for the analysis of similarly rapid processes in sub-Saharan Africa over this same time period. In the first segment, below, I argue for thinking beyond global North theorisation. In the second, I make a case for the value of 'unexpected' comparisons like this (Myers, 2014). Thirdly, I turn to the case study comparison.

2 The Global South and 'Africa Problems' in Urban Theory

One can see an increasing interest in urban Africa across the social sciences in the global North recently. Although the list of exceptions may be growing, there is still little in this work that attends carefully to insights from African urban studies or from the global South more generally. Two very significant arenas of global analysis in urban studies, arenas that ought to have more emphases on African processes of urbanisation, are the works of the Globalization and World Cities (GaWC) group and the scholarship on planetary urbanisation.

The GaWC research group has developed important, data-rich empirical assessments of interconnections between cities in the world economy. I begin with its work, because it is arguably the place where most urban studies scholars start in attempting to come to grips with the interwoven impacts of globalisation and urbanisation. They have filled out previously intimated hierarchies and links resulting from competition between elite enclaves striving for economic command and control (Beaverstock et al., 1999 and 2000; Taylor et al., 2012). GaWC scholars have an ever-widening map of cities—but it is still a map dominated by select global North cities, albeit with a scattering of global South cities beginning to rise. The GaWC group ranks cities 'in terms of their advanced producer services using…[an] interlocking network model. Indirect measures of flows are derived to compute a city's network connectivity – this measures a city's integration into the world city network' (The World According to GaWC[1]). Cities are scored on a scale using the Greek letters Alpha, Beta and Gamma, and both plus and minus signs—the highest scores, for the most integrated or globalised cities, are Alpha ++, and the listing continues through

1 The World According to GaWC, http://www.lboro.ac.uk/gawc/gawcworlds.html (accessed on 3 November 2017).

to Gamma - cities; an increasing number of cities are ranked in two sorts of 'honourable mention' categories, High sufficiency and Sufficiency, below the 'lettered' cities.

Table 10.1 documents the history of Africa's cities in the GaWC rankings, where I abbreviate the rankings' letters with the English rather than the Greek alphabet's first three letters (A, B and C) and the 'honourable mention' categories as HS and S (for High sufficiency and Sufficiency, respectively). As the Table documents, Africa's proportional share of cities listed at all from 2000 through 2016 hardly changed. The 2016 table lists a few more African cities than in previous years, but on a scoreboard with more cities, and almost all the raw total increase is in cities newly listed in the lowest category of global significance, 'Sufficiency'. In 2016 and 2012 the lone African city in the top 'Alpha' levels (A ++, A +, A or A –) was Johannesburg, and there were no Alpha cities on the continent before this. Some massive African cities do not appear at all.

TABLE 10.1 Cities in Africa according to the GaWC ranking

CITY	2016	2012	2008	2004	2000
Johannesburg	A	A –	B +	B +	B +
Cairo	B +	B +	B	B	B
Cape Town	B +	B +	C +	C	C
Lagos	B +	B –	C	HS	HS
Casablanca	B	B	C +	HS	C –
Port Louis	B –	B –	C –	C –	C –
Tunis	B –	B –	HS	HS	HS
Durban	C +	C +	S	S	HS
Kampala	C +	HS	S		S
Accra	C	C –	HS	HS	S
Dar es Salaam	C	C –	S	S	S
Lusaka	C	HS	S		HS
Abidjan	C	HS	S		HS
Harare	C	S	S	S	HS
Luanda	C	S		S	
Gaborone	C –	HS	S	S	S

TABLE 10.1 Cities in Africa according to the GaWC ranking (*cont.*)

CITY	2016	2012	2008	2004	2000
Douala	C –	HS		S	S
Dakar	C –	HS			S
Maputo	C –	S			S
Windhoek	HS	S		S	S
Pretoria	HS	S		S	
Abuja	HS	S			
Nairobi	S	B –	C +	S	C
Libreville	S		S		
Kigali	S				
Port Elizabeth	S				
Blantyre	S				
Tripoli	S				
Kinshasa	S				
Lomé	S				
Antananarivo	S				
African Cities in the...					
Alpha rankings	1	1	0	0	0
Beta rankings	6	7	2	2	2
Gamma rankings	12	3	5	2	4
High sufficiency list	3	6	2	4	6
Sufficiency list	9	6	8	9	8
Total Number of African cities	31	23	17	17	20
Total cities actually listed	359	293	246	225	225
Percentage African in list	**8.6**	**7.8**	**6.9**	**7.6**	**8.8**
Cities in the database	526	526	525	315	315

SOURCE: CREATED BY AUTHOR FROM DATA AVAILABLE ON THE WEBSITE OF THE GLOBALIZATION AND WORLD CITIES RESEARCH GROUP—HTTP://WWW.LBORO.AC.UK/GAWC/GAWCWORLDS.HTML (ACCESSED ON 17 APRIL 2018)

Even where African cities appear, there are oddities that seem inexplicable to African studies scholars. Between the 2012 and 2016 rankings, for example, Nairobi dropped from Beta+ to the lowest ('Sufficiency') category, when very little of the story of Nairobi in those years would indicate to any scholars of Kenyan urbanisation any reasons for a slip in global significance (Myers, 2015). The GaWC database is about office networks for advanced producer services—a very narrow economistic understanding of globalisation, even if more recent lists include data on advertising, accounting and law firms. Yet even so it is an inexplicable oddity that the ranking for Nairobi—which any urbanist of Africa would recognise against any measure of globalisation as consistently one of the continent's most globally networked cities for financial services—has fluctuated radically in the GaWC's calculations and plummeted in those four years. One might claim that the map of GaWC in 2016 has improved on its Africa problem from the 2000 map, but largely by volume, not by intellectual veracity.

That earlier map shaped a critique of the GaWC approach from global South and Africa scholars (e.g. Robinson, 2002 and 2006; Bunnell, 2017). Robinson (2002 and 2006) contended that the GaWC neglected the cities 'off the map' and assumed globalisation and urbanisation to be universal, global North-driven and economistic, and worked out from a game plan of terms that missed key dynamics of globalisation and urbanisation across 'ordinary' cityscapes in the whole world. All this set policymakers in cities on mistaken paths of development that short-changed glaring basic needs for most urbanites and largely ignored histories and specificities, extending the 'unequalization' of cities internally as well (Carmody and Owusu, 2016, 69). The drive to make cities 'global' seems to have had particularly negative consequences in cities in Africa (Myers, 2015).

Criticisms from Robinson and others led the GaWC researchers to expand somewhat their criteria for globalisation, but also to push back (Smith, 2013; McNeill, 2017). This counter-critique often centres on the 'absence of evidence' in the work of 'ordinary cities' scholars (Smith, 2013, 2301) and the vagueness of concepts in 'Southern' urban theory. Yet there is still much to criticise with the GaWC group, despite claims that its scholars have incorporated or surpassed the postcolonial critique, and most notably for urbanists who focus on Africa. Globalisation's impacts go far beyond the range of cities in Africa that GaWC includes in its surveys, to secondary and much smaller cities (Mainet and Racaud, 2015; Choplin and Pliez, 2015). GaWC scholars Caset and Derudder (2017) analyse the 'cultural' manifestations of global-and-world-city status, but their criteria for cultural significance are completely global-North driven. No city in Africa surfaces either in the top 30 of their statistical index or among their

51 global arts 'financial centres' (Caset and Derudder, 2017). Urban Africa's absence is a result that any globally minded comparative understanding should find implausible, given the central importance of Africa for *urban* culture in a long historical–geographical arc (Simone, 2010). Here, the GaWC framework for research into what constitutes urban culture does take note of the rise of Chinese cities as 'cultural' centres, but the framework cannot see African urban culture, or globally significant cultural institutions in Africa (or throughout the global South) that do not adhere to European criteria of culture.

A smorgasbord of more genuinely global urban studies building from Lefebvre has productively sidestepped debates between GaWC and global South scholars (McNeill, 2017). The Lefebvrean concept that the world has entered an era of 'complete, planetary urbanization' has gained great traction in urban studies (Lefebvre, 1970; Brenner and Schmid, 2014 and 2015; Merrifield, 2013; Ruddick, 2015; Millington, 2016; Soja, 1989, 2000 and 2010). The phrase itself is at least a half-century in the making, stretching back to Lefebvre's (1970) hypothesis of it in *The Urban Revolution*. Lefebvre, though, was writing from the vantage point of France. When he discussed the urban outside of Europe in *The Urban Revolution* it was with brief vignettes and broad strokes—Africa did not appear at all, and his analysis of China in 1970 became irrelevant in the era of economic reform there.

The contemporary push to conceptualise a stage of planetary urbanisation is more genuinely planetary in its reach, and more aware of Africa and global South urbanisation. Brenner and Schmid (2015), for example, offer seven theses on planetary urbanisation, the most relevant of which here is thesis three: that 'urbanization involves three mutually constitutive moments', which they call concentrated, extended, and differential urbanisation. They argue that in this era 'the city' is no longer the only or the central concern—concentrated urbanisation, essentially the production of cityness, is but one of three processes of urbanisation taking place. Extended urbanisation and differential urbanisation are occurring in still-under-examined processes across the planet (Murray, 2017). Through theses four through seven, which emphasise the 'multidimensional', 'planetary', 'variegated' and 'contested' character of these three processes of urbanisation, respectively, they invite exploration of the diversity of processes in both global North and global South urban regions.

As Schmid (2016, 30, 33) acknowledges, the 'classic model of urbanity [...] has long been overtaken by worldwide urbanization processes' and 'we are living in a completely different urban world' than Lefebvre in 1970. Brenner and Schmid's (2015, 162) work to address that completely different urban world engages with postcolonial urban theory, but they emphasise the 'urgent task of deciphering' the way 'contemporary forms of neoliberal capitalist urbanization are unfolding across the North/South divide'. They argue that postcolonial or 'Southern' urban theory's emphasis on thick descriptions of everyday life and unique global South specificities leaves out or over-generalises urbanisation processes in global North contexts.

Eurocentric and universalising tendencies in older world/global cities studies were not eradicated with this strong new enthusiasm for Lefebvre (Sheppard et al., 2013; Shaw, 2015). The dominant voices and perspectives of this discussion still belong to the global North, and efforts to reach into the global South for analysis are not aimed at relocating conceptual starting places there. Many global South-oriented scholars have different emphases in mind when exploring the 'planetary' (Jazeel, 2011; Mbembe, 2017). A caution remains for postcolonial, global South and African urbanists with the possibility that 'the universalizing force' in Western thought might 'reduce everything to "the same"' through the Lefebvrean analytical lens of planetary urbanisation (Britton, 1999, 12; Glissant, 1989, 97).

3 Towards an 'Unexpected' Urban Comparativism

There are ways of rethinking the entire discussion that build from outside of global North urban theory, and from an approach that foregrounds postcolonial understandings. Like GaWC scholars, Storper and Scott (2016) and Rizzo (2017, 5–7) criticise postcolonial urban studies for overgeneralising, for selectively criticising modernism, or for weak methodology that make the resulting studies 'woefully vague', lacking in 'empirical data' and 'lacking in [Marxist] attention to the economic and political structures in which the poor are located'. Some of these criticisms may have some validity, but even Storper and Scott (2016, 1121) agree that 'urban theory must now range over the entire world for its sources of data and evidence while remaining fully open to new conceptual insights generated out of the experiences of the cities of the Global South'. There is still much ranging across Southern thinking needed, and openness to its insights for developing global urban studies, to challenge the conceptual assumptions that remain embedded in the field. This need may be felt in many contexts, but it is surely evident for the study of both Chinese and African urbanisation. As the United Nations has noted in outlining Goal 11 (making cities 'inclusive, safe, resilient and sustainable') in the Sustainable Development Goals, '95 per cent of urban expansion in the next decades will take place in the developing world', with China and sub-Saharan Africa very prominent in this expansion process.[2] It is completely logical to begin from analyses and conceptualisations of processes there to attempt to build an understanding of contemporary 'planetary urbanization'.

Processes in China and Africa leading to planetary urbanisation go far back in time, well before this contemporary age of neo-liberal globalisation (which is also too often understood only from the perspective of the global North). There is ample latitude for detailing the specificities of globalising processes over many centuries (Meier, 2016; Prestholdt, 2008). Global South approaches give us tools to see the making of globalised cityscapes differently, from the margins and shadows that run parallel to, connect with or contest Northern understandings of urbanism and urbanisation.

I build on Robinson's broad rubric for global urban comparativism here. Robinson (2016 and forthcoming) proposes remaking comparative global urban studies as multiple variations on 'thinking cities through elsewhere' or 'thinking with elsewhere' (Robinson, 2016). She provides elaborate means for developing robust, historical–geographical comparisons. Comparisons, in her schema, can be genetic or generative, and scholarly tactics can involve tracing, composing or launching these comparisons (Robinson, 2016). This chapter is an exploration of the 'launching' of a comparison that is at once genetic and generative, in Robinson's terminology. The genetic launching starts with a singularity, the southern Chinese idea of a village-in-the-city, but includes 'inserting analysis of this case into wider conversations'. It is generative, too, in that I take a concept out of China that I 'put to work elsewhere'. Since 'a revised comparativism would seek to deliberately stretch concepts' even to the point of breaking them, the experiment here is 'highly revisable', and I have conducted it with what I hope is a 'modest authorial voice' (Robinson, forthcoming).

A vital aspect of my approach to comparison also relies on Glissant's postcolonial Caribbean discourse of 'Relation'. At root, for Glissant, Relation is a form of comparison reliant on 'equality with and respect for the Other as different from oneself' (Britton, 1999, 11). Glissant's vision of comparison is 'nonhierarchical and nonreductive', avoiding a 'universal value system' and acknowledging the 'particular qualities of the community in question' (Britton, 1999, 11). This is a comparativism that makes use of the thick descriptions of particularities in the global South by testing their relation to one another. In Glissant's (1989, 98) vision, comparison celebrates 'diversity [...] without universalist transcendence', where postcolonial societies exist 'no longer as objects to be swallowed up, but with the intention of creating a new relationship'. Glissant

2 *UN Sustainable Development Goals*, Goal 11: Make cities inclusive, safe, resilient and sustainable, http://www.un.org/sustainabledevelopment/cities/, accessed on 18 January 2018.

(1990) resists the colonisers' determination to subsume and excise the 'roots' of other peoples beyond the global North or the West into the 'mono-root' of Western thinking.

To counter any potential criticism that this leads to another 'vague' and 'convoluted' postcolonial approach to urban studies, I put an empirically grounded emphasis into the dynamics of this comparison. To that end, I examine the Chinese terms, *chengzhongcun*, *chengbiancun* and *chengwaicun*—translated as a village 'in-the-city', 'on-the-city-suburb-edge' and 'in the suburb'—in terms of their potential relevance in Africa. They arose as means of describing and analysing what is happening to the small settlements (*cun*) swallowed up all over the Pearl River Delta's megacities as they grow exponentially following China's explosive industrialisation over the last forty years (Al, 2014; Altrock and Schoon, 2014; Chen, 2007; Chen and de'Medici, 2012; de Meulder and Shannon, 2014; Roberts, 2013; Schoon, 2013; Wu et al., 2012). In the Pearl River Delta (PRD) in 2018, hundreds of villages remain inside, on the edges of and in the outskirts of Shenzhen, Guangzhou, Dongguan and other megacities in the region.

The distinctions between the three terms are subtle. The vast majority of all pre-existing villages in the PRD were what are called 'lineage villages', meaning that their residents shared ancestral lineage (Cenzatti, 2014). What happened to the villages with urbanisation partly depended on where they were in relation to industrialisation or urbanisation projects. On one hand, there is a simple spatial distinction: villages that are encased within a fully urban setting are *chengzhongcun*, those which lie firmly outside the urban boundaries are *chengwaicun*, and those in between are *chengbiancun*. This goes together with a continuum of density in both population and structures, from the densely populated built environments of *chengzhongcun* outward to the lesser density of the *chengbiancun* and the least dense *chengwaicun*. As megacities expand in the PRD, though, the spatial separation and density gradation have become more difficult to identify. The implicit assumption of the inevitability of the development of all villages into *chengzhongcun*, villages-in-the-city or urbanised villages, and then their destruction and reconstruction as regularised 'proper' sections of urban areas, ultimately proves problematic. Some *chengwaicun* stabilise as important agricultural producers for the urban cores (Cenzatti, 2014), some *chengzhongcun* reinvent themselves to retain some vestiges of their pre-existing character (Crawford and Wu, 2014; Jun, 2014), and some *chengbiancun* seem to remain in between in both density and urban character (Hao, 2014). Despite the tendency to resort to calling all three types *chengzhongcun*, or rendering all three types in English as urbanised villages, and despite the difficulty occasionally of differentiating the three types, it remains worthwhile to sort them as distinct, both in spatiality and density, and in terms of the intensity at which processes of urban development transpire along the gradient that connects the three.

These concepts of villages in-the-city, on-the-edge, or in-the-suburbs are fascinating for comparative purposes in Africa. As cities have grown throughout the world historically, they have swallowed up the farmlands and hamlets within and around them. In *The Urban Revolution*, Lefebvre (1970) wrote that 'in many places around the world, and most certainly any place with a history, the existence of the city has accompanied or followed that of the village'. He was certainly identifying something akin to what the Chinese terms aim to explain, but within his ultimately Eurocentric framework. One is left to wonder what would have met his definition of a 'place with a history', for example, since the history of cities in Africa did not attract his attention. He does critique the 'ideology' that he associated with the representation here of 'slowly secreted urban reality', but not really for the fact that it 'generalizes from what took place in Europe'. The processes and pathways by which villages evolve into cities or become enmeshed in urban realities have varied tremendously, as has their pace, around the world.

As we look at the urban world of the early twenty-first century, nearly everywhere in the rapidly urbanising portions of the global South we can see places that look like villages in the city, on its edge, or in its suburbs. The literature on South Asian or South-East Asian urbanisation, for instance, has long highlighted these phenomena (Hust and Mann, 2005; McGee, 1997). Here, I take a focused approach of using these types from the Chinese literature and apply them to two urban regions, Dakar and Zanzibar, with the task of comparing how their 'urban villages' have come to be. Example 'villages' like Ouakam, Thiaroye and Keur Massar in and around Dakar, and Kikwajuni, Fuoni and Mwera in Zanzibar are parallel with the three Chinese settings, respectively, as we move out from the city boundary. I am arguing that perhaps this tripartite conceptualisation about the spatiality and pace of the urbanisation process from China, rather than Lefebvre's ideas for 'complete, planetary urbanization', might be of more relevance to the similarly rapid pace and broad sprawl we see in sub-Saharan Africa. In the interest of brevity, I concentrate on the cases of Thiaroye and Fuoni, as villages-on-the-edge (*chengbiancun*) in the Dakar region and Zanzibar, respectively. I compare these with PRD examples in terms of land development, governance and participation in housing and urban development. I contend that, while these two African cases are different from each other and from the PRD cases, the comparability is more enlightening than an attempt to shoehorn either African case into Western-defined processes of globalisation or of planetary urbanisation.

4 Comparing the Edge Urbanisation Processes in the PRD and Sub-Saharan Africa

As Förster (2016, 7) has put it, in Africa 'urbanites make their cities in ways that scholars have yet to comprehend', especially in, around and across the city edges. Might the Chinese concepts take us towards such comprehension? The tripartite division of Chinese processes has the potential to do so, even if there are notable differences. First, however, let me make a more basic case for comparability between the PRD, Dakar, and Zanzibar, particularly in these edge settings. The logic of utilising Dakar and Zanzibar arises not simply because I have conducted fieldwork in urban and peri-urban 'villages' of both contexts. These are also deliberately chosen for being much smaller cities than the PRD's megacities, and therefore representative of cities often left out of the analyses of GaWC or of Lefebvrean planetary urbanisation; but they are also ones which—like the Pearl River Delta region—have been defined around their 'planetary' relationships for centuries. As slave-trading ports and entrepôts of global trade from the 1500s (in the case of Dakar) and 1600s (for Zanzibar), links with Europe, Asia, the Americas and the rest of Africa were crucial to the formation of the urban identities of both cities. These global histories make Zanzibar and Dakar well situated for illustrating different starting places for something we may call 'planetary' urbanisation.

More immediately, all three urban regions (the PRD, Dakar, and Zanzibar) have experienced rapid urbanisation in the last half-century. Within the PRD, the most profound narrative of rapid urbanisation thus far arguably belongs to the megacity of Shenzhen. Shenzhen's urbanisation and industrialisation was transformed by the 1978 decision to establish China's first special economic zone there (Chen and de'Medici, 2012). Shenzhen had a population of around 30,000 people at the time, with the many surrounding villages containing at most 300,000 people. The overall metropolitan area is now around 60 times larger than it was 40 years ago. Much of the growth has been in the population moving to Shenzhen for industrial employment, but with rural *hukou* (registration). People lacking urban *hukou* comprise almost 80 per cent of Shenzhen's population. Many of them reside in urban villages because the lack of urban *hukou* makes obtaining housing elsewhere more difficult; the lower regulation and cost in urban villages produce a market that is available for low-income migrants. However, as urban villages are demolished or gentrified, many of Shenzhen's floating population are pushed farther out to the edge villages or suburban villages (Tian, 2008; Zhang et al., 2016).

Dakar and its satellite city of Pikine have experienced a similar phenomenon, at a relatively slower pace and smaller scale. Dakar's population is currently estimated to be just above 3 million, more than nine times its size at independence in 1960 of around 350,000. The area that is now part of the city of Pikine at its initial establishment in 1952 was home to about 8,000 villagers, in several farming settlements. Thiaroye was the largest of the pre-existing villages. Pikine's population is more than 1.2 million now, and Thiaroye has more than 225,000 inhabitants—around 40 times its size in 1952. Thiaroye has grown largely as a result of displacements due to rising housing costs in Dakar, in combination with rural-to-urban migration caused by stress on Senegal's agricultural economy—rather than as a result of a massive wave of industrialisation.

Zanzibar has also experienced a relatively rapid urbanisation of its edge, in places like Fuoni. The small city proper had a little more than 49,000 inhabitants on the eve of independence in 1958, 115,000 in 1978, and 223,000 in 2012. But West Districts A and B, the edge communities that are now thoroughly morphological and functional parts of urban Zanzibar, grew from a set of rural farming villages with less than 20,000 people in 1958 to 370,678 in 2012 (Myers, 2016). Fuoni went from a tiny village of less than 1,000 people in the 1970s to a village-on-the-edge of 34,774 as of 2012, now subdivided into two enumeration areas. I remember bicycling through coconut plantations and python-rich swamps in Fuoni in 1991, and by 2017 it is essentially the new downtown of the Zanzibar metro area. Fuoni, as with Thiaroye, owes its growth to the high costs of housing in Zanzibar city in combination with rural-to-urban migration, rather than to the Shenzhen sort of industrial explosion.

The reasons for focusing in on Thiaroye and Fuoni are as follows. The most thoroughly studied of the three Chinese categories (*chengzhongcun*, the village-in-the-city or urbanised village) is self-explanatory: these are the pre-existing villages that become quickly surrounded by dense urban development. But it is also the least like most urban African cases. This is because colonialism's restrictions on migration and urban residence caused most cities on the African continent to grow slowly until the waning days of European rule. In that context, pre-existing urban villages either were demolished, slowly eroded away, or ossified. Only very recently, with for instance Huruma in Nairobi, Ouakam in Dakar, or Kariokoo in Dar es Salaam, do we see processes in Africa that might more precisely mirror the *chengzhongcun* of the PRD, in the form of extremely dense, high-rise and low-rent apartment development that accompanies—and forms an intrinsic part of—rapid urbanisation of land and population (Myers, 2016; Huchzermeier, 2011; Seifert, 2011). Massive, nearly instant processes of urbanisation are more common straddling or outside municipal boundaries in Africa, what is often termed the peri-urban zone, and they occur along the two broadly distinct trajectories identified by Chinese scholars as *chengwaicun* and *chengbiancun*—villages on the city edge and villages in the suburbs—but most intensely right along the urban edges.

To go anywhere with this comparison, though, we must recognise that there are important differences. Two overwhelming differences noted already are the overall numbers between the PRD and African urban cases as well as the absence of massive industrial employment growth in the latter. A third lies in the built environment, in the housing stock—the 'handshake-houses' and 'thin-line sky' characteristic of the three 'village' types in China (Roberts, 2013; Al, 2014; de Muelder and Shannon, 2014) are less common in Africa. Handshake-houses are tall, narrow apartment buildings built so close to one another that people say one could reach out a window and shake hands with a resident of the next building. The closeness of these towers leaves an observer in the alley a view of only a thin line of sky above, hence the 'thin-line sky'. Again, there are the beginnings of high-rise developments of a comparable density in African *chengzhongcun*, but far less in the *chengbiancun* or *chengwaicun*.

Still, all three edge-village (*chengbiancun*) settings have experienced rapid urbanisation for at least some comparable reasons, like overcrowding in a nearby city and in-migration from both city and countryside. All three edge-village areas, then, experience overcrowding in substandard housing. All three are full of highly underserviced neighbourhoods. All three have socio-cultural tensions and rising inequalities between villagers and newcomers—and within indigenous village societies—that sometimes spill over into politics. In housing terms, the parameters are similar even if the physical housing stock differs. Even greater commonalties can be found in land development, in the fluid and variable roles of 'village' participation in governance, and in the development processes in these edge areas, as I examine below.

In the PRD, the urbanisation of land starts with the appropriation of agricultural areas by the government—often the local or municipal government (Shin, 2014)—and private interests allied to it, for factories and formally developed urban areas. This 'entrepreneurial push for urban redevelopment' through state-led 'strategic planning' uses land as an accumulation strategy (Shin, 2014, 269). However, because villagers retain the rights to their housing stock, when confronted with the subsequent loss of farming livelihoods many village development committees of residents seek investors to build larger structures for rental to migrants on their housing areas. Villages thus typically retain somewhat the morphological structure of the pre-existing village, with much taller structures (Wiethoff, 2014, 336). Open spaces that passed for a sort of public space between villages steadily disappear at a rapid pace of 'everyday urbanization' (Wiethoff, 2014, 341). This is not a uniform or predictable pace for land urbanisation, and it has a potent mix of 'formal de jure permissions' and 'informal de facto reactions' embedded in it (Wiethoff, 2014, 341).

There are striking parallels here to West District of Zanzibar around Fuoni, and even to some extent with Pikine. The morphological structure of Fuoni and Thiaroye still retains, in segments, a relationship to the built environment of the pre-existing villages. The 'everyday urbanization' in both settings contains a mix of state-led order in the distribution of land and informal reaction. For Fuoni, the 1964 nationalisation of land—here, initially, for a socialist ideological development policy rather than the financialisation of land as an investment—eventually played a part in the urbanisation pattern, but in a manner that is quite relatable to the PRD cases. The long, drawn-out implementation of the 1982 Chinese Master Plan for Zanzibar included development of planned and ordered neighbourhood units (NUs) in Fuoni, but few of these grew in a manner anything like that proposed by the plan. In the 1960s, many properties had been allocated to revolutionary cadres in the government's three-acre allotments, and these were frequently the first areas to be informally urbanised—a process often led, in Fuoni, by the informal plans of three-acre plot holders themselves (Myers, 2016). Land control steadily slipped from a central government intent on allocating it in new, planned NUs into an informal system where land rights became instruments of benefit in the hands of local party officials. Thiaroye experienced no strictly socialistic nationalisation, but it nonetheless developed as a complex mixture of formally and informally organised and controlled urban lands, with segments of state-led, grid-like development surrounded by haphazard construction, particularly in marginal zones.

The participatory governance dynamics in relation to the state in these three contexts may present contrasts, but there is still room for comparability. In the Pearl River Delta, and perhaps especially in Shenzhen, there is a degree of local government autonomy rare in much of urban China. This gives rise to flexibility in *hukou*, for instance, so that Shenzhen's government has been able to grant certificates of residency that amount to a quasi-legal urban *hukou* for many rural-*hukou* residents. The villages in the city, the edge and the suburbs, while varying in the capacity for implementation of planning or governance initiatives in them, also contain governance units with effective opportunities for action, in the form of village development committees. Some are just meant to serve as tools for state actions, such as in Shin's (2014) case study of Enning Road in Guangzhou, where the old village area was scheduled for demolition. Many village committees have more effectively organised villages for collective development action; even in Enning Road, sustained residents' resistance slightly reduced the scope of demolitions and displacements (Shin, 2014, 279; Zhang and Li, 2016). Often, the process has resulted in the development of mid-rise and high-rise apartment buildings on the land formerly occupied by single-story village houses. In some cases, officials cite claims of extraordinary wealth flowing to village development committees (which is occasionally the case) as a way of suggesting that a stand-in for the villagers are benefiting; but in reality most villagers have seen few gains from the process, and migrant residents even less. Inequalities long seen in *chengzhongcun* are now also beginning to rise in edge and suburban villages (Zhang et al., 2016). In Xiaohong and Schoon's (2014) case study of Guangzhou's Liede village, the villagers leading its 'joint-stock company' held the upper hand, but ordinary residents worked hard to participate in decision-making during the redevelopment. There is a high degree of heterogeneity in the capacity for negotiating powerful roles—and the incoming migrants have even less power or capacity than lower-status villagers (Wiethoff, 2014). Still, there are numerous examples throughout the PRD of attempts at more participatory planning of village urbanisation dynamics, variations on what Zhiqiang (2014, 221) refers to as 'gaming' in the decision-making process. A few smaller urban villages stabilised by developing a peculiar economic niche; these include Dafen, the 'Oil Painting Village' of northern Shenzhen. In others, wholesale demolition has taken place or is scheduled for the future. In Hubei, a religious minority community has maintained just over half of its neighbourhood of single-story, closely built humble homes in the shadow of a fancy new shopping district. The local government has long scheduled Hubei for complete demolition. But the recent effort to showcase the vibrancy of *chengzhongcun* and *chengbiancun*—ironically, by having villages host the 2015 Shenzhen architectural biennial—has helped local planners and activists to navigate towards a plan that may preserve approximately one fourth of the original residential space of the village (Fu, pers. comm., 2017).

Local government and developers in the PRD, along with the local media, use the poor physical conditions of villages and their alleged association with unsavoury or even illegal activities as discursive tactics to push for village demolitions. Perhaps the most interesting example of this for this chapter is in Guangzhou, where the *chengzhongcun* of Xiaobei, derided in the local press as 'Chocolate City' for its considerable African population, faces intense pressure for redevelopment (Badgley, pers. comm., 2017; Li et al., 2009; Su, 2016). And in the Pearl River Delta, the forces for demolition and redevelopment allied with and often led by the state, eventually win almost all the battles over *chengzhongcun*, which then leads to the further growth of *chengbiancun* and *chengwaicun*.

On the surface, Thiaroye and Pikine/Dakar present something very different in governance terms. First, the framework for governance is built around a lively multiparty democratic system, rather than China's single-party Communist system. Since the 1998 reorganisation of local government, Pikine has been a city in its own right in the Dakar Region, divided into three *arrondissements*, Dagoudane, Niayes, and Thiaroye. Below this are 16 *communes d'arrondissements*, five of which are in Thiaroye. Each commune has a *chef de quartier*. But there are elements of confusion and varying degrees of incapacity for this governance structure. For example, the *chef de quartier* of Thiaroye Gare in 2013 was at pains to point out that he considered himself a *chef de village*, both in naming the pre-1998 designation of Thiaroye as a village and citing his long connection to the village itself as its *chef*. Yet whether it is in *quartiers* or *villages*, collective action has a strong foothold in Dakar and Pikine politics and governance (Brown, 2015; Fredericks, 2014).

The local state is strangely both more responsive and sensitive to the ordinary people of Thiaroye than the local governments of the PRD are in relation to urban and edge villages, and less capable, largely because of a staggering lack of resources, of meeting their needs. While a major new toll road was built, with Chinese engineers, through Thiaroye without compensation being given to the residents of sixty or so houses that were demolished, the community suffers from near-annual disastrous flooding, an absence of solid waste management, chronic shortages of electricity and water services, a severe environmental health crisis, and haphazard construction. Yet it is, as its *chef de village* put it in 2013, 'the heart of Pikine'. Its largely informal market is one of the largest in Senegal. Politicians, local officials and mosque leaders share with ordinary people a sense of pride in Thiaroye for its welcoming, cosmopolitan character balanced with Lebou village traditions. While a form of gentrification has certainly established a foothold, in the *commune d'arrondissement* of Thiaroye sur Mer, which is technically a part of Thiaroye *arrondissement* but quite geographically distinct on the opposite side of the new toll road, it is nonetheless hard to imagine Thiaroye becoming like Hubei. It might, on the other hand, have more in common with Dafen, as its artists and musicians, such as those based at the artists' cooperative Africulturban, become genuine engines for the populist development of many Pikine neighbourhoods like Thiaroye (Mbaye, 2014). There is much that is parallel to Zhiqiang's (2014) notion of residents' 'gaming' the dynamics.

In Zanzibar, the local government structures lie somewhere in between the more controlled hierarchy of the PRD and the more open democracy of Dakar. Since 1995, Zanzibar has had a multiparty system, but the ruling Revolutionary Party has manipulated all five national elections to stay in power, while bleeding away the powers intended for elected local government into central government-appointed units (Myers, 2016). Zanzibar's 2000 restructuring of local government re-introduced a colonial-era local government representative, called a *sheha*, as an appointment from the central government working under the appointed District Officer. *Masheha* (pl.) have been principal agents of the continued chaotic urbanisation of West District, particularly in the wards of Fuoni and other edge communities. The edge villages of West District, along the line of the official boundary with the municipal government, had by the late 1990s earned the local nickname of the Gaza Strip, as a hotbed of sometimes violent opposition to the Revolutionary Party. In 2012, the government of Zanzibar subdivided West District into an A and a B, but its efforts to provide services in either district have been meagre, just like in Thiaroye, in every sector other than road-building (Myers, 2016). Fuoni in 2016 and 2017 witnessed the massive widening of its main road, replete with the largely uncompensated demolition of its small businesses, and the paving of many of its side streets. It lacks other basic services, but widening the main road greatly enhanced the central route to Zanzibar's southern and central east coast tourism zone and provided an aesthetic mask for tourists over the conditions inside neighbourhoods like Fuoni. That the Revolutionary Party remains one that was modelled on the Chinese Communist Party is clearly reflected in its similar lack of allowance for oppositional voices in planning processes in edge villages. Yet even here there are pathways for the expression of non-compliance, such as in what I have discussed elsewhere as spatial discourses of *fitina* (discord) (Myers, 2016). For instance, in Fuoni and other parts of both West A and West B districts, one often finds, deeper in the alleyways, the light blue-white-and-red banners and insignia of the opposition Civic United Front hanging, tattered, years after an election campaign.

5 Conclusion

Globalisation in cities, the globalising of urban areas or regions, and the 'planetarization' of the urban are all themes that have preoccupied many urbanists over the last four decades. These global North-driven discussions have been late in coming around to urban Africa, and when the attention does come, it is not generally seeking to build from existing African scholarship or Southern analyses or frameworks, instead attempting to fit them into Northern frameworks. One way to address urban theory's enduring problems with Africa, such as what I've argued may be found in the work of the GaWC or Lefebvrean approaches to planetary urbanisation, is to build South–South comparisons that utilise concepts or frameworks designed for explaining Southern urbanisation. The highly comparable rapid urbanisation processes for previously rural village land on the edges of cities provide one empirical context for testing this premise.

In these villages on the edge, we see 'planetary' histories and futures. The processes have great variability and fluidity within and between the settings of this study, but there is much to compare—so much that, in fact, I have merely scratched the surface. For instance, while there is no *hukou* registration system for Senegal or Tanzania, new migrants to Pikine or West District find themselves similarly situated in a divided landscape of insiders and outsiders with varied capacities for belonging. Land development has resulted in notably different urbanising forms, yet through comparably complex pathways that involve variations on limited capacity for local participation and gain from 'gaming' mixed and corrupted systems.

One might counter my examples by saying they are just variegated cases of the 'extended urbanization' of Brenner and Schmid's (2015) Lefebvre-inspired theses on 'planetary urbanization'. But the paths of these 'extensions' are markedly distinct in China, Senegal or Tanzania, respectively, and from global North cases. It is precisely towards thick description of the difference that we must turn, especially if critics of postcolonial or Southern urban studies continue to speak of an absence of evidence or of conceptual vagueness. The ordinary cities that are still too often 'off the map' are telling stories that should change the narrative. After all, if the narrative is about the rapid urbanisation of the planet, that is a narrative that, in the twenty-first century, clearly belongs to South Asia, South-East Asia, China and sub-Saharan Africa. Countries like Senegal and Tanzania have rates of urbanisation that have topped the world for many consecutive decades now.

In thinking with these urban elsewheres, putting the three village-in-the-city concepts to work in African cities, I have certainly stretched the concepts. I have attempted to do so while remaining mindful of Glissant's goal of non-hierarchical, mutually respectful comparison that rejects universality and makes productive use of particularities in the differences. Obviously, there is much more that could be discussed regarding the potential comparability of these neighbourhoods—let alone the comparability of all three of the PRD types. The point is, again, that there are in fact so many realms of comparability. One might just as well start the story from the African settings and use conceptualisations of urbanisation from Senegal or Zanzibar to see how they might help to explain urbanisation in the PRD. I contend that this approach, too, would likely be more enlightening than an effort to apply Lefebvre's ideas about planetary urbanisation from France nearly a half-century ago to these rapidly expanding urban edges in global South contexts. It is through exploration of these seemingly unexpected South–South comparisons that policy makers ought to find more cogent pathways to more sustainable and just urbanisation.

Acknowledgements

Funds for the research for this paper have been provided by the Paul E. Raether Professorship at Trinity College and the Luce Foundation grant to the Center for Urban and Global Studies at Trinity College for the study of East Asian urban environments. I thank Xiangming Chen, Mailys Chauvin, Jenny Robinson, Armelle Choplin, Stina Wolff, Rosalind Fredericks, Jenny Mbaye, Tim Mangin, and Makame Muhajir for their comments in discussing an earlier version.

References

Al, S. (2014) 'Introduction: Villages in the City: A Guide to China's Informal Settlements', in S. Al, (ed.) *Villages in the City: A Guide to South China's Informal Settlements* (Hong Kong: Hong Kong University Press), pp. 3–8.

Altrock, U. and S. Schoon (eds.) (2014) *Maturing Megacities: The Pearl River Delta in Progressive Transformation* (Berlin: Springer).

Badgley, C. (2017) Author's personal communication with Christiane Badgely, documentary filmmaker and director of the documentary film, *Guangzhou Dream Factory*, Basel, Switzerland, 28 June 2017.

Beaverstock, J.R. Smith and P.J. Taylor (2000) 'World-City Network: A New Metageography?', *Annals of the Association of American Geographers*, 90(1), pp. 123–134, DOI: 10.1111/0004-5608.00188.

Beaverstock, J.R. Smith and P.J. Taylor (1999) 'A Roster of World Cities', *Cities*, 16(6), pp. 445–458.

Brenner, N. and C. Schmid (2015) 'Towards a New Epistemology of the Urban?', *City*, 19(2–3), pp. 151–182.

Brenner, N. and C. Schmid (2014) 'The "Urban Age" in Question', *International Journal of Urban and Regional Research*, 38(3), pp. 731–55, DOI: 10.1111/1468-2427.12115.

Britton, C. (1999) *Edouard Glissant and Postcolonial Theory: Strategies of Language and Resistance* (Charlottesville, VA: University of Virginia Press).

Brown, A. (2015) 'Claiming the Streets: Property Rights and Legal Empowerment in the Urban Informal Economy', *World Development*, 76, pp. 238–224, DOI: 10.1016/j.worlddev.2015.07.001.

Bunnell, T. (2017) 'Locating Transnational Urban Connections Beyond World City Networks', in J. Hannigan and G. Richards (eds.) *The SAGE Handbook of New Urban Studies* (London: SAGE), pp. 19–29.

Carmody, P. and F. Owusu (2016) 'Neoliberalism, Urbanization and Change in Africa: the Political Economy of Heterotopia', *Journal of African Development*, 18, 61–73.

Caset, F. and B. Derudder (2017) 'Measurement and Interpretation of "Global Cultural Cities" in a World of Cities', *Area*, 49(2), pp. 238–248, DOI: 10.1111/area.12324.

Cenzatti, M. (2014) 'The City in Between the Villages', in S. Al (ed) *Villages in the City: A Guide to South China's Informal Settlements* (Hong Kong: Hong Kong University Press), pp. 9–18.

Chen, X. (2007) 'A Tale of Two Regions in China: Rapid Economic Development and Slow Industrial Upgrading in the Pearl River and the Yangtze River Deltas', *International Journal of Comparative Sociology*, 48(2–3), pp. 167–201, DOI: 10.1177/0020715207075399.

Chen, X. and T. de'Medici (2012) 'From a Fishing Village via an Instant City to a Secondary Global City: The "Miracle" and Growth Pains of Shenzhen Special Economic Zone in China', in X. Chen and A. Kanna (eds.), *Secondary Cities* (London: Routledge), pp. 107–126.

Choplin, A. and O. Pliez (2015) 'The Inconspicuous Spaces of Globalization', *Articulo: Journal of Urban Research* (online) 12, http://journals.openedition.org/articulo/2905 (accessed on 18 April 2018).

Crawford, M. and J. Wu (2014) 'The Beginning of the End: Planning the Destruction of Guangzhou's Urban Villages', in S. Al (ed.) *Villages in the City: A Guide to South China's Informal Settlements* (Hong Kong: Hong Kong University Press), pp. 19–28.

Fredericks, R. (2014) '"The Old Man is Dead": Hip Hop and the Arts of Citizenship of Senegalese Youth', *Antipode*, 46(1), pp. 130–148, DOI: 10.1111/anti.12036.

Förster, T. (2016) 'Foreword', in A. Simone, *Always Something Else: Urban Asia and Africa as Experiment* (Basel: Basler Afrika Bibliographien), pp. 5–8.

Fu, N. (2017) Author's personal communication with Na Fu, urban planner in Shenzhen.

Glissant, E. (1990) *Poétique de la Relation* (Paris: Gallimard).

Glissant, E. (1989) *Caribbean Discourse: Selected Essays* (Charlottesville, VA: University of Virginia Press).

Hao, F. (2014) 'Spatial Development Patterns', in B. de Muelder, Y. Lin and K. Shannon (eds.) *Village in the City* (Zurich: Park Books), pp. 66–69.

Huchzermeyer, M. (2011) *Tenement Cities: From 19th Century Berlin to 21st Century Nairobi* (Trenton, NJ: Africa World Press).

Hust, E. and M. Mann (eds.) (2005) *Urbanization and Governance in India*(New Delhi: South Asia Institute).

Jazeel, T. (2011) 'Spatializing Difference Beyond Cosmopolitanism: Rethinking Planetary Futures', *Theory, Culture & Society*, 28(5), pp. 75–97, DOI: 10.1177/0263276411410447.

Jun, J. (2014) 'A Village by the Special Economic Zone: The Dafen Paradigm of China's Urbanization', in S. Al (ed.) *Villages in the City: A Guide to South China's Informal Settlements* (Hong Kong: Hong Kong University Press), pp. 42–46.

Lefebvre, H. (2003 [1970]) *The Urban Revolution* (Minneapolis: University of Minnesota Press).

Li, Z., L. Ma and D. Xue (2009) 'An African Enclave in China: The Making of a New Transnational Urban Space', *Eurasian Geography and Economics*, 50(6), pp. 699–719, DOI: 10.2747/1539-7216.50.6.699.

Mainet, H. and S. Racaud (2015) 'Secondary Towns in Globalization: Lessons from East Africa', *Articulo: Journal of Urban Research* (online), 12, DOI: 10.4000/articulo.2880.

Mbaye, J. (2014) 'Hip-Hop Politics: Recognizing Southern Complexity', in S. Parnell and S. Oldfield (eds.) *The Routledge Handbook on Cities of the Global South* (London: Routledge), pp. 396–412.

Mbembe, A. (2017) *Critique of Black Reason*, trans. Laurent DuBois (Durham: Duke University Press).

McGee, T. (1997) *Five Decades of Urbanization in Southeast Asia: A Personal Encounter* (Hong Kong: Institute of Asia-Pacific Studies).

McNeill, D. (2017) *Global Cities and Urban Theory* (Los Angeles and London: Sage).

Meier, P. (2016) *Swahili Port Cities: The Architecture of Elsewhere* (Bloomington, IN: Indiana University Press).

Merrifield, A. (2013) 'The Urban Question under Planetary Urbanization', *International Journal of Urban and Regional Research*, 37(3), pp. 909–922, DOI: 10.1111/j.1468-2427.2012.01189.x.

Millington, G. (2016) 'The Cosmopolitan Contradictions of Planetary Urbanization', *The British Journal of Sociology*, 67(3), pp. 476–495, DOI: 10.1111/1468-4446.12200.

de Muelder, B. and K. Shannon (2014) 'Village in the City as Urbanism in China and Elsewhere', in B. de Muelder, Y. Lin and K. Shannon (eds.) *Village in the City* (Zurich: Park Books), pp. 4–19.

Murray, M. (2017) *The Urbanism of Exception: The Dynamics of Global City Building in the Twenty-First Century* (Cambridge: Cambridge University Press).

Myers, G. (2016) *Urban Environments in Africa: a Critical Analysis of Environmental Politics* (Bristol, UK: Policy Press, University of Bristol).

Myers, G. (2015) 'A World-Class City Region? Envisioning the Nairobi of 2030', *American Behavioral Scientist*, 59(3), pp. 328–346, DOI: 10.1177/0002764214550308.

Myers, G. (2014) 'From Expected to Unexpected Comparison: Changing the Flows of Ideas about Cities in a Post-Colonial Urban World', *Singapore Journal of Tropical Geography*, 35(1), pp. 104–118, DOI: 10.1111/sjtg.12046.

Prestholdt, J. (2008) *Domesticating the World: African Consumerism and the Genealogies of Globalization* (Berkeley: University of California Press).

Rizzo, M. (2017) *Taken for a Ride: Grounding Neoliberalism, Precarious Labour and Public Transport in an African Metropolis* (Oxford: Oxford University Press).

Roberts, N. (2013) 'From Handshake Buildings to Golf Villas: How the Flash Cities of Manchester and Shenzhen Came of Age', in V. Bharne (ed.) *The Emerging Asian City: Concomitant Urbanities and Urbanisms* (London: Routledge), pp. 203–210.

Robinson, J. (Forthcoming) *Comparative Urbanism: Tactics for Global Urban Studies* (Los Angeles: Sage).

Robinson, J. (2016) 'Thinking Cities Through Elsewhere: Comparative Tactics for a More Global Urban Studies', *Progress in Human Geography*, 40(1), pp. 3–29, DOI: 10.1177/0309132515598025.

Robinson, J. (2006) *Ordinary Cities: Between Modernity and Development* (New York: Routledge).

Robinson, J. (2002) 'Global and World Cities: a View from Off the Map', *International Journal of Urban and Regional Research*, 26(3), pp. 531–554, DOI: 10.1111/1468-2427.00397.

Ruddick, S. (2015) 'The 2013 Urban Geography Plenary Lecture: Situating the Anthropocene: Planetary Urbanization and the Anthropological Machine', *Urban Geography*, 36(8), pp. 1113–1130, DOI: 10.1080/02723638.2015.1071993.

Schmid, C. (2016) 'Planetary Urbanization: Henri Lefebvre und das Recht auf die Stadt', in S. Kraft, A. Aichinger and Z. Zhang (eds.) *Planetary Urbanism: The Transformative Power of Cities* (Berlin: Arch+ Verlag GmbH), pp. 26–34.

Schoon, S. (2013) 'Niche Authority in Urbanized Villages: Bottom-up Codetermination in Megacity Developments in China', in N. Perera and W.-S. Tang (eds.) *Transforming Asian Cities: Intellectual Impasse, Asianizing Space, and Emerging Translocalities* (London: Routledge), p. 222–242.

Seifert, A. (ed.) (2011) *Global City – Local Identity?* (Dar es Salaam: Mkuki na Nyota Publishing).

Shaw, K. (2015) 'Planetary Urbanisation: What Does It Matter for Politics or Practice?', *Planning Theory & Practice*, 16(4), pp. 588–593.

Sheppard, E., H. Leitner and A. Maringanti (2013) 'Provincializing Global Urbanism: A Manifesto', *Urban Geography*, 34(7), pp. 893–900, DOI: 10.1080/02723638.2013.807977.

Shin, H.B. (2014) 'Elite Vision before People: State Entrepreneurialism and the Limits of Participation', in U. Altrock and S. Schoon (eds.) *Maturing Megacities: The Pearl River Delta in Progressive Transformation* (Berlin: Springer, pp. 267–285).

Simone, A. (2010) *City Life from Jakarta to Dakar* (New York: Routledge).

Smith, R. (2013) 'The Ordinary City Trap', *Environment and Planning A*, 45, pp. 2290–2304, DOI: 10.1068/a45516.

Soja, E. (2010) *Seeking Spatial Justice* (Minneapolis, MN: University of Minnesota Press).

Soja, E. (2000) *Postmetropolis: Critical Studies of Cities and Regions* (Malden, MA: Blackwell).

Soja, E. (1989) *Postmodern Geographies: The Reassertion of Space in Critical Social Theory* (London: Verso).

Storper, M. and A. Scott (2016) 'Current Debates in Urban Theory: A Critical Assessment', *Urban Studies*, 53(6), pp. 1114–1136, DOI: 10.1177/0042098016634002.

Su, R. (2016) *The Emergence and Shift of the 'Chocolate City': The Socio-Spatial Dimensions of the African Community in Southern China and its Implications*, unpublished BA honors thesis (Hartford, Connecticut: Trinity College).

Taylor, P., P. Ni and B. DeRudder (eds.) (2012) *Global Urban Analysis: A Survey of Cities in Globalization* (New York: Routledge).

Tian, L. (2008) 'The *Chengzhongcun* Land Market in China: Boon or Bane? — A Perspective on Property Rights', *International Journal of Urban and Regional Research*, 32(2), pp. 282–304, DOI: 10.1111/j.1468-2427.2008.00787.x.

Wiethoff, K. (2014) 'The Role of Public Space in the Upgrading of Urbanized Villages', in U. Altrock and S. Schoon (eds.) *Maturing Megacities: The Pearl River Delta in Progressive Transformation* (Berlin: Springer), pp. 335–355.

Wu, F., F. Zhang and C. Webster (2012) 'Informality and the Development and Demolition of Urban Villages in the Chinese Peri-Urban Area', *Urban Studies*, 49, DOI: 10.1177/0042098012466600.

Xiaohong, T. and S. Schoon (2014) 'Villagers' Participation in Mega-Urban Upgrading: Liede Village: Guangzhou's Pioneer', in U. Altrock and S. Schoon (eds.) *Maturing Megacities: The Pearl River Delta in Progressive Transformation* (Berlin: Springer), pp. 247–266.

Zhang, C. and X. Li (2016) 'Urban Redevelopment as Multi-Scalar Planning and Contestation: The Case of Enning Road Project in Guangzhou, China', *Habitat International*, 56, pp. 157–165, DOI: 10.1016/j.habitatint.2016.05.008.

Zhang, L., Y. Ye and J. Chen (2016) 'Urbanization, Informality and Housing Inequality in Indigenous Villages: A Case Study of Guangzhou', *Land Use Policy*, 58, pp. 32–42, DOI: 10.1016/j.landusepol.2016.07.009.

Zhiqiang, Z. (2014) 'Gaming and Decision-Making: Urbanized Village Redevelopment in Guangzhou', in U. Altrock and S. Schoon (eds.) *Maturing Megacities: The Pearl River Delta in Progressive Transformation* (Berlin: Springer), pp. 221–245.

CHAPTER 11

Urban Identities and Belonging: Young Men's Discourses about Pikine (Senegal)

Sebastian Prothmann

Abstract

Suburbs in many parts of the world fall victim to discriminating assessments from the outside. Pikine, an urban area within the Dakar region of Senegal, which was one of urban Africa's major government restructuring projects, is no exception. The frequently evoked and generalised narratives of urban lifeworlds often fail to describe the heterogeneous characteristics of neighbourhoods in precarious large agglomerations throughout the world. In particular, the youth in this urban quarter are important drivers of economic growth and means with which to combat poverty and strengthen social cohesion. This chapter, based on 11 months of ethnographic fieldwork in Pikine between 2011 and 2013, will illustrate how resourceful young men organise their lives. On the one hand, they have equipped themselves with distinct identities and switch them depending on the situation. On the other hand, they have resurrected their feelings of solidarity, courage and local pride in the notion of *Pikinité* as a 'self-revaluation-standard'. Because of increasingly precarious realities and rising unemployment, individualistic tendencies—combined with the aspiration of self-realisation—have gained ground and challenge these stratagems.

1 Introduction

African urban agglomerations are mostly analysed through the narrow lens of developmentalism, which tends to focus only on lack, making them appear 'as imperfect, stunted, and underdeveloped versions of what they ought to be' (Myers and Murray, 2007, 10). These agglomerations come up short if indicators from the global North are applied (Myers, 2011). Also, if the overlapping interconnections of different cities in the world were taken into account, the analyses would look very different (Robinson, 2011). Therefore, alternative readings of the African urban cityscape can help us understand urbanity in all its diversity and productivity by taking the power of disorder into consideration (Myers, 2011).

When reading urban Africa, we also have to be aware of its huge youth population that is trying to make a living within unfavourable and limited socioeconomic structures (Honwana, 2012). This population, which only faces murky prospects of finding work in these inequitable, growing towns, primarily has access to informal structures (the informal employment market, informal property rights, informal transport, etc.). However, for a long time, urban spaces in Africa functioned as 'integration machinery', offering work for graduates of formal education, often in the public sector, although opportunities here have declined. Youth of today, though comprising a much higher proportion of graduates of formal education, are exposed to various forms of marginalisation, exclusion and lack of work. Thus, young people are emerging as a new social group whose common characteristic is that of social deprivation. Because of this, new ways of dealing with problematic situations are also emerging, and these are not necessarily linked with the social expectations of society.

In the 1990s Bayart et al. (1992) posited that young people had shown a great willingness to oppose political regimes but that their power had not sufficed to achieve political revolution. For this reason, assumptions long circulated about the 'lost generation'—weak, marginalised youths debarred from political decision-making processes (Cruise O'Brien, 1996). But earlier the historian Mamadou Diouf had emphasised the pivotal role of the youth (1992; 1996; 2002). In 2018 after the Arab Spring, which has essentially been described as a youth rebellion, and the 'awakening' of urban youth before and during the 2011 elections in Senegal, the power of the young needs rethinking. Nonetheless, in postcolonial debates youths are still viewed as the epitome of both violence and change. If they are, on the one hand, interpreted as offering great hope for the future, on the other they are seen as agents of government instability and protest (Benga, 2001; Diouf, 2003; Durham, 2004). Scholars working on youth have stressed the heterogeneity and ambivalence of youths, depicting them as 'vanguards' and 'vandals' (Abbink and van Kessel, 2005, 22), as 'makers' and 'breakers' of society (de Boeck and Honwana, 2005, 2) or as being 'between Jerusalem and Babylon' (Benga, 2001), drawn from taxonomies between recognition and disparagement.

In general, youth in Africa cannot be determined as a biological entity. They are a cultural construction (Honwana, 2012), one that might easily encompass people who are thirty or even forty years old (Baller, 2010). Youth is, moreover, a fluid category that depends very much on historical, social, cultural and political circumstances (Baller, 2005b). The perception of youth as a time of transition, a constituent element of the concept of youth itself, hinges on the idea of a move from a period of dependency (mainly within the family unit) to the attainment of financial independence through a fixed job and the beginning of one's own family. In the precarious financial context of urban Senegal there is much concern regarding delayed entry or possibly even the impossibility of entry into the labour market. This refused entry and other complications entail a prolonged phase of waiting, resulting in a complex interplay of negotiations between social realities and representations (Baller, 2010).

Based on 11 months of ethnographic fieldwork in the neighbourhoods of Wakhinane II Quartier Mballo Der and Sadio Guissé (Guinaw Rail Nord) in Pikine, a city in the *département* (administrative district) of Pikine within the Dakar region of Senegal, this contribution examines the strategies that young urban men use to deal with their marginalisation and with globalisation. The empirical data will give insight into how young men oscillate between different identities and negotiate urban and religious belongings and thus live urbanity in a productive way. The research shows how local youth in unsteady everyday lifeworlds display their inventiveness by creating stratagems with the help of refined techniques that permit them to cope with constraints and to weave new ideas of being and becoming into their lives. In a broader perspective, this chapter attempts to tackle the question of how young men in the global South approach issues of belonging and identity creation in a globalised world.

2 Dakar and the Infrastructural Vision of a President

For many people, a symbol of the failure of Abdoulaye Wade's regime is the fifty-two-meter-tall bronze statue in socialist realist style that is highly visible from different parts of the Cap Vert Peninsula. Perched on top of one of the Collines des Mamelles, the twin hills in the suburb of Ouakam, geographically the westernmost point of Africa's mainland, overlooking the Atlantic Ocean and dominating the horizon of Dakar, the statue depicts a family: a muscular, half-naked man with broad shoulders and six-pack abdominals holds a nude baby and points resolutely ahead, accompanied by a woman wearing a short skirt. The statue is about half a metre taller than the Statue of Liberty in New York and as such is the tallest sculpture outside of Asia and Eastern Europe (Roberts, 2013). It was meant to symbolise Africa's rebirth after centuries of slavery, colonialism and political domination from the outside (Grabski, 2017). Interestingly, according to official publications from the Senegalese government, the African Renaissance Monument cost nothing. It was built by a company from North Korea (Mansudae Overseas Projects) in exchange for a prime area of land belonging to the Senegalese government (Ritter, 2011). But rumours of a cost of USD 27 million (Arieff, 2012) have provoked a huge controversy on the extravagant and wasteful use of state finances on high-profile architectural and urban projects (Grabski, 2017). It is also alleged that ex-president Abdoulaye Wade claims 35 per cent of the entrance fees to the statue's interior and its museum.

However, in spite of its original intention to mark the rebirth of the continent and to point towards a bright future, in reality little has changed: decay, mismanagement, nepotism, corruption and poverty still abound in Senegal (Gilley, 2010; De Jong and Foucher, 2010). Emblematic of Wade's vision of modernity and the nation and his strategic alignment with foreign investors, the monument therefore represents for many people the 'disjuncture between governmental initiatives and on-the-ground crisis in infrastructure' (Grabski, 2017, 198). It is a glimmering daily reminder of state failure, especially the squandering of public funds and the preferential treatment afforded to select areas of the city.

The *Sopi*[1] election campaign of Abdoulaye Wade in 2000 was perceived as a watershed moment by young people all over Senegal. Although he was almost seventy-four years of age during the election campaign, he succeeded in connecting with the youth of the country. His campaign events were attended by masses of young people. His unctuous speeches, which focused mainly on employment, were warmly welcomed by young people tired of forty years of the inefficient economic policies of Senegal's socialist government. Many youth felt as if Abdoulaye Wade took the words right out of their mouths. He styled himself as their saviour, able to make their biggest unfulfilled wishes come true, by promising universal access to education and greatly increased chances of becoming productive members of society. The time of sitting around passively, drinking endless cups of *àttaaya* (a sugary green tea), was supposed to come to an end. He painted a very rosy picture of Senegal as an emerging country, depicting the youth as the most important actors of his promoted politics of *sopi* (change). Thus, he directly addressed young people's profound lack of societal recognition and self-worth, which was caused by their lack of integration into society due to widespread unemployment and resulting poverty (Sene Absa, 2011; Nelson, 2014; Osmanovic, 2017).

Wade succeeded in creating a feeling of 'legitimate expectation' (Ferguson, 1999) that the precarious situation of the youth would improve, and a feeling of hopefulness and optimism soon spread among Dakar's youth. After his interventions failed to pay off for the young generation, his former supporters

1 *Sopi* literally means 'change' and was used as a strategy to transform Senegal. 'Change' encompassed a complete remaking of political as well as the moral standards of Senegalese society.

felt betrayed. These youth had grown up with higher expectations due to his populist speeches, but after some years the majority of them still did not have steady jobs. They grew increasingly frustrated and fed up with the government, and they talked of an unsuccessful deal (Sene Absa, 2011) and of broken hopes. In January 2011, one year before Abdoulaye Wade confirmed that he planned to run for a third term, artists, intellectuals and activists created the movement *Y'en a marre*[2] (had enough).

Economic redemption was partly translated into large-scale public works[3] mostly funded by foreign capital, but it failed to impact the masses, especially the still-marginalised youth. Wade's concentration on private sector investment in infrastructure instead of in education and social programmes left the young population at the mercy of the neo-liberal free market, in contrast to the forty years of government by the Socialist Party of Léopold Senghor (1960–80) and Abdou Diouf (1981–2000) (Galvan, 2001). On the one hand, Wade's interventions were inflected by globalisation, and he focused on the 'construction of professedly globalized spaces of consumption and circulations […] detached from histories and shared struggles of the past decades' (Melly, 2013, 386) with the help of foreign expertise, capital and international organisations. On the other hand, he engaged in constructing physical manifestations of nationalism in Dakar, such as the Millennium Gate and memorials like the statue *Demba and Dupont*, where a Senegalese infantryman beside a French soldier symbolises the support of Senegal for France during World War II (Diop, 2012). Wade's government's negligence of the periphery across its large-scale urban projects was striking, as was its overlooking of the economic heart of the capital, the Plateau (Grabski, 2017).[4] The Plateau's architecture, which for a long time was redolent of southern France, had become more and more dilapidated, and today it is suggestive of a neglected urban quarter in France to the European

2 *Y'en a marre* is a collective comprising members of the civil society, rappers such as the Kaolack rap duo Keur Gui, Fou Malade, Simon, and Djily Bagdad, among others, and journalists, particularly Fadel Barro. In January 2011 it was launched to oppose political developments, especially around the despotic arrangements of incumbent Abdoulaye Wade. For further information see Savané and Sarr, 2012; Prause, 2012.

3 Projects included the construction of multistorey buildings, roundabouts, ramps and tunnels, which became signs of the modernisation of the city of Dakar. This vision of Abdoulaye Wade's modernisation was crowned by the construction of the Dakar–Diamniadio toll highway and the new airport Blaise Diagne International Airport in Diass, as well as the renovation of the Corniche Ouest (Diouf and Fredericks, 2013).

4 With the construction of new government buildings, museums and monuments, the Plateau was the heart of the postcolonial capital after independence and was shaped by Senghor's idea and vision of postcolonial nationalism and his literary and ideological trend of Negritude (Melly, 2013).

observer. With its throbbing market, Sandaga, at the end of the Avenue Georges Pompidou, referred to as *Ponty*, and its banks and service companies around Independence Square, the Plateau serves until today as the main artery of daily life in Dakar. The street markets and shops here, which are mostly in the hands of religious brotherhoods, were completely absent in Wade's 'soaring oratory about economic emergence' (Melly, 2013, 393) and modernisation.

Many people in Pikine expressed frustration at Wade's exclusive focus on streets and populations in Dakar and his relative neglect of Pikine, which produced further inequalities rather than eradicating them. Furthermore, numerous rumours circulated asserting the embezzlement of resources by Wade's government and the enrichment of plutocrat ministers who siphoned off resources of all sorts. While the political and economic elite enjoyed well-maintained infrastructure along the Corniche and in the neighbourhood of Almadies, the average citizen continued to face an unpredictable future in flood-prone and neglected neighbourhoods with ailing infrastructure and ramshackle houses.

Even today, the glittering manifestations of aggressively promoted modern and globalised 'materiality' scattered throughout the city in the form of new infrastructure, new residential areas, modern supermarkets and other shopping facilities, new gas stations, fast-food restaurants, night clubs, leisure facilities, and so on serve as a constant reminder that the fruits of progress are reserved for a lucky few. When an individual enters Dakar from Pikine via Castor, he or she passes the clean showrooms of EMG Universal Auto (*Voitures de Prestige, Americains, Allemandes*), which display luxury cars in pristine condition. Transnational connections and longings are also symbolised by commercial booths with painted signboards sponsored by international companies. This signage is part of Dakar's own 'language' (Guibbert, 1983). Barbers, garnished with photographs and painted images of bald heads from 50 Cent, 2Pac and other African-American celebrities, and with mural paintings and sophisticated, colourful glass paintings (so-called *suweer*) featuring portraits of famous religious persons, also contribute to the sensory regime of this cluttered 'urban cacophony' (Mustafa, 2001, 49) that shapes a landscape of global and religious longings. Despite their visual prominence, these urban facets are not representative of the experience of the majority of the population of the Dakar region. Or, as Jean and John Comaroff said, here 'the millennial moment has passed without a palpable payback' (1999, 284). The incoming 'neo-liberal logics of global capital flow' (ibid, 396) that shaped Wade's vision of the city's future, and thus that powered the relocation of global city allure from the Plateau as a statement of the post-independence time to the Corniche and Almadies, can also be seen as a brusque rejection of the immediate present with its concrete, precarious and known realities, which are not altered in any respect by these futuristic visions.

3 Pikine, Dakar's Largest Suburb

The city of Pikine was built in the 1950s, as housing problems became more and more urgent on the Cap Vert Peninsula and slums began to appear in neighbourhoods such as Dakar Fass and Colobane, and as the density of the central neighbourhoods of Médina increased. To curb these phenomena the state eventually decided to relocate illegal residents of these areas to outside of the city, in Pikine (Chenal, 2013), which was created under French colonial rule in 1952 and stood about 13 kilometres away from Dakar on a former military site covered with sand dunes (Baller, 2005a, 2007).

At the outset, the site of Pikine was a vast and remote area that was supposed to serve as a dormitory town for those who were relocated from the shanty towns of inner Dakar. Over time, many people started to settle outside the boundaries of Pikine, resulting in rapid urban growth that soon exceeded urban planning (Baller, 2010). During this time, the majority of investments were focused on Dakar, and Pikine and Guédiawaye were not granted the same opportunities and means (Chenal, 2013). Infrastructure—or more explicitly the absence of it—has therefore always been a serious problem in Pikine, and severe problems with sanitation, unemployment, informal uses of space, rapid population growth and an essentially young population (with 60 per cent under the age of twenty-one by 2004) are characteristic of the city.

While only a few years ago the geographer Gérard Salem saw Pikine as a 'city of nothing' and a city 'without a real history' (1998, 271), today Pikine is a vibrant, cosmopolitan satellite town of Dakar, with 1,170,791 inhabitants (estimation for 2015) (ANSD/SRSD, 2015) from a mosaic of different ethnic communities. Pikine is characterised by a diverse conglomeration of formal low-cost housing developments, multi-family abodes, small cement housing blocks and self-constructed multistorey apartment blocks.

3.1 *Pikinité*

The 1990s saw, in particular, the emergence of new forms of juvenile self-identifications. It was during this time that the *Bul Faale* movement[5] started,

5 'Bul Faale' was a song, released in 1994 by Positive Black Soul, one of the first hip-hop groups, founded in Dakar in 1989. Bul Faale served as an empowering slogan that can be translated as

encapsulating the attitude of young Senegalese trying to succeed through effort and work. The most prominent notion for young men in Pikine was *Pikinité*, a term used to describe a feeling of solidarity.

> *Pikinité* is first and foremost dignity. It is to share your own life and to give everything of you, to respect your locality in all its social and professional classes. It is to know to forget and wish only the progress of your fellows.
> LAMINE,[6] Wakhinane II Quartier Mballo Der

Pikinité reveals the awakening, in young people, of pride, and their identification with their locality. In the past, Pikine's negative reputation proved substantial and persistent, even impacting the attitudes of its residents. But it took local figures to overcome residents' denial of their origin. One of the first people who spread a positive message about Pikine was the wrestler Tyson, the nickname of Mouhamed Ndao, a reference to the American boxer Mike Tyson. Previously, successful artists from Pikine had hidden their origins. Eventually reversing this trend, young men started to develop pride and to use the *Pikinois* sense of community as social capital. Artists like Ndongo Lô, Pape Diouf and Ive Niang contributed to improving the reputation of Pikine.

Today young people wear T-shirts with slogans such as *I love Pikine*, *AS Pikine*,[7] *Deuk Pikine Mo Neex* (living in Pikine is cool), *Pikine mo xeew* (Pikine is on top) and *I am from Kinpi*, which can be seen as young men's territorial inscriptions on the city (Lefebvre, 1967). On a more local level, namely on the neighbourhood level, the *nawetaan* soccer clubs convey a strong sense of local connectedness. Pikine also has many wrestlers who participate in *làmb bi* (traditional wrestling).

Today many young people in Pikine attribute to themselves perseverance, smartness and skills of hustling, locally voiced as *esprit banlieue* (suburban mind):

'don't worry', in the sense that despite an ongoing economic crisis you have to keep on living, enjoying life and taking it as it is. You have to work hard and progress (Havard, 2001).

6 The names of informants have been changed in order to protect the anonymity of persons who contributed to this study.

7 AS Pikine is a *nawetaan* football club. In Senegal, youth organised football tournaments during the rainy season (called *nawetaanes*). The Wolof word *nawet* translates as 'rain' or 'rainy season'. In its grammatical form *nawetaan* means 'the one who passes the rainy season'. Initiated in the 1950s, *nawetaan* championships subsumed all neighbourhood teams. By this, more than 2,000 sports and cultural associations (ASC—*Association Sportive et Culturelle*) were formed, which involved not only football but also theatre and local social initiatives (Künzler, 2010).

> If you have a suburban mind, you will have many opportunities, you've seen, you can cope with it, good, quickly-done, what. If you have the strength to move forward, you will have a lot of things. You will persevere, what, because we say *Bul faale* [...], you will have the spirit of coping.
>
> MOUSSA, Sadio Guissé

Speaking in general, for young men the notion of *Pikinité* brings the residents of Pikine together. The residents help each other; they are solidaric. Also, though residents face many challenges in terms of lack of infrastructure, difficult access to education and high youth unemployment, Pikine stands out as one of Senegal's most dynamic fronts of urbanisation and as a very active city with popular urban initiatives. Through the term *Pikinité*, vivid attributions have elevated an urban neighbourhood famous for its bad reputation.

Part of Pikine's wealth is unquestionably its prolific hip-hop scene, mainly in the form of underground hip-hop. This rebellious style actively condemns the poor conditions of Pikine, allowing for the expression of otherwise dormant indignation about an unjust socioeconomic distribution system. Through performative styles, hip-hop provides the youth in Pikine new forms of authority to reinvent and alter their marginal position (Shipley, 2010). The artists Gokh-Bi System featuring Ndongo Lô, Section Jaxanama, Pétaw bi and Nomila featuring Backa have written songs entitled 'Pikine'. These and others, including Pinal Gang, Balvada, Tigrimbi, Wa BMG 44, Matador, Wagëblë, Coalition Niamu Mbaam, J Xaar Under and Sall Ngaary, have contributed to the establishment of a booming local hip-hop scene. Babacar Niang, alias Matador, is one of the most prominent underground rappers in Pikine and a founding member of Wa bmg 44, a hip-hop group hailing from the suburb Thiaroye between Pikine and Rufisque. While performing around the world, he has called attention to the youth of Senegal and the problematic situations faced in its periphery. In 2006 he founded an education centre in Pikine Ouest called Africulturban, which today has about one thousand members and is dedicated to empowering underprivileged youth via a wide range of activities that centre on music production and urban culture.

4 Hustling, 'Killing Time' and Improvising in Pikine

As a result of neo-liberal policies and the gradual withdrawal of the state, hustling has become a means of trying to make a living for young men coping with the emerging social dislocation in Pikine. The phrases 'tey yi ni, town bi dafa metti' (today, the town is difficult), 'damay gerer' (I'm managing) and 'ñépp dañuy taqale' (everyone hustles) all describe a sentiment best summed up in the Senegalese expression of *xoslu.* This expression has become an all-encompassing term that describes the day-to-day lifeworlds of young men in Pikine. Anthropologist Suzanne Scheld (2008) traces the term back to the English word *hustle* and the Wolof word *xoos* (to scratch, to scrape). In 1995, the well-known Montreal-based Senegalese Mbalax[8] musician Oumar Ndiaye, alias *Xosluman,* released the album *Hoslu.* In a personal communication on Facebook, he told me that initially the phenomenon was described by Gambians using the word 'hustle'. He claimed to have wolofised the term as *xoslu* and used it as an album title, which popularised its use in Senegal. *Xoslu* describes the socio-economic predicament of male youth trying by all means to make a living. By the same token, the term *xosluman,* meaning a seasoned struggler, carries connotations of respect and even admiration for an ability to fight one's way through adverse circumstances. It is a very masculine ascription, because the fervour displayed by these men in striving to get by stands in sharp contrast to the helpless passivity of 'effeminate' men in the face of adversity. *Xoslu* therefore suggests empowerment, achieved through living by one's wits and proudly rejecting dependence. Young men describe their daily **resourcefulness with** a powerful youth vocabulary that demonstrates that members of this generation in urban Senegal are trying their best to manage their lives in pursuit of a (better) living (Honwana, 2012), and also that they do not give up easily on their hopes and aspirations. The choice of this jargon around fighting, survival, physical pain and anxieties moreover exalts a certain ethos of toughness that allocates valence and meaningfulness to their lives.

In reality, however, there is a paradox: while work is vital for the economic well-being and for the status of an adult in Pikine, many work opportunities are considered to be beneath these young men's social class. Most of my informants considered notions of social class, dignity and their own position in the neighbourhood to be very important when making choices about pursuing certain income-generating activities in Dakar. Thus, behind the narratives of hard work, suffering and hustling, many urban small-scale activities in the informal sector were associated with a lower rank and therefore with failure and non-advancement. And as occupation indexed a certain rank within the social hierarchy, and many young men were assured of sources of income from other

8 *Mbalax* is syncretic popular music—made world famous by Youssou N'Dour—that combines popular Western music elements with singing in the Wolof language and dances influenced by soul, Latin, jazz, rock and sabar.

members of the family, or in some cases from family members abroad, many work opportunities were not accepted. Most young men I spoke to considered working as a street seller or doing other menial jobs demeaning, and they often thought that physical labour indicated a backwardness inherent to poor and uneducated people; this work was usually referred to as *liggéeyu baadoolo* (the work of the poor). However, young people often taunted other young people for being a *beugge lo yomb*, meaning that they wanted to achieve something or acquire material gain without doing anything for it, dodging responsibilities and hardship (Prothmann, 2017). This tendency resonates with Comaroffian comment on millennial capitalism's 'allure of accruing wealth from nothing' (2000, 313).

One of the most important words among young men was the verb *lijjanti*, which was used to cope with personal and societal demands. The term describes using shrewd and opportunistic scheming to overcome obstacles. For example, *lijjanti* was used when speaking about acquiring or 'organising' a certain sum of money at short notice, or about 'arranging' something. With *lijjanti*, the end—usually—justifies the means. Or, more precisely, the verb serves to obscure the manner in which the end is achieved. Even though it does not necessarily mean transgressing the boundaries of socially and legally acceptable behaviour, it carries the connotation of cunning. As hidden procurement of financial means, it implies a nifty social negotiation, one that is also made in order to circumvent social obligations of sharing. Politicians and sports stars have contributed to the success of the concept of *lijjanti*. Especially influential was the conspicuousness of ministers who posed with their new off-road vehicles and pricey villas. These were people who had nothing before entering politics. Young people started to claim that 'Xaalis ken du ko liggéey danu koy lijjanti' (money is not gained by the fruit of labour, but by resourcefulness). In a newspaper interview, the psychologist Lahbib Ndiaye characterises the Senegalese as people who want to get rich, but who do not want to put any effort into it. He speaks of the philosophy of *kheweul* (godsend), of *coup* (trick), of *wërsëg* (chance) and of 'Yàlla waxul kenn dara' (only God knows what will happen tomorrow). According to him, this philosophy does not embolden individual efforts or recognise the value of work. He quotes histories of fake visas, magical fructifications of businesses and the Senegalese conviction that one can get rich because of a marabout's prayers and occult forces (*Le Soleil*, 2010).

I also frequently encountered the term *nandité* among young men. With this, young people voiced various forms of intelligence, pointing out people who know how to cope with life. *Nandité* normally refers to a Boy Town or a 'gentleman' who both represent a connoisseur: a young man who is clever, well informed, and who knows how to cope with life and is able to manage. He is an urban citizen capable of projecting an image of success. This includes a certain degree of independence and the ability to manage things on one's own. Furthermore, *nandité* status can also be achieved in relation to the female sex—in this regard, a *nandité* is somebody who is able to go on dates with beautiful young women, which is considered to be very costly and demanding.

The expressions *ruse* and *muus* indicate the use of savvy tactics to generate financial gains. Many young men in Pikine tried to survive with *téq deal* in an informal economy. Commodities sent by relatives were often hawked, or articles were bought and immediately sold in an attempt to make a quick profit by inventing stories about the article. As such, articles like laptops or mobile phones can be seen as assets that can be expeditiously sold. This makeshift economy of barter deals can be found among many young males in Pikine. Some of them have developed refined tricks and networks connecting them to the 'right' people; they call themselves *téqat deal* (makers of deal) and use their connections to make a considerable profit by huckstering commodities of inferior quality. During a night interview with an informant in Médina, my interlocutor did not mince matters; he spoke of the cunning stratagems of young men, leaving the specifics of such techniques fuzzy: 'No, but that's it. They rip off. They are scammers. (...) Or they have a brother or a father who is in Europe, who sends materials and they sell them. Most people are like that'. It is through these techniques of hustling that many young men try to navigate through volatile informal economies in order to make a living.

Walking through Pikine, I was often astonished to see young men and women dressed up very fashionably but not holding any formal employment; I wondered where the financial means for these clothes might derive from. As most people were reluctant to admit what they did for a living or felt ashamed to admit that they received financial support from their families, I was not able to gather sufficient data in response to this question. The frequent disguise of income-generating activities also contributed to this vagueness. In any case, most of these strikingly dressed young men spent the whole day among their circle of friends and acquaintances, doing nothing more than talking, sometimes with humorous mischievousness, and eyeing girls walking along the unpaved roads. They sat on makeshift chairs, sharing roasted groundnuts and drinking tea. Young men referred to this as *rey temps bi* or *kill temps bi* (killing time) (Ralph, 2008).

5 Pikine and the Baay Faal Identity Among Young Men: Contrasting Visions

Many young men I met in Pikine blindly admired Baayfaalism, a type of a mendicant suborder of the Murīdiyyah brotherhood[9] and its sheikhs. For young people, torn between their own expectations and those of their kin, ensnared in fickle and problem-ridden secular lifeworlds of reneged promises, the Murīdiyyah and especially Baayfaalism, becomes a rewarding collective identity, based on a glorious past and offering a clear conception of the world and a positive vision of the future. Baayfaalism allows young men to express their religious identity through a 'rudimentary understanding of a "Muslim life"' (Simone, 2010, 148), simplifying for them the concept of a godly life and bolstering their self-esteem.

Thus, among young men the category of the Baay Faal becomes a vessel for aspirations towards goodness. Following the unwritten laws of harmonious outward representations, young men in Pikine display characteristics such as patriotism, sympathy and openness towards other persons, modesty, non-consumerism, humbleness, industriousness, cunning, independence, spirituality, respect and solidarity. Baayfaalism can be considered a moral guide that shepherds young males through the 'ambiguity-filled dilemmas of everyday urban life' (Simone, 2010, 145) and as 'synonymous with personal quest, inner improvement and renunciation, and love of God' (Popovic and Veinstein, 1996, 9). Baay Faal morality re-establishes individual agency and further provides the individual with a meaningful and morally unobjectionable identification.

Baay Faal adherents experience recognition among their peers. Thus, being a Baay Faal means being someone, having a social role and especially being a man of God. A Baay Faal is also authorised to take on menial jobs, *liggéeyu baadoolo*. All this is considered as the opposite of an individualistic, urban version of the self in inner Dakar, which is characterised by a sense of superiority and a blasé attitude. Thus, among marginalised, unemployed young men who hanker for positive change, affiliation to Baayfaalism appears as an emancipating force and enjoys great popularity (Pezeril, 2008). Xavier Audrain (2004) writes that Baayfaalism provides the sense of an alternative moral economy where young men can find their place.

---

9 *Sufi* refers to Sufism or in Arab *taṣawwuf*, which is 'the generally accepted name for Islamic mysticism' (Schimmel, 2011, 3). In Senegal the Sufi orders (*turuq*) the Tijāniyyah, the Qādirīya, the Murīdiyyah and the Layennes are commonly associated with Islam. In total 92 per cent of Muslims are said to be affiliated with Sufi brotherhoods (*Pew Research Center*, 2013). For a presentation of these brotherhoods see Mané, 2012, 7–22.

6 Pikine and the Boy Town Identity Among Young Men

Tshikala Kayembe Biaya (2001) talks of a 'geography of pleasure', referring to tourist sites on the Senegalese coast and certain *Dakarois* nightclubs. He asserts an emasculation of young men, especially concerning their virility. On the other hand, young women, well aware of their own value in this economy, in which shallow appearances and sexualities prevail, know how to exploit this situation for their own benefit, resulting in economic and sexual frustrations among young men. In this economy of appearance, social status is in a Bourdieuian sense an economic variable. Thus, to conceal the humble realities of destitution, profits of any kind are immediately invested in what the Senegalese label the *paraitre* ([*sag*] appearance), which actually hampers opportunities for sustainable accumulation.

> The Boy Town like the ease. They don't like to work. They consider themselves as children from, they behave like Parisians, like rich people.
>
> LAYE, Wakhinane II Quartier Mballo Der

This excerpt from an interview shows the negative perception that my *Pikinois* informants had of this term. The Boy Town is seen as lazy, as a cosmopolitan who knows European etiquette and as a rich person who has had everything handed to him on a silver platter. However, many young men I talked to valued particular characteristics of Boy Town culture, such as having access to luxurious nightclubs, casinos and expensive restaurants in the most sophisticated parts of town. By identifying with these places, the individual transforms himself from an inhabitant of a dilapidated suburb to an inhabitant of a 'hedonopolis' or a 'city of joy' (Ndjio, 2007, 104). This underscores the youth's notion of modernity, as these lifestyles are considered to be progressive (Bahi, 2010). Many of Pikine's youth go to these places, yielding to the temptations of a world of conspicuous consumption and practicing *beugge addina* (living life to the fullest). This life involves going out, enjoying nightlife in discotheques and bars, eating in restaurants, consuming fast food, and so on.

The Boy Town therefore also counts as a prime example of the individualism *à la sénégalaise*. In lieu of family and neighbourhood solidarity there is a new, though partially hidden, attitude of *bopp-sa-bopp* (everyone for himself), a tendency of 'possessive individualism' (Macpherson, 1962) proffered by the neo-liberal regime, infused with values that come from the outside and turn antiquated values upside down. These individualistic tendencies point in the direction of self-realisation and stand in conflict with community- and family-oriented values. The result is expressed in the phrase 'kenn talatul sa mbokk' (nobody has time for neighbours). This can be seen as an adaptation borne from circumstances where urban lifeworlds harshly limit the realisation of solidarity and masculine ideals in the conventional sense. Such circumscription stimulates the formation of a 'singularized, autonomous manhood' (de and Plissart, 2006, 244), which stands in opposition to the identity of the socially responsible male who contributes to a wider social network, such as a kinship network.

However, when asked to characterise Pikine, young men generally refer to solidarity rather than to the individualism often displayed in residential areas and middle-class neighbourhoods. Solidarity thus seems to be highly regarded, although it is mostly displayed when ulterior motives are at play, such as for purposes of personal gain. Nevertheless, it is a prized trait, and visible violation of solidarity norms is viewed unfavourably. Far too often the notion is reduced to antiquated customs around *lekk* (eating) that hold that a guest always eats, regardless of which household they enter. Despite this, solidarity is frequently regarded as the basis of everything and as a value exclusive to Pikine:

> You know, the difference made between us, we the suburbanites and they, that's the difference. We, we have solidarity. And I assure you, from now to any time, if you enter a household and you want to eat, you eat. We don't ask for money. [...] That is what we know. And this is what differentiates us from them. It is the solidarity. It is the basis of all. [...] It is what we live here, and you will find nowhere. [...] Only here in Pikine, there is solidarity. I assure you, there is solidarity here.
>
> DJIBRIL, Wakhinane II Quartier Mballo Der

7 Conclusion: Pikine Read by its Young Men

Situated at the margins of Dakar and therefore in many aspects fairly isolated from the economic activity of the capital city, the inhabitants of Pikine have managed to create different forms of self-organisations, which also foster various forms of urban self-identification and feelings of belonging. The most important notion among young men is *Pikinité*, which provides a feeling of solidarity, courage and local pride. As such, in recent years Pikine has seen a prolific emergence of small-scale initiatives and associations, and Pikine is today the origin of many musicians and sports stars. *Pikinité* offers *Pikinois* youth the opportunity to put their stamp on urban socialities and correct the unilateral and stigmatic image of Pikine. With recourse to antiquated values such as solidarity, the *Pikinois* bring their locality back into a discourse of village-like convictions, but at the same time they are deeply embedded in negotiations of participation and are actors of globalisation. While the first president of Senegal, Leopold Senghor, dreamed that Dakar would—in the year 2000—be like Paris, the question is no longer whether Dakar is like a European city, such as Paris or Berlin, or a North American city, like New York, but how the urban actors themselves experience urban realities and make them fit their needs, and how they negotiate global flows and might say 'We are from Pikine, but just as well we can be inhabitants of Paris or New York!' Through their choice of clothing, young men escape from grim economic realities; more specifically, they transform their outward appearance to convey symbolic representations of what they consider the successful self and to evoke feelings of global belonging (Scheld, 2007, 2008). However, this all is overshadowed by a challenging complex of problems embedded in very weak infrastructure, which includes annual floods and a lack of work opportunities for the young population.

During the administration of former president Abdoulaye Wade, Pikine was marginalised. Wade, with his urban-centric politics, fostered the development of certain urban neighbourhoods and initiated many flagship construction projects, especially ones that served his vision of Dakar as a 'showcase capital' and a global capital city (Melly, 2013, 2017). At the same time, he neglected many problem-afflicted parts of Dakar and failed to tackle the problems of Senegal's youth. In particular, many young men in Pikine felt excluded. An increasing gap between the rich and poor resulted from Wade's neo-liberal economic policy. This has made young males unite to speak out against rampant corruption and rising unemployment and has led to a growing mistrust of the government. It has created an awareness among young males that they are the architects of their own futures and that they cannot depend on the state for this. But this situation also impedes young men from advancing in their lives and becoming social adults who want to start a family and shoulder responsibility for themselves and their kin. However, even if these social conditions speak a very different language, the prevalent urban disorder should not per se be seen as negative; it is the precondition for the young men's spaces in which to manoeuvre.

To survive in this city, young male *Pikinois* show resourcefulness, embedded in an adapted competence for inventing coping strategies that might take surprising or even incomprehensible turns. They have equipped themselves with distinct identities and have cultivated the ability to inhabit the identity that a given occasion requires. Young men switch their identities depending on the situation—for example, a young man may be a pious Muslim in traditional raiment on a religious feast, or a Baay Faal wearing ragged motley garments known as Baye Lahat, or a Boy Town dressed up in fancy clothes in line with American trends on a Saturday evening. Thus, in line with Ferguson's 'performative competence' (1999, 104), young men in Pikine use their attire, consumption practices and also their speech and discursive practices to position themselves in different fields. This helps them to participate in processes of modernity and globalisation, to be in the world, not as passive spectators but as cosmopolitans with the ability to improvise and ultimately take part in building the nation.

References

Abbink, J. and I. Van Kessel (eds.) (2005) *Vanguards or Vandals. Youth, Politics and Conflict in Africa* (Leiden: Brill).

ANSD/SRSD (Agence Nationale de la Statistique et de la Démographie/Services Régionaux de la Statistique et de la Démographie) (2015) *Situation Économique et Sociale régionale – 2013* (Dakar: ANSD).

Arieff, A. (2012) *Senegal: Background and U.S. Relations* (New York: CRS Congressional Research Service Reports on Foreign Policy and Regional Affairs).

Audrain, X. (2004) 'Devenir « Baay-fall » pour être soi: Le religieux comme vecteur d'émancipation individuelle au Sénégal'. *Politique africaine*, 94, pp. 149–165, DOI: 10.3917/polaf.094.0149.

Bahi, A. (2010) 'Jeunes et Imaginaire de la Modernité à Abidjan', *Cadernos de Estudos Africanos*, 18/19, pp. 56–67, DOI: 10.4000/cea.79.

Baller, S. (2010) *Spielfelder der Stadt: Fusball und Jugendpolitik im Senegal seit 1950* (Köln: Böhlau).

Baller, S. (2007) 'Transforming Urban Landscapes: Soccer Fields as Sites of Urban Sociability in the Agglomeration of Dakar', *African Identities*, 5(2), pp. 217–230, DOI: 10.1080/14725840701403473.

Baller, S. (2005a) 'Urbane Zwischen-Räume. Jugendliche der banlieue von Dakar zwischen Lokalität und Globalität', in W. Speitkamp (ed.) *Kommunikationsraume – Erinnerungsraume. Beitrage zur transkulturellen Begegnung in Afrika* (Munich: Meidenbauer), pp. 221–248.

Baller, S. (2005b) 'Creating the Postcolonial City: Urban Youth Clubs in Senegal', in T. Falola and S.J. Salm (eds.) *Urbanization and African Cultures* (Durham, NC: Carolina Academic Press), pp. 139–153.

Bayart, J-F., A. Mbembe and C. Toulabor (eds.) (1992) *Le Politique par le bas en Afrique noire. Contributions à une problématique de la démocratie* (Paris: Karthala).

Benga, N. (2001) 'Entre Jérusalem et Babylon: jeunes et espace public à Dakar', *Autrepart*, 18, pp. 169–178, DOI: 10.3917/autr.018.0169.

Biaya, T.K. (2001) 'Les plaisirs de la ville. Masculinité, sexualité et féminité à Dakar (1997–2000)', *African Studies Review*, 44(2), pp. 71–85, DOI: 10.2307/525575
de Boeck, F. and A.M. Honwana (eds.) (2005) *Makers and Breakers. Children and Youth in Postcolonial Africa* (Oxford: James Currey).
de Boeck, F. and M-F. Plissart (eds.) (2006) *Kinshasa: Tales of the Invisible City* (Antwerp: Ludion).
Chenal, J. (2013) *La Ville Ouest-Africaine: Modèles de planification de l'éspace urbain* (Geneva: MetisPresses).
Comaroff, J. and J. Comaroff (2000) 'Millennial Capitalism: First Thoughts on a Second Coming', *Public Culture*, 12(2), pp. 291–343, DOI: 10.1215/08992363-12-2-291.
Comaroff, J. and J. Comaroff (1999) 'Occult Economies and the Violence of Abstraction: Notes from the South African Postcolony', *American Ethnologist*, 26(2), pp. 279–303, DOI: 10.1525/ae.1999.26.2.279.
Cruise O'Brien, D.B. (1996) 'A Lost Generation? Youth Identity and State Decay in West Africa', in W. Richard and T. Ranger (eds.) *Postcolonial Identities in Africa* (London: Zed Books), pp. 55–74.
Diop, A. (2012) 'Dakar', in S. Bekker and G. Therborn (eds.) *Capital Cities in Africa: Power and Powerlessness* (Cape Town: HSRC Press), pp. 32–44.
Diouf, M. (2003) 'Engaging Postcolonial Cultures: African Youth and Public Space', *African Studies Review*, 46(2), pp. 1–12, DOI: 10.2307/1514823.
Diouf, M. (2002) 'Les jeunes Dakarois dans le champ politique', in M-C Diop, M. Diouf and D.B. Cruise O'Brien (eds.) *La Construction de l'État au Sénégal* (Paris: Karthala) pp. 157–167.
Diouf, M. (1996) 'Urban Youth and Senegalese Politics. Dakar 1988–1994', *Public Culture*, 8(2), pp. 225–249, DOI: 10.1215/08992363-8-2-225.
Diouf, M. (1992) 'Fresques murales et écriture de l'histoire. Le Set/Setal à Dakar', *Politique africaine*, 46, pp. 41–54, http://politique-africaine.com/numeros/pdf/046041.pdf (accessed on 22 April 2018).
Diouf, M. and R. Fredericks (2013) 'Introduction', in M. Diouf and R. Fredericks (eds.) *Les arts de la citoyennete au Senegal: Espaces contestes et civilites urbaines* (Paris: Karthala), pp. 11–44.
Durham, D. (2004) 'Disappearing youth: Youth as a social shifter in Botswana', *American Ethnologist*, 31(4), pp. 589–605, DOI: 10.1525/ae.2004.31.4.589.
Ferguson, J. (1999) *Expectations of Modernity: Myths and Meanings of Urban Life on the Zambian Copperbelt* (Berkeley, CA: University of California Press).
Galvan, D.C (2001) 'Political Turnover and Social Change in Senegal', *Journal of Democracy*, 12(3), pp. 51–62, DOI: 10.1353/jod.2001.0047.
Gilley, B. (2010) 'The end of the African renaissance', *The Washington Quarterly*, 33(4), pp. 87–101, DOI: 10.1080/0163660X.2010.516612.

Grabski, J. (2017) *Art World City: The Creative Economy of Artists and Urban Life in Dakar* (Bloomington, IN: Indiana University Press).

Guibbert, J.-J. (1983) 'Symbols, Signs, Signals: Walls of the City', in B.B. Taylor (ed.) *Reading the Contemporary African City* (Singapore: Concept Media/Aga Khan Award for Architecture), pp. 75–84.

Havard, J.-F. (2001) 'Ethos «bul faale» et nouvelles figures de la réussite au Sénégal', *Politique africaine*, 82, pp. 63–77, DOI: 10.3917/polaf.082.0063.

Honwana, A.M. (2012) *The Time of Youth: Work, Social Change, and Politics in Africa* (Sterling, VA: Kumarian Press. Stylus Publishing).

de Jong, F. and V. Foucher (2010) 'La tragédie du roi Abdoulaye? Néomodernisme et Renaissance africaine dans le Sénégal contemporain', *Politique africaine*, 2, pp. 187–204, DOI: 10.3917/polaf.118.0187

Künzler, D. (2010) 'Des événements du Cabinda à la star Drogba: Les évolutions du football africain à l'aune de la Coupe du monde 2010', *Afrique contemporaine*, 233, pp. 15–24, DOI : 10.3917/afco.233.0015.

Le Soleil (2010) 'Interview avec Lahbib Ndiaye "L'homme sénégalais aime s'enrichir sans travailler"', Week-End. 13–14 Mars.

Lefebvre, H. (1967) *Le droit à la ville* (Paris: Éditions Anthropos).

Macpherson, C.B. (1962) *The Political Theory of Possessive Individualism: Hobbes to Locke* (Oxford: Oxford University Press).

Mané, M. (2012) *Les valeurs culturelles des confréries musulmanes au Sénégal* (Dakar: UNESCO), http://www.unesco.org/new/fileadmin/MULTIMEDIA/FIELD/Dakar/pdf/EtudeconfreriesSenegal4Dec2012.pdf (accessed on 22 April 2018).

Myers, G. (2011) *African Cities: Alternative visions of urban theory and practice* (London/New York: Zed Books).

Myers, G. and M. Murray (2007) 'Introduction: Situating Contemporary Cities in Africa', in *Cities in Contemporary Africa* (Basingstoke, UK: Palgrave Macmillan), pp. 1–25.

Melly, C. (2017) *Bottleneck: Moving, Building & Belonging in an African City* (Chicago, IL; London: The University of Chicago Press).

Melly, C. (2013) 'Ethnography on the Road: Infrastructural Vision and the Unruly Present in Contemporary Dakar', *Africa: Journal of the International African Institute*, 83(3), pp. 385–402, DOI: 10.1017/S0001972013000235.

Mustafa, H.N. (2001) 'Ruins and Spectacles: Fashion and City Life in Contemporary Senegal', *Nka: Journal of Contemporary African Art*, 15, pp. 47–53, DOI: 10.1215/10757163-15-1-47.

Ndjio, B. (2007) 'Douala: Inventing Life in an African Necropolis', in G.A. Myers and M.J. Murray (eds.) *Cities in Contemporary Africa* (Basingstoke, UK: Palgrave Macmillan), pp. 103–118.

Nelson, S. (2014) 'The New Type of Senegalese under Construction: Fadel Barro and Aliou Sané on *Yenamarrisme* after Wade', *African Studies Quarterly*, 14(3), pp. 13–32, http://asq.africa.ufl.edu/files/Volume-14-Issue-3-Nelson.pdf (accessed on 22 April 2018).

Pezeril, C. (2008) *Islam, Mysticisme et Marginalite: les Baay Faal du Senegal* (Paris: L'Harmattan).

Pew Research Center (2013) *The World's Muslims: Unity and Diversity*, April 30, http://www.pewforum.org/the-worlds-muslims (accessed on 5 June 2017).

Prause, L. (2012) 'Y'en a marre: Wer sind sie, wie mobilisieren sie und was fordern sie?' *Standpunkte International*, 2/2012, (Berlin: Rosa Luxemburg Stiftung), https://www.rosalux.de/publikation/id/5783/ (accessed on 22 April 2018).

Prothmann, S. (2017) 'Migration, masculinity and social class: Insights from Pikine, Senegal', *International Migration*, DOI: 10.1111/imig.12385.

Popovic, A. and G. Veinstein (1996) *Les voies d'Allah: les ordres mystiques dans le monde musulman des origines a aujourd'hui* (Paris: Fayard).

Ralph, M. (2008) 'Killing Time', *Social Text 97*, 26(4), pp. 1–29, DOI: 10.1215/01642472-2008-008.

Ritter, J.W.A. (2011) 'National Symbol or a National Frustration: Academic, Artistic, and Political Perspectives of the African Renaissance Monument', *Independent Study Project (ISP) Collection.* Paper 1200, http://www.digitalcollections.sit.edu/isp_collection/1200 (accessed on 5 June 2017).

Roberts, A.F. (2013) 'Citoyennetés visuelles en compétition dans le Sénégal contemporain', in M. Diouf and R. Fredericks (eds.) *Les arts de la citoyennete au Senegal: Espaces contestes et civilites urbaines* (Paris: Karthala), pp. 195–235.

Robinson, J. (2011) 'Cities in a World of Cities: The Comparative Gesture', *International Journal of Urban and Regional Research*, 35(1), pp. 1–23, DOI: 10.1111/j.1468-2427.2010.00982.x.

Salem, G. (1998) *La sante dans la ville: Geographie d'un petit espace dense: Pikine (Senegal)* (Paris: Karthala-Orstrom).

Savané, V. and B.M. Sarr (eds.) (2012) *Y'en a marre: Radioscopie d'une jeunesse insurgée au Sénégal* (Paris: Harmattan).

Scheld, S. (2007) 'Youth Cosmopolitanism: Clothing, the City and Globalization in Dakar, Senegal', *City and Society*, 19(2), pp. 232–253, DOI: 10.1525/city.2007.19.2.232.

Scheld, S. (2008) 'The City in a Shoe: redefining urban Africa through Sebago footwear consumption', *City and Society*, 15(1), pp. 109–130, DOI: 10.1525/city.2003.15.1.109.

Schimmel, A. (2011) *Mystical Dimensions of Islam* (Berkeley, CA: University of California Press).

Sene Absa, M. (2011) *Yoole – Le Sacrifice* (Dakar: Absa Films).

Shipley, J.W. (2010) 'Self-Sovereignty and Creativity in Ghanaian Public Culture', in A.-M. Makhulu, B. Buggenhagen and S. Jackson (eds.) *Hard Work, Hard Times: Global Volatility and African Subjectivities* (Berkeley, CA: University of California Press), pp. 91–112.

Simone, A. (2010) 'Reaching a Larger World: Muslim Youth and Expanding Circuits of Operation', in A. Bayat and L. Herrera (eds.) *Being Young and Muslim: New Cultural Politics in the Global South and North* (New York: Oxford University Press), pp. 145–159.

Osmanovic, A. (2017) *"Sénégal Émergent": State Building between Empire and Islam* (Dakar: Rosa Luxemburg Stiftung West Africa).

CHAPTER 12

The City and Its Ways of Life: Local Influences on Middle-Income Milieus in Nairobi

Florian Stoll

Abstract

How is it possible to study the 'cityness' of cities, their particular character and the locally specific actions of their residents? One crucial aspect that distinguishes cities from one another is how social phenomena are embedded in a particular city's built environment, its economy, and particular horizons of meanings.

To analyse a significant example of this embeddedness, this chapter examines Kenya's Nairobi through the lens of social milieus in the middle-income stratum, the so-called 'middle classes'.[1] Moreover, the milieu concept enables the identification of social groups that share sociocultural features such as specific ways of life, professional and leisure activities, and forms of consumption and investment. The text studies which local aspects are significant for milieus in Nairobi in comparison to Mombasa and other Kenyan cities. And using two case studies, the *Christian Religious Milieu* and the milieu of the *Young Professionals,* it illustrates how the particular city modifies these milieus.

Such an approach not only allows for a better understanding of the 'middle classes' in African cities as comprised of different identifiable milieus, it also yields a method for analysing the local particularities of a city, whether in Africa or other parts of the world. The chapter is significant for policy and practice because it introduces with the concept of social milieus a nuanced alternative to (middle) class approaches that distinguishes lifestyles, aims in life and forms of consumption. Also, the chapter discusses, using the example of Nairobi, how milieus are bound to specific structures of a city and might offer—from the perspective of basic research—suggestions for practical use.

1 Parts of this text refer to the working paper *How to be Middle Class in Nairobi* (Stoll, 2018). The sections that overlap are indicated by references at the beginning of the section.

 | DOI:10.1163/9789004387942_013

> How to spot a Nairobian:
>
> You should see Nairobians leaving the City. Once past Ruiru or the Great Wall,[2] it is all systems go. Ask any "ocha"[3] dude or dudette about Nairobi dressing and they will probably tell you girls wear hot pants and the boys are forever in vests and shorts and that clothing is never complete without an alcoholic drink in hand.
>
> We are never like that here. The girls are always struggling to walk in heels and the dudes with their protruding bellies are always testing the limits of buttons. [...]
>
> We are not loud, no, not when we are looking for money to go splurge in some other "ocha" county and show others how well we are living. When someone lands in Nairobi for the first time, expecting the good life, they are met by a people who are always in a hurry and very unfriendly.
>
> Someone will collapse on the streets and people will give him bad looks, like how dare he fall in front of us, can't he go somewhere deserted and fall there?
>
> 'HOW TO SPOT A NAIROBIAN', Philip Mwaniki in *Daily Nation*, 3.10.2014

1 Introduction

Some of the most iconic images of cities come from classical songs. Frank Sinatra sings about New York as the city that never sleeps; Dean Martin makes 'Volare' (to fly) a unique experience of Rome; Andre Filho honoured Rio de Janeiro as the 'Cidade Maravilhosa' (wonderful city) and contributed thus to its myth as a place for all kind of pleasures. These and many other songs construct vivid images of what it means to participate in the life of a particular city. Likewise, it is a matter of common knowledge that Lagos is very different from Cape Town and that the inhabitants of both cities vary in their everyday life routines. Looking at residents of Nairobi, there are also local particularities—but why is this the case? And how is it possible to go beyond stating merely differences and to study, instead, the 'cityness' of cities, including their characteristic features and the specific actions of their residents? This text contributes to a conceptual discussion about the urban in Africa and is, therefore, more than a case study.

2 Ruiru and 'the Great Wall' are both districts on the outskirts of Nairobi.

3 '*Ocha*' is a common expression in the Nairobi slang, Sheng, and refers to a rural area or someone's rural home.

The starting point for this chapter are two developments that have taken place in many parts of Africa over recent decades and that overlap to a high degree. The first development is the increasing significance of cities and a tendency towards urbanisation. The second aspect is the rise of millions of families out of poverty as a result of economic growth. In the shadow of debates on 'Africa Rising' and 'Lions on the Move' (McKinsey, 2010), the middle-income group was coined in a rather popularising manner as 'the African middle-class' (AfDB, 2011; Ncube and Lufumpa, 2015).[4] Such research focused on quantitative income and consumption rates but resulted in a poorly defined concept of economic class. In spite of the substantial critique of the use of the middle-class concept in Africa (Lentz, 2015; Melber, 2016; Darbon and Toulabour, 2013), there are few alternatives for studying middle-income strata.[5] The majority of contributions are either ethnographic case studies of micro-groups (Spronk, 2012; Budniok and Noll, 2016) or large-scale quantitative studies on 'middle classes' that primarily look at the national level (AfDB, 2011).

Therefore, the starting point of this chapter is the large-scale critique of the debate on 'middle classes' in Africa that the author developed in several, partly co-authored publications (Neubert and Stoll, 2015; Daniel et al., 2016; Stoll, 2018; Neubert and Stoll, 2018). Transferring the term 'middle class' from the Euro–American context to Africa suggests that individuals in these income groups have sociocultural attributes such as typical values but also a financially stable position. While these attributes are considered essential characteristics of the 'middle class' in Europe and North America, they are often missing in the African middle-income strata. In contrast to the widespread characterisation of individuals with a daily consumption rate over the poverty level as 'the African middle-class' (AfDB, 2011), this text uses the terms 'middle-income strata' and 'middle strata', which are more precise characterisations than the well-established but weakly defined 'middle classes' in the social sciences.

4 The definition of the African Development Bank (AfDB) considers individuals with an average income of between two and twenty US dollars per day as 'middle class', with the stratum between two and four US dollars as an insecure floating class. Like other quantitative definitions of 'middle class' (see Neubert and Stoll, 2018), this economic range gives an orientation of who is neither poor nor rich. However, this text aims to elaborate qualitative aspects of diversity and the local embeddedness of middle-income strata and will therefore not discuss margins of economic definitions.

5 An exception is the concept of 'moderate prosperity groups' proposed by Andrianampiarivo (2016), who develops a multidimensional approach referenced by Darbon and Toulabour (2013) for middle-income strata. An interesting case study with the potential for a conceptualisation of middle-income groups is Claire Mercer's (2014) study on different types of living rooms in Tanzania.

As an alternative to class, we have also introduced the *milieu* approach developed by German sociologists since the 1980s (Keim, 1979; Hradil, 1987; Grathoff, 1989; Schulze, 1993; Vester et al., 2001). The study of milieu allows us to distinguish meso-groups according to their particular priorities in life, such as ties to the rural and ethnic community, individual advancement, or religion (Neubert and Stoll, 2015; Stoll, 2016). The argument is that there is not one homogenous African or even Kenyan 'middle class' but that it is necessary, instead, to consider socio-culturally differentiated middle-income strata that are to a high degree locally embedded. As the chapter demonstrates using the example of Nairobi and other Kenyan cities, there are local differences in the composition of the milieus that can be linked systematically to a city.

The author will not only use milieu studies to provide a more nuanced picture of social groups and lifestyles in urban Kenya but will also investigate how these milieus are locally embedded in a particular setting and demonstrate how milieu studies also offer the possibility to consider particularities of a specific city. Comparisons are very helpful to identify general and unique local aspects of milieus and cities. We have considered in our research Nairobi and Mombasa, and to a lesser degree other Kenyan cities. This text focuses, however, on Nairobi and takes references to other cities only as points of comparison.

Recently, Jennifer Robinson (2006) made a major statement with regard to the study of urban African contexts when she claimed that it is necessary to treat them as ordinary cities and not just as the underdeveloped other of Euro–American urban settings. Robinson criticises the hegemonic developmental view in Urban Studies because it suggests the existence of a shared quality of African urbanity, without or even against empirical proof. She emphasises that it is crucial to investigate the local conditions of African contexts, instead of making assumptions based on an untenable theory. As such, Robinson set a new standard in the study of the urban in Africa by stressing that it is necessary to research cities on the continent in a similar way as anywhere else in the world. Robinson's approach thus encourages a localised approach, for it would be problematic to assume that the same or very similar 'classes' or milieus exist in African cities as many stratification theories tacitly assume for European states (e.g. Vester et al., 2001, for Germany).

Similar to language, which is always highly localised through dialects, slang and typical phrases, other aspects of social life are also bound to the economic, symbolic, political and historical environment of a city. The literature on Nairobi and other Kenyan cities shows how elements of the environment determine the lifestyles of members of specific milieus or the city in general. For instance, one volume (Charton-Bigot and Rodriguez-Torres, 2010) gives insights into different aspects of life in Nairobi, such as public politics, group identities, and spatial structures. Other research focuses on Young Professionals and their sex lives (Spronk, 2012), elite clubs (Connan, 2015) or the local dialect Sheng (Beck, 2015). Similarly, research on Mombasa has sought to establish the elements that influence city life using the methodology of the *distinctiveness of cities* (Berking, 2012).

A further strand of research emerged in the last decade (for an overview see Parnell and Pieterse, 2016; Ricci, 2016, 11–16; Werthmann, 2014) and conceptualises cities in Africa beyond isolated case studies. Authors from this field of study oppose the dominant negative characterisations of urban African contexts, which focus on supposed 'deficits' or the lack of order. Such attributes focus mostly on the weak organisation or bad performance of cities (Ricci, 2016, 13 f.). The author of this chapter also aims at developing an understanding of the urban in Africa that describes and analyses cities on the continent through empirical research and not as 'negative' or deficient in comparison to models of Northern cities.

Therefore, this chapter provides a case study with the milieu approach, which clarifies how local particularities modify group structures and interact with the space of the city. The highly diverse local precolonial, colonial, and postcolonial influences make it necessary to think of urban Africa in the plural, in a similar way as we differentiate contexts in Europe, the Americas and Asia. Accordingly, the composition of middle-income strata differs significantly due to local influences. Firstly, this chapter discusses why it is thus useful to examine milieus in the middle-income stratum and not 'middle classes'. Secondly, it provides an overview of the methodology of the research and the data. Thirdly, the chapter discusses Nairobi's 'middle strata' in the context of the city. For a better understanding, the text zooms in on the milieus of the *Christian Religious* and *Young Professionals* as case studies.

2 Why Milieus and not 'Middle Classes'

Other publications by the author have criticised the use of the concept of middle class in Kenya and other African countries because this approach does not consider the diversity of sociocultural groups in the middle-income stratum (Neubert and Stoll, 2015; Stoll, 2016; Stoll, 2017; Neubert and Stoll, 2018). This chapter adds a related critique that studies how the differentiation of social groups is bound to a certain place and its particularities. Following this argument, this section introduces milieu study as an alternative to class and the next sections demonstrate how a conceptualisation of cities can improve research on milieus, describing two milieus in Nairobi.

In contrast to class, milieu study builds on shared cultural orientations, structures of meaning and characteristics (for this chapter cf. Stoll, 2018, and Neubert and Stoll, 2018). Class concepts aggregate vertical groups that are supposed to have similar structural characteristics such as income, occupations and lifestyles. In contrast, the idea of milieu is to identify horizontally differentiated groups with similar values, actions and aims in life. Milieu does not presuppose similar income and occupations but focuses on sociocultural elements. Class, and more particularly 'middle class', evokes ideas of a stable future and the possibility of saving and consumption. It is not clear, however, if it is possible to describe African societies in general and urban Kenya in particular with a vertical concept like class. According to Dieter Neubert, class is not an adequate analytical tool to study social groups in Africa as influences such as ethnicity, economic relations to the extended family, and urban–rural ties transcend a vertical analysis (cf. Neubert, 2005, 182–189). Studies of vertical class structures with clearly separated poor-, middle-, and high-income households of nuclear families do not describe social relations in African societies convincingly. In many African countries, complex forms of urban–rural connections and ethnic differentiation exist, which do not necessarily overlap with socioeconomic boundaries. The class concept implies more than being part of a certain income stratum. Since Karl Marx, class has been described as a group in the same socioeconomic position that shares certain interests but also cultural characteristics such as values, typical habits, and political views. In particular, in English-speaking academia, the term 'class' is not only used for group definitions but also for economic strata without acknowledging the cultural implications of the class notion sufficiently. Moreover, the class concept is not a flexible approach to studying groups but is bound to a vertical analysis. It is appropriate to studying forms of stratification that focus on high, middle and low strata but has difficulties to include horizontal forms of differentiation. The conceptual limitations of class affect research that is committed to examining also different lifestyles and sociocultural factors. Famous studies such as Bourdieu's *Distinction* (1984) or Leela Fernandes' (2006) work on middle classes in India analyse also sociocultural aspects and lifestyles. However, they do not introduce an alternative conceptualisation that goes beyond vertical group analysis.

Due to conceptual flaws of class, German sociologists have, since the 1980s, begun to discuss alternatives. It had become more and more evident that an analysis of vertical classes is not sufficient to understand social structure and lifestyles in late capitalism. In European societies of the nineteenth and early twentieth centuries, socioeconomic positions, professions, and lifestyles mostly overlapped. However, since the 1960s, the impacts of deindustrialisation, the rise of post-materialism and other developments such as the dissolution of previous forms of class solidarity have led to new lifestyles in Germany and other Western democracies. Therefore, German sociology developed new concepts to examine sociocultural groups that share values, aims in life and leisure activities. These aspects do not necessarily correlate with income levels or professions, as the class concept assumes. While these approaches are very common in German social sciences, they are unknown in international contexts and it is necessary to introduce them here. The milieu concept and the more flexible notion of *Lebensstile* (lifestyles) are the most common tools for sociocultural analysis (for an overview on milieus see Isenböck et al., 2014; Rebstein and Schnettler 2014; Neubert and Stoll, 2015, 11 ff.; for lifestyles see Otte and Rössel, 2012).

While Pierre Bourdieu's study of culture in *Distinction* (1984) has been important for this debate, milieu theorists refer to Bourdieu and other vertical approaches in very different ways. Michael Vester et al. (2001) see for Germany a strong connection between class and the realities of life. They assume that milieus correspond strongly with vertical differences in the same income stratum including structure, values or leisure activities. Other versions of milieu have a stronger empirical orientation and study sociocultural elements like attitudes or forms of leisure activities with a stronger horizontal than vertical conceptualisation (cf. Hradil, 1987; Schulze, 1993). Likewise, the development of the milieu concept is closely linked to social and market research, for instance by the SIGMA-Institute (cf. Ascheberg, 2006) and the SINUS-Institute (cf. Flaig et al., 1993; Sinus, 2015). All versions of milieu analysis mentioned here aim to study lifestyle groups of a significant size in a certain setting. While milieu perspectives include ethnographic descriptions, they generally focus on the meso-level of reconstructed groups who share crucial sets of characteristics. Consequently, the analysis is situated between city, society or nation-state as possible macro-level and the individual at the micro-level.

This text puts more general conceptions of milieu into dialogue with local particularities. Due to the focus on milieus and specific elements of Nairobi, the chapter does not discuss the conceptualisation of cities and other elements of urban theory in detail. It is, however, possible to develop a more elaborated framework for the study of social milieus. Ash Amin and Nigel Thrift stress, in *Seeing Like a City* (2016), that cities consist of multiple networks, from everyday routines to politics and the economy, and thus assume a particular shape. Daniel A. Bell and Avner de-Shalit (2011) discuss the particularities of different cities under conditions of accelerated global connections in *The Spirit of Cities. Why the Identity of a City Matters in a Global Age*. A recent systematic approach is also offered, for instance, with the *distinctiveness of cities/Eigenlogik der Städte* (Berking, 2012; Löw, 2012),[6] which studies how an understanding of the everyday knowledge and locally specific structures of meaning by residents can explain differences between urban settings. This research programme focuses on the question of how a city influences the ways of thinking, acting, and grouping that are crucial to the life of its inhabitants. Other works that study 'the cityness' of cities include Ulf Hannerz's *Exploring the City* (1980) or Janet Abu-Lughod's *New York, Chicago, Los Angeles* (1999). As the disputably most important theory of space and urbanity, it is also possible to consider cities as multidimensional constructs in the line of Henri Lefebvre's *The Production of Space* (1991 [1974]). In particular, Christian Schmid's (2005) interpretation of Lefebvre contextualises and clarifies the framework in such a way that it becomes possible to study cities as socio-spatial conglomerates. Another, already classic work is Doreen Massey's (2005) *For Space*, which develops a dynamic approach to space and place because she considers the concepts in a relational understanding as the outcome of contextual influences ranging from global impacts to economic policies and particular local forms of meaning making.

This study applies a descriptive version of the milieu concept that does not presuppose a vertical stratification (Hradil, 1987; Sinus, 2015). 'Descriptive' means the reconstruction of milieus results from empirical research, instead of deducing it from theory. The advantage of such an empirical focus is that it can integrate African, Kenyan, and specific local characteristics such as the importance of the extended family or religion for certain milieus.

3 Methodology and Data

The data was gathered mostly during nine months of fieldwork by the author in Nairobi and Mombasa. During five field stays between 2013 and 2016, the author conducted observations in significant places such as churches, restaurants and private homes, and carried out 97 biographical interviews in both cities. This data collection aimed at identifying groups with distinctive sociocultural orientations in life: social milieus. The research followed a contrastive approach that aims at differentiating milieus with distinctive traits. For this purpose, the study began examining publicly visible groups and contrasted them with a revised multilayered matrix developed by the SINUS-Institut

6 There are two English translations for the German *Eigenlogik der Städte*. While 'distinctive logic of cities' (Löw, 2012) emphasises the emergence of phenomena from a particular setting, the other translation, 'distinctiveness' (Berking, 2012), stresses rather the particular character of a city.

that covers the most significant areas of life (Flaig et al., 1993, 71; Neubert and Stoll, 2015, 8 ff.): demography/social position, space and places, aims in life, work/performance, ideals and role models, image of society, family/partnership, leisure/communication and everyday aesthetics. In the next steps, the research examined more difficult to access groups that spend, for example, most of their time in family circles or closed ethnic networks. Also, data from media reports or other studies (Spronk, 2012) contributed to constructing the milieus.

The methodology of this study considers milieus in the middle-stratum as particular to Nairobi and Mombasa. It also contrasts the differentiation of milieus to distinguish between identical and unique elements. The differences in size, density, heterogeneity of the population and city type are no obstacle for the comparison as they can be part of specific features of a city. With milieu studies, it is possible to interpret the particular ideas and actions of a milieu in relation to a city. In the case of the *Young Professionals,* these actions include visits to certain clubs wearing typical outfits. Thus, the milieu of the *Young Professionals* depends on an urbanised youth culture and club scene, which exists in Nairobi but not in Mombasa. It is important that the milieus have their starting point in the middle-income stratum but are not limited to it as sociocultural commonalities are the defining criterion.

The reconstruction of milieus and their particular local embeddedness methodologically builds on two combined analytical foci. Whereas both foci are in the research intertwined, an analytical separation clarifies the process of milieu generation. The first focus concentrates on the construction of milieus and uses field data to identify characteristics and elaborate milieus in Nairobi and Mombasa. The second focus combines these results with a study of Nairobi as a multidimensional space that influences the size and also certain characteristics of milieus. Such aspects range from the significance of clothes as markers of membership in a milieu to a particular career orientation that distinguishes Nairobi from Mombasa. Many other aspects such as job opportunities, the relation of religious communities or the proximity to the home areas of certain ethnic groups influence city structures and the composition of milieus as well. The description of milieus presents the results in Sections 3 to 5 in a more readable way and not according to the foci of analysis.

Focus I opposes the widespread, mostly implicit assumption that there is a culturally uniform African or Kenyan 'middle class', an assumption that economic definitions seem to make when they ignore sociocultural influences (AfDB, 2011; for the critique see Neubert and Stoll, 2018). The study examines in the first focus to which degree groups of significant size differ in their orientations in life, values, and consumption habits. For highlighting differences, the research referred to the matrix mentioned earlier (Neubert and Stoll, 2015, 8 ff.). The data collection aimed at identifying milieus by sets of distinctive characteristics such as values, orientations and activities in comparison with other milieus. The process of milieu construction does not concentrate on local particularities, but it can also consider features and mechanisms that are unique to Nairobi or Mombasa, locally adapted to a city, or identical in both cities.

Focus II links the empirical data on milieus from Focus I systematically to particularities of Nairobi and Mombasa. This part examines how milieus relate to existing structures of a city and adds more information from historical and other sources that explain continuities and new developments. The study examines characteristics such as typical beliefs and practices but also the demarcation lines between milieus. Also, this part considers historical influences and events in a diachronic perspective that is still significant today. In the best case, it would be possible to identify routinised patterns as the outcome of historical paths. For instance, the emergence of a new urbanised part of Nairobi's middle stratum during the last two decades resulted from the growth of the city, the emergence of a new generation of urban-born Kenyans, and new opportunities for migrants from other cities.

4 Middle-Income Milieus in Nairobi

Nairobi is Kenya's economic centre, the seat of the national government and the preferred destination for work migration (for this chapter cf. Stoll, 2018). The city is a place for all kinds of industrial labour, trade and businesses of different sizes. It hosts several universities and government institutions that attract many ambitious young people. Nairobi is also home to thousands of international companies and non-governmental organisations that offer well-paid jobs in internationally connected fields. With more than three million inhabitants, the city is by far Kenya's biggest urban agglomeration. Nairobi is a classic example of the rapid growth of an African city that lacked sufficient industrialisation to include the rising number of rural migrants. The Metropolitan region constantly grew from its beginnings as a small settlement in 1900, counting 510,000 inhabitants in the year 1970 and 1.35 million in 1980. Even though official statistics vary, the city may at present have a population of more than three million, and between 4.5 million (UN-Habitat, 2016) and six million (Amis, 2006, 173; Kenya National Bureau of Statistics, 2009) may live in the Metropolitan area. While statistics are unreliable, international organisations estimate that up to 60 percent of the city's population live in slums

(UN-Habitat, 2013) and that about half of its residents are poor (Oxfam, 2009; UN-Habitat, 2013). This also means that a considerable share of its population lives above the poverty line, with around one-third in the middle-income stratum.

For decades, migrants from all parts of Kenya lived in Nairobi as 'Peasants in Cities' (Mangin, 1970). People earned money in urban occupations and reinvested in their rural home areas. Today, this is no longer the dominant mode of living but one of many possibilities. In the last two decades, a generation of 'middle class' Nairobians emerged with different basic orientations in life. For instance, some members of this middle stratum have a highly urban and others a stronger rural focus. The only feature that they share is a similar income above the poverty line. These economic opportunities leave space for different forms of consumption, according to specific priorities in life.

While not everyone in the statistical middle-income stratum has sufficient means to purchase costly goods, consumption and investment preferences show central orientations of milieus. Some members of the 'middle class' prefer to buy land in the countryside, whereas others invest in business activities and again others prefer to buy stylish clothes and smartphones. Members of the middle-income stratum differ in their lifestyles, which include values, future orientations, and many other aspects. It is crucial, nevertheless, to consider all milieus as part of contemporary, modern Nairobi. In particular, a common distinction between modern and traditional is misleading because all milieus are in many ways modern as their members use digital communication, participate in global discussions and are highly mobile.

Through empirical fieldwork, Dieter Neubert and the author have identified six milieus in Nairobi (cf. Neubert and Stoll, 2015, 8; see also graphic 1):

- *Neo-traditionals*[7] have close ties with members of their extended family and their rural and ethnic community. This includes a strong emotional bond but also sharing of finances. Also, members of this milieu often take political positions that favour their ethnic group.
- *Social Climbers* focus on saving to advance individually and to improve the situation of their nuclear family. Many of them work long hours and save a high percentage of their income for investing in a business or for studying.

7 It is crucial that there is no distinction between more or less modern or traditional milieus. We call this milieu 'Neo-traditionalists' as they refer in a particular way to traditions. This does not mean that these traditions have existed for a very long time. The crucial point is the subjective orientation towards such values and their significance for the conduct of life in this milieu.

- Members of the *Stability-Oriented Pragmatic milieu* try to maintain their current position and have fewer aspirations than members of other milieus. This includes moderate consumption with their family with whom they spend most of their time out of work at home.
- Characteristics of the *Cosmopolitan-Liberal milieu* are a clear stance for civil values and against corruption and tribalism, combined with career ambitions. Members of this milieu often work in non-government organisations and are active in human rights or environmental groups.
- Members of the *Christian milieu* (also *Christian Religious*) regularly participate in church-related activities and spend a large part of their leisure time away from their families with other parish members. Their orientation in life focuses on religion, the church, and economic success.
- *Young Professionals* are between 20 and 35 years old and come mostly from privileged families in upper or upper-middle strata. They combine hedonistic consumption, an international orientation and career ambition in economically well-paid fields.

In addition to the listed milieus, there are also Muslim and Hindu micro-milieus in Nairobi for which there are not sufficient data. These micro-milieus are, however, considerably smaller than the *Christian Milieu*. The *Young Professionals* and the *Cosmopolitan Liberals* are limited to Nairobi and do not exist as milieus of a significant size in other Kenyan cities.

The composition of milieus in Mombasa's middle-income stratum differs significantly due to economic, cultural and other factors. Mombasa is Kenya's access point to the Indian Ocean and also a hotspot for global tourism. It is a port city with a long history of overseas trade to the Middle East and to India, and a large Muslim community. There are divisive lines between Muslims and Christians that overlap often with ethnicity. Members of ethnic groups such as the Swahili and Michikenda have been in Mombasa for generations; they are Muslims and are also bound by lifestyles to Mombasa's old town. In contrast, members of other ethnic groups such as Kikuyu or Luo are mostly Christian migrants to Mombasa of the first or second generation. These migrants usually come for work at touristic spots or the port.

There are partly different milieus in Mombasa's middle-income stratum but also the size of certain milieus varies. In contrast to Nairobi, there is a *Swahili* milieu with a distinctive lifestyle that is limited to Mombasa. The *Christian Milieu* is considerably smaller and there is no milieu of *Young Professionals* because Mombasa has neither the professional opportunities nor the club scene and cultural life that attracts the ambitious members of this milieu.

Figure 1 visualises the milieus in Nairobi. The size of the bubbles does not represent the actual size of milieus as there is not sufficient data. There is also

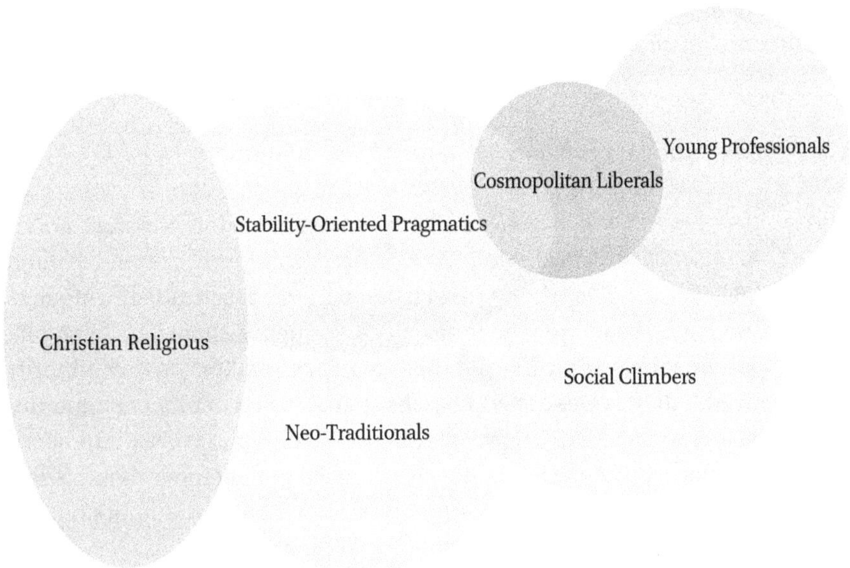

FIGURE 12.1 Milieus in Nairobi's middle-income stratum.
SOURCE: AUTHOR

not enough information to determine the socioeconomic positions of milieus precisely but it is possible to give an idea which milieu is limited to one vertical stratum and which milieu comprises several strata. The y-axis describes based on estimates basis roughly the socioeconomic position of the milieus. There is no linear x-axis as it is not possible to reduce the different qualitative orientations of milieus to one linear continuum (such as more or less socioeconomic resources on the y-axis). Not everyone is clearly a member of only one milieu but may draw on two or even more groups. The overlapping areas of milieu circles express these possibilities. However, the two-dimensional figure cannot cover all possible overlaps between milieus.

This text reconstructs the *Christian Religious* and the *Young Nairobi Professionals* as empirical examples. Both milieus show different city-specific influences. The *Christian Milieu* can be found in all Kenyan cities, but apart from general characteristics it shows particular influences of Nairobi. For instance, the importance placed on the display of material prosperity is typical for inhabitants of Kenya's capital. Demonstrations of wealth are less important among *Christian Religious* in other cities like Mombasa where a large part of the population consists of Muslims and where the author found less competition for members among Christian communities. This competition includes spiritual programmes but also the promise of material wealth as the next section on the *Christian Religious Milieu* demonstrates.

5 Case Study 1: *Christian Religious Milieu* in Nairobi

This section describes first general characteristics that the *Christian Milieu* (also *Christian Religious*) (cf. Stoll, 2018) in Nairobi, Mombasa and Eldoret share (Niechoj, 2016). The second part elaborates which features are unique to Nairobi and how they are related to the city's distinctive character. Being religious is part of almost every Kenyan's self-definition, and only a tiny minority do not consider themselves as part of a Christian, Muslim or other community. Religion and church activities have, therefore, a high significance in the social and symbolic order of Kenya. It is, however, crucial to remember that this section does not study religious groups such as Pentecostals or Catholics but describes individuals with a similar lifestyle that differs from the lifestyles among other milieus. Moreover, the case study is limited to the *Christian Milieu*, as the author does not have enough data on Muslim or Hindu groups in Nairobi to make reliable categorisations.

In contrast to many Kenyans who would call themselves Christians, members of this milieu are more dedicated to their church and follow religious rules in a more consequent way (cf. Neubert and Stoll, 2015, 11f.; Stoll, 2018). *Christian Religious* are active in their church community and engage in several meetings per week, such as Bible study, the counselling of troubled church members and service-based worship. Apart from with their families, members of this milieu spend a large share of their leisure time in religious networks and often have close friends in church. Frequently, work or business are intertwined with religion. Another distinctive trait is that members of this milieu follow norms of their community with greater consequence than less dedicated Christians. For example, members of the *Christian Milieu* distance themselves in interviews from premarital sex and say they avoid places that sell alcohol. Another characteristic is that they regularly pay the tithe, ten percent of their income, to their parish. The foundation for their actions is—in contrast to the *Neo-traditional* milieu for example—the Bible and not the values of their ethnic community. In spite of the existence of connections to the extended family in the countryside, these ties are not the main orientation in the life of *Christian Religious*.

By their religious convictions, most members of this milieu have strong career ambitions. Economic success is, unlike in the majority of European Christian denominations, not interpreted as materialism or a lack of spirituality. Rather, it is common in many Kenyan churches to display financial well-being by wearing expensive clothes, driving prestigious-brand cars and donating to the community. All of these actions can raise a church member's status. In spite of differences between Christian groups in Kenya, the milieu analysis focuses on the commonalities in the lifestyle of committed church members—as they are distinct from members of other described milieus.

The previous part elaborated general elements of *Christian Religious* that are common in Nairobi, Mombasa, Kisumu and Eldoret. The next sections give examples of unique influences in Nairobi. Information from interviews and observation shows that the ambition and the business focus of many *Christian Religious* are on the average more intense—or, in the language of many Nairobians, 'more aggressive', with a positive connotation—than those of their counterparts in other Kenyan cities. This will to obtain economic success is a local meaning structure that is also very strong in most other middle-income milieus in Nairobi. Individuals perceive Nairobi as a place that offers economic opportunities and a good environment for life but is also competitive and expensive. The city attracts individuals from all parts of Kenya and East Africa with its promise of social advancement by economic success and the opportunity to study at a university. Residents of Nairobi and Mombasa perceive Kenya's capital as much faster and higher paced than Mombasa, which people in both towns describe as a relaxed beach town.

Correspondingly, expectations of prosperity are essential parts of church programmes and are more important than in Mombasa. Many churches in Nairobi are strongly affected by the competitive atmosphere of the city as they are often much bigger than the churches in other cities and they try, with very particular programmes, to attract new members. Another aspect is the comparatively higher acceptance of changing one's church affiliation as a life reform in Nairobi. A number of churches offer not only spiritual guidance but a life plan for social advancement, although this is especially true of Pentecostal churches (for Pentecostalism in Nairobi see Droz, 2010). This focus on success is particularly visible in some Pentecostal communities in Nairobi, communities whose idea systems combine an intense spiritual programme with an appreciation of personal development and economic improvement. These Pentecostals, and to a lesser degree many other communities, interpret professional success as an expression of God's favour. In some big churches, pastors even ask their congregants to be dressed well, and in this way exclude poor people from attending.[8] Some pastors receive so many donations from church members that they build mansions and buy private jets.

8 There is a debate about the head of the Jubilee Christian Church Parklands, reverend Kathy Kiuna, who has made comments about dressing and the economic status of church members.

Obviously, individuals in Nairobi are expected not only to be successful but also to show this in a particular way. While members of church programmes for individual advancement do not always succeed in improving economically, they are, nevertheless, supposed to demonstrate status by good looks, high-brand cars and huge donations. In certain churches, showing one's good situation can even overcome the moral boundaries of sexual restrictions; at Sunday services, young women wear short skirts to display, by their good looks, their elevated social position. Such a proof of God's favour would not be acceptable in many churches, especially in other cities. Here, the emphasis on prosperity has become stronger than the control of sexuality. With their entanglement of faith and success orientation, these churches are bound to Nairobi: it is a locally embedded norm in Nairobi to demonstrate status through appearance, exclusive clothing, and conspicuous consumption. The Sunday services of many church communities in Nairobi are known as catwalks with a spiritual background, for instance in Parklands, Westlands or Kilimani. Such visual displays of well-being also have the aim of illustrating the dominance of Christians in Kenya's capital. Another important aspect is that many churches in Nairobi demand considerable donations. The contrast to Mombasa with its higher share of Muslims is a good point of comparison. For instance, in Mombasa clothes do not mark social differences to the same degree as they do in Nairobi. Also, interviews with members of church communities in Mombasa reveal that many of them do not feel as secure as their counterparts in Nairobi. In 2014, attacks by Al-Shabaab on churches in Mombasa produced considerable uneasiness among Christians. Additionally, witchcraft was a more frequently mentioned topic in interviews in Mombasa than in Nairobi.

One result returned by the research is that in Nairobi different areas of life frequently mix although they are rather separate in other cities. For instance, members of the *Christian Religious Milieu* in Nairobi frequently work in areas where they come into contact with behaviours that show little respect for central Christian norms. The consequences for life are illustrated by the example of Jennifer, a religious, 24-year-old student who sings not only in church but also as a professional backing singer for bands. Many situations in the music business are related to sex:

'Yeah, it's the popular music in Kenya is about that. Basically like [...], it's about party life and women, and all those things. [...] Yeah, 'cause you know being like a background vocalist, for some people they want to dictate what you'll wear, they want to dictate how you should dance on stage, they can even push you to dance with someone. I have seen it happening in concerts. [...] And that for me is something I really didn't look forward to being or doing, cause I really—first impressions are everything. Yeah. So, I may, today you're maybe somebody's background vocalist, but tomorrow you may want a job in a good organisation. And maybe somebody saw you dancing in a, in an otherwise, not so proper manner with someone. And this happens to be a director of a company and he'd have problems hiring you. 'Cause he feels like you would change the company's imagination'. (Interview with Jennifer, 13.09.2013)

To earn money, Jennifer is often at places where she must interact with people who consume much alcohol and where casual sex is normal. She does not drink and emphasises in the quote above, that she does not want to dress provocatively or dance with men because concert organisers ask for it. However, Jennifer not only draws a moral boundary, she is also worried about spoiling her future employment prospects if someone sees her. Many members of the *Christian Milieu* in Nairobi face similar problems because they work in environments where drinking, partying and one-night stands are usual. In a similar way to the music scene, many companies in Nairobi have an after-work culture of going out together and celebrating until late into the night. *Religious Christians* such as Jennifer must develop particular strategies to deal with such situations. In comparison, despite large amounts of club life and prostitution in Mombasa, there seem to be fewer overlaps in the everyday situations of inhabitants in the coastal town, by and large. In Mombasa, clubs and places for prostitution are concentrated in parts of town such as Mtwapa and Nyali, which are far away from the homes and jobs of most inhabitants, including the *Christian Milieu*. Professional areas and clubs are socially and spatially more separated than in Nairobi, possibly also as a result of the connection to domestic and international tourism present in Mombasa.

6 Case Study II: *Young* Nairobi *Professionals*

Nairobi is the only city in Kenya where *Young Professionals* exist as a milieu of considerable size (cf. Stoll, 2018). The emergence of this milieu is no coincidence but is closely related to the city's special character as a national and regional economic and cultural hub for Kenya and even neighbouring countries. The milieu of the *Young Professionals* has taken shape in the last two decades and is an expression of new urbanisation processes that are significant for present day Nairobi. To many young adults, Nairobi promises individual success and a hedonistic urban life without subordination to the extended family or to ethnic or religious community. *Young Professionals* are between 20 and 35 years old and grew up mostly in middle-income or even rich families from Nairobi or other cities. Nevertheless, there are also members of this milieu from rural areas who migrated to Nairobi. As 'Young *Nairobi* Professionals'

(Spronk, 2009, 501—emphasis added), this group of well-educated young employees, entrepreneurs or students (cf. Spronk, 2012) differ—mostly in their financial possibilities and their everyday lives—strongly from the poor majority of the city.

The *Young Professionals* are often self-employed in areas with good financial returns such as finance, information technology or resource trading. They work in globally operating firms and institutions such as non-governmental organisations, the United Nations or multinational companies. Many of them travel regularly to Europe or North America. *Young Professionals* are famous for forms of conspicuous consumption, with colourful clothes, the newest electronic gadgets such as the latest phones, and partying in clubs and bars. Members of this milieu must have the financial means to pay for elegant clothes, for drinks in bars and clubs, and for restaurants in the city centre or districts like Westlands or Kilimani. Moreover, members of this milieu attend events such as the monthly 'Blankets and Wine' Festival, the 'Koroga' Festival, the Nairobi fashion market and shiny parties or art festivals. The role models of those in this milieu are successful business people and celebrities. In public, the lifestyle of *Young Professionals* sometimes clashes with the ideals of other milieus. As an example, since 2014 groups of men have attacked, on several occasions, women and tried to strip them naked in public places because they wore, in their opinion, too short skirts and acted in an immoral way.

Young Professionals have a weaker affiliation to rural and ethnic communities, and to their extended families, than members of most other milieus. A considerable number of them try to cut the ties to their extended families to escape social control and financial obligations. In this way, they distance themselves from the moral economy of rural villages and avoid forms of mutual solidarity.

Structural and cultural factors make Nairobi attractive for *Young Professionals*. The milieu is bound to the city because the well-paid jobs in international companies and non-governmental organisations are located here. Similarly, Nairobi has a uniquely vibrant nightlife. Style and looks are crucial for members of this milieu. They are the spearheading group of Nairobi's specific form of visual boundary-making by aesthetics. To be 'hip' in Nairobi it is not enough to merely have money for the latest style and mobile phone. It is crucial in this environment to also know what to wear, how, and when and where to wear it. Their well-paid jobs—but also money from their well-established families and from bank loans—give *Young Professionals* economic opportunities and allow them to display exclusive taste. This is a privileged situation that distinguishes them from the majority of Nairobi's young inhabitants. All these aspects produce symbolic economic and cultural boundaries (cf. Lamont, 1992, 4). High economic and cultural hurdles make it difficult for migrants from rural locations and for Nairobi's poor to become part of this milieu.

Rachel Spronk (2012) has written a comprehensive study of this milieu and its members' sex lives. According to Spronk, the rise of the *Young Professionals* is intertwined with the economic growth and the new job opportunities that have emerged since around 2000. She also shows how these young Nairobians maintain their gender-specific identities by going to popular places. Part of typical interactions is having certain types of relationships, including those that enable casual sex. In spite of possible conflicts with social conventions, sex has—for many yuppies—an important psychological and social function: 'Sex, which is central to self-expression, is somehow associated with "being modern", while at the same time it feels "natural". In their self-expression, their notions of self are "African", "non-Western", "nontraditional"' (Spronk, 2012, 14). This quote shows that sex can bridge, at least partly, the contradictions that young people feel as they become part of a globally integrated Kenya and when they fear they might lose connection to their African background.

Biographical data show how Nairobi's urban environment gives Zara, a 31 year old business consultant and owner of a small travel booking company, freedom from the moral and monetary expectations of her family. She does not own a car or even a fridge, probably to hide her good financial situation from relatives. For instance, she not only goes to clubs and restaurants but also travels to lodges in the Masai Mara and to European countries. Her individualised lifestyle not only gives her financial opportunities, she can also hide her love life from her family and avoids questions about marriage and children. Although Zara does not mention it in the interview, she has—according to friends—successive and sometimes multiple boyfriends.

Another interviewee, Adrian, is a 27-year old graphic designer who grew up in Karen, one of Nairobi's best areas. He is a co-owner and co-director of a small marketing and event company, which he founded together with a friend three years before the interview. After attending expensive schools and securing a diploma as a graphic designer, he started working for a Chinese pay-TV company in Nairobi. With some years' work experience, he decided to bring his knowledge of photography, advertising and digital marketing to his own company. Adrian is well-dressed in colourful outfits or, if necessary, more formal business clothes. He wears his hair in well-kept dreadlocks, exercises several times a week at the gym and goes regularly to popular bars and festivals. As a graphic designer, he owns a MacBook and a digital camera with several lenses. Additionally, he often goes on holidays in various places in Kenya.

In contrast to members of other milieus, *Young Professionals* follow a generational, individualised lifestyle that focuses on hedonistic consumption and career, not on church-related activities as is the case for the *Christian Milieu*. Most *Young Professionals* leave this milieu or reduce, at least, their visits to bars and festivals before they reach 35 years of age. Usually, the reason is that they get married and have children.

7 Conclusion: Nairobi's Distinctive Middle-Income Milieus

This chapter has examined middle-income milieus (sociocultural groups with similar lifestyles) in Nairobi to demonstrate how such a conceptualisation can include specific local aspects. The milieu concept is an alternative to the popular but not very nuanced concept of the 'middle class' and considers the most significant aspects of life in order to construct social groups. Moreover, due to their focus on empirical findings, milieu studies are able to consider, likewise, particular aspects of a city, such as local subcultures, economic branches or particular forms of global connections.

By examining middle-income milieus and their relation to Nairobi as an example, the text contributes to the debate on cities in Africa. It has become widely accepted that it is necessary to study African cities as 'ordinary cities' (Robinson, 2006) and not as the 'other' of cities in the global North as developmental views suggested for a long time. Robinson (2006) stresses that we must approach each city as a particular constellation, and build on empirical research and not on untenable theory from 'EuroAmerica'. It is necessary to study cities in Africa without assumptions that have no empirical proof, such as underdevelopment as an alleged commonality of urban Africa. Similar to Robinson's claim, milieu theory demands we consider social groups according to local findings and study them, therefore, in forms other than vertical, economic strata or 'classes'. In particular, the concept of the 'middle class' has so many, often contradictory connotations that its transfer to Africa invites one to make assumptions before one has even begun to learn anything about the groups that lie between the poor and the rich. From a typical 'middle class' lifestyle to a financially stable situation and moderate political views, there are many attributes that are not necessarily found in the middle-income strata of African countries. Moreover, it is doubtful if vertical categorisations such as 'middle class' or 'working class' can grasp the most distinctive realities of life in twenty-first century Kenya and other African settings. Including sociocultural aspects in the process of group construction is, on the African continent, particularly important because many features such as ongoing urban–rural connections, the affiliation to the extended family but also the emergence of new urban lifestyles are frequent there but missing in class studies and Northern social theory in general. These aspects influence individuals' lives on a horizontal level that income distribution has difficulties analysing. In contrast to class, milieu refers to the most significant sociocultural characteristics and may offer an alternative. Also, due to their empirical perspective, milieu studies are open to local particularities and do not transfer the same model of stratification to each city in a certain country or region.

This chapter illustrates how the *Christian Milieu* and the milieu of *Young Professionals* are bound in specific ways to Nairobi. But what do these descriptions of milieus in the middle stratum tell us about Nairobi as a city? The *Christian Milieu* in Nairobi is different from its counterparts in other Kenyan cities in terms of its greater orientation to economic success and its degree of organisation. The *Young Professionals* exist as a milieu of significant size only in Nairobi, where many companies and non-governmental organisations, an entrepreneurial environment and a lively club scene attract young, well-educated Kenyans. In Kenya's capital they can follow their career paths and live a hedonistic, individualised lifestyle.

The text has portrayed Nairobi as an 'ordinary city', without deductive theoretical assumptions about a specific African urban quality—admittedly, from a particular sociological perspective with a focus on lifestyles, meanings and culture. Likewise, the study of middle-income milieus provides particular insights into aspects such as urbanism and urban–rural ties, which are crucial parts of most African cities but may manifest themselves there in ways very different to those found in Nairobi. A short discussion with a focus on urbanism and urban–rural ties demonstrates the usefulness of the milieu approach. As a result, the differentiation of milieus in the middle stratum results from Nairobi's unique form of urbanism.

For instance, the *Young Professionals*' highly individualised lifestyle cannot be explained merely by structural conditions such as the size of Nairobi or the job opportunities and good salaries. Rather, the cultural importance of entrepreneurial success and the material display of wealth provide the symbolic basis for the existence of the *Young Professionals* as a milieu. A strong entrepreneurial attitude and a tendency to display visible symbols of one's success are characteristic of many residents of Nairobi, also among the *Christian Religious*. Because the *Young Professionals* do not exist as a milieu in Mombasa and even members of the *Christian Religious Milieu*, by and large, do not show similar career ambitions in Mombasa, it is highly plausible to consider the strong orientation towards economic success and demonstrations of well-being as characteristics of Nairobi. For the inhabitants of most cities in sub-Saharan Africa, urban–rural ties are significant, but the way in which milieus relate to them is revealing with regard to specific forms of urban life. There are different ways in which residents of Nairobi relate to their extended families and the rural communities of the countryside. *Young Professionals* focus on their individual lives in the city, and they either have few connections to their extended family or even try to escape the financial obligations attached to kinship. For members of the *Christian Religious Milieu*, strong relations with the extended family and rural community are possible, but they are—mostly—less important for their lifestyle than the activities that take place in their church. In contrast, ties to the extended family and ethnic group in their rural home form a central part of life for another milieu, the *Neo-traditionals*. They share a considerable proportion of their income with relatives, and the development of their local communities is also crucial to them. Urban–rural ties are one significant aspect that all milieus deal with, but they do so in very different ways.

The milieu perspective demonstrates how urban–rural ties are enacted on the level of meso-groups in Nairobi and how this relates to their lifestyles. Furthermore, it is possible to study other significant aspects of African cities by a focused research into milieus, from economic practices to movement patterns, and the use of infrastructure in a wide sense that includes housing, education or forms of social security. Many new developments have deeply changed lives in African cities over the last two decades, and the milieu perspective may help us to study these. For instance, such different aspects as growing digitalisation and changing global–local relations, but also gender, affect individuals in specific ways according to their lifestyles. How and for which purpose do members of a milieu use smartphones, social media and messengers in a certain city? Which specific global influences affect members of which milieu in a certain city? From new Chinese economic activities to mass tourism, there are many aspects on the global level that change the realities of life on the local level. Nevertheless, field research is necessary to understand how global developments are being integrated into the routines of cities.

Further, gender relations are a very important topic that differs significantly across different cities. The milieu approach widens scope and allows one to study gender relations in certain groups and with respect to particular features of places. As an example, gender roles and related ideas differ strongly between the *Christian Religious Milieu* and among the *Young Professionals* in Nairobi. Relations to aspects such as sexuality and expectations with regard to women and men, but also attitudes towards homosexuality, differ strongly between these and other milieus. Finally, milieu studies can increase our understanding of certain cities for future comparative research. Also, comparing ways of life among middle-income milieus in selected African cities will reveal local particularities. Which milieus exist in Lagos and Cape Town, which similarities and differences are there in comparison to Nairobi, and how do these findings relate to the general characteristics of these cities? Furthermore, comparisons of milieus in different parts of the global South and North may provide new forms of knowledge—for example, with a focus on selected topics such as the use of digitalisation and gender. The milieu concept can be a fine bedfellow for the study of the urban. In Africa, but even elsewhere in the world.

Acknowledgements

I am grateful for the support of the German Ministry of Research for the project 'Middle Classes on the Rise', which was part of the Bayreuth Academy of Advanced African Studies, and for the support of the Volkswagen Foundation for a postdoc scholarship at the Center for Cultural Sociology, Yale University. The chapter was written in Bayreuth and at Yale. The team of the project 'Middle Classes on the Rise' has a sociological part (Dieter Neubert and Florian Stoll) and an anthropological part (Erdmute Alber, Lena Kroeker and Maike Voigt).

References

Abu-Lughod, J. (1999) *New York, Chicago, Los Angeles.* (Minneapolis, MN: University of Minnesota Press).

AfDB (African Development Bank) (2011) *The Middle of the Pyramid: Dynamics of the Middle Class in Africa*, Market Brief (Abidjan: AfDB), https://www.afdb.org/fileadmin/uploads/afdb/Documents/Publications/The%20Middle%20of%20the%20Pyramid_The%20Middle%20of%20the%20Pyramid.pdf (accessed on 10 May 2018).

Amin, A. and N. Thrift (2016) *Seeing Like a City* (Cambridge: Polity Press).

Amis, P. (2006) 'Urban Poverty in East Africa. Nairobi and Kampala's Comparative Trajectories', in D.F. Bryceson and D.H. Potts, (eds.) *African Urban Economies. Viability, Vitality or Vitiation?* (Basingstoke and New York: Palgrave Macmillan), pp. 169–183.

Andrianampiarivo, T. (2016) 'Moderate Prosperity: An Adaptation of the Middle Class Concept to a Malagasy Rural Area. The Case of Itasy', *Review of Social Economy* 75(1), pp. 26–48, DOI: 10.1080/00346764.2016.1171384.

Ascheberg, C. (2006) 'Milieuforschung und Transnationales Zielgruppenmarketing', *Aus Politik und Zeitgeschichte*, 44–45, pp. 18–25.

Beck, R.M. (2015) 'Sheng: An Urban Variety of Swahili in Kenya', in N. Nassenstein and A. Hollington (eds.) *Global Repertoires and Urban Fluidity. Youth Languages in Africa*, pp. 51–79.

Bell, D.A. and de-Shalit, A. (2011) *The Spirit of Cities. Why the Identity of a City Matters in a Global Age* (Princeton, NJ: Princeton University Press).

Berking, H. (2012) 'The Distinctiveness of Cities: Outline of a Research Programme', *Urban Research & Practice*, 5(3), pp. 316–324, DOI: 10.1080/17535069.2012.727549.

Bourdieu, P. (1984) *Distinction. A Social Critique of the Judgement of Taste* (Cambridge, MA: Harvard University Press).

Budniok, J. and A. Noll (2016) 'Konsum und Distinktion. Verortungen der ghanaischen Mittelklasse', in A. Daniel, S. Müller, F. Stoll and R. Öhlschläger (eds.) *Mittelklassen, Mittelschichten oder Milieus in Afrika? Gesellschaften im Wandel*, Politik und Gesellschaft in Afrika, 2 (Baden-Baden: Nomos), pp. 111–132.

Charton-Bigot, H. and Rodriguez-Torres, D. (eds.) (2010) *Nairobi Today. The Paradox of a Fragmented City* (Dar es Salam: Mkuki na Nyota Publishers).

Connan, D. (2015) *The Decolonization of Private Members Clubs Socialization, Respectability and Elite Formation in Modern Kenya*. Unpublished dissertation.

Daniel, A., S. Müller, F. Stoll and R. Öhlschläger (eds.) (2016) *Mittelklassen, Mittelschichten oder Milieus in Afrika? Gesellschaften im Wandel*, Politik und Gesellschaft in Afrika, 2 (Baden-Baden: Nomos Verlagsgesellschaft).

Darbon, D. and C. Toulabour (2013) *Quelle(s) Classe(s) Moyenne(s) en Afrique? Une Revue de Littérature*, Document de travail, 118 (Paris: Agence Française de Développement).

Droz, Y. (2010) 'Pentecostalism in Nairobi', in H. Charton-Bigot and D. Rodriguez-Torres (eds.) (2010) *Nairobi Today. The Paradox of a Fragmented City* (Dar es Salam: Mkuki na Nyota Publishers).

Fernandes, L. (2006) *India's New Middle Class: Democratic Politics in an Era of Economic Reform* (Minneapolis: University of Minnesota Press).

Flaig, B.B., T. Meyer and J. Ueltzhöffer (1993) *Alltagsästhetik und politische Kultur. Zur ästhetischen Dimension politischer Bildung und politischer Kommunikation* (Bonn: Dietz).

Grathoff, R. (1989) *Milieu und Lebenswelt* (Frankfurt am Main: Suhrkamp).

Hannerz, U. (1980) *Exploring the City. Inquiries Towards an Urban Anthropology* (New York: Columbia University Press).

Hradil, S. (1987) *Sozialstrukturanalyse in einer fortgeschrittenen Gesellschaft. Von Klassen und Schichten zu Lagen und Milieus* (Opladen: Leske + Budrich).

Isenböck, P., L. Nell and J. Renn (eds.) (2014) *Die Form des Milieus. Zum Verhältnis von gesellschaftlicher Differenzierung und Formen der Vergemeinschaftung*, Zeitschrift für theoretische Soziologie, Sonderband 1 (Weinheim: Beltz Juventa).

Keim, K.-D. (1979) *Milieu in der Stadt. Ein Konzept zur Analyse älterer Wohnquartiere* (Stuttgart: Kohlhammer).

Kenya National Bureau of Statistics (2009) *2009 Kenya Population and Housing Census Analytical Reports*, https://www.knbs.or.ke/2009-kenya-population-and-housing-census-analytical-reports/ (accessed 1 November 2017).

Lamont, M. (1992) *Money, Morals, and Manners. The Culture of the French and American Upper-Middle Class* (Chicago: University of Chicago Press).

Lefebvre, H. (1991 [1974]) *The Production of Space* (New York: John Wiley & Sons).

Lentz, C. (2015) *Elites or Middle Classes? Lessons from Transnational Research for the Study of Social Stratification in Africa,* Working Paper of the Department of Anthropology and African Studies, 161 (Mainz: Institut für Ethnologie und Afrikastudien, Johannes Gutenberg Universität), http://www.ifeas.uni-mainz.de/Dateien/AP_161.pdf (accessed on 1 September 2017).

Löw, M. (2012) 'The Intrinsic Logic of Cities: Towards a new theory on urbanism' *Urban Research & Practice*, 5(3), pp. 303–315, DOI: 10.1080/17535069.2012.727545.

Mangin, W. (ed.) (1970) *Peasants in Cities: Readings in the Anthropology of Urbanization* (Boston: Houghton Mifflin).

Massey, D. (2005) *For Space* (London: Sage).

McKinsey Global Institute (2010) *Lions on the Move: The Progress and Potential of African Economies* (Seoul, San Francisco, London, Washington D.C.: McKinsey). http://www.mckinsey.com/global-themes/middle-east-and-africa/lions-on-the-move (accessed on 1 September 2017).

Melber, H. (ed.) (2016) *The Rise of Africa's Middle Class: Myths, Realities and Critical Engagements*, Nordiska Afrikainstitutet, (London, Uppsala: Zed Books).

Mercer, C. (2014) 'Middle Class Construction. Domestic Architecture, Aesthetics and Anxieties in Tanzania', *Journal of Modern African Studies*, 52(2), pp. 227–250, DOI: 10.1017/S0022278X14000068.

Mwaniki, P. (2014) 'How to Spot a Nairobian', *Daily Nation*, 3 October.

Ncube, M. and C.L. Lufumpa (2015) *The Emerging Middle Class in Africa* (London and New York: Routledge).

Neubert, D. (2005) 'Kulturelle Differenz und soziale Strukturierung in Afrika', in R. Kössler, D. Kumitz and U. Schultz (eds.) *Gesellschaftstheorie und Provokationen der Moderne. Gerhard Hauck zum 65. Geburtstag*, Peripherie. Sonderband, No. 1 (Münster: Westfälisches Dampfboot), pp. 178–192.

Neubert, D. and F. Stoll (2018) 'The Narrative of "the African Middle Class" and its Conceptual Limitations', in L. Kroeker, D. O'Kane and T. Scharrer (eds.) *Middle Classes in Africa. Changing Lives and Conceptual Challenges* (Basingstoke and New York: Palgrave Macmillan), pp. 57–79.

Neubert, D. and F. Stoll (2015) 'Socio-Cultural Diversity of the African Middle Class: The Case of Urban Kenya', *Academy Reflects*, No. 1, *IAS Working Paper Series*, No. 14 (Bayreuth: Institut für Afrika Studien, Universität Bayreuth).

Niechoj, K. (2016) *Das christlich engagierte Milieu in Eldoret, Kenia*, http://www.bayreuth-academy.uni-bayreuth.de/resources/Masterarbeit_Niechoj.pdf (accessed 1 September 2017).

Oxfam (2009) *Urban Poverty and Vulnerability in Kenya. Background Analysis for the Preparation of an Oxfam GB Urban Programme Focused on Nairobi*, https://urbanhealthupdates.files.wordpress.com/2009/09/urban_poverty_and_vulnerability_in_kenya1.pdf (accessed on 1 September 2017).

Otte, G. and J. Rössel, J. (eds.) (2012) *Lebensstilforschung*, Kölner Zeitschrift für Soziologie und Sozialpsychologie, Sonderheft, 51 (Wiesbaden: Springer).

Parnell, S. and E. Pieterse (2016) 'Translational Global Praxis: Rethinking Methods and Modes of African Urban Research' *International Journal of Urban & Regional Research* 40(1), pp. 236–246, DOI: 10.1111/1468-2427.12278.

Rebstein, B. and B. Schnettler (2014) 'Sozialstrukturanalyse "feiner Körnung" oder subjektzentrierte Lebensweltanalyse? Ungleichheitsbezogene und wissenssoziologische Ansätze der Milieuanalyse', in P. Isenböck, L. Nell and J. Renn (eds.) *Die Form des Milieus. Zum Verhältnis von gesellschaftlicher Differenzierung und Formen der Vergemeinschaftung*, Zeitschrift für theoretische Soziologie, Sonderband, 1, pp. 46–68.

Ricci, L. (2016) 'Reinterpreting Sub-Saharan Cities through the Concept of Adaptive Capacity: An Analysis of Autonomous Adaptation in Response to Environmental Changes in Peri-Urban Areas', *SpringerBriefs in Environment, Security, Development and Peace*, 26 (Cham, Heidelberg, New York, Dordrecht, London: Springer).

Robinson, J. (2006) *Ordinary Cities. Between Modernity and Development: Questioning Cities* (London and New York: Routledge).

Schmid, C. (2005) *Stadt, Raum und Gesellschaft. Henri Lefebvre und die Theorie der Produktion des Raumes* (Stuttgart: Franz Steiner).

Schulze, G. (1993) *Die Erlebnisgesellschaft. Kultursoziologie der Gegenwart* (Frankfurt am Main: Campus Verlag).

Sinus (2015) *Informationen zu den Sinus-Milieus 2015* (Heidelberg: SINUS) https://www.sinus-institut.de/fileadmin/user_data/sinus-institut/Downloadcenter/Informationen_zu_den_Sinus-Milieus.pdf (accessed on 1 September 2017).

Spronk, R. (2012) *Ambiguous Pleasures. Sexuality and Middle Class Self-Perceptions in Nairobi* (New York: Berghahn Books).

Spronk, R. (2009) 'Sex, Sexuality and Negotiating Africanness in Nairobi', *Africa* 79(04), pp. 500–519, DOI: 10.3366/E0001972009001041.

Stoll, F. (2018) 'How to be middle class in Nairobi: Lifestyles of middle-income milieus and their relation to Nairobi's city structure' in A. Ahmad, D. Nicoue, J. Riess, J. Sarre and F. Stoll, *Living in African Cities: Urban Spaces, Lifestyles and Social Practices in Everyday Life*, Bigsas Works, Bayreuth African Studies Working Paper Series.

Stoll, F. (2017) 'Middle Classes', in G. Antonelli and B. Rehbein, *Inequality in Economics and Sociology: New Perspectives* (London and New York: Routledge), pp. 81–97.

Stoll, F. (2016) 'Lebensweisen von Mittelschicht-Milieus in Nairobi: Eine Analyse mit Randall Collins' Interaction Ritual Chains', in A. Daniel, S. Müller, F. Stoll and R.

Öhlschläger (eds.) *Mittelklassen, Mittelschichten oder Milieus in Afrika? Gesellschaften im Wandel*, Politik und Gesellschaft in Afrika, Vol. 2 (Baden-Baden: Nomos), pp. 195–216.

UN-Habitat (2016) *Urban Data* (Nairobi: UN-Habitat), http://urbandata.unhabitat.org (accessed on 1 September 2017).

UN-Habitat (2013) *The State of Urban Youth 2012/2013: Youth in the Prosperity of Cities*, (Nairobi: UN-Habitat) https://unhabitat.org/books/the-state-of-urban-youth-20122013-youth-in-the-prosperity-of-cities/ (accessed on 1 September 2017).

Vester, M., H. Geiling, T. Hermann, D. Müller and P. von Oertzen (2001) *Soziale Milieus im gesellschaftlichen Strukturwandel. Zwischen Integration und Ausgrenzung*, Suhrkamp Taschenbuch Wissenschaft, No. 1312 (Frankfurt am Main: Suhrkamp).

Werthmann, K. (2014) 'Sind Städte in Afrika „unkennbar"? Ethnologische Stadtforschung in Afrika', in *Zeitschrift für Ethnologie*, 139 (2), pp. 159–178.

CHAPTER 13

Urbanisation and the Political Geographies of Violent Struggle for Power and Control: Mining Boomtowns in Eastern Congo

Karen Büscher

Abstract

This chapter addresses rural–urban transformations in the Kivu provinces, Democratic Republic of Congo (DRC), and more particularly focuses on the complex relationship between dynamics of violent conflict and the emergence of urban mining 'boomtowns'. Mining towns offer fascinating sites from which to investigate the socio-economic and spatial effects of a protracted history of violence, displacement and militarisation. They are the spatial outcomes of dynamics of the transformative power of violent conflict. Moreover, this chapter demonstrates how they also offer interesting spatial as well as analytical starting points from which to study the political geographies of war dynamics in Eastern DRC. It will be argued that the reason why these mining towns evolve into strategic 'resources' in violent struggles for power and control is to be found in their urban character as much as in the presence of natural resources. As such, this chapter analyses the process of mining urbanisation in the Kivu provinces as part of (armed) elites' spatial politics of power and control. As demographic concentrations and economic nodes, mining towns represent important political, economic and social resources for 'big men', armed groups and the Congolese state in their broader political struggles for power, legitimacy and authority. In a context of fragmented and multi-scalar governance, the urbanisation process of these towns is the outcome of a complex interaction and contestation of different forms of agency. Based on three ethnographic cases of mining towns that emerged from diverse dynamics of artisanal mining activities and forced displacement, this chapter contributes to broader academic and policy debates on the political nature of mining urbanisation in a context of conflict and fragmented governance.

1 Introduction: Mining Towns as Critical Locations of (Violent) Political Struggle in the DRC

On June 19, 2014, a local radio station *Amani* ('peace' in Swahili) was inaugurated in Rubaya, a mining town situated in the hills of Masisi, North Kivu, in

Eastern Congo. The inauguration ceremony, which took place in heavy rain, was widely attended, not least by a big delegation of Congolese government representatives. As part of a larger project on community peace consolidation set up by the American NGO Search for Common Ground, *Radio Amani* was financed by the Japanese government and launched in cooperation with the United Nations Development Programme (UNDP) and the UN peacekeeping force United Nations Organization Stabilization Mission in Democratic Republic of the Congo (MONUSCO). In front of the cameras and microphones documenting this mediatised event, donors, provincial ministers, as well as local inhabitants expressed their hopes that this 'intercommunity radio', an 'apolitical radio of proximity', would bring together people from different communities to overcome distrust and violence and to build together on the consolidation of peace in the region.[1]

The event is informative of the general image of the mining town of Rubaya, a site of interethnic land conflicts, rebel rule and a militarised economy of natural resources. It presents one of those local sites at which the broader dynamics of violent conflict characterising Eastern Congo's Kivu provinces come together and are being translated into local precarities, conflicts and violent livelihoods. The choice of Rubaya as one of the stations for the intercommunity peace-building radio project is further informed by the fact that this mining town presents an ideal site for a broad reach: in contrast to its rural surroundings, Rubaya is marked by a dense demographic concentration and a relatively well-developed radio and mobile data network. With its estimated 70,000 inhabitants, this mining town is a crowded centre, where miners, traders, state officials, IDPs (internally displaced persons) and taxi drivers from very different places and ethnic backgrounds meet in search of livelihoods, protection or leisure. Further, the event also points at the position of this mining town on the map of international humanitarian, development and peacebuilding interventions. The presence of IDP camps in the vicinity of the town, but especially the militarisation of artisanal mining activities, has attracted the attention of several international actors. In recent years, several NGOs, advocacy organisations and activists have engaged in the struggle against so-called conflict minerals. Since it is the first North Kivu 'sector' in the so-called traceability process,[2] Rubaya has been put on the international map by a wide variety of researchers, activists, journalists and NGO staff. Rubaya's appearance

1 See *Radio Okapi* (2014) 'Nord-Kivu: Création d'une radio communautaire à Rubaya' https://www.radiookapi.net/regions/nord-kivu/2014/06/20/nord-kivu-creation-dune-radio-communautaire-rubaya (accessed on 1 November 2017).

2 Organised by International Tin Association (ITA) Ltd. See Verbrugge et al. (2011) and Geenen (2016) for more information on this supply chain traceability initiative.

in US campaigns, for example, has largely reproduced the dominant narrative of 'blood minerals' and interethnic conflict (Vogel and Radley, 2014).

As the presence of Congolese state representatives at the inauguration ceremony shows, it is not only on the international level that Rubaya is clearly on the map. The presence of important economic and military 'big men' (owning, for example, much of the land on which Rubaya is developing) with ties in Goma as well as in the capital city, Kinshasa, makes this place less 'remote' than it seems and it actually becomes a nodal point in politico-military networks of power and control. At the same time, the presence of state representatives at the ceremony is contradictory. Despite the state's economic and political interest in the town, not even the minimum in terms of state investment has been made in Rubaya's development. As is the case for other mining boomtowns (and any other form of urbanisation) in the region, the Congolese state is rather absent from processes of urbanisation, planning or infrastructure provision. Inauguration ceremonies, performed with grotesque grandeur by Congolese ministers who have never invested one single dollar in projects or places like this, have become painful moments of magnification of state failure and the transfer of the state's legitimacy to other actors, such as international donors (Trefon, 2011). Instead of being the result of a state-led urbanisation process, mining towns like Rubaya are the outcome of a complex interaction of different kinds of agency, in which non-state actors play an important role.

Rubaya's development is not unique in the region. It is one of several urban centres that developed around artisanal mining sites and were transformed into boomtowns during the early 2000s. Rising market values of minerals such as cassiterite and coltan attracted many people to dig in the mines; at the same time, violent clashes between different armed groups pushed IDPs into these centres in search of security and a livelihood. Increasing economic activity has transformed the town into a vibrant commercial centre, with its packed houses, its colourful shops and its noisy bars standing in sharp contrast to its rural surroundings. Boomtowns such as Rubaya illustrate the profound reconfiguration of the Kivu landscape in a context of war, violence, repeated displacement and transforming livelihoods. Over the past twenty years, Eastern DRC has become increasingly urbanised, strongly affecting local economies, administrations, landscapes, cultures and identities (Büscher, 2015, 2016).

When places like Rubaya, Kamituga, Numbi or Nyabibwe are mentioned in the academic and policy literature on Eastern DRC, the focus is put on their artisanal mining activity and its role in the broader political economy of natural resources (Cuvelier, 2010; Geenen, 2014; Radley and Vogel, 2015; Vogel and Raeymaekers, 2016). While a lot of attention has been given to local livelihoods and the different forms of agency behind the natural resource economies and networks, the dynamics of boomtown urbanisation around these artisanal mines have gone largely unstudied. Instead of the mine itself, mineral extraction and the mine's artisanal miners, this chapter focuses on the town that has developed around them. Its urbanisation will be perceived as a dynamic, transformative process in its own right. In the current Congolese context of a confusing, half-implemented decentralisation law, the expansion of the centre itself becomes a highly political process, involving different state and non-state actors at the local, provincial and national levels. It will be argued that in this political context of war, the establishment, expansion and administrative recognition of these centres represent important political, economic and social resources for multi-scalar alliances of elites, customary authorities, armed groups and the Congolese state in their broader political struggles for power, legitimacy and control. Mining boomtowns represent, for example, significant bases for taxation, electoral politics and ethnic mobilisation.

By presenting mining towns as not only spatial but also analytical starting points from which to study dynamics of power and (violent) control in the Kivu provinces, this chapter speaks to both academic and policy debates. For both debates, this chapter wishes to add an urban dimension to the study of the relationship between conflict and mineral extraction. Academically, the chapter contributes to discussions of urbanity and its 'critical significance' in settings of war (Beall et al., 2011). In Congo's Kivu provinces, urban sites embody 'safe' spatial environments for IDPs or refugees, at the same time being safe havens or strongholds for rebel movements, strategic targets, economic hubs, or hotspots for the humanitarian industry (Büscher, 2016). Further, this chapter adds a missing spatial and particularly urban element to the current debates on violent conflict and the production of public authority in Eastern DRC (Hoffmann and Vlassenroot, 2014). As complex 'laboratories' (Robinson, 2006; Simone, 2004), urban centres embody the spatial, political, social and economic agency of a wide range of actors (state and non-state, formal and informal, public and private, civil and armed). As the chapter illustrates, the distinction between these categories is in reality extremely blurred. With regard to policy debates, the chapter draws attention to the crucial political character of these places as well as of their urbanisation process. Different actors involved in their regulatory frameworks are in fierce competition over power and control, a competition that is often violently mobilised along ethnic lines.

This paper is based on extensive ethnographic fieldwork carried out (by the author and/or by Congolese colleagues) between 2010 and 2017 in Numbi, Nyabibwe (South Kivu) and Rubaya (North Kivu). Fieldwork in these different sites consisted of in-depth interviews with key stakeholders (administrative and customary authorities, members of local civil society, heads of mining and commercial associations, representatives of the Congolese security forces and NGO staff), focus-group discussions with different target groups (such as, for example, miners, traders and transporters), social mapping exercises, the consultation of local administrative reports, observational walks and informal discussions.

2 Mining Urbanisation in the DRC

It is only recently that in academic writings special attention has been paid to the complex relation between mining and urbanisation in Africa. While much has been written on mining and land use/conflicts, mining and mobility, as well as on mining and human settlement patterns, the connection between mining and urban transformation has been largely ignored. Yet both processes make an important contribution to Africa's current transformation of local societies in a global era, as they both produce fundamental demographic, economic, spatial and sociocultural changes. The first attempt to bring together specific studies on the intersection of mining and urbanisation in Africa was made by Bryceson and MacKinnon (2012): from a collection of case studies on Zambia, Tanzania, Ghana, South Africa, Sierra Leone, and the DRC, the editors centred their analysis around what they call 'mineralised urbanisation', or the influence of mineral production cycles and commodity chains on urban growth and settlement patterns at local, regional and national levels. On the one hand, these studies present a clear picture of the diverse settlement trajectories, livelihoods and welfare paths of mining towns; on the other hand, they make an important attempt to examine the current sense of 'mining place' (Bryceson and MacKinnon, 2012, 514).

The issue of mining urbanisation also occupies a central place in the broader theoretical debates on the interaction between global markets and rural–urban dynamics and shifts. In their edited volume, Agergaard et al. (2010) analyse trends of mining urbanisation within the context of the 'frontier', being a region where linkages to global markets are dominated by one particular economic product. Just like other frontier economies (such as cash crop economies linked to the world market), mining frontiers are particularly dynamic spaces characterised by rapid changes in demographic structure, economic basis, occupational opportunities, settlement patterns and land use, where one observes livelihoods being transformed through the establishment of new commercial activities (Agergaard et al., 2010, 3). These dynamics strongly impact rural–urban linkages and processes of urbanisation, metamorphosing from remote 'deep rural' to pulsating urban centres of goods and services provision (Bryceson and Mwaipopo, 2010, 158). The concept of frontier urbanisation enables us to investigate mining towns in Eastern DRC as distinctive political, economic and sociocultural spaces (Werthmann and Grätz, 2012) as well as spaces of intense transformation. It is beyond the scope of this chapter to fully engage with the frontier literature on Eastern DRC, but it reinforces our understanding of frontier towns as spaces marked by fierce (often violent) contest over control and authority in the geographic periphery of the state, yet often at its political centre (Raeymaekers, 2014). Further, the literature enables us to see those places as nodes within the political projects of a wide range of actors, such as miners, mining cooperatives, all sorts of local, national and foreign corporations and governments, NGOs, and numerous middlemen, all of them negotiating local governance (Vogel and Raeymaekers, 2016).

A number of researchers has been inspired to ethnographically study the unique environment of these boomtowns and the identities, cultures and lifestyles that they develop (De Boeck, 2001; Werthmann and Grätz, 2012). The case studies of Numbi, Nyabibwe, and Rubaya largely correspond with the findings of this research and of the literature on mining urbanism in general. Attractive because of their 'frontier mystique' (Agergaard et al., 2010) and as centres of rapid in-migration, these settlements have served as 'destinations of desire' (Bryceson and Mwaipopo, 2010, 168), setting in motion dynamics of change, rapid growth and expansion. With a few exceptions, (see, for example, Büscher et al., 2014; De Boeck, 2001; Kabamba, 2012; Vlassenroot and Raeymaekers, 2004; Vwakyanakazi, 1992), mining urbanisation in the DRC has not been explicitly documented. Yet the academic interest in artisanal mining in the DRC is well developed, and several researchers have extensively studied the ways in which, in the context of state crisis and civil war, artisanal mining has become a livelihood strategy for very different civil and military actors (see, for example, Ansoms and Marysse, 2011; Bashwira, 2017; Geenen, 2013). The Kivu provinces, where this research is located, are extremely rich in natural resources such as gold, colombo-tantalite (coltan) and cassiterite (tin). At the same time, these provinces have been characterised by a protracted situation of violent conflict. The dwindling power and role of formal state institutions have been the result of a profound economic and political crisis that was already set in motion in the mid-1990s at the end of the Mobutu era. A civil war that started in the second half of the 1990s has evolved over the last 20 years into a complex jumble of dynamics of violence and conflict and a proliferation of armed groups in the Kivu provinces. During the different episodes of the war, mining towns have been strongly influenced by dynamics of forced displacement, violence and militarisation. The massive arrival of Hutu refugees in 1994, fleeing Rwanda (after the political changes following the end of the genocide), strongly impacted on such towns' demographic composition, local economies and political constellations. As has been extensively documented, these 1994 dynamics set in motion the start of a series of violent conflicts in the broader region (see, for example, Turner, 2007), and throughout the war towns like Numbi and Nyabibwe have been an operational ground for multiple armed groups.

Dynamics of violence and conflict have produced social transformation and generated a number of important shifts in the socio-economic sphere (Vlassenroot and Raeymaekers, 2004, 14). These shifts, with regard to issues such as access to land and the structure of public authoritym for example, should not be explained as temporary effects of a context of violence and war but as elements of a general transformation of local society. In earlier works I have argued that rural–urban shifts and the emergence of boomtowns in the Kivu provinces should be understood as a spatial aspect of this transformative power of violent conflict (Büscher, 2011, 2016). This transformation of peripheral rural mining sites into urbanised centres of (largely informal) accumulation and survival has resulted in a profound socio-economic, spatial and political reorganisation of local society.

The thriving forces behind the fast expansion of these mining agglomerations are multiple, and a combination of structural processes and people's agency. Like booming mining towns elsewhere, not only does the arrival of large groups of artisanal miners gave a considerable boost to local economic activity (Cuvelier, 2010; Walsh, 2003; Werthmann, 2003), these boomtowns also serve as a place of refuge for people seeking to rebuild their lives after having been marginalised in their communities of origin (Fisher, 2007; Grätz, 2009; Werthmann, 2009). Kivu's mining towns have attracted important numbers of rural poor and urban unemployed in search of their fortunes, but at the same time the ongoing violence has pushed large parts of the rural population to the same centres in search of physical security (Vlassenroot and Raeymaekers, 2004, 143).[3] Mining towns often form attractive 'safe havens' for refugees (coming from Rwanda) and IDPs (coming from Kivu's rural hinterlands), who settle in camps or in the town itself. The more these centres grow and develop, the more miners and IDPs have been followed by an influx of all kinds of other 'migrants' seeking to integrate into and invest in these emerging semi-urban

3 Urban centres providing a haven in civil conflicts is fairly common (Beall et al., 2011). The urban features of inclusiveness, freedom, global connections and cosmopolitism mark the attractiveness of cities. In the Kivu provinces, urbanised areas have become attractive poles for IDPs because of their ethnically more diversified demographic profiles (compared to surrounding villages), the higher presence of NGOs or humanitarian agencies, and the higher presence of Congolese (as well as UN) security forces.

economies. This has led (in some cases more than others) to the creation of an ethnically and economically diverse demography, the development of new markets, increased circulation of money and goods and the spontaneous development of infrastructure and services. Traders, transporters, hotel and bar managers, butchers, pharmacists, etc. gradually settle and start their businesses in these highly populated spaces. Although much of the mining extraction itself is largely carried out by men, these boomtowns are far from being a 'man's world', and women play important roles in local economies and occupy a variety of positions (Bashwira et al., 2014).[4] In a short time, these former villages transform into booming agglomerations with an increasingly 'urban' character (Büscher et al., 2014; Mususa, 2012). What makes these places 'urban' or 'semi-urban' is not only a matter of demographic size and density; it is also a matter of demographic composition, economic accumulation, livelihood diversification, public service provision, settlement patterns and political organisation (Dobler, 2009; Werthmann, 2009).

A fact that is often overlooked in academic debates is that the process of mining urbanisation is not only a demographic, administrative, spatial and economic process, but is a political process as well. This chapter, analysing mining boomtowns in a context of violent conflict, will contribute to the understanding of the politics of mining urbanisation and boomtown urbanisation in general. Through a long history of political and economic crisis and war, mining urbanism came to involve particular types of stakeholders—formal and informal, civilian and military. This particular setting generates distinctive patterns of urbanisation, settlement, governance and livelihoods, generating an urbanisation process that is often of a highly unstable and conflictual nature (Büscher, forthcoming).

Further, this urbanisation process is inevitably interwoven with agendas of political, military and ethnic mobilisation. To recognise mining urbanisation as a political process, it is important to understand the mining town as the spatial arena of political constellations and to understand the process of urbanisation as a part of political mechanisms. A case illustrative of the political aspect of the urbanisation of these boomtowns is the process of their administrative transformation from the status of a 'centre' or village, towards the status of a 'commune'. According to the decentralisation law of the DRC, agglomerations

4 A study undertaken by the gender section of MONUSCO in 2010 in six Congolese provinces found that women mostly work in the processing of mineral tailings (e.g. sieving, sorting, transporting and washing), followed by activities related indirectly to mineral exploitation (e.g. as small goods traders, housewives or prostitutes) (MONUSCO, 2010, cited in Bashwira, 2017, 109).

change administrative status according to their demographic statistics. With, for example, more than 20,000 inhabitants, a village can be recognised as a 'commune'. From our cases, it will become clear how this process is more than an administrative mechanism: it is a highly political issue, creating fierce power contestation and conflicts.

3 The Case of Nyabibwe and Numbi (Kalehe, South Kivu)

Kalehe territory in South Kivu has served as a case study to look at a variety of conflict dynamics that have become hot topics in the literature and in knowledge production with regard to the war in Eastern DRC, such as the proliferation of armed groups (Hoffmann and Vlassenroot, 2014), the struggle over citizenship (Vlassenroot, 2013), land issues (Ansoms et al., 2012) and the political economy of natural resources (Jackson, 2006; Cuvelier, 2010). Until the present, the region has been characterised by the mobilisation of armed groups, strong ethnic tensions, violent struggles over public authority and militarised land conflicts. In the early years of the new millennium, during the RCD rebellion[5] that coincided with the global boom in demand for coltan and cassiterite, several boomtowns emerged around artisanal mining sites in Kalehe. Both Nyabibwe and Numbi have experienced spectacular growth over the last two decades, transforming from small villages into extended 'urbanised' agglomerations.

Nyabibwe, with approximately 25,000 inhabitants in 2015,[6] is situated on the main road that runs along the shores of Lake Kivu and connects the two main cities in the Kivu region: Goma (capital city of North Kivu province) and Bukavu (capital of South Kivu province). The town emerged in proximity to the Kalimbi mines, which were exploited from the mid-1970s on, in an industrial manner. From the end of the 1980s, detrimental economic nationalisation policies in Zaire, and further economic decay throughout the 1990s, resulted in the gradual informalisation of mineral extraction. The 'big boom' occurred in 2000–01, when the war pushed, and global mineral prices attracted, thousands of miners to the town, resulting in a quadrupling of its population. The town distinguishes itself from its rural surroundings by its 'cosmopolitan' character, including the different ethnic groups to be found in the region. Hutu comprise

5 *Rassemblement Congolais pour la Democratie* (RCD), a Rwandan and Ugandan backed rebel movement that controlled large parts of Eastern Congo between 1998 and 2004. For more information see Tull (2003) and Vlassenroot and Raeymaekers (2004).

6 Statistics provided by the local health centre of Nyabibwe.

the largest group, and other well-represented communities are Havu, Tembo, Bashi and Tutsi. A historical friction between, on the one hand, Hutu and, on the other, Tembo and Havu has been reinforced by dynamics of conflict and militarisation. Administratively, Nyabibwe is governed by two layers of authority: customary (traditional) authority in the form of a customary chief, and state (administrative) authority in the form of a *chef du poste*. The former is traditionally the realm of the Tembo and Havu community, while the latter is locally elected and thus represents the Hutu majority. In light of regional (violent) ethnic politics, this fragmented leadership has been often conflictual. Mining activities have had an important impact on the local leadership; the mining cooperatives Coopérative Minière de Kalimbi (COMIKA) and Coopérative Minière du Bien-Être Communautaire de Kalehe (COOMBECKA), who control and govern these activities, have an important stake in local politics, and are in their turn strongly influenced by regional and national elites in the larger cities of Goma and Bukavu (Cuvelier, 2013).

Numbi, with an estimated number of inhabitants between 10,000 and 11,000,[7] is situated in the highlands (*Hauts Plateaux*) of Kalehe, some 30 km from the main road that runs along Lake Kivu. Compared to Nyabibwe (which is located on the main road) and because of almost non-existent road access (most of the time it inaccessible to cars), Numbi is an extremely isolated place. It is surrounded by huge pasture concessions, owned by influential Tutsi elites that emerged during the RCD rebellion (1998–2004). As we observe in other mining towns, the involvement of such politico-military elites, connected to local, provincial, national and even trans-border power networks, strongly contests the 'isolated' nature of the place. Administered under the status of a 'village', it is headed by a customary chief from the Tutsi community and a state authority from the Tembo community. As is the case in Nyabibwe, a fierce conflict between these two layers of authority over the control of the town (and crucial mechanisms such as land distribution or taxation revenues) has known very violent episodes. During the RCD period, as part of the group's efforts to establish its parallel administration, Numbi was administratively 'upgraded' and came under the control of a Tutsi chief close to the rebel movement. In 2006, after the peace process and the country's reunification, this chief was replaced by a Hutu chief. In 2012, the former Tutsi chief, by influencing provincial political and ex-rebel elites in Bukavu, regained control thanks to the appointment of his own brother as the new chief. The local Hutu population, who perceived

7 In 2014, the figure of 8900 inhabitants was provided by the local health centre. According to Numbi's local authorities, the actual number was around 11,000 or 12,000 inhabitants (interviews with village chief and *chef de poste*, Numbi, April 2014).

this as an orchestrated Tutsi coup d'état, strongly opposed his rule, a situation which created strong ethnic tensions.[8] Further, Numbi is known for its violent land conflicts, which are being significantly politicised by elites (urban-based elites in Goma, for example) through the political and military connections of the landowners (Ansoms et al., 2012). As was equally the case for Nyabibwe, mining activities in the nearby pits had been informalised since the 90s, and were very small scale. Also similarly, a mining boom occurred at the turn of the new millennium.

Much of its urbanisation process initially unfolded in an organic, spontaneous and unplanned way, yet various actors have increasingly tried to incorporate the process, as a spatial mechanism of control, into their own political or economic ambitions. In Numbi, local elites have, on the one hand, tried to invest in a minimum of infrastructure (to anticipate an administrative upgrade within the decentralisation process—see below). On the other hand, rumours circulate about other elites at the provincial and national level blocking investments in urban expansion (such as the road, which is in a perpetual state of disrepair), to prevent external actors, including the Congolese state, from interference.[9]

Numbi and, to a lesser extent, Nyabibwe are situated in areas that have experienced significant levels of armed mobilisation for at least two decades. Both 'autochthonous' militia (such as Mai-Mai groups in the second Congo war and *Raia Mutomboki* factions thereafter) as well as different trajectories of Congolese Hutu mobilisation (branches of the Coalition of Congolese Patriotic Resistance (PARECO) and, more recently, different *Nyatura* groups) deploy a degree of influence to these urban centres and their surroundings. Violent and militarised struggle for control over these centres of course needs to be understood in the light of their strategic significance as mining towns. From 2010 onwards, Nyabibwe was selected as one of the first pilot cases for the 'traceability process' organised by the International Tin Research Institute (ITRI).[10] In Numbi, which is far less state controlled and more isolated, armed groups like Nyatura were, until 2012 involved in taxation mechanisms applied to

8 For example, the local chief of a nearby village, put in place by the Tutsi chief, was murdered a couple of days after his appointment, allegedly by members of the armed Hutu franchise group *Nyatura* ('hit hard' in Kinyarwanda). Interview with an entrepreneur (Numbi, April 2014); interview with a mineral buyer (or middleman (*négotiant*)) (Numbi, April 2014). See also Pole Institute (2012).

9 Focus group with mineral buyers/middlemen (*négociants*) (Numbi, April 2014); interview with an entrepreneur (Numbi, April 2014).

10 Since February 2018 known as International Tin Association (ITA) Ltd. For more information on this supply chain traceability initiative, see Verbrugge et al. (2011) and Geenen (2016).

mining incomes, although not present in the mines themselves. Until the present day, despite the different disarmament initiatives, the circulation of arms remains an important challenge, and local, everyday conflicts often escalate as violence remains an important means in daily livelihood strategies.[11]

The urbanisation process of these towns was further shaped by the vast influx of internally displaced people. In both Nyabibwe and Numbi, IDPs settled within the mining agglomeration. Many of them went to work in the mines, others integrating into other economic sectors. In Nyabibwe, for example, IDPs coming from Masisi introduced 'new' commercial activities such as the exploitation of small cafeterias where people can consume milk and a small breakfast. Apart from mining, inhabitants of Nyabibwe and Numbi are engaged in a number of secondary activities, such as small trading in staple goods, transport, trading in wood, and—of course—in the proliferation of very lucrative activities catering for the food and entertainment needs of the mine workers. With a purchasing power far in excess of farmers in the surrounding countryside, the presence of miners in these towns has resulted in the emergence of a highly profitable 'entertainment infrastructure' and a sharp increase of the numbers of bars, cinemas and restaurants since the start of the new millennium.[12] It is this proliferation of secondary activities (butchers' shops, hairdressers, other shops), services (pharmacies, hotels) and entertainment infrastructure (cinemas, bars) and the large diversity of traded products that shape these mining towns' semi-urban character. As local traders in Nyabibwe told me: 'today in Nyabibwe one can find almost everything one can find in the city'.[13] One example of an economic sector that spectacularly expanded due to the process of mining urbanisation was the transport sector. Operating motorcycle taxis is a lucrative livelihood option for many youngsters and IDPs, as well as an attractive market for investment because of its high returns.[14] This economic transformation went hand in hand with a material reconfiguration of the villages' landscapes, increasingly evolving towards 'urbanised' settlements (with 'durable' housing materials, multi-storey houses and relatively extensive infrastructure).

The expansion of these dynamic mining towns did not only attract armed groups, miners, traders and IDPs; it also encouraged the Congolese state to settle at these sites, presenting—as they do—interesting economic and political

11 Focus group discussion with miners (Numbi, April 2014); interview with a village chief (Numbi, April 2014); author's own observations.

12 Interview with the manager of a *Nganda* or 'popular bar' (Nyabibwe, May 2013).

13 Focus group with traders (Nyabibwe, May 2013).

14 Focus group with motorcycle riders and interview with an FEC representative (Nyabibwe, May 2013). Since the purchase price of a motorcycle in Goma is only USD 1,500, not only urban-based elites but also local miners and middlemen can easily invest in this 'market'.

opportunities. In Nyabibwe, from around 2005 onwards, state offices increasingly installed themselves in the town, opening local branches of the Divisions of Hygiene, Tourism, Urbanisation, etc. In fact, these branches are often no more than a barely equipped 'office' (often a small wooden room) run by badly paid staff. The official discourse of 'better coordinating and organizing the town's expansion and urbanisation'[15] masks the real desires to get a piece of the massive cash flows and financial interests generated by these boomtowns. In Numbi, not only established elites but also new big men (most of them with high ranking positions in the Congolese army) have heavily invested in real estate. Most of the houses and hotels are owned by colonels, captains, and others in the Armed Forces of the Democratic Republic of the Congo (FARDC)—investments that somehow 'assure' the local population of a stable future.[16]

In 2013, in the context of the decentralisation reforms,[17] Nyabibwe was in the process of being recognised as a 'commune' in a decree from the central government. On June 13, the First Minister of the central government and the Minister of the Interior signed the decree, fixing the geographic limits of the agglomeration.[18] The transformation of Nyabibwe into a commune is the direct consequence of its growth. The law, on paper, grants an important degree of autonomy to the decentralised entity, in terms of its governance of human, economic and financial resources (Englebert, 2012). One consequence of this shift was that the customary authorities would lose administrative control to an elected state agent or a '*bourgemestre*'. Afraid he would lose the right to collect fees, taxes and royalties on mining and other commercial activities in the most important economic centre of his chieftaincy, the customary chief undertook various steps to preserve his influence. Büscher et al. (2014) have described in detail how, by for example influencing 'connected' politicians on the provincial level or by strategically selling off his land and intervening in the local political economy of the town's mining activities, the chief's strategies of maintaining power and authority have laid the basis for further local political

15 Interview with an official from the Division of Urbanisation and Habitat (Kalehe, May 2013).

16 Interview with an entrepreneur (Numbi, April 2014).

17 These reforms were launched in 2006 to improve governance and accountability, undermine predation, corruption, and personal rule, bring government closer to the people, and promote local development. However, as Englebert and Kasongo Mungongo (2016, 1) have argued: 'As of 2014, despite some regional variations, Congolese decentralisation had instead increased the degree to which the state extracts the resources and incomes of its citizens'.

18 *Décret n°13/029 du 13 juin 2013 conférant le statut de ville et de commune à certaines agglomérations de la province du Sud-Kivu.*

conflicts. In the meantime, the decentralisation law has been suspended. Since 2014, Numbi has been waiting to also be granted the status of a 'commune', yet until this day this process has not been further implemented as local elections are repeatedly postponed. As I will further demonstrate through the case of Rubaya, this half-implemented decentralisation law creates confusion, offering room for manoeuvre that enables the state and other actors, such as economic and military big men, to exercise their power over these places. Urbanisation is in itself a process characterised by contestation; these political mechanisms have strongly reinforced these conflicts.

4 The Case of Rubaya (Masisi, North Kivu)

Rubaya, a town currently estimated to have a population of 70,000,[19] is situated in Masisi (North Kivu), a region known for its violent history of identity politics. Originally, Rubaya emerged around a transit point for Rwandan labourers 'exported' into Congo (Hutu and Tutsi; today locally referred to as '*Banyarwanda*') by the Belgian colonisers in the 1930s and 40s to sustain the colonial plantation economy in the Masisi highlands. Ethnic tensions between these *Banyarwanda* and the so-called autochthonous populations (status claimed by people from the Hunde and Tembo community) rose in the aftermath of the Rwandan genocide, when hundreds of thousands of Hutu sought refuge in the Kivu provinces. Their arrival in Rubaya caused many Tutsi and Hunde to flee,[20] and in parallel with the wider region had a general destabilising effect.

Rubaya knew its real 'boom' phase during the RCD period, when coltan had been discovered three kilometres from the town's centre. Local big men from the Hutu community saw their positions reinforced by the political–economic Hutu elite that was installed in the North Kivu province under the provincial governor Eugène Serufuli, controlling the main administrative posts and key economic sectors.[21] In this period of rapid expansion, several neighbourhoods were constructed and the reconfiguration of Rubaya's landscape was also visible in the transformation of wooden shacks into constructions in more durable housing materials and the erection of multi-storey buildings. In 2001 Rubaya was administratively recognised as a commercial centre and a *chef de*

19 Activity Report of a local health centre; local electoral inscription centre.
20 Interview with a former *chef de poste* (Rubaya, June 2017).
21 Focus group discussion with Rubaya mineral buyers and middlemen (*négociants*) (Goma, May 2016).

centre was appointed from the provincial administration. Eugène Serufuli himself invested in the centre with the installation of a radio mast.[22]

The National Congress for the Defence of the People (CNDP) rebellion introduced a new phase of military conflict in Rubaya, with heavy clashes between the CNDP and the Congolese army as well as the PARECO armed group. As one of the CNDP's strongholds, mining activities were controlled by the Congress and the town of Rubaya was governed through a parallel rebel administration, which 'elevated' it to the administrative status of a '*cité*' (resulting, amongst other things, in more power and autonomy for rebel-appointed officials over customary authorities).[23] Even today, armed groups such as *Nyatura* and the Alliance of Patriots for a Free and Sovereign Congo (APCLS)[24] remain active in Rubaya's immediate proximity (United Nations Security Council, 2015). This complex history of violent conflict, in which the town has occupied different positions, from rebel stronghold to a safe haven for IDPs, has generated a process of urbanisation that is highly militarised. Now that armed groups are no longer physically present in the town itself, a heavy presence from police and soldiers has taken over.[25] Rubaya, just like Numbi, suffers from a vast proliferation of arms among its inhabitants. This results in a constant fear of violence and casualties in the case of (even very banal) conflicts.[26] Rumours regarding the creation of a new rebel movement in Rubaya are illustrative of this volatile situation.[27]

More than Numbi and Nyabibwe, Rubaya's evolution has been marked by processes of forced displacement and an influx of IDPs and refugees. Through the different phases of the violent conflict, IDPs and refugees have installed themselves in camps around the centre and in the centre itself. In 2016, the last IDP camp inside the town was closed by the provincial governor and today two camps remain, at four and seven kilometres from the town, respectively. Their

22 Interview with a teacher and interview with a priest (Rubaya, June 2017).

23 Interview with a former *chef de poste* (Rubaya, June 2017).

24 Essentially Hunde; emerged in 2008. Like many of these other militias, it mobilised its forces on the basis of popular resistance to the return of Tutsi refugees, the defence of traditional Hunde land rights, and defence against the expansion of the influence of *Banyarwanda* in Masisi territory.

25 This presence is not constant however, and fluctuates with periods of tension.

26 See, for example, *Radio Okapi* (2016) 'Nord-Kivu : 9 blessés dans une fusillade à Masisi', https://www.radiookapi.net/2016/01/14/actualite/societe/nord-kivu-9-blesses-dans-une-fusillade-masisi (accessed on 1 November 2017).

27 *Radio Okapi* (2014) 'Nord-Kivu : soupçons d'une présumée reconstitution du M23 à Rubaya', https://www.radiookapi.net/actualite/2014/08/30/nord-kivu-soupcons-dune-presumee-reconstitution-du-m23-rubaya (accessed on 1 November 2017).

inhabitants (mainly Hutu) represent a pool of cheap labour for employment in cultivating the land surrounding Rubaya.[28]

Rubaya's big man is Robert Habinshuti Seninga—a Hutu and a much-discussed figure in the region's recent history. As one of former governor Serufuli's close allies during the RCD period, he has remained in power and has continued to use his influence (Cuvelier et al., 2014). He is the president of COOPERAMMA, the mining cooperative in Rubaya, and just like in Nyabibwe and Numbi, the cooperative is a major player in local governance. It has an important stake in local politics and is itself significantly influenced by regional and national elites (Cuvelier, 2013). One several occasions COOPERAMMA has engaged in the physical development of the town. In 2014, the organisation bought a large piece of land, baptised it *quartier COOPERAMMA*, and put together its own commission (with Seninga himself at its head) to parcel it out. In 2015, under the same commission, two more neighbourhoods were developed on land belonging to a FARDC general.[29] These neighbourhoods are generally referred to as the 'best developed' in town, with more or less good roads, a health centre and spacious parcels. Further, COOPERAMMA also regularly invests in road repairs and maintenance, and in 2014 it installed a small hydropower plant to provide the town with electricity (a project that largely failed, partially because the Congolese state imposed heavy taxes on the electricity produced).[30] COOPERAMMA's involvement in Rubaya's development is again illustrative of an urbanisation process that unfolds outside formal state planning and is the outcome of the agency of different non-state actors. Furthermore, the involvement of big men as key actors in this development illustrates that it is a political process, used in strategies of legitimacy and control. The position of these key actors within political and military networks reaching the provincial and national levels reinforces this political character. This is further illustrated in the struggle for administrative control over the town in the current context of the controversial decentralisation process.

Rubaya is a town with a mixed ethnic profile, with Tutsi, Hunde, Tembo, Shi and Kano, but with a strong Hutu dominance. With its considerable size and number of inhabitants, Rubaya is in the process of becoming a 'commune' in the context of the decentralisation law. Although customary power is less strong in Rubaya than it is, for example, in Nyabibwe, this would still influence

28 Interview with a customary chief (Rubaya, June 2017).

29 Focus group discussion with Rubaya middlemen (*négociants*) (Goma, May 2016); interview with a COOPERAMMA representative (Rubaya, June 2017).

30 Focus group discussion with Rubaya mineral buyers/middlemen (*négociants*) (Goma, May 2016).

the balance of power in the area. Within the complex history of violent conflict in Masisi, this balance of power is heavily coloured by the continuous power struggles between the so-called autochthonous population and the *Banyarwanda*, and internally between the Hutu and Tutsi communities. In the first place, it was Rubaya's *chef de poste* (a Hutu), who made the 'commune' request to the provincial government, believing he would be appointed as the head of the new administrative entity.[31] The demand was further encouraged by the town's economic Hutu elite.[32] However, the '*postes de territoires*' were being abolished in North Kivu, and shortly after any further implementation of the decentralisation law was suspended. In the context of this administrative vacuum, a 'provincial delegate' was appointed by the provincial governor. To this day, this delegate, Bihami Serkali (a former administrator from the RCD period) is the only official administrative representative in Rubaya, yet he has very little legitimacy given his unclear mandate and his equally unclear juridical status. Because Serkali is a close ally of Seninga, his appointment is generally viewed as a result of Seninga's political lobbying efforts and mechanisms of control.[33] Especially among the local Hunde and their customary chief, there is strong resentment regarding his appointment, as they perceive it as a Hutu strategy to seize control over resources, such as land and taxes, from the customary authorities.[34]

5 Conclusion

These current political struggles over mining towns point to a number of dimensions of mining urbanisation in a context of violent conflict that are of crucial academic as well as policy importance.

First of all, they underline the fact that these places represent strategic nodes in the dynamics of development and accumulation, as well as in the dynamics of political and military control. These towns attract huge numbers of people from rural as well as urban environments in the Kivu provinces and they grow at great speed. As attractive poles of investment and livelihood diversification,

31 Interview with a former *chef de poste* (Rubaya, June 2017).

32 Interview with a representative of the Federation of Economics and Commerce (FEC) (Rubaya, June 2017).

33 Focus group discussion with miners (Rubaya, June 2017); focus group discussion with Rubaya mineral buyers/middlemen (*négociants*) (Goma, May 2016). We see the same dynamics in other urbanising and fast-growing towns in North Kivu, including in Kitchanga (Mathys and Büscher, forthcoming).

34 Interview with a customary chief (Rubaya, June 2017).

for researchers as well as for policy makers, it is crucial to look at these places, given their transformative power in processes of development, social change and stability. The 'urban' has for a long time been largely ignored in academic and policy studies on conflict and development in Eastern Congo. Secondary urban centres in particular have received only minor attention, yet as this research demonstrates, they may play a central role in dynamics of conflict and peace. An urban reading of wartime economic, spatial as well as political transformation is necessary if we are to understand current processes of rural–urban development as well as the production of order and public authority in Eastern DRC.

Second, what this chapter has demonstrated and what should further inform academic and policy engagement with this topic is that these boomtowns represent attractive resources to tap into for a wide range of actors. Mining urbanisation involves intense interaction between an extremely varied set of actors (political, economic, humanitarian, civil, military, formal, informal, state and non-state) and offers extensive room for manoeuvre for their diverse agencies. This applies not only to the rural migrants or displaced people seeking security and income opportunities, but also to armed groups integrating into ethnic groups for the purpose of violent mobilisation, or to the Congolese state profiting from tax benefits, or to political and economic elites tapping into economic resources such as land or mining activities, or political resources such as electoral bases. These attractive spaces of rural–urban transformation display interesting governance arrangements between customary authorities, state institutions, state and non-state military actors, big men and IDPs.

Third, given the fact that these governance arrangements are part of multi-scalar alliances involving actors in Goma or Kinshasa or abroad, the socio-economic and political dynamics emerging from mining urbanisation are less local than they may appear at first sight. Many of these alliances are the outcome of a historical process of armed conflict, state fragmentation and the ethnic logics of protection.[35] In ethnic struggles for access to political and economic resources, these political and military alliances are easily mobilised. In a setting where mining cooperatives have major stakes in urban planning and urban governance, the local regulatory framework of this boomtown process is influenced by the political stakes of external elites. Conflicts arising from the transformation of rural villages into mining boomtowns are as such easily politicized at different levels, reinforcing the towns' larger regional influence. This has influenced the political character of mining urbanisation. The case studies of Numbi, Nyabibwe and Rubaya have underlined the importance of

35 On these historical processes, see for example Raeymaekers (2010) and Tull (2003).

understanding the rapid development of these towns not only as a demographic, economic and spatial process, but as a political process as well.

The effects of the decentralisation reforms that change the administrative status of these boomtowns uncover broader violent struggles for power and control, often fought along ethnic lines. They also illustrate that interventions in these places can trigger existing tensions and render them more violent. To capitalise upon the transformative capacity of these places, a profound understanding is indispensable regarding their position and role in the complex political geography of the Kivu region.

Acknowledgements

This research has been carried out with the financial support of the Flanders Research Foundation. The data was collected in collaboration with our Congolese partners from APC (Action pour la Paix et la Concorde) in Bukavu. I would like to thank Christoph Vogel for his critical input on this paper.

References

Agergaard, J, N. Fold and K. Gough (eds.) (2010), *Rural-urban dynamics: Livelihoods, mobility and markets in African and Asian Frontiers* (London: Routledge).

Ansoms, A., K. Claessens and E. Mudinga (2012) 'L'accarpement des terres par des élites en térritoire de Kalehe, RDC', in F. Reyntjens, S. Vandeginste and M. Verpoorten (eds.) *Afrique des Grands Lacs, Annuaire, 2011–2012* (Paris: L'Harmattan), pp. 205–226.

Ansoms, A. and S. Marysse, (2011) *Natural resources and local livelihoods in de Great Lakes Region of Africa; a political economy perspective* (Basingstoke: Palgrave Macmillan).

Bashwira, M.R. (2017) *Navigating obstacles, opportunities and reforms, woman's lives and livelihoods in artisanal mining communities in eastern DRC*, PhD Dissertation (Wageningen: Wageningen University), http://edepot.wur.nl/413901.

Bashwira, M.R., C. Cuvelier, T. Hilhorst and G. Van der Haar (2014) 'Not only a man's world: women's involvement in artisanal mining in eastern DRC', *Resources Policy*, 40, pp. 109–116, DOI: 10.1016/j.resourpol.2013.11.002.

Beall, J., T. Goodfellow and D. Rodgers (eds.) (2011) *Cities, Conflict and State Fragility*, Working paper, 85 (London: LSE), https://www.files.ethz.ch/isn/136064/wp852.pdf (accessed on 28 May 2018).

Bryceson, D. and D. Mackinnon (2012) 'Eureka and beyond: mining's impact on African urbanisation', *Journal of Contemporary African Studies*, 30(4), pp. 513–537.

Bryceson, D. and R. Mwaipopo (2010) 'Rural-urban transitions in Tanzania's northwest mining frontier', in J. Agergaard, N. Fold and K. Gough (eds.) *Rural-urban dynamics: Livelihoods, mobility and markets in African and Asian Frontiers* (London: Routledge), pp. 158–173.

Büscher, K. (2018) 'War, displacement and rural-urban transformation: Kivu's boomtowns, Eastern D.R. Congo' (manuscript submitted for publication).

Büscher, K. (2016) 'Reading urban landscapes of war and peace: the case of Goma, DRC', in A. Björkdahl and S. Buckley-Zistel (eds) *Spatializing Peace and Conflict; Mapping the production of places, sites and scales of violence* (Basingstoke: Palgrave Macmillan), pp. 79–97.

Büscher, K. (2015) 'On-Going Crisis in Eastern DR Congo: The Need for an Urban Perspective', *Urban Africa*, 11 August, https://www.urbanafrica.net/urban-voices/on-going-crisis-in-eastern-d-r-congo-the-need-for-an-urban-perspective/ (accessed on 5 November 2017).

Büscher, K. (2011) *Violent conflict, state weakening and processes of urban transformation in the Eastern Congolese periphery; the case of Goma*, unpublished PhD dissertation (Ghent: Ghent University), https://biblio.ugent.be/publication/2092391/file/4335807 (accessed on 28 May 2018).

Büscher, K., J. Cuvelier and F. Mushobekwa (2014) 'La dimension politique de l'urbanisme minière dans un context fragile de conflict armé; le cas de Nyabibwe', in M. Verpoorten, S. Vandeginste and F. Reyntjens (eds.) *Annuaire de l'Afrique des Grands Lacs*, 2013–2014 (Paris : L'Harmattan), pp. 243–268.

Cuvelier, J. (2013) 'Conflict Minerals in Eastern Democratic Republic of Congo: planned interventions and unexpected outcomes', in T. Hilhorst (ed.), *Disaster, Conflict and Society in Crisis* (London: Routledge), pp. 132–148.

Cuvelier, J. (ed.) (2010) *The complexity of resource governance in a context of state fragility: the case of Eastern DRC*, Report International Alert (London: International Alert) http://www.international-alert.org/publications/complexity-resource-governance-context-state-fragility-case-eastern-drc (accessed on 6 November 2017).

Cuvelier, J., S. Van Bockstael, K. Vlassenroot and C. Iguma (2014) *Analyzing the Impact of the Dodd-Frank Act on Congolese Livelihoods*, CPPF Conflict Prevention and Peace Forum Report (New York: SSRC), https://biblio.ugent.be/publication/5766410/file/5766411.pdf (accessed on 6 November 2017).

De Boeck, F. (2001) 'Garimpeiro Worlds: Digging, Dying and "Hunting" for Diamonds in Angola', *Review of African Political Economy*, 28(90), pp. 549–562, DOI: 10.1080/03056240108704565.

Dobler, G. (2009) 'Oshikango: The Dynamics of Growth and Regulation in a Namibian Boom Town', *Journal of Southern African Studies*, 35, pp. 115–131, DOI: 10.1080/03057070802685601.

Englebert, P. (2012) 'Incertitude, autonomie et parasitisme : les entités territoriales décentralisées et l'état en République Démocratique du Congo', *Politique africaine*, 125, pp . 169–188, DOI: 10.3917/polaf.125.0169.

Englebert, P. and E. Kasongo Mungongo (2016) 'Misguided and Misdiagnosed: The Failure of Decentralization Reforms in the DR Congo', *African Studies Review*, 59(1), pp. 5–32, DOI: 10.1017/asr.2016.5.

Fisher, E. (2007) 'Occupying the margins: labour integration and social exclusion in artisanal mining in Tanzania', *Development and Change*, 38(4), pp. 735–760, DOI: 10.1111/j.1467-7660.2007.00431.x.

Geenen, S. (2016) *African Artisanal Mining from the Inside Out; Access norms and power in Congo's Gold Sector* (London: Routledge).

Geenen, S. (2014) 'Dispossession, displacement and resistance: artisanal miners in a gold concession in South-Kivu, Democratic Republic of Congo', *Resources Policy*, 40, pp. 90–99, DOI: 10.1016/j.resourpol.2013.03.004.

Geenen, S. (2013) 'Who seeks, finds: how artisanal miners and traders benefit from gold in the Eastern Democratic Republic of Congo', *European Journal of Development Research*, 25, pp. 197–212, DOI: 10.1057/ejdr.2012.19.

Grätz, T. (2009) 'Moralities, risk and rules in West African artisanal gold mining communities: A case study of Northern Benin', *Resources Policy*, 34(1), pp. 12–17, http://hdl.handle.net/11858/00-001M-0000-0011-92C3-8.

Hoffmann, K. and K. Vlassenroot (2014) 'Armed groups and the exercise of public authority: the cases of the Mayi- Mayi and Raya Mutomboki in Kalehe, South Kivu', *Peacebuilding* 2(2), pp. 202–220, DOI: 10.1080/21647259.2014.910384.

Jackson, S. (2006) 'Sons of Which Soil? The Language and Politics of Autochthony in Eastern D.R. Congo', *African Studies Review*, 49(2) pp. 95–123, DOI: 10.1353/arw.2006.0107.

Kabamba, P. (2012) 'A tale of two cities: urban transformation in gold-centered Butembo and diamond-rich Mbuji-Mayi, Democratic Republic of the Congo', *Journal of Contemporary African Studies*, 30(4), pp. 669–685, DOI: 10.1080/02589001.2012.724870.

Matthys, G. and K. Büscher (2018) 'Violent conflict, displacement and urbanisation in Eastern Congo: the case of Kitchanga' *Journal of Eastern African Studies*, 12 (2), pp. 232–253.

Mususa, P. (2012) 'Mining, welfare and urbanisation: the wavering urban character if Zambia's Copperbelt', *Journal of Contemporary African Studies*, 30(4), pp. 571–588, DOI: 10.1080/02589001.2012.724873.

Pole Institute (2012) *Numbi: Entre richesses potentielles et carences réelles de l'Etat en territoire de Kalehe/Sud Kivu* (Goma : Pole Institute, Institut Interculturel pour la paix dans la Région des Grands Lacs), http://pole-institute.org/article/numbi-entre-richesses-potentielles-et-carences-réelles-de-l'etat-en-territoire-de-kalehe-sud (accessed on 6 November 2017).

Radley, B. and C. Vogel (2015) 'Fighting Windmills in Eastern Congo? The ambiguous impact of the "conflict minerals" movement', *The Extractive Industries and Society,* 2(3), pp. 406–410.

Raeymaekers, T. (2014) *Violent Capitalism and Hybrid Identity in the Eastern Congo: Power to the Margins* (New York: Cambridge University Press).

Raeymaekers, T. (2010) 'Protection for sale? War and the transformation of regulation on the Congo-Ugandan border', *Development and Change*, 41(4), pp. 563–587, DOI: 10.1111/j.1467-7660.2010.01655.x.

Robinson, J. (2006) 'Inventions and Interventions: Transforming Cities - An Introduction', *Urban Studies,* 43(2), pp. 251–258, DOI: 10.1080/00420980500495812.

Simone, A. (2004) *For the City Yet to Come. Changing African Life in Four Cities* (Durham and London: Duke University Press).

Trefon, T. (2011) *Congo Masquerade: the political culture of aid inefficiency and reform failure,* (London, New York and Kampala: Zed Books, Fountain Publishers).

Tull, D. (2003) 'A reconfiguration of political order? The state of the state in North Kivu', *African Affairs,* 102(308), pp. 429–446, DOI:10.1093/afraf/adg046.

Turner, T. (2007) *The Congo Wars: Conflict, Myth and Reality* (London: Zed Books).

United Nations Security Council (2015) *Rapport Final du Groupe d'Experts sur la République Démocratique du Congo*, S/2015/19, (New York: United Nations).

Verbrugge, D., E. Francq and J. Cuvelier (2011) *Guide to current mining reform initiatives in Eastern DRC*, IPIS report, https://biblio.ugent.be/publication/1863693/file/1864032 (accessed on 6 November 2017).

Vlassenroot, K. (2013) *South Kivu: identity, territory and power in Eastern Congo* (London: Rift Valley Institute).

Vlassenroot, K. and T. Raeymaekers (2004) *Conflict and social transformation in Eastern D.R. Congo* (Ghent: Academia Press).

Vogel, C. and T. Raeymaekers (2016) 'Terr(it)or(ies) of Peace? The Congolese Mining Frontier and the Fight Against "Conflict Minerals"', *Antipode* 48 (4), pp. 1102–1121.

Vogel, C. and B. Radley (2014) 'In Eastern Congo, economic colonialism in the guise of ethical consumption?', *Washington Post,* 10 September, https://www.washingtonpost.com/news/monkey-cage/wp/2014/09/10/in-eastern-congo-economic-colonialism-in-the-guise-of-ethical-consumption/?utm_term=.49b40ef128c1 (accessed on 6 November 2017).

Vwakyanakazi, M. (1992) 'Creuseurs d'or et crise socio-économique au Nord Kivu en République du Zaire', *Africa,* 47(3), pp. 75–391.

Walsh, A. (2003) ' "Hot Money" and daring consumption in a northern Malagasy sapphire-town', *American Ethnologist,* 3(2), pp. 290–305, DOI: 10.1525/ae.2003.30.2.290.

Werthmann, K. (2009) 'Working in a boom-town: Female perspectives on gold-mining in Burkina Faso', *Resources Policy*, 34, pp. 18–23, DOI: 10.1016/j.resourpol.2008.09.002.

Werthmann, K. (2003) 'Cowries, gold and bitter money: gold mining and notions of ill-gotten wealth in Burkina Faso', *Paideuma* 49, pp. 105–124.

Werthmann, K. and T. Grätz (2012) *Mining Frontiers in Africa. Anthropological and Historical Perspectives* (Köln: Rüdiger Köppe Verlag).

Index

www.ingramcontent.com/pod-product-compliance
Lightning Source LLC
Chambersburg PA
CBHW071422230926
51846CB00001B/113
9789004387928